Buddhism and Psychotherapy Across Cultures

BUDDHISM AND PSYCHOTHERAPY
Across Cultures

ESSAYS ON THEORIES AND PRACTICES

Edited by Mark Unno

WISDOM PUBLICATIONS • BOSTON

Wisdom Publications, Inc.
199 Elm Street
Somerville MA 02144 USA
www.wisdompubs.org

Library of Congress Cataloging-in-Publication Data
Buddhism and psychotherapy across cultures : essays on theories and
    practices / edited by Mark Unno.
    p. cm.
    Edited from conference presentations at Boston University, Sept.
10–11, 2004.
    Includes bibliographical references and index.
    ISBN 0-86171-507-1 (pbk. : alk. paper)
      1. Psychotherapy—Religious aspects—Buddhism—Congresses.
    2. Buddhism—Psychology—Congresses. 3. Death—Religious aspects
    —Shin (Sect)—Congresses. 4. Shin (Sect)—Psychology—Congresses.
    I. Unno, Mark.
    BQ4570.P76B795 2006
    294.3'3615—dc22

                                                    2006009978

ISBN 0–86171–507–1

First Printing
10   09   08   07   06
5   4   3   2   1

Cover design by Suzanne Heiser. Interior by Gopa & Ted2, Inc.
Set in AGaramond 10.75pt/14pt.

Wisdom Publications' books are printed on acid-free paper and meet the guidelines for permanence and durability of the Production Guidelines for Book Longevity set by the Council on Library Resources.

Printed in the United States of America.

This book was produced with environmental mindfulness. We have elected to print this title on 50% PCW recycled paper. As a result, we have saved the following resources: 34 trees, 23 million BTUs of energy, 2,949 lbs. of greenhouse gases, 12,239 gallons of water, and 1,572 lbs. of solid waste. For more information, please visit our web site, www.wisdompubs.org

Contents

Acknowledgments

T HIS VOLUME is truly the collaborative result of many. On the few occasions when I am able to go enjoy a film at the theater, I am always amazed to see the number of people involved as the final credits roll. It seems similarly remarkable how many people have been involved in this work. It would not have been possible without all of the contributors; the organizers, staff, and supporters of the conference from which these papers were drawn; the expert editorial staff at Wisdom Publications; and others beyond who have come together to play essential roles.

Although it is impossible to list everyone here, I would like to express my heartfelt appreciation to the following, in addition to all of the authors of the individual articles: David Eckel, Director of the Boston University Institute for Religion and Philosophy, a most wonderful host for the conference and final banquet; Takeda Ryusei, Director of the Open Research Center (ORC), Ryūkoku University, for his sustaining sponsorship and support; Nabeshima Naoki, Vice Director of the ORC, for coordinating everything on the Japan side; Richard Payne, Dean of the Institute of Buddhist Studies (IBS), for providing the impetus, support, and direction for the conference; Lisa Grumbach, Assistant Professor of Buddhism and Religions of Japan, IBS, for expert assistance in translating papers and interpreting at the conference; Boston University doctoral student David Nichols for attending to all of the details of the conference so efficiently; Ty Unno, Jill Ker Conway Professor Emeritus of Religion and East Asian Studies, for invaluable editorial assistance on the bibliography; all of the conference participants who did not contribute a paper to this volume but whose presence is felt in so many ways; Megumi, for her patient, steadying hand; and Onyx and Taata, for much-needed comic relief.

In addition, I wish to express my deep thanks to the following conference sponsors: Boston University Humanities Foundation; Boston University Institute for Religion and Philosophy; Institute of Buddhist Studies,

Graduate Theological Union; The Kyoto Institute; Open Research Center, Ryūkoku University; Department of Religious Studies at the University of Oregon.

Special thanks to Josh Bartok, Tony Lulek, and Rod Meade Sperry of Wisdom Publications for their wonderful attention to this volume, and to John LeRoy for his copyediting.

Notes on Names and Romanization

Chinese, Japanese, and Korean names are given in the usual order, surnames first followed by given names, except in cases where authors and thinkers are regularly known to Western audiences according to English name order, that is, given names followed by surnames.

Terms and titles in various Asian languages are sometimes specified in terms of the language through the following abbreviations: "Ch." for Chinese, "Jpn." for Japanese, and "Skt." for Sanskrit. In other cases, the specified language is fully spelled out or omitted because obvious by context.

Introduction

MARK UNNO

T HE CHAPTERS IN THIS VOLUME have been collected from "Between Cultures: Buddhism and Psychotherapy in the Twenty-First Century," a conference held at Boston University, September 10–11, 2004. The conference, which brought together a score of scholars and specialists from Japan and North America, had two parts. First, we met in a seminar format, the participants having submitted their papers beforehand. With the opportunity to read one another's work ahead of time, we were able to devote the majority of the proceedings to discussion and conversation. Although this meant extra work on the part of the presenters, the effort was rewarded with rich, intimate dialogue. Second, we held a public plenary session featuring five keynote speakers that included stimulating exchanges with the audience.

The title of the conference signifies first of all the cross-cultural interaction between Buddhism and psychotherapy. As Jeremy Safran states, "Both Buddhism and psychotherapy are cultural institutions that originally developed as expressions of the values and the complex tensions and contradictions within their cultures of origins. Both are systems of healing that have evolved over time as culture has evolved, as the configurations of the self have evolved, and as new cultures have assimilated them. *And both have transformed the cultures in which they have evolved*" (italics added).[1] As this statement implies, cross-cultural interaction occurs not only between the two *disciplines* of Buddhist and psychotherapeutic practice (involving various schools and approaches within each) but also across *geographical* and *ethnic* boundaries. Thus, participating in the conference were clinicians, Buddhists, and scholars of Buddhism and psychotherapy from both Japan and North America, often with two or more specializations represented in a single participant. For example, Jeremy Safran is on the Graduate Faculty of the New School University, a clinical psychotherapist, and a Buddhist practitioner in multiple lineages. Richard Payne is dean of the Institute of Buddhist Studies, a consortium member of the Graduate Theological Union, and also a practicing Shingon Buddhist. Nabeshima Naoki is a scholar of Buddhism from Ryūkoku University but also an ordained priest and an end-of-life counselor. Okada Yasunobu is dean of the Counseling and Psychotherapy Program at Kyoto University and also a clinical Sandplay therapist. And Seigen Yamaoka, former bishop of the Buddhist Churches of America, is currently the resident minister of the Oakland Buddhist Church involved in counseling terminally ill patients. The existence of multiple disciplines within individual participants means that cross-cultural dialogue occurs not only between individuals but even within each person. This interaction of multiple cultural factors between and within individuals is both historic and timely. Never before have so many different sects and schools of Buddhism and psychotherapy come together in so many ways.

In the early history of the interaction between Buddhism and psychotherapy that began over a half-century ago, Buddhist teachers tended to be Asian and the psychotherapists European or North American. As both Buddhism and psychotherapy have grown and diversified in Asia as well as in the West, so too has the literature dealing with their interaction. Today, Japan and the United States are the two largest psychotherapeutic cultures in the world. The Association for Japanese Clinical Psychology, with over fifteen thousand members including psychotherapists, psychiatrists, counselors, and other clinicians, is one of the largest bodies of its kind in the world. The United States has by far the largest number of certified specialists in various clinical fields. Japan and the United States have, within their respective geographical regions, the largest numbers of ordained Buddhist priests, monks, and nuns, as well as academic researchers of Buddhism.

Sheer numbers by themselves mean little. Beyond the numbers, there is the tremendous influence exerted in other cultures and regions. Just as Japan has served as a bridge to Western culture for other Asian cultures in such fields as business, technology, and pop culture, the Association for Japanese Clinical Psychology is becoming a significant resource for the development of clinical practice in other Asian cultures such as China and Korea. While Europe is the birthplace of psychoanalysis, psychotherapy in the United States exerts considerable influence in other Western cultures as well. Interestingly, Buddhists from many Asian cultures have begun to interact on North American soil in ways that they historically had not in Asia. Japan is also now becoming a significant locus of interaction for Buddhists from various parts of Asia.

Until recently, however, the interaction between Buddhism, psychology, and psychotherapy has been developing largely in parallel in Japan and the United States, in the East and West, with relatively little interaction.[2] We are finally reaching a stage of critical mass in the historical interaction between specialists in these two areas in Asia and the West, and in Japan and the United States in particular. This volume, and the conference from which it derives, represent a timely beginning that should stimulate further work and reflection. The papers range from complex theoretical analyses to historical reflections and discussions of practical problems of clinical and religious practice. Regardless of genre, however, almost all of the papers contain concrete case studies or illustrations. This volume makes several particular contributions. First, it brings together specialists from diverse disciplines from both Japan and North America and provides a forum for their interaction. Many of the following chapters have been revised to include references to the proceedings of the conference and to the participants' insights or disagreements. Second, this volume includes substantial discussion of the problems that both Buddhists and psychotherapists have encountered in each other's language and practice. Third, several contributors explore the creative possibilities emerging from the synergy of Buddhism and psychotherapy.

Many conference participants came from a Pure Land Buddhist background, specifically that of Jōdo-shin (commonly known as Shin Buddhism), although Buddhist teachers and scholars of the Zen, Tibetan, and Vipassana traditions were also well represented. Less well known in the American mainstream than the Zen, Tibetan, and Vipassana forms, Pure Land Buddhism is based on entrusting to and ultimately identifying with the liberating power of Amida Buddha. It is the largest stream of Buddhism in East Asia, and Shin Buddhism is the largest sect of Japanese Buddhism and one of the largest followings of any form of Buddhism outside of Asia as well. Additionally, several chapters are devoted to the topic of death and dying in Pure Land Buddhism, although they are broadly framed in terms applicable beyond the specific context of Pure Land or of Shin.

The chapters in Part I address the problems and pitfalls that psychotherapists and Buddhists encounter when they exchange ideas. "Being somebody and being nobody," the now-famous phrase coined by Jack Engler, has become emblematic of the diverse tendencies and aims of psychotherapy and Buddhist practice: to establish a healthy self, and to realize no-self, respectively. We decided to take Engler's excellent discussion of the issue, presented in his essay (in Jeremy Safran's watershed anthology) "Being Somebody and Being Nobody: A Reexamination of the Understanding of Self in Psychoanalysis and Buddhism,"[3] as a starting point for our discussions by having everyone read the piece in preparation for the conference. We were delighted that Engler accepted our invitation to be a keynote speaker. His chapter, "Promises and Perils of the Spiritual Path," is a refinement of that speech. Although he covers considerable ground already addressed in the prior piece, he shifts his focus to examine the ways that Western practitioners of Buddhism tend to subvert Buddhist practice by using it to avoid facing issues that are often also the subject of psychotherapy—employing, for example, "practices like meditation in the service of defense, rather than self-awareness." He shows just how deeply embedded issues such as avoidance of responsibility and fear of intimacy can be, and how easy it is to escape into new and exotic religious practices. Concrete and incisive, Engler's analysis may be likened to Mañjuśrī's sword that cuts in order to heal.

Richard Payne's "Individuation and Awakening: Romantic Narrative and the Psychological Interpretation of Buddhism" provides a historical framework for understanding the problems of the Western self in engaging Buddhism. Drawing on the work of Suzanne R. Kirschner,[4] he suggests that Western Buddhists' narcissistic self-avoidance as described by Engler is due at least in part to the psychologization of Buddhism in a "romantic atonement narrative." Taking Jung's model of individuation as emblematic, he describes what he sees as the reduction of Buddhism to a humanized version of the Western religious narrative, in particular that of Christianity. He suggests that Western students of Buddhism too often reduce Buddhism to a narrative of self-alienation (previously Christian sin), atonement (repentance), and self-redemption (divine redemption).

As an alternative, he presents the bodhisattva path described by the Indian master Śāntideva in his *Bodhicaryāvatāra* as a typical Buddhist narrative.[5] In contrast to the humanistic, individualistic atonement narrative of the psychologized self, he describes the bodhisattva path as a structured, progressive ritual practice culminating in awakening and the directing of bodhisattva virtues in the service of liberating all sentient beings. There is no fall or alienation, no repentance or atonement as the decisive turning point, and thus no redemption, divine or human. Rather, it is a gradual progression that is ritually/liturgically rigorous and is designed to take practitioners *beyond* themselves in the service of all beings.

Payne is careful to distinguish Jung himself from "Jungians" whom he takes to particular task for their simplistic reduction of Buddhism to an instance of Jungian individuation. Jung himself, in fact, seemed to anticipate some of Payne's criticisms. Of Zen Buddhism he wrote: "Great as is the value of Zen Buddhism for understanding the religious transformational process, its use among Western people is very problematical. The mental education necessary for Zen is lacking in the West. Who among us would place such implicit trust in a superior Master and his incomprehensible ways?"[6] Yet, Payne does not let Jung off the hook entirely, for he sees Jung as implicated in the problematic appropriation of Eastern, and specifically Buddhist, thought into the framework of his psychological theories. Rather than trying to decide whether Payne is praising or blaming Jung, we might take his ambivalence as indicative of something deeper, and that is the difficulty of coming to terms with the "other." Textually and historically, one might be able to isolate Buddhism in its "pure state," untainted by westernizing projections, but as a human being, one unavoidably brings with one the tools and baggage of a particular cultural perspective. In seeking to integrate the understanding of the other into one's worldview, one draws on one's best tools to craft a bridge, but that bridge is necessarily distorted by those very same tools. One way to view this challenge is: Can one craft a bridge that is strong and serviceable enough to convey what is most important about the other?

Jeremy Safran, largely responding to Payne, seeks to point the way to such bridges in his essay "Cross-Cultural Dialogue and the Resonance of Narrative Strands." He makes two major points, illustrating them with concrete instances. First, religious traditions and practices, including those of Buddhism and psychotherapy, are never static or fixed. Second, there are many versions or "narratives" of the Buddhist path as well as courses of psychotherapy. Combining these two points, he suggests that (*a*) neither Buddhism nor psychotherapy can be reduced to an essential narrative, and (*b*) points of resonance, or bridges to understanding, between various schools of Buddhism and of psychotherapy can be found if one is only open to them. He suggests, for example, pointing to the work of Franz Metcalf, a conference participant, that Zen and object-relations psychotherapy share similar views of the realization of the naturally or inherently awakened self-in-relational-process (rather than a fixed or essential self). Neither of these, he argues, fits either the liturgical self of the bodhisattva path or the atonement self of individuation.

Safran does not argue against the idea that one must become aware of cultural presuppositions or that one must avoid inappropriate projections and appropriations. Rather, by remaining open and flexible one can better see both one's own assumptions and creative possibilities for building bridges and synthesizing. Echoing some of the themes enunciated in his introduction to *Buddhism and Psychoanalysis,*[7] his is a forward-looking essay that endeavors to see *how* Buddhism and psychotherapy might be brought together rather than *whether* they might be.

Harvey Aronson, in "Buddhist Practice in Relation to Self-Representation: A Cross-Cultural Dialogue," argues both how difficult *and* how fruitful it is to bring psychotherapy and Buddhism together. Like Payne, he describes the two fields in terms of narratives, in his case as *karmic* versus *psychological.* Drawing on the work of the anthropologist Richard Schweder, he outlines four ways of relating to and integrating the other, the most appropriate and effective being a self-reflexive engagement that leads to a new synthesis. Properly pursued, this leads to self-critical awareness of both the possibilities and limits of integration and synthesis. In addition to the issues discussed by other authors, he examines the diverse sociological contexts of traditionally communal Asian Buddhist cultures and of the individualistic modern West. Showing that "self" concepts or "self-representations" are inseparable from the world in which one is socialized, Aronson describes several instances of cognitive dissonance and mis- or noncommunication between Asian Buddhist teachers and Western students embedded in a psychological narrative. Citing the work of the spiritual teacher A. H. Almaas, Aronson also describes how moments of release from obsession with self-image in psychotherapy can be akin to and open windows into the type of samādhi or meditative release realized in Buddhist practice. Among other things, he suggests that psychotherapy independent of any Buddhist practice may be necessary for students who are interested in Buddhism; psychotherapy undergone together with Buddhist practice can be beneficial for progress in both; there are points of resonance between Buddhism and psychotherapy that can enhance the understanding and practice of both in a Western context; and understanding underlying karmic and psychological narratives may be essential for effective engagement of Buddhist practice in the West.

William Waldron's "On Selves and Selfless Discourse" offers philosophical, textual, and linguistic analyses of what is meant by "self" and "no-self" *(atman* and *anatman)*, Engler's "somebody" and "nobody." Waldron's essay is among the most theoretically involved in this collection, and it provides a framework for examining the logical and cultural assumptions behind much Buddhist and psychotherapeutic thought.

He begins by examining this analysis as a problem of consciousness. In Buddhism, Abhidharma, and especially Yogācāra, also known as the Mind-Only School *(Cittamatra)*, provide models of Buddhist practice based on cognition and consciousness. Specifically, Waldron compares and contrasts the Yogācāra notion of the storehouse consciousness, the *ālaya-vijñāna*, to models of consciousness offered by depth psychology (Freud, Jung) and cognitive science. The *ālaya-vijñāna* is a subjectless flow of mutually conditioning events that momentarily constitute at the surface level of consciousness something akin to an ego that experiences and reflects. On the one hand, compared to the *ālaya-vijñāna*, depth psychology, Waldron finds, is too personalistic and subjectivistic to be a good bridge for understanding; depth psychology seems always to assume *personality* to be at work, even at the deepest levels of the psyche, such that there seems to be a kind of "ghost in the machine" of consciousness, a person hidden down there somewhere. On the other hand, cognitive science seems to be too impersonal and objectivistic to account for the human suffering and spiritual liberation that form the basis of virtually all of Buddhism including the Yogācāra theory of the *ālaya-vijñāna:* "Thus, like depth psychology, cognitive science also seems inadequate for conveying *both* the impersonality of Buddhist discourse and its essential ameliorative aim: that one seeks to understand how the mind works in order to alleviate human ignorance and suffering." He goes on to describe *how* the theory of consciousness found in Yogācāra makes possible addressing both the impersonal process of consciousness unfolding and the subjective experience of personal suffering and release. At the heart of his analysis is his presentation of the classical Buddhist notion of dependent co-origination *(pratītya-samudpada)* through which impersonal causes and conditions give rise to the temporary experience of personal suffering and through which the same suffering can be dissolved into the awareness of the impersonal or nonpersonal.

The second part of Waldron's essay is devoted to a textual and linguistic examination of the evolution of this kind of personal/impersonal discourse and syntax in Indian Sanskrit literature. This discussion, like the essay as a whole, is quite erudite; it explains compellingly how religious culture helps to create language including syntax as well as how language and syntax help to create religious and philosophical thought and culture. There is nothing essential about language, whether Sanskrit or English, that would go against the very notion of dependent co-origination. Nevertheless, Waldron's chapter leads one to seriously consider the profound conditioning effect that cultural discourse has upon the habits of consciousness, and how consciousness helps to shape discourse and language, including that of the Buddhist religion as it is assimilated into Western culture.

Tarutani Shigehiro, in "Transcendence and Immanence: Buddhism and Psychotherapy in Japan," provides a view from the other side of the Pacific Ocean. Reading the preceding chapters, one is apt to assume that Buddhism in Asia continues in its traditional forms uninterrupted. Tarutani describes in vivid terms how this is not the case. Through his analysis of Asahara Shōkō, the leader of the Aum Shinrikyō cult that was responsible for the sarin gas attacks in the Tokyo subway in 1995, he shows how the particular Japanese appropriation of Western individualism and secularism has led to the creation of a distinct set of problems socially, psychologically, and spiritually. Japan as well as other Asian cultures cannot (and probably would not wish to) return to the close-knit agrarian societies of the past any more than Western cultures can revert to their agrarian pasts. The question, then, becomes one of how to move forward in today's global society.

Tracing the history of the emergence of Japan's version of the modern self, Tarutani argues that today even the mother-child bond, which traditionally served as the secure ground of connection to both the human and religious realms, has been broken. In order to overturn the current perversion of consciousness and spiritual life, he advocates the cultivation of a nondiscursive awareness akin to Freud's "evenly suspended attention" and the activation of the trickster figure such as found in Jungian psychology. According to him, a nondiscursive awareness is needed to gain a foothold against the rising tide of a fragmenting society, and a trickster consciousness is necessary to unmask and overturn false consciousness. Overall, the essay presents a tantalizing look into the "other" that shows just how different and how similar are the situations in Japan and North America.

The essays in Part II explore the possible synergy of Buddhism and psychotherapy. In "Psychotherapy and Buddhism: Attending to Sand," Okada

Yasunobu meditates on the religious and psychotherapeutic significance of sand. Beginning with some reflections on the specific qualities of sand, Okada goes on to describe the Shingon Buddhist practice of the Mantra of Light and Sand, one of the most widely disseminated practices of Japanese esoteric Buddhism, in which the practitioners carry, apply, and sprinkle grains of sand to alleviate suffering of all kinds and to purify the karma of the practitioner. Next, Okada gives an overview of Sandplay therapy, one of the fastest-growing forms of psychotherapy in the world, with Japan at the hub of this explosion. He provides case studies with illustrations, and he notes both similarities and differences between the use of sand in the Mantra of Light ritual and in Sandplay. He also discusses the mandalic use of sand in the general training of counselors and psychotherapists at Kyoto University and concludes with reflections on sand as a literary motif in Japanese and Western literature.

Sand is so ordinary and plentiful; yet when one looks closely, it is so extraordinary and precious. Okada's chapter offers an opportunity to consider this almost eerie juxtaposition of the ordinary and extraordinary, the ubiquitous and precious—juxtapositions that, upon consideration, also seem to be at the heart of other forms of psychotherapy and Buddhist practice.

In "The Borderline between Buddhism and Psychotherapy," I consider four areas where these two disciplines meet or diverge. First, they both attempt to meet the immediate practical suffering and needs of people while remaining grounded in a larger theoretical framework or worldview. Second, the effectiveness of both requires deep listening and deep hearing. Third, this deep hearing, whether in therapy or in Buddhist practice, often involves unexpected insights and approaches, or "rule-breaking." And finally, both psychotherapy and Buddhist practice face challenges posed by a global society that exhibits some of the characteristics of the borderline personality. I explore these four areas using examples and illustrations from: Albert Camus's novel *The Plague;* the life of Kisa Gotami, a laywoman and eventual nun in the community of the historical Buddha Śākyamuni; case studies by the American psychotherapist Milton Erickson; the life of Shinran, the founding figure of Shin Buddhism; and my own modest experiences.

In "Naikan Therapy and Shin Buddhism," Taitetsu Unno undertakes a comparative study of Naikan therapy, a distinctly Japanese form of psychotherapy that has begun to take root in North America, and the Shin Buddhist tradition out of which Naikan grew. Placing the development of each in historical context, he describes the practice of *mi-shirabe*, or self-reflection, that has been characteristic of both. In Naikan, this self-reflection is formalized into intensive guided individual retreats in which the participant is asked to reflect on indebtedness to others, beginning with family members, especially parents. In Shin Buddhism, this occurs more organically in a process of religious awakening that recognizes the unique internal time frame that exists for each religious seeker.

In a number of prominent forms of Western psychotherapy, one often begins by recognizing and describing *difficulties* suffered at the hands of family members, especially parents. The diametrically opposed emphases of Asian forms of psychotherapy such as Naikan and Western psychoanalysis reflect precisely the kinds of cultural differences and cognitive dissonances examined by Engler, Aronson, and others. These differences between Japanese and Western psychotherapies parallel the differences that Aronson says often exist between the expectations of Asian Buddhist teachers and Western students: "Depending on who the specific traditional teacher is," Aronson writes, "we may hear traditional *moral* advice about pride and be less likely to hear psychologically sensitive responses that address the *psychological* dilemmas of self-assertion and self-abnegation." It is an interesting twist, then, that a form of psychotherapy that seems so alien to the American mind-set has begun to take root here.

In this chapter, Unno also introduces some of the basic elements of the Shin Buddhist path, such as intoning the Name of Amida Buddha, "Namu Amida Butsu," based on the hearing of the Name as the embodiment of boundless compassion. To articulate these themes Unno gives an outline of Shin religious thought, offers examples of religious awareness in Shin poetry, and reflects on his experiences with D. T. Suzuki, a devoted student of the Shin tradition as well as a noted scholar of Zen.

Anne Klein in her essay "Psychology, the Sacred, and Energetic Sensing" proposes that spiritual energy and the faculty of energetic sensing, as found in the *prāna, rlung,* and *qi* of Indian, Tibetan, and Chinese Buddhism, respectively, may provide the basis for a psychology of the sacred, a psychology in which the *logos* emphasis of psychotherapy as the "talking cure" and the body or somatic practices of Buddhism can be bridged. Drawing on the work of A. H. Almaas as well as mystics in wisdom traditions around the world, Klein describes an unbounded wholeness that resonates with the Shin theme of boundless compassion and that expresses the effortless, spontaneous realization of sacred energy permeating body, heart, and mind. Using case studies, poetry, and metaphor as well as psychological and philosophical analyses, Klein seeks to delineate the logic of this psychology of the sacred and evoke its sensibility in the reader.

A key element of this sacred psychology is the realization of the womb-matrix and the maternal as the mature or ultimate stage of awakening. She relates this to, but also contrasts it with, infantile or regressive urges to return to the warm embrace of the biological mother's womb. There are similarities in the palpable, somatic qualities of awakening and regression, but they are diametrically opposed in the directionality of their development. The realization of the sacred maternal as found in the Buddhist womb-matrix signifies the ability to encompass and nurture all beings in their own mature realization of cosmic responsibility.

The essays collected in Part III explore themes of death and dying. They discuss Buddhist doctrine, history, and current practices in both Japan and North America. The focus is on Pure Land Buddhism, in particular the Shin tradition, but much of the discussion is applicable to broader Buddhist and religious contexts of facing death, care for the dying, and grief following death. Julie Hanada-Lee, an ordained Shin Buddhist minister, is currently a supervisor-in-training with Clinical Pastoral Education, a nondenominational program that is nevertheless taught through Christian-affiliated institutions. In "Shandao's Verses on Guiding Others and Healing the Heart," Hanada-Lee gives a personal account of the challenges and rewards of learning how to train others in clinical pastoral care involving loss, grief, and death. Using the Four Noble Truths and Shin Buddhist teachings of compassion as its framework, her essay vividly illustrates several points discussed in earlier chapters. These include the misuse of religious practice as a means of avoiding personal issues, the importance of deep listening and deep hearing, and the unexpected nature of religious insight that unfolds within a structured path but that paradoxically cannot be programmed or intentionally sought. Although she herself is still in training, she conveys naturally and in ordinary language what are often discussed more technically and abstractly as issues of projection, transference, and countertransference.

Seigen Yamaoka, a Shin minister in Oakland, California, presents the Six Aspects, part of a larger program called MAP (Meaning and Process), that he has developed to provide guidance for a distinctly North American Shin

Buddhist ministry.[8] Yamaoka, who received his religious training in Japan, initially found himself lost in attempting to minister to North American congregations, precisely because of the kinds of cultural disjunction and cognitive dissonances described in earlier chapters. Drawing on traditional doctrine but reformulating and adjusting for a vastly different culture, Yamaoka presents through theory and case studies how MAP works, especially in relation to the terminally ill and their families. If there is any moment that tests the Western narrative of romantic self-redemption described by Payne, surely death must be it. Although many of the members of Oakland Buddhist Church were raised in ethnic Asian households with strong Buddhist values, as Americans they have been deeply steeped in the romantic narrative of self-redemption. In the face of death, however, this narrative fails for many of them (although it may very well work for others), leaving them with great fear, anxiety, and confusion. Some of the case studies Yamaoka presents illustrate this failure vividly, and they show how MAP serves as a bridge to the core of the Shin path of realizing deep oneness beyond life and death, the boundless compassion of Amida Buddha.

In "A Buddhist Perspective on Death and Compassion: End-of-Life Care in Japanese Pure Land Buddhism," Nabeshima Naoki describes the development of end-of-life care in Shin Buddhism, the intellectual history of death and dying in Pure Land Buddhism, and contemporary case studies that illustrate current Shin practice, including the program of Vihara Care. One of Nabeshima's points is applicable to other areas of social engagement: Buddhism is sometimes criticized for the lack of a more proactive, programmatic approach to social issues. Certainly, such criticisms are warranted, and one of the characteristics of Buddhism in the West has been to develop this dimension of its practices, resulting in what has come to be known as "engaged Buddhism," including Buddhist-oriented hospice programs.

As Nabeshima points out, however, traditionally in Japan (and also in other traditional Buddhist cultures), strong networks of local support in the form of extended families, temples, and villages provided the setting in which individuals were able to meet the end of life in a supportive environment surrounded by human love and Buddhist compassion. This was also the case with other social issues such as care for the mentally ill, the physically disabled, and the poor. When Buddhism first spread to foreign lands, it tended to blend with local beliefs and cultures. To a significant degree, this allowed organic, local networks of social support to continue, and in the best cases Buddhism helped them to flourish. This is in contrast with Christianity, which, seeking to displace local religions, often provided *alternative* social services and institutions. Both the Buddhist and the Christian models surely have their strengths and weaknesses, and it is therefore important to recognize their differing histories and approaches.

However, as Japanese society has become increasingly compartmentalized, following first the Christian pattern and then the secular West, Japanese Buddhists have increasingly found it necessary to develop institutionally organized programs for addressing social needs including those at the end of life. According to Nabeshima, Buddhists have done so in a distinctly Buddhist manner. "Hospice care or palliative care aims to care for and support patients and their families with compassion until the patient dies. [Buddhist] Vihara Care shares this same goal, but secondly also seeks to care for and support bereaved families during their grief after a loved one's death. The Vihara movement aims to link grieving people with deceased loved ones through memories even after death, [understanding that all beings are mothers and fathers, brothers and sisters, in the timeless process of rebirth]."

In addition to the essays in the main body of this volume, two articles and a list of key terms are included as special appendices. In "Illusions of the Self in Buddhism and Winnicott" Franz Metcalf considers the possibility of bridging the language of Zen Buddhist practice with that of object-relations psychotherapy. The article is written largely as a response to Jack Engler's article "Being Somebody and Being Nobody: A Reexamination of the Understanding of Self in Psychoanalysis and Buddhism," included in Safran's *Buddhism and Psychoanalysis,* and secondarily to some of the views articulated by Jeremy Safran's introduction to the same volume. The Metcalf piece constitutes part of a dialogue that continues through the present volume, and those unfamiliar with Engler and Safran's work may find it a bit hard to follow in isolation. Its unusual "call-and-response" format makes clear its dialogical character.

Naitō Chikō's essay "Shinran's Thought Regarding Birth in the Pure Land" offers an account of such birth according to a traditional Japanese sectarian presentation of Shinran's thought. Of particular note are Naitō's treatment of how to understand the moment of death, which is said to be the moment of birth in Amida's Pure Land; how this moment relates to the working of *shinjin,* or true entrusting, that occurs as the Shin practicer entrusts her- or himself to Amida's boundless compassion; how this true entrusting ultimately comes from Amida as one's own deepest and truest reality; and how the best preparation for death is thus not to think of death but to focus on realizing *shinjin,* true entrusting, in the present moment, here and now. Although this essay does not address the specific topic of Buddhism and psychotherapy, it provides helpful background for those unfamiliar with Shinran's thought, as noted by some of the authors in this volume.

For those unfamiliar with Pure Land Buddhism generally and Shin Buddhism in particular, an overview of some of the key terms is also provided as an appendix.

As a beginning rather than a culmination, the chapters included in this collection reflect the enthusiasm, collaborative spirit, and meanderings of those moving together into relatively uncharted waters. In that sense, they may raise more questions than they answer, and even raise some eyebrows. But we will have done our job if that is the case, for the issues discussed herein call for attention and some eyebrow-raising. As the old Zen proverb says, we are all the blind leading the blind, and perhaps some good will have been done if we find the contours of our blindness illuminated by the brilliant light of awakening, Buddhist, psychotherapeutic, or otherwise.

PART I

PROMISES AND PITFALLS: DIALOGUE
AT THE CROSSROADS

1

Promises and Perils of the Spiritual Path

JACK ENGLER

T HERE IS A DISCOVERY we Western practitioners of Buddhism have come to, somewhat reluctantly, as we have gained more experience in practice, particularly meditation practice. What first drew us, and may continue to draw us, was Buddhism's promise of liberation from suffering, and from the painful sense of incompleteness and limited satisfaction in life. And most of us were not disappointed. We did find a path and a liberation in Buddha-dharma that we have not found anywhere else. That is why we continue to practice. But as time has gone on, we have discovered something else about practice: it is not immune from our personal history, our character, our inner conflicts, and our defensive styles. Just as with psychotherapy and other healing interventions, we are learning that *vipassanā, zazen, nundro, tong-len, mettā*—the whole range of Buddhist practices, in fact—can be undertaken in ways that are directly opposed to their purpose and design. This most radical agent for personal transformation can be used unwittingly to prevent genuine transformation—to avoid our issues, while making it look like, and feel like, we're addressing them—and so perpetuate our suffering instead of liberating us from it. This has been an unwelcome and disconcerting discovery. We started out thinking that spiritual practice would dissolve all our emotional problems. Perhaps this was typical Western hubris or naïveté, our inveterate belief in human perfectibility and the right to happiness. But at the same time, it has forced us to become much more sophisticated about how we practice, about motivations behind practice, and about discerning what practice can do and what it can't.

The psychoanalyst Robert Langs wrote a fascinating little book some years ago entitled *Rating Your Psychotherapist.*[1] His basic assumption flies in the face of common sense. It says that you cannot rate your therapist by any scheme that relies on conscious, rational appraisal—the usual kind of commonsense assessment. This is because our conscious mind just wants relief; we just want to feel better. This part of us isn't very interested in doing the hard work of coming to know ourselves and genuinely facing our issues—in fact, we would rather avoid it if we could. Further, the part of us that just wants relief, as Langs saw it, will tend to collude with that part of us that retains, unconsciously, a memory of every significant hurt we've ever suffered. That part of our unconscious is interested only in survival and in avoiding retraumatization. Now, there is a still deeper part of us, also unconscious, call it our wisdom mind, that always knows the emotional truth of every situation and cannot deceive or be deceived. This part of us always pushes toward full conscious awareness. But our conscious desire for relief at any cost, and our unconscious fear of retraumatization, tend to gang up on and repress the part of us that knows the truth and wants to know it in full awareness.

Langs's radical conclusion is that we can rate our therapists only by accessing our unconscious perception of them. I wonder if this isn't the case with spiritual teachers as well. The point is that we have a deeply ambivalent attitude toward any process of change. In Langs's phrase, we enter upon it with a "mind divided." Part of us wants to know, part of us doesn't. Part of us wants to change, part of us is deeply frightened at the prospect of change and will often settle for the illusion of change instead of the real thing.

The part of us we might call the ego—the part that is willing to settle for the devil we know rather than risk the devil we don't—can use practice for its own advantage. It's just as well we are forewarned of its machinations—though the ego, clever as it is, can take this same forewarning and use it to protect itself: "See, I told you it was going to be difficult. Why don't you wait until you feel better before engaging in serious practice?" There is something analogous in traditional Asian Buddhism—a way of thinking about the goal of practice which the anthropologist Melford Spiro termed "kammatic Buddhism": the practitioner decides that the goal of liberation in this very life is unattainable and tries instead to do meritorious works that will lead to a better rebirth. With a better rebirth, one might then be able to practice for liberation. This is both sincerely meant and an acceptable position to take in Asian Buddhism, where life circumstances may actually not be supportive of practice. But waiting for a better rebirth, like waiting until you feel better, can rationalize avoidance of the hard work of change.

This is remarkable when you think about it: Without being aware of it, we can use a practice designed to liberate us from ego to shore up ego. But is this really surprising? Have you ever found anything in your life that you couldn't—or haven't—conscripted into the service of your own neuroses? I did this at the very beginning of Buddhist practice with the way part of me responded to hearing the First Noble Truth—the truth of suffering. My conscious reaction, and a genuine and accurate one as far as it went, was "Thank God, someone is finally telling it like it is!" "Suffering" fit the ego's need for a perfect explanation of life's ills and offered a neat remedy. My mother's favorite word was "perfect." There was no place for imperfection or unhappiness in her worldview or in our home. It took many years in therapy before I understood a deeper and darker resonance with the Truth of Suffering: my mother's and my own pleasure in suffering, because it provided leverage and power and expiated guilt. Without awareness of these unconscious motives and meanings, the First Noble Truth legitimated and perpetuated neurotic needs for a long time.

It's just that we'd like to believe spiritual practice is the exception. We want to be assured that there is at least one path that we can't screw up, that is immune from our capacity for self-deception and self-sabotage, some practice we can just do and be assured it will "work." The fact seems to be that there isn't. There's no way to practice meditation or any spiritual path that is immune from the anxieties, needs, belief structures, emotional patterns, or dynamics of our own personal history and our own character. At the end of the day, we still have to work with sides of ourselves we perhaps hoped spiritual practice would make unnecessary.

Phillip Kapleau relates this exchange with a student during a question-and-answer session in a Zen workshop:[2]

QUESTIONER: But doesn't enlightenment clear away imperfections and personality flaws?

ROSHI: No, it shows them up! Before awakening, one can easily ignore or rationalize his shortcomings, but after enlightenment this is no longer possible. One's failings are painfully evident. Yet at the time a strong determination develops to rid oneself of them. Even opening the Mind's eye fully does not at one fell swoop purify the emotions. Continuous training after enlightenment is required to purify the emotions so that our behavior

accords with our understanding. This vital point must
be understood.

This is not what the student wanted to hear. He desperately hoped that
becoming enlightened, experiencing *kenshō*, would solve all his personal
problems and doubts.

The enlightenment traditions often seem to promise this. In an interview
for the spring 2001 issue of his journal *What Is Enlightenment?*, devoted to
the question "What is Ego?," Andrew Cohen asked me, "Don't you agree
that if one's enlightenment is deep enough, wouldn't the fixation on the personal self and all the suffering associated with it disappear because one's perspective would shift completely—from seeing oneself as the one who was
wounded to recognizing oneself to be that which was never wounded by
anything? Won't realization of the emptiness and ultimate insubstantiality
of the personal self and its suffering completely change one's relationship to
personal experience?" My reply was that this is an idealized view. In practice, it just doesn't seem to work that way.

The radical change Cohen foresaw happens only when one has truly gone
to the end of the path and can then say with all buddhas, "The holy life has
been lived. What needed to be done has been done." In the Theravada tradition of Buddhism, for instance, freedom from self-generated suffering
doesn't happen all at once. It occurs by stages or increments. The entire
group of unwholesome mental factors (*saṃyojanas,* or "fetters," so called
because they bind one to the wheel of life and death) that produce suffering are not extinguished all at once. Rather, four different clusters of these
factors are extinguished sequentially in four separate enlightenment experiences.[3] The first cluster has to do with mistaken beliefs, the second and third
with unwholesome affects and motivations, and the fourth with narcissistic attachments to self. Along the way, much work remains. In Western experience, some of that work must be personal work. As Kapleau's reply
suggests, it isn't simply a matter of applying spiritual insight to the rest of
one's life. Yet if the "continuous training" that he says is necessary after initial enlightenment is just more spiritual practice—more sitting, more
retreats, more meditation—then that can leave one's character flaws and personal conflicts and difficulties untouched.

I want to suggest several reasons for this.

One is that we cannot help but assimilate our approach to Buddhist practice into our preexisting emotional patterns, some of which are inevitably maladaptive. Assimilation is inevitable. It unavoidably affects not only our work and relationships but the way we understand, practice, and experience Buddhist teaching. This is one answer to the question Harvey Aronson asks in his excellent book *Buddhist Practice on Western Ground:* "Why is it that meditation in the absence of psychotherapy or personal work does not prevent or reduce mental anguish for some people?"[4]

A second reason why personal work is often necessary is that awareness in one area of life doesn't automatically transfer into other areas. Spiritual awareness, as Buddhism defines it, doesn't automatically yield psychological and emotional awareness in a Western sense. The profound need to defend against retraumatization, as well as our capacity for horizontal and vertical splits in personality, leave sequestered compartments where the memories of past injury and the anticipation of future hurt are deepest. Entrenched characterological defenses and flaws can remain untouched. So, for instance, we encounter teachers who have deep insight into the nature of self and reality, but who encourage dependent guru-disciple relationships with students, at worst sleep with them, need uncritical admiration, are intolerant of criticism or dissent, or insist on a rigidly hierarchical structure in their community. Or more simply, we encounter teachers who are powerful in the front of a zendo but can be anxious, confused, immature, or at worse violate boundaries and take advantage of their students.

In the inaugural conference I moderated at the Barre Center for Buddhist Studies between teachers from different Buddhist traditions, a recently disrobed Tibetan lama admitted, quite courageously, that although he had no difficulty generating compassion toward the "thousand beings of light" in traditional Tibetan visualization practice, he found it much more difficult, now that he was no longer a monk, to deal with the real person in front of him.

Jack Kornfield writes in *A Path with Heart,* "Only a deep attention to the whole of our life can bring us the capacity to love well and live freely. . . . If our spiritual practice does not enable us to function wisely, to love and work and connect with the whole of our life, then we must include forms of practice that heal our problems in other ways."[5] And in fact, in Buddhist societies this has always been the case. One never took every problem in love and work to the spiritual teacher.

The psychological self also seems to be a much more individualistic concept in the West than in traditional Buddhist societies. It is much less embedded for us in a preexisting social and cultural matrix that defines and supports it. Therefore, practice also seems to unfold differently for Western practitioners. This is a whole topic and issue in itself, and I cannot do more than suggest it here. But let me share several observations.

First, even in spiritual practice, the need to deal with emotional and relational issues seems to be more the rule for Westerners than the exception. Practice itself tends to uncover personal issues for us by holding a mirror to our mind. But uncovering these issues in meditation doesn't automatically bring insight in a psychodynamic sense. It may for some, but this depends on how psychologically minded you are, on how much you have worked with this kind of material in the past, on how your teacher responds to it, and most important, on whether you yourself choose to work with it. The classical meditation traditions themselves discourage working with what they refer to as "mental content."

Two vignettes: Among the Buddhist vipassanā practitioners I interviewed in India, those who had experienced at least the first stage of enlightenment were noteworthy for the absence of personal content when they described their meditation practice. The kind of material that surfaces for Western students was simply not reported. This raises several important questions. Was it that personal issues simply didn't come up? If not, why not? Did this have to do with the way the practice was taught? Were personal issues considered so insignificant compared to the experience of enlightenment, for instance, that they didn't deserve much mention? Or did they not come up because of a different, less individuated, sense of self?

A second vignette: In the course of my study in India, I had the good fortune to do intensive practice with the Venerable Mahasi Sayadaw at his meditation center in Rangoon. He was the root teacher of this tradition of *satipaṭṭhāna-vipassanā* and the most venerated monk, scholar, and meditation master in Theravada Buddhism. By the third day, the senior sayadaw (teacher) taking my daily report of practice was asking me, "Have you seen the great light yet?" This is a very advanced stage of practice—the fourth *ñana,* in the classical "stages of insight." Apparently he thought three days were sufficient to get there!

In her wonderful little biography of the Buddha, Karen Armstrong points out how little the scriptures tell us of the Buddha as a person.[6] They tell us next to nothing of his personality, for instance. We know more about the person of Ananda than about his teacher. It is as if the personality of one who has awakened is not only unimportant but has disappeared.

But whether explicitly worked with or not, practice for Westerners will more often than not access personal material long before there is any experience of the great light. Jack Kornfield found the same thing Dan Brown and I did ten years earlier in a Rorschach study of vipassanā meditators before and after a three-month retreat.[7] About half the practitioners found it hard to sustain mindfulness practice in its pure form because they encountered so much unresolved grief, fear, wounding, and unfinished developmental business with parents, siblings, friends, spouses, children, and others. Trying to get them to redirect their attention to note simple arising and passing away is usually unsuccessful. The press of personal issues is just too great. Even advanced Western students find that periods of powerful practice and deep insight will often be followed by periods in which they reencounter painful patterns, fears, and conflicts. Or they may come to some important understanding and balance in formal practice but find that, when they return home to the problems of day-to-day living, relationships, and career, old neurotic or dysfunctional patterns of behavior are as strong as ever and have to be faced. If they do not face them, there is a good likelihood they will unconsciously use their practice to avoid dealing with them. And if that happens, their practice itself will eventually become dry or sterile and increasingly unrewarding. Emotional issues that aren't addressed can infuse daily meditation practice with anxiety, agitation, discomfort, or dullness.

Second, we continue to find that many of these personal issues aren't healed simply by more meditation or other forms of spiritual practice alone. Specific problems such as early abuse, addiction, conflicts in love and sexuality, depression, struggles with aggression and the expression of anger, problematic personality traits, and certainly mental illness all require specific attention, and probably ongoing personal, professional, and communal support to resolve. This is particularly true of issues around trust and intimacy in relationships. These issues can't be resolved simply by watching the moment-to-moment flow of thoughts, feelings, and sensations in the mind. These problems arise in relationships; they have to be healed in relationships.

In 1980, in the course of a retreat in Yucca Valley during the Venerable Mahasi Sayadaw's only visit to the United States, Jack Kornfield, in his intrepid way, asked the sayadaw in a teachers' meeting, "What do you do

when students bring psychological problems?" There was a hurried conference between the sayadaws. The Venerable Mahasi Sayadaw turned back to
face the Western teachers: "What psychological problems?" he asked. In one
of his last talks before leaving the United States, the sayadaw said he had
discovered a new form of dukkha called "psychological suffering."

The wish that spiritual practice could, by itself, prove a panacea for all
psychic suffering is widespread and understandable. But unfortunately it
prevents teachers and students from making use of other resources. Worse,
students are sometimes led to believe that if they encounter difficulties, it's
because they haven't practiced long enough or they haven't been practicing
correctly or wholeheartedly enough. The message too often is that the problem is in the quality of the student's practice, rather than in the mistaken
assumption that practice should cure all.

Also, not everyone is capable or ready to devote themselves exclusively to
spiritual practice, or to pursue it single-mindedly to its depth. If they try to
force themselves, or if teachers push too hard, there is a risk of serious dis-
organization, decompensation, regression, or loss of function. Most will simply give up, but then may carry the burden of shame and guilt for "failing."
Others will get discouraged and quit, giving up a practice and a community that could have been immensely helpful to them.

Third, when basic developmental tasks are neglected or remain largely
unfinished, Western students often find it difficult to deepen their practice
beyond a certain point. They start to have problems focusing and concentrating. They become irritated and discontent with practice. "Under these
circumstances," Harvey Aronson observes, "attempts at barreling through,
toughing it out, or just practicing more can lead to derailment."[8] Students
stop bringing practice into daily life.

Arnold Toynbee's dictum seems to apply in spiritual life as well, at least
for Westerners: those who don't remember history are compelled to repeat
it. If personal conflictual patterns, of whatever origin, aren't consciously
faced and worked with, they continue to repeat in practitioners and their
communities. As Jack Kornfield writes, "The need to reclaim and develop
a healthy sense of self and self-esteem, a capacity for intimacy, and a creative
and fulfilling way to live in the world can't be and shouldn't be separated
from spiritual practice."[9] The Buddhist teaching that I neither have nor am
an enduring self should not be taken to mean that I do not need to struggle to find out who I am, what my desires and aspirations are, what my needs

are, what my capabilities and responsibilities are, how I am relating to others, and what I could or should do with my life. Ontological emptiness does not mean psychological emptiness.

In his great sixth-century compendium of classical Theravada Buddhist philosophy, psychology, and practice, Buddhaghosa called practice a *visuddhimagga* or "path of purification." Practice is like refining an alloy in fire until the impurities are burned way, leaving the pure metal. He was pointing out, in less psychological language than ours, that we bring a mixture of motivations to practice. Some are healthy: to genuinely see, know, and deeply understand ourselves; to change for the better; to be more kind and compassionate. And there is the most simple and fundamental of all human desires: the desire to be happy and free from suffering, along with the desire that others likewise be happy.

But these healthy motives are typically interlaced with one or more other motivations, other meanings practice can have for us, which reflect our fear of change, our fear of freedom, and our grasping at self to allay our anxiety. Some of these motives and meanings are idiosyncratic, rooted in personal history—the kind of preexisting emotional patterns Harvey Aronson pointed to. But others are more universal, and these underlie the attraction Eastern forms of spiritual practice have for many Westerners.[10] They also predispose us to employ practices like meditation in the service of defense, rather than self-awareness. We need to be aware of them, not as personal faults or failings, but as the irreducible "impurities" that need to be refined in the fire of practice. I want to say a few words about these ten unhealthy motivations.

1. *A quest for perfection and invulnerability.* Enlightenment can be imagined as a heaven-sent embodiment of a core Western narcissistic ideal: a state of personal perfection from which all our badness, all our faults and defilements, have been expelled, a state in which we will finally become self-sufficient, not needing anyone or anything, above criticism and reproach, and above all, immune to further hurts or disappointments. Practice can be motivated in part by this secret wish to be special, if not superior: enlightenment will finally elicit the acknowledgment and admiration that have been lacking. Because narcissistic issues are so pervasive in character development and across every level functioning, this is usually the most important of the ten issues.

2. *A fear of individuation.* Fears, conflicts, and felt doubts and deficiencies—around assuming responsibility, being assertive and competent, living our own life and making our own choices—can be avoided through a defensive pursuit of an idealized "egolessness" or "selflessness."

3. *Avoidance of responsibility and accountability.* The Buddhist goal of freeing oneself from egocentric needs and desires can rationalize our avoidance of anxiety-producing situations: making decisions, accepting responsibility for them, and taking charge of our life.

4. *Fear of intimacy and closeness.* A stance of "nonattachment" can rationalize fears of closeness and the anxieties associated with intimacy: fear of feeling exposed, vulnerable, humiliated, shamed, hurt, rejected, or abandoned. It can rationalize feelings of estrangement and loneliness. It can absolve us from fears and conflicts over sexuality.

5. *A substitute for grief and mourning.* Significant personal loss often brings people into practice, but practice itself can be used defensively to avoid the personal issues and feelings associated with real loss. Mindfulness can be practiced in a way that either dissociates the important affects of mourning—anger, confusion, withdrawal, sadness—or acknowledges them only from a safe distance. Or they can be neutralized through escape into no-self. The longing for reunion with the loved one can be displaced onto the quest for mystical oneness and union.

6. *Avoidance of feelings.* The labeling of aversive emotions as "defilements" or "unwholesome" in Buddhist practice can lead to thinking the goal is not to feel any disturbing emotion, and then feeling guilty if you do. Western practitioners often have a problem with anger and its derivatives. An earnest and sincere Vajrayana student started therapy with me with the request that I help him get rid of his anger, that is, collude with his attempt to avoid facing it.

7. *Passivity and dependence.* Fear and denial of anger, competitiveness, and self-assertion (often masked by a passive-dependent or passive-aggressive style) can be mistakenly viewed as the practice of egolessness and detachment from personal desire. Passivity can also be used to rationalize the fear of disagreeing or taking an independent stance. Codependency can be mistakenly seen as compassionate service.

8. *Self-punitive guilt.* Desirelessness and nonattachment can become the arena for acting out underlying feelings of unworthiness and guilt, as well as superego needs for punishment. "Needs are bad, and I'm bad for having them."

9. *Devaluing of reason and intellect.* The emphasis on immediate, nonverbal experience in meditation, and the axiom that "those who speak do not know, those who know do not speak," can justify the histrionic defense of "having experiences" without reflecting on their meanings. It can also seem to promise resolution of obsessional rumination by saying, "Don't think," and thereby reinforce the defensive avoidance of thinking to block self-understanding. On the contrary, "Do not dislike even the world of senses and ideas," the *Hsinhsin ming* (Song of Faith) says, and "Indeed, to accept them fully is identical with true enlightenment."[11]

10. *Escape from intrapsychic experience.* By trying to "let go" of all aspects of psychological selfhood, we can justify the suppression or repression of anything that arouses anxiety or insecurity, and anything that may stimulate self-awareness. States of samādhi that have the power to suppress perception, thinking, imagery, and aversive emotions can be used to keep the mind relatively free of unwanted thoughts and feelings, substituting "bliss" instead.

One or more of these motives can continue to influence us for a long time. Traditional Buddhist Abhidhamma explains the process of spiritual growth in terms of what Western psychology calls the principle of reciprocal inhibition: opposing wholesome and unwholesome mental factors cannot arise in the same state of consciousness. Anger and loving-kindness cannot arise together. Generosity and selfishness cannot be present in the mind at the same time. But reciprocal inhibition cannot explain or account for this mix of motivations and meanings that Western students bring to and encounter in practice. This requires another principle of mental functioning that Western psychology has called attention to and sees as central to mental and emotional life: the principle of multiple determination. This principle states that all action, all behavior, is determined by multiple motives, that we often have different and opposing reasons for doing what we do, some conscious, some unconscious: that we can be loving, for instance, and at the same time very angry, and our loving is a defense, a reaction formation against feelings of anger that are too unacceptable or dangerous to feel. The principle of multiple determination also involves a recognition that some of our motives for a given action will be conscious, and others will be unconscious—outside conscious awareness, but influencing volition, choice, affect, mood, and the meaning of our behavior nonetheless. Multiple determination helps us to understand that our unconscious motives can be in conflict with our conscious ones—or even in conflict with other unconscious motivations and meanings.

Spiritual practice, of whatever kind, is not exempt from this law of multiple determination. It is noteworthy that Buddhist psychology, at least as formulated in the Abhidhamma, does not seem to have a theory of intrapsychic conflict and resistance in a psychodynamic sense. The paradigm of the Five Hindrances to practice is the closest it comes. These are mental factors that are considered particular obstacles to practice: sense desire, anger, boredom (traditionally, "sloth and torpor"), worry and agitation, and skeptical doubt. They could be read as "resistances," and they often function that way in actual practice: sense desire or sexual attraction, for instance, can distract from or defend against self-realization or insight. But at this existential level of experience, what is defended against is not insight into personal motives and emotional patterns but insight into the three "marks" of phenomenal existence: unsatisfactoriness, impermanence, and insubstantiality. However, this is not resistance in a psychodynamic sense, and it is not at this existential level that most Western practitioners first encounter resistance. Without an understanding of multiple determination and the resistance that ensues, it is difficult to understand Western practitioners' experience with spiritual practice and the problems they and their teachers encounter. At least for Westerners, Buddhist practice is not immune from the same resistance, defenses, and distortions that have to be worked through, for instance, in psychotherapy. And therapy for some can be a resource in identifying resistance and working through it. The mystic poet Kabir complains, with some humor:

Friend, please tell me what I can do about this world
I hold on to, and keep spinning out!

I gave up sewn clothes, and wore a robe,
But I noticed one day the cloth was well woven.

So I bought some burlap, but I still
Throw it elegantly over my left shoulder.

I pulled back my sexual longings,
And now I discover that I'm angry a lot.

I gave up rage, and now I notice
That I'm greedy all day.

I worked hard at dissolving the greed,
And now I'm proud of myself.

While the mind wants to break its link to the world,
It still holds on to one thing![12]

It takes effort and courage and willingness to look at our motives again and again before this "holding on" becomes apparent in all its many and subtle guises. Often it requires the guidance of a good teacher or therapist, or a *kalyāna mitta*, a good friend. Or it may take some disappointment in our progress, or feeling stuck for a long time—the Christian mystic Ruysbroeck reportedly remained stuck in the stage of the Dark Night for close to twenty years. Or it may take some exceptionally painful event like the loss of a child or a spouse, a major depression, or a teacher's betrayal of trust to wake us up and force us to look and see.

But this is the work and always the work: removing the obstructions and obfuscations. Parting the clouds so the sun can shine through. Clearing the dust and dirt from the mirror so we can get an accurate reflection of ourselves. We can't remove what we don't see. Such habits of mind are difficult to see, not only because they are like the air we breathe, but because we rely on them for self-protection—literally—to protect whatever self we are invested in at the moment. Among the many things it can do, practice can be a powerful and effective vehicle for bringing our mixed motives to awareness, and giving us the means and opportunity to confront them in this ongoing "path of purification." It will do this only if we truly want to know and see. Aronson writes, "The critical psychospiritual question is how to stop translating new content into old patterns and actually start experiencing things in a fresh way. . . . The first step in this process is to become experientially aware of what until now have been unconscious processes of assimilation."[13]

The Indian saint Ramakrishna was once asked why there was evil in the world. He answered, "To thicken the plot!" These very plot thickeners, often the most difficult and most insistent ones, can either lead to more suffering or to the end of suffering—to opening all of us to what is true and real if we face them honestly, opening to what they have to teach us. Then, as Jack Kornfield says, "We will discover that they never were our true identity."[14] Precisely through the fear and hurt and anger we have contracted around and tried to deny and avoid, we can find freedom, ease, unshakable peace, and a deep, deep joy.

2

*Individuation and Awakening: Romantic Narrative
and the Psychological Interpretation of Buddhism*

RICHARD K. PAYNE

A Personal Reflection

S EVERAL YEARS AGO, while still a struggling doctoral candidate anxious
for things that I could add to my curriculum vitae, I was asked to participate in a day-long session for the general public conducted in Berkeley
by a group whose name I seem to have purposely forgotten. I was requested
to act as a representative not of Japanese Buddhism, a topic with which I
had some personal experience, but rather of Shinto, with which I had only
a rather general familiarity. Despite my demurral, the person inviting me
persisted, and I finally agreed.

As the day unfolded I found the unspoken theme was the unity of all religions. It is popular in some circles—not only among New Age adherents
but also more generally among many of the religiously liberal—to claim that
all religions ultimately teach the same thing, that all of the great mystics
have accessed the same higher truth, and that these higher, mystical teachings form the true essence of each and all religions—an esoteric teaching or
"perennial philosophy," accessible only to the initiate.[1] One of the most common metaphors for this view is that although there are many paths up the
mountain, they all lead to the one peak.

I resisted fitting Shinto into this view. Although one can find some traditional shrines and some new Shinto-derived religions that do have spiritual traditions and practices—often characterized by traditional concepts of
purity and pollution—these seem to be the exceptions. The vast majority
of the shrines popular both with native Japanese and with tourists offer no
program of individual perfection, no esoteric truths to be acquired by meditative practice, no mystical texts revealing the experiences of ancient masters. From my own admittedly casual observations it seemed that the

concerns of the vast majority of visitors to Shinto shrines are highly pragmatic—good health, safety, prosperity, progeny, admission to a desirable
university, success in business (or warfare), and so on. Indeed, I have been
shown one shrine whose deity specializes in curing insomnia, and another—
reputedly popular with geisha—whose deity specializes in preserving feminine beauty. Buddhism is also filled with petitionary prayer, and Japanese
Buddhism in particular has been further characterized as overly preoccu-
pied with death rituals, hence the term *sōshiki Bukkyō,* or "funerary
Buddhism." My point is not to define Buddhism as spiritually superior to
Shinto but rather to point out that Shinto priests and shrines themselves
generally do not make some kind of path to spiritual realization integral or
central to their mission, as Buddhists do, at least formally, through doctrine
and their training centers.

During the discussion period, one of the audience members commented
that all of the speakers made sense to her—"except that fellow who spoke
about Shinto." It seemed that the perennialist assumption was so strong that
any other view was simply incoherent to her. It was not a topic the session
leader wanted to follow up on.

While I can hardly claim that this one event produced a sudden and
blinding change in my way of thinking, it has contributed to my own present insistence that being a Buddhist makes a difference, and to my own project of attempting to peel back the layers of the popular view of Buddhism.
After all, if all religions are ultimately the same, then why should one adhere
to one rather than another? Why actually expose oneself to a tradition that
is radically different, one that challenges many of the fundamental assumptions of popular religious culture? If one prefers not to be challenged, one
can assume that one already knows, because one knows that all religions are
ultimately the same. Although the metaphor is at least dubious, if not fatu-
ous, it seems to me that not only are there many paths but that there are
also many mountains—as well as no shortage of swamps, dead ends, char-
latans, poison oak, and mosquitoes along the way.

Introduction

Beginning in the second half of the nineteenth century—and continuing
into the present—Buddhist modernism has recast the representation of
Buddhism. This trend arose out of the interaction between the traditionally

Buddhist cultures of South, Southeast, and East Asia on the one hand, and Euro-American imperialism on the other. The expansion of Euro-American power throughout the world was fueled by an evangelical triumphalism that presumed the authority not only to bring the Christian good news to the heathens but also to systematically transform these societies according to the model of Euro-American culture.[2] In the wake of this religio-cultural expansion, traditionally Buddhist cultures were confronted by new conceptions of what constitutes religion and its place in society.[3]

The creation of Buddhist modernism and its role in the construction of a particular conception of Buddhism modeled on liberal evangelical Protestantism has in the last few decades become a focus of scholarly attention.[4] This reflexive scholarship, that is, one that self-critically examines its own presuppositions, is essential to the project of understanding Buddhism as it is, rather than as we want it to be.

One of the strongest strands in the tangled web of Buddhist modernism has been the creation of a psychological interpretation of Buddhism. While we cannot here examine the entire history of this psychologized Buddhism, we can focus on one particular aspect by asking the question, "Is it appropriate to equate the Jungian concept of individuation with the Buddhist concept of awakening?" This question is personally important to me because for years I assumed that there was such an equation, suggesting that Jungian psychology provides a metalanguage for making comparisons between religious traditions. Specifically, individuation as a process moving a person toward a state of wholeness may be seen as providing a tradition-neutral way of talking about any religious tradition that has a notion of human life having a goal toward which one should be moving.[5] However, the question that now arises for me is whether or not individuation is in fact "tradition-neutral."

Jung himself seems to have thought of individuation as universally applicable, that is, as an appropriate way of thinking about the developmental process of all humans.[6] In his foreword to D. T. Suzuki's *Introduction to Zen Buddhism*, Jung explains that "the individuation process" is his "term for 'becoming whole.'"[7] He then goes on almost immediately to suggest that Zen is committed to the goal of "becoming whole" as well. J. J. Clarke asserts that Jung was more sympathetic toward Buddhism than other Asian religions, and that one of the reasons for this greater sympathy is that what he found in Buddhism "was a method which was built on the self's capacity and urge to realize itself through its own efforts to seek individuation."[8]

However, whether or not individuation as understood in analytic psychology can be universalized needs to be questioned.

To pursue these questions—whether individuation is tradition neutral and can therefore be unproblematically equated with awakening—this essay will first examine the religious and Romantic origins of modern psychology. This takes the form of examining the common narrative structure of an idealized original state, followed by the loss of that state, ending in reattaining that state at a higher level. We will then look at the presence of this narrative structure in the Jungian concept of individuation. Lastly, we will propose an alternative narrative structure based on Śāntideva's *Bodhicaryāvatāra*. The contrast between the two narrative structures will allow us in conclusion to consider more generally the problematic character of a psychologized Buddhism.

The Romantic Narrative

The importance of critically examining the ideologies that inform our models of human development lies in the power that they have as implicit assumptions, not only to limit the range of solutions considered and mold the nature of the solutions offered, but more importantly to create the self-conception that there is some problem to be solved. The fundamental narrative structure originating in biblical history and carried forward through Neoplatonism and Romanticism into modern psychological conceptions of development is that of creation, fall, and redemption. The apparent function of this narrative is to offer an answer to the problem of the human condition. However, what is left unspoken, and is therefore all the more powerful because unspoken, is the way in which this narrative constructs the human condition, defining it as problematic in such a fashion as to entail what is then offered as a solution to the problem. Suzanne R. Kirschner has examined the religious origins of psychoanalysis and has made this point in passing: "Biblical history can be understood in terms of the 'problem' that it at once constructs and attempts to resolve."[9] Writing on the Book of Revelation, Leonard L. Thompson has made this point more strongly: "An apocalypse thus functions in a social situation not only to bring comfort, hope, perseverance, and the like, but also to cause people to see their situation as one in which such functions are needed and appropriate. An apocalypse can create the perception that a situation is one of crisis and then offer hope, assurance, and support for faithful behavior in dealing with the crisis."[10] The role of systems of thought not only in offering solutions but also in creating and defining the problem to be solved is as true of Buddhism as it is of biblical history, Neoplatonism, Romanticism, and psychotherapy. The differences between how systems of thought define the human condition as problematic, the nature of the solution to that problem, and the means to reach that solution are central to considering any comparison between Buddhism and Jungian psychology.

The Romantic background of Jung's psychology has been discussed by several authors and is not in need of demonstration here.[11] A discussion of one specific aspect of Romanticism that continues to inform analytic psychology, however, reveals how the assumptions of Western religious culture have structured the psychological representation of Buddhism over the last century or more. This aspect is the Romantic narrative of self-redemption.

M. H. Abrams has described the structure of the Judaeo-Christian atonement narrative and its historical development up to Romanticism. The structure of the Romantic narrative of self-redemption naturalizes the biblical narrative of an initial state of grace, a fall into alienation, and finally atonement. Naturalizing the atonement narrative means that it is not alienation from God that needs to be overcome through atonement for sin, but rather alienation from one's true, natural self that needs to be overcome by a higher reintegration of the individual self with the larger whole of nature, or the state.

Drawing on the work of Abrams, Kirschner has demonstrated that this narrative continues its historical development.[12] While the fundamental narrative structure of creation, fall, and redemption has its origins in biblical history and is carried forward through Neoplatonism and Romanticism, it goes on to inform contemporary psychological conceptions of individual development. The underlying narrative of psychological development that is found in depth psychology has been described by Kirschner as "the story of a progression from an originally undifferentiated unity, through a painful-but-necessary chain of ruptures, losses, and differentiations, towards a culmination . . . in which the severed elements are reunited, by means of an integration that preserves their differentiated distinctiveness."[13] Kirschner's point is that this narrative structure of human development was not discovered by psychologists but is a new, psychological interpretation of the atonement narrative, which they have inherited from biblical, Neoplatonic, and Romantic sources.

While the roots of this narrative are ultimately biblical, it provides a structure that becomes paradigmatic for Western culture: creation, fall, and redemption. At the creation there is a harmonious unity between God and his creation, but a harmony created by the absence of differentiation. The fall is initiated by sinful willfulness to not be obedient to God. And redemption is the return to harmony, but at a higher level of integration in which the separate will is retained.[14] Of course, the characterization of this narrative structure as comprising three parts is a convention, and is subject to further refinement and nuance. For example, in his historical study of the cult of the Sacred Heart, Raymond Jonas describes the narrative structure of "a salvation story" as comprising four parts: "an original state of harmony → transgression and rupture → decadence and chastisement → atonement and redemption."[15] Kirschner's three-part narrative structure, which we will continue to employ here, basically treats as a single stage the moments Jonas separates as the second and third stages.

As Kirschner says, this movement from creation through the fall to redemption is "a distinctive historical narrative design, [that] is detectable in many of our most taken-for-granted ideas about history, society, and psychology."[16] As implied by the last item in her list—psychology—the biblical narrative of creation, fall, and redemption is taken both as a description of the past, present, and future of the human race as a whole and as a model for interpreting the life history of the individual. Kirschner summarizes the complex later history of this narrative as

> a series of cultural transformations in which a Judaeo-Christian narrative was made more worldly (and in some cases interiorized) in the form of Protestant doctrines and then was fully secularized in eighteenth and nineteenth century movements in philosophy, arts, and letters. In the case of non-psychoanalytic (social and psychological) developmentalisms there is a stronger inheritance from Enlightenment and nineteenth-century positivist/evolutionist doctrines, whereas in the case of contemporary psychoanalytic developmental psychology there is a stronger inheritance from Romantic doctrines.[17]

Romanticism transformed the narrative of redemption, particularly in its quest version, into interiorized forms of development of the self. Emphasizing the individualistic character of Romanticism, Harold Bloom has described the movement as "an internalization of romance, particularly of the quest variety, an internalization made for more than therapeutic purposes, because made in the name of a humanizing hope that approaches apocalyptic intensity."[18] This was a shift, in other words, from the social and political to the individual and mental. "For the Romantics, [the biblical] historical narrative is transmuted into the story of the unfolding and realization of the mind or self."[19] It is this naturalized story of the individual originating in and developing out of an undifferentiated sense of unity, moving through separation and alienation, to achieve a higher reintegration with the other characterized by "constancy, authenticity, creativity, intimacy"[20] that came to provide the fundamental narrative for psychotherapeutic understandings of development. The higher reintegration sought, however, is ambivalent or paradoxical—the greater whole threatening to absorb the separate individual. This fear of absorption into the greater whole has often been projected onto Indic religions, which are seen as promoting a loss of separate self-consciousness, a merger back into the amniotic bliss—Freud's "oceanic" feeling.[21] Gerald N. Izenberg summarizes this ambivalence in the Romantic view, saying that while the individual is dependent upon "an all-inclusive totality other and greater than the self," it is also the case that the creative potency of the individual is absolute. At the same time, however, the individual "is also held to be superior to, even the very source of, the overarching totality to which it submits itself."[22] This ambivalence applied equally to nature and to the state, as discussed by Izenberg.[23] As Harold Bloom puts it, the "program of Romanticism . . . demands something more than a natural man to carry it through," this expansion necessitating "enlarged and more numerous senses."[24] In this demand for a more-than-natural humanity we can hear the theme of human perfectibility, or self-transcendence, found in much of American folk religion, including New Age thought.[25] The theme of human perfectibility as it is found in popular spirituality is simply the Romantic individualistic and naturalistic interpretation of the atonement narrative. Although this is not the same as the psychologized version, it does provide one of the strongest links in popular culture between spirituality and psychology.

The narrative structure of idealized origin, fall or alienation, and restoration of harmony is so pervasive that it seems to structure almost all aspects of Western historiography. Despite the opposition to Hegel by later Romantic thinkers because of his supposedly excessive rationalism, Hegel's philosophy of history shares the Romantic assumptions regarding an original time of harmony, followed by an alienation, and reaching toward a final time in which harmony is restored. Abstracted from the specifics of his philosophy of history, this becomes the three-part dialectic which is the motive force for the spiritual development of human society. Marx's philosophy of history is also structured by this three-part movement, in his case from social harmony of primitive communism through the intervening fallen periods of feudal and capitalist exploitation, culminating in the recovered harmony of the classless society of the future. Though the motive force has changed from spiritual to material, the narrative structure remains the same. Likewise, even the most self-consciously critical postmodern thinkers reveal the influence of this narrative structure, growing out of their own Romantic and Marxist roots. Commenting on a work by Fredric Jameson, Stephen Greenblatt states,

> The whole passage has the resonance of an allegory of the fall of man: once we were whole, agile, integrated; we were individual subjects but not individuals, we had no psychology distinct from the shared life of the society; politics and poetry were one. Then capitalism arose and shattered this luminous, benign totality. The myth echoes throughout Jameson's book, though by the close it has been eschatologically reoriented so that the totality lies not in a past revealed to have always already fallen but in the classless future. A philosophical claim then appeals to an absent empirical event.[26]

It seems as if all such analyses begin in the middle of the narrative—describing the current situation as a fallen one in which we are "plagued" by alienation. It is the pervasive quality of such historiographic assumptions that motivates the frequent rhetorical breast-beating about how modern America, one of the most religious nations in the contemporary world, has lost its direction due to secularization. Such reiterations, or variations on the same theme, demonstrate how deeply this narrative structure works within Western culture.

In summary, the narrative structure informing depth psychology's conception of development has a history of reinterpretation, moving through a series of distinguishable stages of interpretation. Beginning with the idea of collective redemption in history as found in the Hebrew Bible, the narrative becomes spiritualized when interpreted by Christian thinkers. This spiritualized version becomes specifically individualized in Protestant interpretations.[27] Then the Protestant, individual, spiritualized narrative is naturalized by the Romantics. Once naturalized, the narrative has become psychologized by depth psychologists as what we may call the narrative of self-development.

The Narrative Structure of Individuation

Individuation is the key element in any consideration of the relation between analytic psychology and Buddhism, especially the cross-cultural application of analytic psychology to Buddhism. All of the other elements of analytic psychology—type theory, archetypes, and the like—are effectively subtheories within the broader theory of personal development found in analytic psychology. Change in one of these can be absorbed without endangering the entire system. However, individuation so integrates the other elements into a coherent system that changes in it do constitute a threat to the integrity of the whole system. In a recent introductory survey Murray Stein employs the metaphor of a map to describe the various elements of the psyche (the archetypes etc.) as the terrain, while individuation is identified as the journey across this terrain.[28]

In a review of Jung's writings on the subject of individuation Kenneth Lambert has identified three different usages of the term "individuation."[29] The first is "differentiation of the individual from the collective." This does not, however, necessarily imply that the individual takes an oppositional stance to the collective, only that the two are differentiated. The second usage is related to the first but is used to identify the "relationship of the individual to the collective," meaning that there is a relation of complementarity and mutual interdependence between the individual and the collective. The third usage is the one that will be the focus of our attention—the "nature and conditions of the development of individuation," that is, the process of individuation. This is understood to be a spontaneous process, ordering "the multitudinous instincts, tendencies and oppositions of the personality into a unique and meaningful whole. Jung considered that he had assembled enough evidence to suggest that this may be thought of as an innate power of the self rather than as a contrivance of ego-consciousness. For him the function of the latter was to come to terms with these unifying processes and, in a discriminating way, to cooperate with them as they emerged."[30]

For those having a religious orientation, individuation appears to be the most appealing aspect of Jungian thought. Individuation seems to offer a psychologically based model of human development analogous to religious conceptions of human life as having some purpose, some goal beyond the condition in which one finds oneself. Expressed abstractly enough, such a conception would seem to apply equally well to both Christian conceptions of salvific redemption and Buddhist conceptions of the path to awakening. Indeed, the ideas of Jungian thought may appear to be abstract enough to form a metalanguage in terms of which all religious traditions could be equally well described and compared.

This use of Jungian thought as a metalanguage for religion has the same appeal as any hegemonic metanarrative—by claiming that all religions are properly within its purview, it establishes a commanding position over those traditions. As is by now well known from postmodern critiques, however, any discourse that claims the status of a hegemonic metanarrative is itself located relative to other narratives—not only socioculturally but also politically and historically. Comparing individuation with the narrative of self-development reveals the locatedness of individuation.

Although Kirschner has been concerned with contemporary psychoanalysis, for example, Mahler, Kohut, Fairbairn, and Winnicott, this same pattern is certainly familiar from the writings of some Jungians in describing the process of individuation. The pervasive character of the narrative of self-development and its effect on molding the way in which individuation is interpreted can be seen more clearly in the works of some of Jung's followers than in Jung's own writings. The development of Jung's ideas took place over more than half a century, and a thorough study would require placing his formulations of the idea of individuation into that history. In the work of his interpreters, however, we find Jung's complex, changing conceptualizations reduced to a version more in conformity with the cultural assumptions concerning personal development.

For example, Edward Edinger's description of the individuation process is fully informed by the narrative of self-development, and indeed by the explicitly religious atonement narrative. For Edinger, the original condition for human infants is one in which there is no real ego, and the "latent ego is in complete identification with the Self."[31] This primal identification

between the ego and the Self is one that Edinger identifies as inflationary—
the ego ascribes to itself the deity-like powers of the Self. He explicates this
by reference to myths of an original paradisal age, including an extended
discussion of the Garden of Eden myth as an "excellent example" of this
original inflation. Edinger's description of inflation parallels exactly the sin
of Adam and Eve—the presumption to acquire the power that is properly
God's: "We can identify a state of inflation whenever we see someone
(including ourselves) living out an attribute of deity, i.e., whenever one is
transcending proper human limits."[32] Such an inflated condition, however,
cannot be sustained in interaction with the realities of the world and, in
Edinger's view, leads inevitably to a deflationary alienation. Continuing with
his alignment of the individuation process with the myth of Eden, he says
that the "myth depicts the birth of consciousness as a crime which alienates
man from God and from his original preconscious wholeness."[33] This movement from inflation to alienation is followed by another inflation, creating
a dialectic that is the driving force of human development. "As this cycle
repeats itself again and again throughout psychic development it brings
about a progressive differentiation of the ego and the Self. In the early phases,
representing approximately the first half of life, the cycle is experienced as
an alternation between two states of being, namely inflation and alienation.
Later a third state appears when the ego-Self axis reaches consciousness . . .
which is characterized by a conscious dialectic relationship between ego and
Self. This state is individuation."[34]

Successful repetition of this cycle is supposed to lead eventually to a
healthy conscious awareness of the ego-Self axis, which is how Edinger—
apparently following Neumann[35]—defines individuation. The religious character of Edinger's conception of individuation is made further evident by
his explanation of the motivating force leading toward individuation. Rather
than a natural process of the psyche, as one most commonly finds it in Jung,
for Edinger individuation is motivated by a transcendent mystical power:
"The transpersonal life energy, in the process of self-unfolding, uses human
consciousness, a product of itself, as an instrument for its own self-
realization."[36] In Kirschner's terms the final, individuated relation between
ego and Self described by Edinger is "an integration that preserves their differentiated distinctiveness." Quite clearly, Edinger's interpretation of individuation is simply the biblical atonement narrative presented as if it were
a psychological theory.

In some discussions of individuation, however, while there are echoes of the atonement narrative, it has been freed from its ties to the Eden myth, so that individuation is more explicitly a theory rather than an interpretive presumption. Thus, there is a recognizable similarity between the work of some analytic psychologists who in recent research have focused on developmental issues (self-object relations) and Edinger's description of individuation in that both emphasize the dialectical character of the individuation process. But there are also key differences, particularly in the characterization of the initial state. For example, basing himself on Michael Fordham's work, Kenneth Lambert describes individuation as a "deintegrative–reintegrative process" and elaborates on this by saying that it is "a kind of breathing process, [in which] the self deintegrates and reintegrates at appropriate times in the developmental process, and accordingly, the reintegrated self contains progressively more and more archetypal realized objects that have been internalized—a very different matter from either formal potentialities or even potentialities presenting themselves as *images* only and devoid of real experience."[37]

An accompanying diagram, which looks very similar to a diagram Edinger employs, outlines this dialectic process in three stages.[38] In Lambert's diagram the initial stage of development postulates the individual as being centered in the unconscious. The unconscious contains within itself archetypal potentialities and is separate from the external world, existing in a state of "undifferentiated potentiality." In early years interaction with the external world motivates the dialectic of deintegration and reintegration. This creates an intermediating psychic range in which the known objects of the external world have become internalized as they relate to archetypal potentialities. These internalized archetypal objects comprise archetypes, defenses, actual objects of the external world, and ego fragments. At this second stage the center of the self is still in the unconscious. Finally, in later life an ego-inclusive self is created as a result of the ongoing dialectical interaction. The ego-fragments coalesce as an ego in the psychic midrange, along with the other internalized archetypal objects, and now the center of the self is also located in this psychic midrange.

While there are clear similarities between the Romantic narrative structure and the three stages described by Lambert—an original unconscious unity, a period of disruptive interaction with the actualities of the world, and a final reintegration at a higher state—it seems that these may be simply the result of Lambert's use of the notion of the dialectic as a motivating force of development, rather than as simply a psychological version of the biblical atonement narrative. Missing is both the idealization of the original unconscious unity as Edenic and the final reintegration as motivated by God.

As with Romanticism's ambivalence about losing one's separate identity into the greater whole, some versions of the individuation process reveal a comparable ambivalence about the relation between the ego and the psyche. This ambivalence has been discussed by George E. Atwood and Robert D. Stolorow. They have pointed out that the theme of self-dissolution as threat is found in Jung's own conceptualizations of individuation. It is perhaps most obvious that an "omnipotently bad object" may threaten "self-boundary destruction and self-object dedifferentiation."[39] However, such "threats to the self representation lurk, not only in the dangerous, negative manifestations of the archetypes, but in the positive, idealized ones as well."[40] While both self-surrender and self-inflation can lead to self-loss, individuation is the goal of establishing "a cohesive, bounded self representation sharply differentiated from the omnipotent object representations."[41] As we saw above, the Romantics were ambivalent in their relation to nature. It both posed a threat to individuality if one merged into the natural, and constituted the greater whole since by integrating with it one achieves one's full potential. Now, instead of nature, it is the psyche that poses this ambivalence.

While the three-part narrative structure of creation, fall, and redemption has undergone repeated reinterpretation from a collective, historical redemption to an individualized, psychological one, this does not mean that its earlier versions have disappeared from the culture. Indeed, the more various the realms to which the narrative is applied, the more pervasive its presumptive power. For example, the biblical version of collective, historical redemption has been applied to the societal role of analytic psychology itself by Ann Ulanov. Presenting this as Jung's own view, she constructs a mythic history in which we find analytic psychology replacing religion. Although she does not explicitly express the analogy, it seems clear that, for her, just as Christ the Redeemer brings a new message, a new testament, to replace the old testament which has now become decadent and no longer effective, so analytic psychology plays the role of a second redeemer for contemporary society, displacing a religion that has become decadent and no longer effective.

The first movement in the three-part narrative constructed by Ulanov is the assertion that "for centuries the symbols, rituals, and dogmas of religions, East and West, gathered the psychic energy of individuals and nations alike into traditions that bore witness to life's meaning and acted as underground springs nourishing different civilizations."[42] Here is the image of primal harmony, the mythic *in illo tempore* or "once upon a time." Our contemporary, fallen condition, is one in which "the energy [that was once] channeled into religious containers [has been] poured back into the human psyche with disastrous effect. Deprived of its proper outlet in religious experience, it assumes negative forms." Our contemporary condition is characterized as one in which "we feel afflicted by a deadening malaise, unable to effect healing measures against rising crime, ecological depredation, and mental illness." Thus, in this view all the ills of contemporary society are the result of loss of religious faith, of secularization. But, fortunately, redemption is at hand: "There is also, however, a positive effect in the pouring back of all this psychic energy into human beings. It is nothing less than the emergence of a new discipline, that of depth psychology, which is a new collective way of exploring and acknowledging the fact that the nature of our access to God has fundamentally changed. Our own psyche, which is part of the collective psyche, is now a medium through which we can experience the divine."[43] Given the religious purpose in this portrayal of analytic psychology, it might seem appropriate to coin a new term, "psychotheology," for conflations of psychology and religion of this sort.

Some interpretations of individuation are quite clearly versions of the atonement narrative that have been filtered through the process described by Kirschner. Having been first individualized and then naturalized, it has now been psychologized. As a theory of human development, such a view insinuates a deeply religious set of assumptions into a supposedly secular view of the person. While those assumptions are largely shared throughout Western culture, they are limited to that culture. Buddhist religious conceptions of human development derive from radically different assumptions.

The Narrative Structure of the Bodhisattva Path

Given the long history of Buddhism, its extensive scholastic literature, and its transmission to so many different religious cultures, it should not be surprising that there are many different descriptions of the path to awakening.[44] In the West, one of the best known is the sequence of Ten Oxherding

Pictures of Chan Buddhism. These are well known in analytic psychology due to the work of D. T. Suzuki, who both commented on the sequence and was a participant along with Jung in the Eranos symposia. Indeed, Suzuki's commentary on the Ten Oxherding Pictures was given at Eranos in 1954.[45] The interest in the Ten Oxherding Pictures among analytical psychologists is reflected in the fact that there are commentaries on the Ten Oxherding Pictures by two analytic psychologists, J. Marvin Spiegelman and Hayao Kawai.[46] The series of pictures was so influential in the history of Chinese religion that it is replicated in a Taoist version in which the animal is a horse instead of an ox. A similar sequence is also found in Tibetan Buddhism. In this case, however, the animal is an elephant that gradually changes from black to white as the process of meditative training proceeds.[47]

Whereas these are all pictorial representations of the path, there are also extensive philosophic expositions of the path as well.[48] These are in some cases quite extensive and detailed studies. For example, the Theravada tradition has both the *Vimuttimagga* and the *Visuddhimagga*. The latter is the better known and is the work of one of the most revered Theravada masters, Buddhaghosa. It is basically structured on the former, earlier work, but expands it greatly. It is likewise the case that many of the most important Mahayana Buddhist philosophical treatises are structured around discussions of the path. Writings on the path *(marga)* become a major literary genre in Tibetan Buddhism and assume various forms, such as the stages of the path *(lam rim)*, which discusses the full range of development from the preliminary practices preceding meditative training up to tantric practice, and the stages of the doctrine *(bstan rim),* which focuses on the bodhisattva path per se.[49] Several such works have recently become available in English translation.[50]

For our purposes, the *Bodhicaryāvatāra* by Śāntideva provides a concise treatment of one version of the Buddhist path without being so succinct as to be open to projective misinterpretation. Śāntideva lived in the high medieval period of Indian Buddhism. It is generally thought that his life extended from the latter part of the seventh century to the middle of the eighth.[51] The work came to be held in particular importance among Tibetan Buddhists. Its popularity in Tibet is reflected by the attention it has received in the diasporic spread of Tibetan Buddhism.[52]

Like all medieval Buddhist works, the textual history of the *Bodhicaryāvatāra* is quite complex, but the version that is best known today has ten chapters. Enclosed within a familiar liturgical structure, the core comprises five chapters expounding the six perfections *(pāramitās)*. The liturgical framework is not to be discounted as merely a literary device, however. The process of practice replicates movement on the path. In other words, practice is not only intended to move one on the path, but being a recapitulation of the entire path, practice *is* realization. Adopting the translations of Crosby and Skilton, the ten chapters are:

1. Praise of the Awakening Mind
2. Confession of Faults
3. Adopting the Awakening Mind
4. Vigilance Regarding the Awakening Mind
5. The Guarding of Awareness
6. The Perfection of Forbearance
7. The Perfection of Vigor
8. The Perfection of Meditative Absorption
9. The Perfection of Understanding
10. Dedication

The liturgical program that informs Śāntideva's work is known as the "unsurpassed worship" *(anuttarapūjā)*.[53] The work opens with praises to the primary object of veneration, which in this case is the "awakening mind" or *bodhicitta*. This is a key concept in Mahāyāna Buddhism, as establishing the mind intent upon awakening is both necessary and sufficient for at least eventually achieving full awakening—for becoming a buddha. Such praises are frequently found at the beginning of both Buddhist liturgies and Buddhist literary works, and in this case are then followed in chapters 2 and 3 with a series of liturgical actions. These include worship of the buddhas, their teaching (dharma), and the community of those who adhere to the teachings (sangha); going for refuge to the Triple Jewel (buddha, dharma, and sangha); confession of faults (not in the sense of atonement for sinful disobedience but rather in the sense of what might be called, in the terminology of the 1970s, "consciousness raising");[54] rejoicing in the meritorious actions of others; requesting the buddhas to not abandon the world, that is, to not enter final cessation; dedicating whatever merit one's own actions may create to the benefit of all living beings; and arousing one's own mind of awakening. The fourth chapter encourages perseverance in working toward awakening. At this point the liturgical ground has been established for movement through the path, in this case structured in terms of the six perfections. These are qualities that someone seeking full awakening, a bodhisattva, needs to bring to full perfection.

The six perfections are generosity, morality (these first two found together in chapter five), forbearance, vigor, meditative absorption, and wisdom. The six perfections are found as an organized group in the Perfection of Wisdom *(prajñāpāramitā)* literature, which has its origins several centuries prior to Śāntideva. The six perfections are a progressive sequence leading to awakening, and the six are, therefore, always found in this order.[55] Generosity *(dāna)* is the willingness to give one's material goods and time and, most importantly, to share the teachings of the buddha (buddha-dharma) without reservation. Morality *(śīla)* means restraining oneself from actions that are harmful to others, such as killing, stealing, illicit sex, lying, pointless criticism and complaining, instigating conflict between others, gossip and rumor-mongering, greed, anger, and asserting mistaken conceptions of human existence. Forbearance *(kṣāti)* is the ability to persevere through difficulties and to refrain from becoming angry with those who cause you harm. Vigor *(vīrya)* is necessary as the ability to sustain one's efforts, even when life is difficult—or boring and pointless, which can be even more subversive of one's good intentions. Meditative absorption *(dhyāna)* refers to a very wide range of meditative techniques, all of which may be interpreted either as developing the ability to focus one's attention on some object for a sustained period of time, or as developing a decentered attention on the present moment. Wisdom *(prajñā)* is insight into the absence of any permanent, eternal, absolute or unchanging essence in any and all existing things—that is, the insight that all existing things are empty.

As in the Perfection of Wisdom literature, Śāntideva's text treats the first five of the six perfections as forms of mental training contributing to the perfection of wisdom, and the perfection of wisdom as what is needed in order to perfect the other five. What makes it possible to perfect generosity, for example, is insight into the nature of the giver, the gift, and the recipient of the gift as empty, as lacking any permanent, eternal, absolute, or unchanging essence. Such insight is wisdom. The perfection of wisdom, which means living from an awareness of all things as empty, is awakening. For this reason, the perfection of wisdom is sometimes called "the mother of buddhas."

The final chapter continues the liturgical structure of the text. Once again the practitioner—now having realized awakening—dedicates the merit of his or her efforts to the benefit of all living beings. The progressive movement through the six perfections has culminated in awakening. Having developed wisdom, one has overcome the fundamental ignorance that keeps one repeating habitual behaviors that are self-frustrating. That ignorance is the mistaken conception that anything can provide permanent satisfaction, permanent security. Mistaken conceptions of this kind lead to misplaced affections—desires for that which will not in fact actually satisfy one's desires, and hatred of those things that threaten our self-centered projects. In Śāntideva's version of the path to awakening, repetitive ignorant action is interrupted by establishing the mind intent upon awakening, the mind that forms the basis for practice, e.g., the six perfections, leading to insight into emptiness. Drawing on Śāntideva's version of the path, we can propose one possible Buddhist narrative structure as an alternative to the biblical redemption narrative and its psychological reinterpretation. This narrative structure would start with a primal condition of ignorance and its consequent suffering, move into an arising of the intent to awaken, and culminate in insight into the emptiness of all conditioned existence and the liberation of all sentient beings.

Buddhism as Psychology, Psychology as Buddhism?

The Western representation of Buddhism has also been directly influenced by Romanticism. For example, the Western discourse on Buddhism is usually characterized as having nirvana, or cessation, as its goal. As a result of the misappropriation of Buddhism by Schopenhauer, during Jung's time cessation was understood as cessation of the ego. Schopenhauer's interpretation of Buddhism as motivated by the desire to escape from the sufferings of cyclic existence (samsara) through the eradication of the ego was extremely influential, leading to the allegation, still commonly heard, that Buddhism is nihilistic.[56] This characterization of Buddhism results not simply from a failure to discriminate between Buddhist teachings and those of various Hindu schools, such as the Samkhya, but more importantly in Schopenhauer's case from his appropriation of the authority of the exotic to justify his own views. This understanding of Buddhism as a "world-denying ascetic faith"[57] continued well into the second half of the twentieth century, a reflection of the influence of Schopenhauer on the perception of Buddhism.

However, categorizing Buddhism as a "world-denying ascetic faith" conflates concepts that need to be kept distinct. There is the teaching of *anātman*, which is the rejection of metaphysical essences: nothing is permanent, eternal, absolute, or unchanging. Frequent, albeit literalist, translations of *anātman* are "no-self" and "selflessness," phrases easily misunderstood as indicating a rejection of the personal ego as purely illusory. This latter interpretation is then linked with nirvana, which is consequently understood as cessation of the ego or self. A closer reading of Buddhist literature, however, reveals that what is brought to an end are the *kleśas*, the obscurations, those mental and emotional factors that keep us from engaging with the world as it actually is. (In a different interpretation, action, or karma, is brought to an end. These two interpretations have led to debates about the nature of awakening in China.) The *kleśas* are defined as being of two kinds: mistaken conceptions and misplaced affections. The fundamental mistaken conception is that there is anything permanently satisfying, and the fundamental misplaced affection is our desire for that illusive something.

Nirvana, then, is not the cessation of the ego but rather the cessation of the obscurations. Nirvana itself is not the goal of Buddhist practice but rather the means by which one attains to the state of awakening, *bodhi*. This distinction is analogous to pointing out that the reason one cleans a mirror (brings about the extinction of the obscurations) is for the sake of seeing clearly (awakening). When mistaken concepts and misplaced affections end, then we awaken to the way things really are: empty of any metaphysical essence.[58]

We can clarify the difference between Buddhism and this Romantic version by first noting what Buddhism is not. This can be done by highlighting how fundamentally different its view of human existence and the nature of religion is from Christian views. Christian religious anthropology minimally involves the elements of the atonement narrative: God as the transcendent creator, creation as a primal harmony, sin as willful disobedience, alienation from God as the result of sin, redemptive sacrifice— which God himself provides—as atoning for human sin, leading to a restored harmony between the human creature and the transcendent creator. In contrast, Buddhism does not hypothesize a transcendent creator god responsible for the existence of the world but rather interprets the universe as having existed from "beginningless time." Human beings have always been deluded about the nature of their own existence, but such delusion is not the result of sinfulness, and it is neither essential nor irremediable. What is needed is not a redemptive sacrifice leading to atonement but rather a transforming epistemological insight into how things actually exist—empty of any absolute, eternal, unchanging, or permanent essence. What is attained is not a restoration of harmony, but rather insight into the emptiness of everything that exists. So instead of the atonement narrative, Buddhism interprets human existence and development as the path leading from ignorance to the cultivation of the six perfections to an awakened mind. Rather than the sequence of creation, fall, and redemptive atonement, we have ignorance, intent to awaken, and insight into emptiness.

An important qualifying consideration for this critique of the equation of individuation and awakening is a therapeutic one. Someone whose cultural background is Western, having been raised in a culture deeply imbued with the atonement narrative, will have absorbed this narrative and its assumptions. In a therapeutic situation, then, use of a concept of development that replicates the structure of the atonement narrative, such as individuation, may in fact be the most effective course of action. A different developmental conception, such as awakening as it has been described here, may prove to be unproductive and confusing for those neither ready nor willing to step outside the foundational assumptions of their own culture.[59] This therapeutic consideration, however, does not negate the violence done to the constellation of concepts that comprise the path to awakening when it is misinterpreted as simply another instance of the psychologized, neoromantic version of the atonement narrative.

In the late nineteenth century and early twentieth, several Buddhist apologists and reformers attempted to respond to Western criticisms of Buddhism by creating a loose international movement that is now referred to as "Buddhist modernism." Buddhist modernism moved to naturalize Buddhism, stripping it of all supernatural, devotional, and intercessionary aspects. These were considered irrational, regressive, and superstitious. Instead, a rational, moralistic, and humanistic version of Buddhism was promoted. Often one hears vestiges of this rhetoric in assertions that Buddhism is not a religion but rather a philosophy of life. As Kirschner has pointed out, the Romantics' naturalization of the atonement narrative was a necessary step between the Protestant individualizing and the psychological internalization of the narrative. In the same way, the naturalized Buddhism created by modernist reformers transformed Buddhism into something that could be internalized as a psychologized Buddhism.

However, if awakening is glossed according to Romantic presumptions of the narrative of individual development, and the concept of individuation is structured according to those same Romantic presumptions, then the resulting convergence—Buddhism interpreted as psychology—has the appearance of being valid, when it is actually little more than an elaborate *petitio principii* fallacy: the atonement narrative stands behind both individuation and the psychologized interpretation of awakening, thus creating the illusory appearance that individuation and awakening are the same.

3

Cross-Cultural Dialogue and the Resonance of Narrative Strands

JEREMY D. SAFRAN

THE CONVERSATION between Buddhism and Western psychotherapy, while hardly new, is currently accelerating at a rapid pace. While much of this conversation has focused on issues such as commonalities, differences, complementarity, and so on, I think it is also important to step back and reflect on the nature of the discourse as well. Like any type of cross-cultural conversation, the encounter between Buddhism and psychotherapy is fundamentally about the confrontation with the other, and there are various common forms that this type of encounter can take.

One common form consists of the distorted construction and marginalization of the other as a means of validating one's own world view. Although historically speaking this was certainly the response of Western theologians to Buddhism, I do not believe that this is a dominant theme in contemporary discourse.

Another common tendency is to idealize the other. My sense is that there is still considerable evidence of this type of idealization in the approach of Western psychotherapists to Buddhism, although fortunately a number of authors have recently pointed to its pitfalls.[1] Another approach consists of looking for commonalities or common principles. For example, some have argued (e.g., Aronson, this volume) that disidentification from self-representations is a common principle in both Buddhism and Western psychotherapy. I believe that this approach can be of value in some contexts. Especially at an early point in the conversation, the exploration of common principles can facilitate dialogue by rendering the alien more familiar. The exploration of common principles, however, can also function at a sufficiently high level of abstraction that it forecloses deeper understanding. As cultural anthropologists such as Clifford Geertz suggest, it is only through understanding what is most unique about each culture that we can understand human beings in all their complexity. To this end, we need a type of *thick description* that explores in detail and with nuance both similarities and differences between traditions.

Another common form of conversation consists of the co-opting of one culture by another through the imposition of one's own preexisting cultural narrative upon the other's. For example, John Reynolds has demonstrated the way in which Evans-Wentz's translation of *The Tibetan Book of the Great Liberation* was strongly influenced and distorted by Theosophy and Neoplatonic philosophy and popularized Advaita Vedanta.[2] Similarly, he demonstrated the way in which Jung's introduction to the translation distorts the Dzogchen teachings through the lens of both Evans-Wentz's distorted translation and Jungian psychology.

Richard Payne (this volume) has made the case that Western psychology tends to view Buddhism through the lens of a Romantic "atonement" narrative that has become paradigmatic for modern psychology. His thesis, in short, is that much of modern psychology is shaped by a secularized version of a Biblical atonement narrative that is paradigmatic in Western culture, and that there is a tendency for modern psychotherapy to impose this narrative on Buddhist teachings, thereby distorting their fundamental meaning. I believe that Payne's caution about the risk of imposing one's own cultural narratives upon another tradition serves as a valuable warning. At the same time I would like to use Payne's thesis as a point of departure for questioning the idea that there is any one dominant cultural narrative in either Western psychotherapy or Buddhism, and to argue that the encounter between different cultures always involves the conversation between multiple cultural narratives.

Payne follows Suzanne Kirschner in arguing that much of modern psychoanalysis has been influenced by a psychologized version of an atonement narrative that derives from Judaeo-Christian sources.[3] According to this argument, the structure of the original atonement narrative consists of the following stages: an initial state of grace (harmony with God), a fall into alienation (from the divine), and finally a culminating stage of atonement or redemption. This narrative was subsequently naturalized or secularized by Romantic and Neoplatonic traditions that reconceptualized the alienation from God as a type of alienation from a *true* or natural self. This naturalized atonement narrative, it is argued, influences much of contemporary psychoanalytic thinking. Thus, Payne argues that the Jungian notion of individuation, which emphasizes the integration of multiple, opposing tendencies of the self into a meaningful whole, provides a good example of this type of naturalized, romanticized atonement narrative. He goes on to contrast this narrative with the kind of Buddhist narrative structure that can be found in Shantideva, which consists of the following stages: a primal condition of ignorance and its consequent suffering, the arising of the intent to awaken, and a culminating stage of insight into the emptiness of all conditioned existence. According to Payne, the tendency to equate the Jungian concept of individuation with the Buddhist notion of awakening involves the imposition of one cultural narrative upon another and thus an unconscious cultural imperialism.

While Payne's cautions regarding the dangers of unconscious cultural imperialism are well taken, I want to argue that both Buddhism and Western psychotherapy are living and evolving cultural institutions that are each characterized by multiple narrative structures. In order to simplify my task I will focus primarily on Western psychotherapy and only secondarily on Buddhism, and within Western psychotherapy I will restrict my focus to psychoanalysis.

I will start by briefly describing the approach of D. W. Winnicott, an influential British psychoanalyst, whose perspective does to some extent conform to the structure of the Romantic, naturalized atonement narrative as described by Payne. According to Winnicott, the goal of treatment is to facilitate the growth of the true self. From his perspective, the development of this true self is stunted through the impingement of the needs of others. Because of this impingement we learn to relate to others through a false self that is overly responsive to the needs of the other. The problem here is thus an overadaptation to society and the needs of the other. As Franz Metcalf points out, Winnicott's true self should not be interpreted as a pristine, substantial, fixed entity but rather as kind of ongoing, evolving process—what he referred to as a "going-on-being."[4] Again, as Metcalf points out, Winnicott's notion of unintegration, a state in which there is no need to have a fixed sense of self or self-representation, is resonant in some ways with the Buddhist notion of no-self, at least as conceptualized in the Zen tradition.

While Winnicott's vision can be seen as a Romantic one, many other psychoanalytic perspectives cannot. For example, Freud, the father of psychoanalysis, had a vision of life that can hardly be called Romantic. According to Freud, there is an inevitable conflict between the individual and society or between instinct and civilization. This conflict can *never* be resolved, although we can make more or less adaptive compromises. Change takes place through making our unconscious instincts conscious, and then taming and renouncing them to an acceptable degree. Freud was not particularly sanguine about the prospects of dramatic change and believed that psychoanalysis transforms "neurotic misery into ordinary unhappiness." Thus, Freud's perspective is more accurately conceptualized as a tragic perspective than as a Romantic one. One can also see the emphasis of the Enlightenment tradition on Freudian thinking. Although he emphasized the importance of recognizing that we are driven by unconscious animal passions and instinctual forces, he ultimately believed that reason and intellect could triumph over instinct. An important part of analytic change for Freud involves recognizing and coming to accept that many of our wishes and fantasies will never be fulfilled, which requires replacing the "pleasure principle" with the "reality principle." Although I can only touch on this briefly here, one can see certain resonances between the Freudian emphasis on accepting the "reality principle" and the first noble truth of Buddhism, the inevitability of suffering.

One of the most influential psychoanalysts in Europe, Latin America, and increasingly the United States is Melanie Klein. Once again, it is difficult to see the narrative structure of Kleinian thinking as Romantic in nature or as fitting the structure of a secularized atonement narrative. Klein believed that the root of our problems is innate aggression, and that the young infant needs to disown this aggression by projecting it onto the mother. He or she then engages in a defense called splitting, which involves experiencing the mother as two distinct individuals: a good, loving mother and an aggressive, persecutory one. In healthy development the individual is gradually able to integrate his or her feelings of love and hate for the mother and perceive the mother as a whole, integrated being who can be both loving and aggressive. Maturation takes place through accepting responsibility for one's aggression and coming to experience genuine concern for the mother and gratitude for what she has provided. In psychoanalysis, this maturational process needs to be worked through in the relationship with the analyst. Again, it is difficult to see this as a Romantic narrative or a secularized atonement narrative. There is no fall from an original state of grace and no alienation from a true or natural self. If anything, aspects of the Kleinian narrative seem reminiscent of the Christian narrative of original sin. We are born with the stain of original sin (innate aggression) and it is only through acknowledging our sinfulness that we can be redeemed. Ultimately love needs to triumph over hate. I am also intrigued by certain resonances between the Kleinian emphasis on the importance of coming to experience genuine concern for the other and the Mahayana Buddhist emphasis on the development of compassion. The ability to experience genuine gratitude toward others is an important part of the Kleinian narrative, just as it is in contemporary Japanese therapies influenced by Buddhist principles (e.g., Morita and Naikan therapies).

Currently, the most influential psychoanalytic tradition in North America is what is referred to as the relational tradition. Some of the major contributors to this tradition have been Stephen Mitchell, Lewis Aron, Jessica Benjamin, Philip Bromberg, and Irwin Hoffman. There are two major narratives within this tradition. The first is that the self becomes deadened and devitalized as a result of the breakdown of traditional structures of meaning, the progressive development of the importance of the individual within Western society, and the attempt to adapt to social conventions. There is thus a need for the individual to find ways of revitalizing the self through the creation of personally meaningful narratives in collaboration with the analyst. The second narrative is that the self is in a sense inhabited by alien presences in the form of harmful internalized relationships with others. According to this perspective, the self is inevitably constituted through relationships. Thus we can never find a true self in Winnicott's sense. But we can internalize new, healthier relationships by working out new, healthier ways of being through the relationship with the analyst. This type of narrative has a more Romantic tone to it than Freud's or Klein's perspectives. But it is hardly a Romantic narrative in the sense that Jung's or Winnicott's perspectives are. And again, it is hard to see this as a narrative of atonement (even when broadly defined). There is no fall from an original state of grace and no return to harmony at a higher level of integration. If anything, relational psychoanalysis emphasizes the acknowledgment of the existence of multiple, competing self-states and their acceptance, rather than their integration into a meaningful whole.[5]

As a final example of a different psychoanalytic narrative, let us consider the approach of the important French analyst Jacques Lacan. Lacan had an extremely important influence on the development of French psychoanalysis and is becoming increasingly influential in various parts of Europe, Latin

America, and the United States. According to Lacan, human beings live in a state of fundamental alienation from the self. This is true for the following reasons. First, we can only express ourselves through the medium of language. For this reason, there is an aspect of our experience that will never be symbolized, since language inevitably involves some transformation and distortion of our experience. Second, because we can only represent ourselves through the eyes of others, there can be no pure or true self independent of the other's perception (or our internalization of it). We thus experience a fundamental sense of emptiness or lack (the Lacanian term), and we spend our lives trying to fill this lack through symbolic forms of satisfaction or completion. These attempts are inevitably doomed to failure. The task is thus one of recognizing and accepting the inevitability of this lack rather than attempting to fill it. There is an interesting resonance here with the Buddhist notion of no-self that has a different feeling to it than the resonance between Winnicott's thinking and the notion of no-self.

Now let us look at the Buddhist tradition (and here I admit to being on less safe ground, since I am a psychoanalyst and not a scholar of Buddhism). One common narrative (mentioned by Richard Payne in this volume) is ignorance, intent to awaken, and awakening. There are, however, other narratives within Buddhism as well, and I would argue that some of these narratives are resonant with some of the more Romantic narratives found in the Western tradition. For example, there is a strand in the Zen tradition that emphasizes the importance of trust in the natural mind and the recovery of one's natural state of harmony with the universe. For example, the Zen literature speaks about the original mind, the buddha-mind, or no-mind as synonymous. In this tradition, emptiness takes on a more positive quality. There is a faith in the intuitive, spontaneous, and non-self-preoccupied state of being.

For example, the Chinese Zen master Linji said: "There is no place in Buddhism for using effort. Just be ordinary and nothing special. Relieve your bowels, pass water, put clothes on, and eat food." Or, consider the following example: The eighth-century Zen master Zhaozhou asked his teacher, Nanquan: "What is the Dao?" Nanquan replied: "Your ordinary mind is the Dao." "Then how can you return into accord with it?" asked Zhaozhou. Nanquan responded: " By intending to accord you immediately deviate. But without intention, how can you know the Dao? The Dao belongs neither to knowing or not knowing. Knowing is false understanding; not knowing is blind ignorance. If you really understand the Dao without doubt, it is like the empty sky. Why drag in right or wrong?"

I don't think it is too much of a stretch to see a consistency between this type of narrative and the secularized atonement narrative described by Payne: An original or natural state of harmony which is lost and then recovered. But there is an important paradoxical element here as well: "By intending to accord you immediately deviate. But without intention how can you know the Dao?" Now one can argue that this stance is a distortion of the original Buddhism resulting from the synthesis of Indian Buddhism with Chinese Daoism. Long before Buddhism came to China, the indigenous Daoist teachings had a long tradition of emphasizing that awakening has to do with achieving a natural, uncontrived state of being—with letting the mind alone.

Eventually, this led to the emergence of the debate between sudden enlightenment and gradual enlightenment, after which the paradigm of sudden enlightenment came to dominate many schools of East Asian Buddhism. In this paradigm there is an emphasis on the view that all beings have buddha-nature, or inherent enlightenment, and a tendency to negate graduated, hierarchical models of practice. Payne (with his reference to Shantideva) reflects a more gradualist approach, and his presentation of Buddhist narratives reflects this as well. In contrast Zen Buddhism tends to adopt a different, more nondualistic narrative. But this emphasis can be found in some strands of Indian Buddhism as well. The idea that all beings have buddha-nature can be traced back to the Tathagatagarbha doctrine that originated in India as early as the third century C.E.[6] And it is certainly present in the Vajrayana tradition which had developed in India by the tenth century C.E. For example, the Tantric master Saraha states, "If the truth is already manifest, what's the point of meditation? And if it's hidden one is just measuring darkness. Mantras and tantras, meditation and concentration, they are all causes for self-deception. Do not defile in contemplation thought that is pure by its own nature. Whatever you see that is it. In front, behind, in all ten directions, the nature of the sky is always clear. But by gazing and gazing the sight becomes obscured."

My point is that Zen is not just a distortion of Buddhism resulting from the imposition of one cultural narrative upon another. There were some resonances between specific aspects of indigenous Chinese culture and specific narrative strands already present in Indian Buddhism that led to the creative evolution of Zen. And by the same token I would argue that the current conversation between Buddhism and Western psychotherapy involves conversations among multiple narrative strands existing within each of these traditions. While in some cases gross distortions emerge from the unconscious imposition of a particular Western cultural narrative on Buddhist teachings, in other cases the resonance between particular narratives emerging from Buddhism and Western psychology can lead to a creative evolution and revitalization of both cultures. To my mind this is what the conversation between Buddhism and psychotherapy is all about. It is not a search for superficial similarities, a colonization of Buddhism by Western psychology, or vice versa. It is about a mutual and genuine confrontation with the complexity and otherness in each of these two traditions that can ultimately lead to the evolution and enrichment of both.

There is always the danger that the psychologization of Buddhism will lead to the corruption or distortion of its original message. And I believe there is an important role for critical scholarship in helping us to reflect carefully on ways in which both Buddhism and psychotherapy are subtly changed by this ongoing encounter. At the same time, I believe it is important for us to recognize important ways in which this process can contribute to the perpetuation and revitalization of the essential spirit of the dharma. As Stephen Batchelor puts it,

> A culture of awakening is forged from the tension between an indebtedness to the past and a responsibility to the future. . . . A culture of awakening cannot exist independently of the specific social, religious, artistic, and ethnic cultures in which it is embedded. It emerges out of creative interactions with these cultures without either rejecting or being absorbed by them. It will inevitably assume certain features of contemporary culture, perhaps inspiring and revitalizing some dimensions of it, while maintaining a critical perspective.[7]

4

*Buddhist Practice in Relation to Self-Representation: A Cross-Cultural Dialogue**

HARVEY ARONSON

T HERE IS MUCH TALK in Buddhism and psychotherapy about the *self.* Elsewhere I have explored at length some of the linguistic and cultural issues distinguishing the meaning of this term in Buddhist and psychotherapeutic contexts.[1] Here, I would like to consider issues related to psychological difficulty, narcissism, identification, and self-representation and their significance in a dialogue between Buddhism and psychotherapy. Kyabje Kalu Rinpoche states in *Luminous Mind,*

> Our mind can be compared to a hand that is bound or tied up, as much by the representation of our "me," of the ego or self, as by the conceptions and fixations belonging to this idea. Little by little, Dharma practice eliminates these self-cherishing fixations and conceptions, and, just as an unbound hand can open, the mind opens and gains all kinds of possibilities for activity. It then discovers many qualities and skills, like the hand freed from its ties. The qualities that are slowly revealed are those of enlightenment, of pure mind.[2]

The originator of self-psychology, Heinz Kohut, identifies the self as a concept: "The self . . . emerges in the psychoanalytic situation and is conceptualized, in the mode of a comparatively low level, i.e., comparatively experience-near, psychoanalytic abstraction as a content of the mental apparatus."[3]

Nowadays there is a strong interest in the issues that occur in relation to

*The research for this essay was made possible by a generous grant from the Ford Foundation, with this particular project being guided by the supportive oversight of Constance Buchanan.

the sense of self; much of this work is around issues pertaining to *narcissism*. Narcissistic difficulties may be manifest in the need for exhibition, for fame, success, power, or in the need to serve, follow, or be tied into an individual or organization that leads.[4] Typically, these concerns have been the main focus of psychotherapy, which has not, for the most part, ventured into the area described by Kalu Rinpoche as the pure mind, the mind of enlightenment.

How do psychotherapy and the pure mind interrelate? Meditation, which is a means for achieving a pure mind, has been imported into a variety of psychotherapeutic arenas.[5] A smaller but burgeoning number of voices have talked about the necessity of therapy for those who are seeking enlightenment yet facing emotional difficulties.[6]

The spiritual teacher A. H. Almaas observes that traditionally the quest for the pure mind was done phenomenologically, by which he means working with the bare nature of mental phenomena, looking at them extensively in order to understand them.[7] This phenomenological way of realizing pure mind did not include the type of narrative exploration and developmental understanding that informs modern psychotherapy.

Even if, for the moment, we limit ourselves to those forms of Buddhist practice that traditionally have most emphasized phenomenological approaches—mindfulness *(satipatthana)*, *maha-mudra*, dzogchen, *lam-dre*, Chan/Son/Zen—numerous questions arise in the importation of these practices to the West. One set of questions has to do with why it is that Westerners undertaking these practices are still beset by psychological problems.[8] A second set concerns how the endeavors of psychotherapy and the various phenomenological approaches found in Buddhism are related to one another.[9] With respect to both sets of question, I would like to make use of some material developed by the cultural psychologist Richard Shweder and the philosopher Charles Taylor to contextualize our reflections. And with respect to the second question, I would like to make use of some of the material developed by A. H. Almaas and Jack Engler to explore some of the fundamental differences that have been enunciated to date between traditional Buddhist practice and modern psychotherapy and the ways in which they can ultimately be integrated.

The Cross-Cultural Context of Buddhist Meditation and Psychotherapy

In reflecting on psychotherapeutic issues related to modern Westerners and specifically North Americans who are practicing traditional Buddhist phenomenological approaches, it is helpful to understand something of the cultural differences that obtain between the two milieus. Richard Shweder articulates four significant movements in the process that occurs in considering other cultures:

1. Thinking by means of the other.
2. Getting the other straight.
3. Deconstructing and going beyond the other.
4. Witnessing in the context of engagement with the other.[10]

The first is using the other's conception of things to become more aware of aspects of life that are less conscious to us. Information about the possibility of developing particular spiritual realizations through meditation is one such form of knowledge that had been generally unavailable to modern North Americans. As Shweder so aptly states, we may participate in this first movement "to recognize the other as a specialist or expert on some aspect of human experience whose reflective consciousness and system or representation and discourse can be used to reveal hidden dimensions of our selves."[11]

The second movement, "getting the other straight," means placing ourselves in the internal logic of the world as constructed by the other, in order to make sense of their beliefs and motivations. The third movement entails seeing the incompleteness of the other, what has been hidden from their world view. The fourth has to do with the way in which we are ineluctably self-illuminated by any careful consideration of the other. Shweder sees this movement as including acts of criticism, liberation and discovery, all flowing from an "open-ended self-reflexive dialogic turn of mind."[12]

When we consider another vision of the world, we inevitably become clearer about those who hold that vision, and ourselves. I see the writing of this essay and the reader's response as part of an ongoing process in which we in the West are considering the nature of traditional Buddhist practice and its importation into our culture.

We can use this particular analysis of the movements in cultural reflection in conjunction with material that Shweder has developed on "narrative" to see how our context here in North America may be radically different from that of traditional Buddhists and how that difference sets the stage for the articulation of a unique set of psychological concerns in practicing meditation.

Typically in traditional Buddhist literature enlightenment was articulated in the context of understanding the absence of the metaphysical self. This understanding in turn was developed on the basis of moral behavior that served as a support for mindfulness, concentration, and insight. Right intentions, otherwise known as wholesome karma, create the context for practice which ultimately leads to burning up the karmic seeds *(bīja)* that eventuate in negative and positive rebirths, leaving the sage free from the cycle of rebirth.

Examining the path of practice in terms of karma can be especially fruitful for grasping some of the cross-cultural issues involved for individuals in North America when they adopt the traditional forms of practice. Shweder helps to place karma in context as the narrative frame for dealing with cross-cultural issues. He says that around the world individuals have always been faced with experiences that are not immediately comprehensible.[13] For example, when we wake up and feel heavy, or we have some type of fear or anxiety that seems to pop out of nowhere, we call upon some significant explanatory motif to understand this event. Such motifs vary across cultures.

One mode of explanation for such events is the *karma* narrative that sees the current quality of our experience as influenced by the moral quality of our actions in the past. In this mode of understanding, current discomfort would be related in some way to negative, harmful, or disruptive actions in the past. Another significant way of understanding such events, though fairly rare in the modern scientific West, is the *bewitchment* narrative, in which our current state of being would be seen as due to the intervention of some second party who is wishing us well or ill. A third way is through a *psycho-somatic* narrative. This can take the form of a psychological narrative, when, for example, I explore whether I had some unsatisfying emotional interaction recently in which I could not express myself or my boundaries were violated. Or it can be a *somatic* narrative, in which I look for an explanation in such factors as my blood chemistry, diet, or exercise routine, among a host of others.

The self in narrative: karmic versus psychological. Those of us familiar with Buddhist material know that a large part of its narrative is karmically oriented. A much smaller number of bewitchment narratives and somatic narratives can be found that (a) provide instructions for magic, (b) prescribe medicinal teachings and the use of herbs, and (c) delineate yogic teachings about working with the breath and internal energies. Buddhism certainly has psychological narratives, such as found in its Abhidharma literature. This is a psychology that is cognitive in nature, dealing with the conscious intentionality of subjects, yet subsumes the workings of psychology into the frame of karmic wholesomeness and unwholesomeness. There is no coherent body of Buddhist material equivalent to our modern psychodynamic developmental psychology.

How is this discussion of narrative relevant to the relationship between Buddhist practice and psychotherapy? The dominant narratives in our culture are psychological and somatic (medical), not karma or bewitchment narratives. It is hard to appreciate how much we swim in these waters unless we have an opportunity to swim in those of another culture. We can take, for example, traditional Tibetan Buddhism as providing the context for the type of dialogic self-reflection that Shweder describes as "witnessing in the context of engagement with the other." Having spent three years in India and Nepal and lived for many years in close proximity with Tibetans, I know that their narratives are different from ours. Tibetans do not routinely feel it is necessary to verbally share their inner states with one another as is so typical of us in the modern West.[14]

We can see the clear difference in narrative styles when considering Jack Engler's thoughtful essay on self, object relations (i.e., psychological relations between self and other), and Buddhist practice in juxtaposition with a traditional presentation.[15] For native Buddhists, writing or speaking in the karmic narrative, the first transformative stage of insight practice—"entering the stream" of realization (sotapanna)—assures eventual escape from the cycle of samsara, a decisive karmic event. One is no longer a "worldling" (puthujjana) but rather a Noble One (ariya). For Engler, writing in a psychological narrative frame about this same stage of practice, the significant karmic accomplishment escapes mention altogether, in favor of a discussion of the "maladaptive cognitions" abandoned at this stage of practice.[16] Engler situates his discussion in terms easily understood and of interest to individuals in the West. Karma, rebirth, and liberation from samsara involve narratives and worldviews that many Westerners find foreign and difficult to understand or believe. But the danger in our sometimes exclusive use of the psychological narrative, as Franz Metcalf points out, is that practitioners may lose all contact with the root tradition and the contributions that it can make to our seeing things in a new and different way.[17]

The autonomous self of the modern West. There has been some nascent research on how in the modern situation our sense of self differs from that of individuals in Asia. This work is of great interest insofar as it points to a more holistic group-oriented identity in Asia versus the individual self that has developed in the West.[18]

Shweder, for example, contrasts traditional culture and the modern West starting with the instance of India. "Like most peoples, Indians do have a concept of a person-in-society, but a person-in-society is not an autonomous individual. He or she is regulated by strict rules of interdependence that are context specific and particularistic, rules governing exchanges of services, rules governing behavior to kinsmen, rules governing marriage, and so on." He contrasts this traditional holistic vision with the autonomous values of the West: "Free to undertake projects of personal expression—personal narratives, autobiographies, diaries, mirrors, separate rooms, early separation from bed, body, and breast, of mother, personal space—the autonomous individual imagines the incredible, that he or she lives in an inviolate region (the extended boundaries of the self) where he or she is free to choose . . . , where what he does is his own business."[19]

Because of our immersion in autonomy and the psychological narrative, a host of issues related to how we think and experience—our sense of independence, choices, feelings, ambivalences, and understandings of unconscious dynamics—are foreign to traditional Asian teachers. This leads to occasional disappointments in expectations and communication between North American students and traditional Asian teachers.[20] In order to understand the contexts of these problems, one must examine some of the root assumptions behind the Western "self" concept.

In a masterful study, the philosopher Charles Taylor has identified some of the historical roots and intellectual articulations of the type of self we have in the West today.[21] This self is characterized by looking inward, finding its moral sources internally, and engaging in self-reflexivity. There are several beliefs and perspectives related to our modern Western sense of self.

Self as source and as instrument. The first two beliefs that inform the modern Western self emerging from Taylor's study are contrary. The first has to do with the drive for power and control. During the seventeenth century an appreciation began to emerge for the significance of instrumentality (how to effectively make things happen) in the fields of health, warfare, and administration.[22] Beginning with the work of Descartes, the individual was increasingly emboldened to become the source of moral choices as well as scientific observation. Following Descartes and Locke we begin to see a move away from the centrality of God in the moral universe and a greater emphasis on the self to exercise its capacity or even responsibility for managing itself as opposed to looking for guidance to an external authority. These same authors emphasized the individual's capacity to make choices, and be instrumental with respect to itself in terms of the person's capacity to free themselves of traditional beliefs and unruly or superstitious emotional reactions.[23] This vision of the person, emerging both in the culture and among the philosophers, supports a sense of self which is in control—a master of nature and emotion. It is out of these sources that we in the West come to have the type of self identified by Clifford Geertz: "The Western conception of the person as a bounded, unique, more or less integrated motivational and cognitive universe, a dynamic center of awareness, emotion, judgment, and action organized into a distinctive whole and set contrastively both against other such wholes and against a social and natural background is, however incorrigible it may seem to us, a rather peculiar idea within the context of the world's cultures."[24]

In the religious world this type of instrumental self-management can be seen in the Puritan forefathers who had the sense of encouraging self-scrutiny and self-help.[25] And it is within the context of a belief in self-help that many in the West are drawn to certain kinds of Buddhist practice.

Self in conflict: intention versus performance. However, as anyone knows who has tried to help themselves to stop smoking, or drinking, or take up a practice like meditation, the mind may be strong but the heart weak. This brings us to a second set of belifes in considering the self in the West. This is the conflict between intention and performance that we see at least as far back as Paul in Romans 7: "For that which I do I allow not; for what I would, that do I not; but what I hate, that I do." This highlights something of a tragic vision concerning the individual's capacity to rationally move themselves forward. Such self-doubt receives scant attention in the rather exuberant avowals of rationality and instrumentality in the later works of Descartes and Locke. This Pauline vision of self-deficit was elaborated in the work of Augustine, who articulated the place of grace in overcoming the war between positive and negative will. For Augustine, it is only through the unpredictable grace of God that one can overcome the types of perversity, weakness, and derailment that occur due to the negative will.[26]

Self-reflexivity and the creation of self-identity. Another significant perspective on the self that Taylor identifies is Augustine's articulation of the individual's capacity for radical self-reflexivity. This is different from the early Greek "care for oneself," which meant that one should care for one's soul more than one's property. In contrast, modern radical self-reflexivity "brings to the fore a kind of presence to oneself which is inseparable from one's being the agent of experience." That reflexivity, according to Taylor, is developed in two dominant modes. One is in the type of isolated, philosophical, disengaged self-reflection epitomized by Descartes and Locke that leans toward self-mastery. The other is a type of self-reflection that many would identify as emerging with the confessions of Augustine and which is oriented to establishing our identities today: "It consists in exploring what we are in order to establish this identity, because the assumption behind modern self-exploration is that we don't already know who we are."[27]

This type of self-reflection begins with an individual's consideration of events in their personal life. Significant signposts in the development of this form of reflection can be found in the work of Montaigne, in the recorded confessions of religious French women who had dramatic visions, and in the Puritan writings of self-scrutiny.[28] The enormous impact of the printing press and the development of mass media on this emergent model cannot be overestimated.[29] In these instances what begins to emerge is a form of self-reflection that centers on the narrative of the *individual's* self-reflection on their thoughts, feelings, and personal history. This enshrinement of the individual and the valuation of the details of their thoughts and feelings are part and parcel of cultural developments stemming from Augustine, the elevation of the individual through the reformation and democratic revolutions in the West, and the significance of the everyday supported by both Protestant polemics and the Romantic celebration of feelings.[30]

Psychoanalytic self. These various beliefs and perspectives came together in the institution of psychoanalysis, which can be seen as a secularized attempt to solve the Pauline and Augustinian dilemma of our positive intentionality being undermined by the perversion of our behavior. In Freudian psychoanalysis, however, the conscious ego is the good will, the unconscious is what motivates behavior that is out of tune with our conscious intentions—and so is the bad will. It is psychoanalytic understanding, which emerges gracefully in the dialogic framework between therapist and client, that allows for more autonomous mastery over that which has historically derailed us.

We are immersed in these cultural waters. Our sense of self, the joys and burdens of autonomy, the expectation that we should know our feelings and be individually assertive in expressing them, and the imperative to follow our personal vision of life all flow from specific elements in our cultural past. While certain pieces of our cultural values may be shared in traditional Buddhist cultures, the psychoanalytic self is a distinctive result emerging out of the matrix of specific influences: democracy, the Protestant reformation, and Romanticism. We are furthermore oriented toward hedonic satisfaction, pragmatic real-world success, and successful union of our aims and actions in the world.[31] All these values create a unique framework for our sense of self that is dramatically different from the sense of self developed in traditional Asian cultures.

We in the West, when compared to those in traditional Asia, do not have much sense of a communal self, do not have access to the unique supports of being part of a long-standing, communally embedded culture with clearly defined rules and roles and a sense of human, environmental, and spiritual interdependence. The emotional burdens imposed on our independent self are far different from the holistic, communally embedded self that is typical of more traditional Asian Buddhist cultures.[32] This is not a value-judgment, since many advances tied to the modern Western idea of the self, in areas such as technology, medicine, and art, are remarkable achievements.

Nevertheless, we may speculate that in more traditional cultures, the support of the community may have minimized certain kinds of mental stress. Traditionally, individuals in distress may have understood their situation through a karmic or bewitchment narrative, experienced their difficulties mostly in somatic versus emotional terms, and had recourse to spiritual resources as well as traditional herbal remedies.[33] Traditional practitioners, furthermore, had capacities based in faith, tradition, and social stability to make use of the authority of the tradition to ward off unwanted states.[34]

The modern Westerner's construction of self is at once autonomous yet beset with tragic flaws, be they called "evil will" or "the unconscious," and brings with it uniquely configured sets of problems and demands.

The Need to Address Psychological Issues
When Engaged in Traditional Practice

If, during the course of practicing traditional meditation, we modern North American students have some untoward emotional experience, our first line of defense may be to strengthen our sitting by lengthening it or sharpening our focus. We may focus more on openhearted reception of blessings from buddhas and bodhisattvas, for instance. If this fails, we have in our culture psychotherapeutic tools that have emerged out of the very source material of our culture, reflecting our values, perspectives, and concerns. The psychological concerns that we find in our practice will emerge from within the nexus of our sense of self—from the object-relational sense of self that has arisen in our particular Western setting (i.e., self as understood primarily in psychological relation to our internalized images [objects] of other human selves). Taking many of our uniquely configured object-relational dilemmas to a traditional teacher may expose us to compassionate acceptance. If we are talking about wanting to succeed at a worldly endeavor in an appropriately assertive manner, depending on who the specific traditional teacher is, we may hear traditional *moral* advice about pride and be less likely to hear psychologically sensitive responses that address the *psychological* dilemmas of self-assertion and self-abnegation. Absent such psychological support, we may end up feeling confused or guilty, and find ourselves stuck in psychological paralysis or cultural confusion. There is, therefore, definitely a place for culturally sensitive psychotherapeutic intervention for individuals pursuing traditional Buddhist practices. In our culture we have a uniquely configured set of solutions emerging from our understanding of psychology that can be very relevant to engaging effectively in life and ultimately in spiritual development.

When we North Americans take up the practice of traditional Buddhist meditation, we, on the one hand, may think it is like going to the store and picking up some more things (in this case a set of techniques) to nourish us and make us feel better. The traditional understanding of Buddhist religious life, on the other hand, would see its practices much more like the central area of a spider web thoroughly and inextricably linked to supporting threads of history, culture and language. As an individual involved with the translation of Buddhism into American life for decades, I would like to think that a metaphoric picture for successful translation of Buddhist culture to the West is somewhere between these two. We do not need to take on the burden of adopting traditional language and culture to practice, but it is very important to understand or appreciate as much as possible about the linguistic, cultural, and historical threads that support traditional Buddhist practice to have a full and robust appreciation for its purpose. Such a contextualized understanding allows us to appreciate the deep meaning of Buddhism as a path of liberation, and keeps us from reducing it to the fulfillment of our perceived psychological needs. The latter can happen when we equate this vast spiritual tradition to a single practice such as simple mindfulness of the breath—a discrete item off the shelf—or limit our expectations to our culturally mandated desire for wellness and mental health, without becoming aware of, or having respect for, the treasures of liberating insight.[35]

With a culturally nuanced understanding of Buddhist practice, we recognize as well that this is not necessarily just one more thing we take off a shelf ready to consume; we see, rather, that we may need supplements, or enzymatic assistance, in learning how to assimilate what actually is a rich and complex foreign food.

It is not uncommon for individuals first exposed to Buddhism to see it in an idealized way and expect it to address both spiritual and psychological issues thoroughly.[36] I am reminded of a diehard Alcoholics Anonymous member who insisted that if someone just worked the steps of AA with sincerity they would never be bothered with the need for antidepressants. Would that it were so. Despite a bevy of early idealizations of Buddhist meditation, over the years a number of books have alerted us to the types of psychological digestive enzymes that individuals may need when taking up the practice of Buddhist meditation. These books explore the situations that arise when individuals involved with Buddhist practice have a need for psychotherapeutic assistance—when, as Jack Engler states, practitioners come to see that their practice in itself does not "manage problems in day-to-day living or provide direction in love and work."[37]

One way of understanding the difficulties we encounter during practice is to see them as related to problematic object relations. We can have a problematic object relation when either our sense of self, our sense of some internalized other, or some overwhelming affect associated with these relationships is causing us difficulty. We saw earlier that Kyabje Kalu Rinpoche articulated the Buddhist path as one in which we move beyond living through our self-representations, which are constructed by memory and occlude seeing things as they are *(yathabhutam)*.[38] In Theravada this eventuates in the realization of nirvana; in Mahayana, one's buddha-nature.

In traditional Buddhist practice a central approach to reach this goal makes use of phenomenological analyses to critically assess self-representations. Within the phenomenological approach itself, however, there are divergent emphases, with some employing the direct experiential observation of mindfulness, some using conceptual/experiential analysis of Abhidharma or Madhyamika, and some wherein a teacher may dialogue with students and have them contemplate what they discuss, inspired and supported by the tools and vision of the first two approaches.

There are also significant and effective approaches that work more indirectly with self-representations: techniques such as evocatively experiencing oneself as a Buddha, or as some say "sitting as a Buddha"; ways of transforming *(bodhicitta/tonglen)* and transmuting *(tantra)* the affects that are supported in particular self-representations; and a broad range of approaches that employ faith and gratitude as a mode of disengaging from the willful activities that are inextricably linked up with particular kinds of self-representation.[39]

I am not as familiar with how the approaches of faith are working among North Americans, but I can say from familiarity with those using other approaches that they do not alone resolve preexisting psychological issues. Dan Brown and Jack Engler found that some insight meditators of substantial development, while endowed with greater awareness of their patterns, were still exhibiting states such as "fear of rejection; struggles with dependency and needs for nurturance; fear and doubt regarding . . . relationships; fear of destructiveness."[40] The vipassana teacher Jack Kornfield also speaks of having made advances in meditation but recognizing that deeper patterns of isolation and defendedness remained.[41] At least in the case of modern North Americans, it seems safe to say that there can be progress in the traditional stages of realization while substantial psychological patterning remains intact.

In modern North America, when experiencing distress we tend to experience it in emotional or somatic terms, resort to psychological and medical narratives for explanation, and seek mental health or medical interventions for alleviation. Individuals who cannot or will not access such resources often ruminate in tremendously painful cycles of self-recrimination—"I should practice more or better or harder," "I should have more faith"—or give up the path altogether. For those who enter a practice of meditation to sidestep psychological issues, if the calming, clarifying effects of meditation do not resolve those issues, there may be a need for therapeutic intervention.[42]

Spiritual Practice Brings Forward Emotional Issues

To those solidly based in the psychological world, and those only familiar with modern psychologized presentations of Buddhism, it may come as a surprise to know that among some individuals practicing traditional Buddhist practice there has been some resistance to psychotherapy. I think traditional teachers, upon hearing student descriptions of the psychotherapeutic process, mistakenly felt it might exacerbate proliferation of thoughts or preoccupation with self and discouraged engagement with psychotherapy. I have heard such discouragement myself directly from teachers and indirectly from students. While therapy might indeed transitionally intensify reflection and emotional fluctuation—as a therapist, I know I hope it will—I think that successful therapy actually allows many kinds of repetitive ruminations and anxieties to be lowered in frequency and allows for a synthesis of thought and emotion, appropriate experience of affect, and more capacity for empathy and regard for others. We continue to support a synthesis worthy of further dissemination when we advocate the conjunction of therapy with traditional Buddhist practice to deal with issues that arise during the course of practice.

A. H. Almaas makes a startling but significant contribution when he states during the course of an ongoing spiritual path that psychological, physical, and functional difficulties are "actually produced" by spiritual experience.[43] I would say from personal experience and observation of others that this assessment is worthy of serious reflection. Much like pressure on a seemingly intact ceramic will reveal underlying fissures and cracks, the clarity of insight practices will illuminate areas of blockage, defense, and contraction. Engler cites Kapleau Roshi's similar idea about higher stages of realization: "Before awakening, one can easily ignore or rationalize [one's] shortcomings, but after enlightenment this is no longer possible."[44]

It is very brave for spiritual writers to articulate these difficultes, as this flies in the face of the considerable literature that makes a simple correspondence between spiritual engagement and improvement in mental health. There are, of course, often many positives that flow from spiritual practice. It is just more realistic to acknowledge what any long-term practitioner has seen; that is, with progress, and in particular with intense practice, come a variety of seemingly positive and negative experiences as epiphenomena. In Tibetan Buddhism, these are simply known as "meditative experiences" (nyams); it is always emphasized they can feel both positive and negative.

Jack Engler mentions a variety of ways in which specific Buddhist teachings may be used to support or strengthen particularly unworkable patterns of behavior that predate involvement with practice. Teachings on no-self can be used to rationalize a lack of integration or cohesive self; teachings on nonattachment can rationalize an inability to form relationships; enlightenment can be used as some type of idealized grandiose self; and devotion to a teacher can allow one to feel special in mirroring the idealized other and masking internal feelings of inferiority. In brief, Engler correctly observes that spirituality, like psychotherapy, can serve defensive purposes.[45]

Almaas mentions a variety of issues that can be brought to the surface freshly in spiritual practice.[46] During spiritual practice, individuals working on issues related to love may get in touch with the quality of the love they did or did not receive as a child. Individuals dealing with issues of faith will confront issues of trust that arose for them as young children. Through the immediacy of presence, a practitioner might feel some anxiety due to a sense of separation from his internalized image of his mother. Or a practitioner seeing an aspect of internal nature not seen before might activate issues related to not having been seen in the past. Finally, individuals working on issues of self and self-representation will deal with an entire panoply of issues including inner support, the need to be seen, and questions of meaning and value.[47]

While many of us in the West approach Asian spirituality as a conscious or unconscious alternative to dealing with our psychological issues, there are ways in which these types of issues will just not come to rest through practice, and in fact may become more or newly clarified and due to that clarification be felt more intensely.

As a Western author well versed with the psychological narrative prevalent in our modern culture, Almaas points out that there are "environmental factors" related to an individual's involvement with her parents that contribute to the development of the vast array of narcissistic issues that are stimulated during spiritual practice:[48]

Most spiritual teaching methods do not address these factors and do not envision psychological understanding that can free the individual from the influences of early childhood. In fact, the common position in traditional teachings is that dealing with the epistemological-phenomenological and representational factors is sufficient to dissolve blockages caused by the environmental factors. This is because the former factors are more fundamental and actually function as the ground of the psychological issues and conflicts related to the latter. Most traditional methods of self-realization are based on moving beyond representation and the associated psychic structures.[49]

Almaas correctly points out that structural difficulties and psychodynamic issues pose significant barriers to self-realization, certainly for modern North American practitioners, and that most traditional spiritual teachings do not have the context and perspective to address these. In particular he states he has found the barriers to self-realization to be the "complex and intertwined reflections of all the factors in the development of narcissism."[50] Here he is in tune with Engler, who states, *"Narcissistic dynamics are probably far more intertwined with everyone's spiritual practice than I originally thought"* (italics added).[51]

The ways in which various needs have not been met at various specific developmental stages lead to patterns of reactivity that, in turn, obscure or prevent a settling into presence. Furthermore, the various defenses that are developed to prevent contact with overwhelming feelings also tend to obscure immediacy. Each pattern of reactivity and mode of defense in its own way contributes to the lack of contact with our true nature, and this is constitutive of "narcissism."[52] In contrast to a symptomatic or even structural definition of narcissism, Almaas broadens our understanding of this phenomenon when he places it in a spiritual frame and sees narcissism as stemming from "disconnection from the essential core of the self" and consisting in "identification with mental representations."[53] Ultimately this definition in psychological terms is very much in parallel with the vision Kalu Rinpoche articulates when he discriminates bondage and freedom in more epistemological terms.

It is important to note a few things about this. The first is that lacking the cultural developments found in the West, and absent an emphasis on the psychological narrative and our understanding of psychology that is prevalent now, there is no way that traditional teachers could articulate any meaningful observations about psychological problems and narcissistic issues in the developmental terms we are familiar with. It may also be worthy of speculation that a culture that emphasizes autonomy, independence, and self-reliance might bring additional value to the whole constellation of concerns that occur in creating self-identity. An Asian Buddhist meditator may also face some of the concerns we are talking about here, but I think we can suspect that the weight, intensity, and meaning of these concerns would be different, and the meditator would address them much more in the moral/karmic mode of giving up "pride," abandoning "self-cherishing," or criticizing overinvolvement with the "I and mine," or else in an epistemological frame of analyzing the "self"-image that one is attached to.[54]

There would clearly be differences between what Western and Asian meditators are concerned about. However, I'm not sure that Engler is quite right when he says that Asian individuals never took their problems in love and work to their spiritual teachers,[55] and therefore when we in the West have such problems, he implies, we shouldn't either. This was perhaps true for certainly highly structured Asian meditation environments where the focus of conversation was implicitly restricted. But I have seen many Tibetans and Vietnamese bring everyday issues to teachers for counsel. It would be more accurate to say that if we take our issues of love and work to a teacher, we should expect them to respond with (*a*) advice coming from some intuitive position hard to evaluate, (*b*) suggestions based on the moral metaphors of traditional teaching, or (*c*) blessings to assure a positive outcome or avert calamity (a variant on the bewitchment narrative).[56] Unless they have been schooled for a long time in the West, however, such teachers surely will not address our issues of love and work in terms that resemble anything like the modern psychological narrative.

As cited above, Almaas gives examples of individuals achieving some state of presence and as a consequence experiencing difficulties that should be understood as normal aspects of practice. In traditional practice, I suspect that sheer sitting time worked through some of these issues. In the conference where this essay was presented, Victor Sogen Hori stated that Western Buddhists have imported two of the Three Jewels—the Buddha and the Dharma—but not the Sangha. In traditional practice, the Sangha, due to social and cultural practices, may have in fact contained or restrained certain types of emotional disruptions. How we in the West can "import" the Sangha, and truly embody a community that honors the tradition of community and our values of autonomy, is a large project and one that might ultimately keep certain psychological issues—for example, feelings of aloneness and alienation—from becoming exacerbated in practice. In the West, however, our meditative "stuff" may often bleed into the normal reactivity of everyday life because we typically do not sit as professionals, are not embedded in a traditional culture with its communal sense of self and system of social support, and find our selves in a culture that values feelings, autonomy, and action.

The arising of such issues makes pursuing spiritual practice difficult. As Almaas correctly points out, in some instances the feelings that spiritual practice may stimulate, such as separation anxiety (from, for example, a familiar sense of self), may not be felt consciously or understood but rather be acted out, when, for example, the practitioner pursues a relationship instead of continuing meditation practice. When students limit themselves to a phenomenological/epistemological approach such as traditional mindfulness/insight practice, the emotional issues that arise can lead to enormous disruptions in practice, absent the assistance of psychological intervention.[57] As Engler states, while there is uncovering in mindfulness practice, "it doesn't automatically facilitate insight in a psychodynamic sense."[58]

In light of this additional information about the function of meditation in relation to emotional issues, we may need to augment our earlier "digestion" metaphor of meditation practice being like a food that requires the digestive enzymes to assist in assimilation in our cultural context. Now we see that meditation practice, in particular intensive meditation practice, may serve as a cathartic or emetic, causing issues to arise or to be brought into relief. It seems clear that in some instances such upward/downward swelling of emotional issues, especially for those with some experience in therapeutic self-reflection, may, itself, result in some type of resolution. It may also be the case that for full-time meditators the sheer force of sitting may allow for some gradual and utter disidentification from whatever issues come to the surface. As Franz Metcalf pointed out in responding to this essay, it is important to distinguish this liberating *disidentification* from *disembodied dissociation*. The former is a gradual, often emotionally rich, process of disentangling one's personal sense of self from particular thoughts, feelings, or self-representations. The latter is the often unconscious, defensive movement away from disturbing feelings, thoughts, or self-representations that are felt as frightening, overwhelming, traumatic, or incongruent and therefore *not allowed* into full awareness. For modern Westerners, who do not become clear of emergent issues during emesis or catharsis, exploration of one's full emotional experiences in some context such as psychotherapy may be extremely beneficial in advancing the process of liberating disidentification.[59]

Identification and Disidentification, Error and Freedom: Epistemological-Phenomenological Aspects

A. H. Almaas makes some very helpful observations about identification and disidentification that help us understand the ways in which psycho-therapeutic success and Buddhist realization relate to one another. In a departure from the more psychologically oriented approaches to narcissism which would look at grandiosity or the need to serve of the so-called "closet narcissist," Almaas gives a psycho-spiritual definition of narcissism: "Narcissism is the condition that results when the self identifies with any content of experience to the exclusion of awareness of its fundamental Being."[60] The beauty of this definition is that it not only includes all the inflated or deflated self-representations that are central to pathological forms of narcissism but also alerts us to a much broader array of issues relating to identification and disidentification.

Identification is the mind's capacity to identify with any of its manifestations, impressions, or images.[61] "To identify with anything, any state, means simply that your mind takes a certain state for identity. Your mind holds on to an expression, or a feeling, or a state, and uses it to define you. It is thus to take any concept and say, 'That's me,' or 'That relates to me.'"[62] If we translate Kalu Rinpoche's phenomenological/epistemological statement quoted at the beginning of this chapter into this psychologically informed language, it would say: *identifying* with any experience as "I" or "mine" serves as an obstruction to realizing our inner true nature.

An appreciation of disidentification can be found in the earliest recorded discourses of Buddhism. In the *suttas* of the Theravada tradition, Gautama is shown modeling a particular type of dialogical inquiry that is ultimately internalized during the course of mindfulness meditation.

> "What do you think, O monks? Is form . . . feeling . . . perception . . . the conditioning mental factors . . . consciousness permanent, or transitory?"

"It is transitory, Your Reverence."

"And that which is transitory—is it negative, or good?"

"It is negative, Your Reverence."

"And that which is transitory, negative and liable to change—is it possible to say of it: 'This is mine; this am I; this is my Self'?"[63]

Here in a dialogical approach focused on phenomenology and epistemology, Gautama pithily indicates an approach to disidentification that is central to the subjective inquiry fostered in a variety of Buddhist meditation techniques.

I may have an image of myself as small and weak and identify with that even though I have sufficient physical capacity. Many psychotherapists are familiar with the issue of anorectic individuals who, though thin in actuality, have a sense of identity of being fat. Over and over in therapy I see talented and attractive individuals who feel like failures and consider themselves unattractive. This is due to identification with an internal image of themselves as deficient. The process of identification usually occurs outside of awareness; when we become fully aware of an identification, it often breaks down and no longer has a grip on us.[64]

Disidentification in the Spiritual Context Goes Further

Going beyond the position of modern psychotherapy, and siding more with the traditional spiritual disciplines Almaas differs in two key respects from the psychotherapeutic tradition.

The process of psychotherapy can be seen as moving toward more flexibility in one's self-image, and more realism in one's self-representation—two forms of modulating one's identifications. In contrast, Almaas sees psycho-spiritual development as leading beyond identification with self-representation altogether.[65] This is his first major difference with the more widely accepted view of therapists. The accepted view in therapy is that at the end point of successful therapy there is some alignment between the reality of the normal self and the self-representation that continues to function.[66] In therapy just this modification and alignment of the self-representation is the accepted end point, and it is conceived of as possible and desirable. According to Almaas, however, full psycho-spiritual development entails disidentification with self-representation altogether, and this more unencumbered goal is seen as possible and enriching.[67]

Informed by Almaas's language for the path of psycho-spiritual development, we can see therapy and meditational practice on a continuum, with therapy leading to flexibility of identity and meditation having the capacity to thoroughly free the practitioner from identification with self-representation. Those familiar with Buddhist material will not be surprised to reflect that it advocates, in its language, abandoning all self-representation. This is typically discussed in terms of the karmic project of giving up pride (Skt. *mana;* Tib. *nga rygal*). In the Theravada tradition "pride" is glossed as a sense of "I am higher," "I am lower," or just "I am." *Mana* clearly can be understood as "self-representation." With awareness of Almaas's psychological language of "self-representation" we can see a translation of the karmic task into a psychological one. It also allows us to see a relationship between psychotherapeutic work, on the one hand, and psycho-spiritual work (in general) and Buddhist insight practice (in particular), on the other.[68]

Almaas correctly points out that spiritual traditions have many practices oriented toward disidentification—that is, the ceasing of the mental activity of identification, even if the identification is accurate in a conventional sense: identifying as a wife, husband, colleague, teammate, and so on. In this description, he is emphasizing that *disidentification is a cessation* of a certain kind of intentionality, not just a case of intending one identity rather than another. In this he is subtly and profoundly pointing out that ultimately in practice such disidentification must occur, absent some sense of intender and intended goal; otherwise, one is merely substituting one form of identification for another— the identification of oneself as a seeker who is abandoning. Traditional practices contribute to disidentification through enhancing awareness of the content and process of identification and identifying.[69] In Theravada, we see much attention given to (*a*) looking at the nature of our experience, its evanescent content, in relation to the construct of a permanent self *(atta);* (*b*) the emotional glue in the process of identifying in its teaching on attachment; and (*c*) identification with self-representations in its teachings on pride *(mana).* In later Mahayana, the analysis of the self continues and is presented in analyses of self with respect to the person (Skt. *pudgala;* Tib. *gang bzag*), phenomena (Skt. *dharma;* Tib. *chos*) and own-being (Skt. *svabhava;* Tib. *rang bzhin*), and there is also discussion of the activity of holding things as self (Skt. *atmagraha;* Tib. *bdag 'dzin*) (one traditional way of describing the process of identification).

Almaas states that regardless of tradition, one can, through the application of penetrating insight, experience the dissolution of various kinds of identification in stages. Consequently one may experience inner spaciousness devoid of any self-images, first temporarily and then in a more ongoing way.[70] Here Almaas is aligning himself with those spiritual traditions that consider any holding to self-representation to be an unfaithful rendering of our innermost nature, as found in the passage by Kyabje Kalu Rinpoche cited at the outset.

One of the first concerns people have, when hearing that the goal of spiritual practice is "the abandonment of self-representation," is that they will lose their past and their memory. Interestingly enough, during the course of Buddha's enlightenment experience, he was said to have remembered not only his present life but prior lives as well.[71] It is not the function of memory that gets altered during the course of enlightenment but the *identification* with self-representations and memories—being identified as strong, weak, victimized, or victorious—that is altered.[72]

The ultimate unreality of identification with self-representation becomes apparent with deeper spiritual experience.[73] Almaas, using terms consonant with the Buddhist philosophical perspective, states that self-representations made up of images are not able to reveal a reality beyond concepts or images. The immediacy of inner reality cannot be captured by any memory. "Awareness of oneself as presence is the immediate experience of beingness, while retained impressions are many steps removed from this immediacy."[74] It is the very act of identification and living through self-representation, versus being grounded in one's fundamental nature, that Almaas details over and over as the core narcissistic quandary that can manifest in more severe forms in what are typically designated narcissistic traits.[75]

"Self-realization" is in fact the process by which individuals move from immersion in the world of images to the world of deeper reality. Quoting one of his students, Almaas describes it as *a major transformation or rather a shift of awareness from personality to something much more real.*[76] The major point is one moves beyond conventional identification with self-representation to something of a qualitatively different order: a spiritual reality, a state independent of the content of identifications. "The awareness of fundamental presence, with no activity in the mind (which may be felt as emptiness or spaciousness), results when self-images are dissolved by explicit awareness of them."[77]

Our sense of self is something that may be discussed objectively but can also very much affect our subjective experience, like the living lens of our eye. Our sense of self originates from the various experiences we have had with others. As Almaas remarks, in consonance with the Buddhist spiritual tradition, the disappearance of our identification with the familiar sense of self, or identity, is something that our ordinary mind will quite naturally resist. That is why such experiences are not easy to achieve, and generally occur only in the context of lengthy, dedicated practice.[78]

The process of disidentification with representations of the self is subtle. Jack Engler alerts us to this in what I see as the beginnings of a qualitative analysis (as in *abhidharma*) of diverse mental states in which the sense of self is diminished, or one feels nondual in relation to experience. I think further productive work can be done on considering the varieties of nondual experiences—pathological, ordinary, peak, meditative, and insight derived—and how they are similar, dissimilar, or may overlap. Engler identifies several. First, are those states where there is "full awareness without any reflexive consciousness of self." Examples he cites include responding to our name without thought, doing something readily that was difficult earlier, and a fresh moment of contact with another. A second, related category consists of "peak experiences" wherein individuals feel more alive and at one with what they are doing.[79] This might be the spontaneous release of the Zen archer, the child who balances on his roller skates, or the artist absorbing experience or creating art.

Engler correctly points out that it confuses the issue to conceptualize these states in terms of "loss of self-differentiation" insofar as the self is not "lost."[80] Using both Almaas's language of identification and some traditional categories may help here. In these nondual states our identifications with our self-representation as separate might be dormant, or we might have an expanded self-representation, but we certainly do not through such experiences wholly abandon the *process of identification* with self-representation; nor do we lose a *metaphysical* self, which from the Buddhist perspective we do not have to begin with.[81] Furthermore, ego functions that constitute the *empirical* or *psychologically functioning self* are not "lost."[82]

Let's for the moment accept that *mana* (pride), the sense that I am higher, lower, or simply "am," is a mental function that is sometimes present and sometimes absent from our consciousness. The states Engler describes may be instances when the mental function of *mana* is not operative; it is temporarily dispelled *(tadanga-pahana)*.[83] As Engler correctly argues, to speak of these nondual states as "loss of differentiation" is to imply diminishment of ego functioning; clearly such diminishment is not occurring in these states.[84] We continue to struggle in the West to move beyond earlier models that pathologized non-ordinary states. Our inquiry would be more productive if we focused on discriminating clearly how spiritual states may retain ordinary functions yet complement these functions with other qualities.

The next form of nondual awareness that Engler mentions has to do with the meditative absorptions, that is, states of concentration during which the sense of self *(mana)* is absent, technically identified as abandoned through suppression *(vikkhambhana-pahana)*.[85] The last form of nondual awareness is insight realization. There actually are a variety of nondual states here: states in the higher stages of insight, states related to path and fruition consciousness, and those following full realization. In particular, during and succeeding full enlightenment, identification with a particular sense of self *(mana)* would be given up through eradication *(samuccheda-pahana)* leaving the practitioner free of such identification.[86] Once meditators have embarked on practice and become familiar with the orientation of Buddhist inquiry, they may from time to time have a variety of less-dual or nondual meditative experiences in and out of meditation (Tibetan: *nyams*) that will reflect ever-deepening realization, cognitive and affective, and culminate in disidentification with the core sense of self.[87]

The Therapeutic Relationship Offers Surprises

Almaas, however, opens a valuable window when he points out that even in traditional psychotherapy, there are unintended and unnoticed moments of freedom from self-representation. This is his second major departure from the accepted therapeutic view. "The dissolution of self-images upon their becoming clearly conscious is actually involved in the uncovering techniques used in depth psychological work," he writes. "This dissolution makes it possible for distorted images of oneself to change when they emerge in consciousness."[88] During the course of therapy, with the dissolution of one self-image there is the immediate arising of another, so that much attention is not paid to the intervening absence of self-image. Even if no self-image is present for some duration, the person will not attend to it or grasp its significance, since their presuppositions will not typically include the possibility of experiencing inner boundless space. Jack Engler supports this when he says of the *absence of self-representation* that "there is no natural place for this mode of self-organization in the standard model of psychological functioning. It does not inform the core of psychoanalytic thinking about the person."[89]

Almaas's observation that there is a dissolution of self-representation at times in psychotherapy is no small matter, insofar as he is suggesting that the milieu of psychotherapy can provide an experiential opening to states of freedom supportive of burgeoning spiritual development. In ordinary psychotherapy, our conceptions, presuppositions, and self-images keep us from becoming aware of our experience of temporary freedom from self-representation. As Albert Einstein perceptively noted, "It is the theory which decides what we can observe"![90] In general, at the coarse conceptual level, one set of conceptions will block us from considering other conceptual models. Here, in the context of actual therapy or therapeutic self-reflection, our preconceptions block us from the riches and mysteries of spiritual immediacy.

Almaas thus reveals that certain features of the uncovering techniques of therapy yield results exceeding those usually mentioned. In his approach to spiritual development he uses elements of psychodynamic theory and therapeutic modes of self-reflection as elements in his larger process of inquiry. For those who follow Almaas, this form of inquiry is contextualized in an ongoing relationship with a spiritual teacher, a practice of meditation, and a school dedicated to the logos of "a love of truth."[91] Practitioners use self-reflection, reflection with colleagues, and dialogue with teachers, informed by the insights of modern psychoanalysts and therapists, and they become aware of the content and process of identification. They can thereby experience the dissolution of self-representation.[92] Thus, the uncovering approach that was pioneered in psychotherapy, a therapeutic approach that is based on our modern Western sense of self, can be used to construct a new psychological narrative that serves as a bridge and complement to the traditional Buddhist enterprise of disidentification with any conventional notion of self. That is, the psychotherapeutic narrative can be reframed to articulate elements of the non-narrative, non-self-representational state.

Things do not have to turn out as feared by traditional teachers who see therapy as an avenue of proliferating conceptions and further destructive involvement with self. Rather, this approach—when skillfully applied, with its valuation of personal history, thought, and feeling so germane to Western practitioners—can be effectively harnessed to a task that Buddhism shares with other spiritual traditions, that of reducing our identification with and attachment to our self-representations.[93] The possibility that this may occur is much enhanced when a practitioner is experienced in self-inquiry and particularly if she or he is in dialogue, or engaged in verbal self-reflection in the company of someone who can mirror, hold, or identify spiritual states such as spaciousness, clarity, or presence.

In sum, I have illustrated a process of "dialogical self-reflection" inspired by Richard Shweder's work. When applied to Buddhist meditation, it reminds us not to lose sight of the unique perspectives and contributions inherent to the karmic presentation of the path, while alerting us to the fact that Western students may benefit from our translating elements of the path into more easily assimilated, but accurately reflective, psychological terms. Furthermore, I have supported the now more widely recognized position that meditators with preexisting manifest psychological issues can benefit from adjunctive psychotherapy.

Two salient points have been identified. First, we should not see psychological issues as untoward exceptions to the path but rather understand that any good spiritual practice stimulates emotional and psychological issues. Not all of these issues would require therapy, but they would require attention of some kind. Second, taking a lead from Almaas and Engler, we can see spiritual practice as leading to a disidentification from self-representation altogether, in contrast to therapy where the goal is greater flexibility and realism in one's self-representation. In a groundbreaking contribution, Almaas points out that even though it is not part of the therapeutic agenda, psychological inquiry itself can also lead to such disidentification and I would add thus serve as an ally to traditional Buddhist practice. Working with detrimental and benign self-representations—their evolution, their maintenance, their ways of impeding us, and their eventual demise when identification with them weakens—may be a highly meaningful area for dialogue between Buddhists and psychotherapists.

5

On Selves and Selfless Discourse

WILLIAM S. WALDRON

THERE IS A DEEP and underlying tension between two equally essential discourses within Indian Buddhist thought, a tension paralleled to a certain extent in psychology and cognitive science as well. One discourse treats the *person* as the autonomous agent of his or her own actions, of karma, and by implication the effective subject of samsara as well as the crucial locus of self-transformation. The second discourse treats even psychological processes as an *impersonal* play of cause and effect and denies the ultimate reality of any agent or subject, which is considered at best either a convenient fiction, as in cognitive science, or at worst the core illusion that keeps one caught in the cycle of compulsory behavioral patterns (samsara), as in most Buddhist perspectives. Though distinct, these two discourses are also closely intertwined, for the second only aims to analyze and describe, theoretically, how cognitive and emotional processes impersonally arise in order to serve, pragmatically, the ameliorative aims of the first—the transformations that *persons* undergo in attaining understanding and freedom from cognitive obscurations and emotional obsessions. Indian Buddhist traditions distinguish these distinct kinds of discourse by the theory of two truths: *conventional* truths that pragmatically acknowledge and work with notions of persons and things, and the *ultimate* truth that disavows their reality.

This distinction between the two truths in Indian Buddhism—between the personal and impersonal forms of discourse—is essential not only for understanding how Buddhists can analyze personal experience without positing an inherent subject as the enduring locus of that experience, it is also essential for elucidating both where and to what degree Buddhist thought and practice is commensurate with various Western ways of thinking and working with mind, such as psychoanalysis and cognitive science—

the two areas most often compared with Buddhism. This distinction clarifies both the challenges and promises of engaging Buddhist ideas and practices with our thoroughly "psychologized" culture. It also sheds interesting, and I believe essential, light on the current and seemingly interminable debates in the West regarding the status of a self in Buddhism. To exemplify all these points, I will briefly outline my own evolving understanding of Indian Buddhist concepts of consciousness *(vijñāna)* in general and the Yogācāra notion of unconscious mind *(ālaya-vijñāna)* in particular, noting where they are similar to or different from psychoanalytic concepts of the unconscious and more modern notions of a 'cognitive unconscious.' Ultimately, I will note the advantages of traditional Buddhist modes of analyzing mental processes for bridging both the personal and impersonal discourses of mind.

At the outset of my studies I found it useful to consider the conception of *ālaya-vijñāna* in comparison with Freud's and Jung's conceptions of the unconscious, which were similar enough to help, heuristically, in introducing the concept of *ālaya-vijñāna* to Western audiences.[1] I gradually became dissatisfied, however, with the implicit subjectivism informing depth psychology's conception of the self, for I sensed that the homunculus, "the little man within," had not disappeared so much as withdrawn. I realized that depth psychology's conceptions of unconscious mind were unsuitable for expressing the deeply impersonal view of experience, the utter absence of any experiencing subject, that is favored by so much of Indian Buddhism. This aspect of Indian Buddhist thought, I increasingly found, was more easily expressed, again heuristically, by reference to cognitive science, which relies upon the typically impersonal discourse of natural laws rather than the personal discourse of intentional agents.[2] Cognitive science, though, has its own limitations. It tends to throw the baby out with the bath water, expunging in its impersonal approach the very sense of experience—concrete, immediate, human experience—that it set out to explain in the first place. Thus, like depth psychology, cognitive science also seemed inadequate for conveying *both* the impersonality of Buddhist discourse *and* its essential ameliorative aim: that one seeks to understand how mind works in order to alleviate human ignorance and suffering. In short, there is no current Western discourse, as far as I know,[3] that adequately expresses the distinct yet delicate balance that Indian Buddhist thought has forged between personal and impersonal forms of discourse. This absence alone recommends our serious consideration of Buddhist causal discourses.

The notion of *ālaya-vijñāna*, a "store-house" or "home" consciousness, serves as a useful example for this investigation since it is a theory of unconscious mental processes that is described in decidedly impersonal Buddhist terms, yet developed within a context of religious practice *(yogācāra)* explicitly aimed toward the amelioration of suffering. And since it shares more than a passing resemblance to Western notions of unconscious mental processes, it should be of considerable interest to psychotherapists in its own right.

Comparing Conceptions of Unconscious Mind

It is readily apparent why *ālaya-vijñāna* is compared with depth psychology's notions of unconscious mental processes, of mental processes operating outside of or below our conscious awareness. Both of these concepts address questions concerning the continuity and influence of underlying mental processes, such as memory and dispositions, that had become problematic within their own philosophical milieus—Abhidharmic analysis and Cartesian subjectivity, respectively. Both of these milieus tended to equate consciousness with immediate awareness,[4] a narrow conception of consciousness that made it difficult to explain many ordinary mental processes, such as memory and language, as well as extraordinary ones such as hypnotic and meditative trances. How, after all, could we account for the processes subserving learning, memory, or the continuity of one's dispositions if we had to be constantly aware of them?[5] How, indeed, could we even function if we were? Such considerations were only exacerbated by the radical *dis*continuities in conscious awareness experienced in hypnosis and meditative cessation, interruptions that were cited by psychoanalysts and Indian Buddhists, respectively.[6] As a consequence, conceptions of continuous yet *unconscious* mental processes arose in both traditions as obvious responses to, as well as natural corollaries with, conceptions of consciousness as necessarily accompanied by immediate awareness.

It was further inferred that unconscious processes must be continuously influencing all conscious ones, even ordinary sense perception, albeit mostly without our knowing it.[7] Who, for example, could possibly be consciously aware of the underlying processes by which the disparate visual stimuli that impact upon countless retinal rods and cones are processed in multiple areas throughout the brain and synthesized into recognizable forms, processes that we now know are of mind-boggling complexity? Yet we effortlessly see, hear and touch all the time. What we are consciously aware of represents but the tip of the iceberg of all the mental processes that are necessary for even ordinary perception to occur. Both the Buddhist *ālaya-vijñāna* and the modern notion of unconscious mental processes were thus conceived as continuously underlying and influencing conscious mental processes, which in turn influence them—making all ordinary experience a product of an ongoing and inseparable interaction between conscious and unconscious processes.[8]

These unconscious processes thus constitute cognitive activities in their own right, and it is here that our two notions of unconscious mind begin to diverge. Among the unconscious cognitive activities, Buddhists and depth psychologists maintain, are most of the same processes that occur consciously. In the *Yogācārabhūmi*, a fifth-century Yogācāra text, *ālaya-vijñāna* is said to be accompanied by the same five 'mental factors' *(caitta)* that accompany every other moment of mind *(citta)* in the Yogācāra tradition: attention, sensation, feeling, perception, and intention.[9] Seemingly similar, Jung also claims that unconscious processes replicate conscious ones in that they include "perception, thinking, feeling, volition, and intention, *just as though a subject were present*" [emphasis added].[10] This latter statement faithfully expresses, I believe, an implicit yet nearly inextricable assumption in most Western thinking: that underlying all experience, whether conscious or not, there must be a distinct subject, a real "someone," who is the agent of action and the subject of experience.[11] This assumption, and the grammatical syntax in which it is enshrined and expressed, demarcates the boundary of useful comparisons between *ālaya-vijñāna* and depth psychology's conception of unconscious mental processes (and perhaps, for that matter, between most Western and Indian Buddhist psychological discourses). For, we know, Indian Buddhists repeatedly rejected the reality of a substantive subject, an enduring locus of action and experience, considering it a pernicious fiction, a false view *(satkāya-dṛṣṭi)* that binds beings to the vicious cycle of repetitive behavior patterns *(saṃsāra)* and that must therefore be overcome in order to see things as they truly become *(yātham bhūtam)*. How, then, in Indian Buddhist terms, do things become? How is there experience without an experiencer?

Impersonal Discourse: Buddhism

> For there is suffering, but none who suffers; Doing exists although
> there is no doer.
> Extinction is but no extinguished person; Although there is a path,
> there is no goer.
>
> *Visuddhimagga*[12]

Though many find the very idea of experience without an experiencer nearly incomprehensible, if not self-contradictory, this way of analyzing experience is arguably the most distinctive feature of Indian Buddhist discourse. It is clearly expressed in the form of analysis favored by the Buddha and generations of his followers,[13] that of dependent arising:

> When this is, that comes to be; with the arising of this, that arises.
> When this is not, that does not come to be; with the cessation of
> this, that ceases.[14]

Consciousness or cognitive awareness *(vijñāna)* is also analyzed in this way: "Visual cognitive awareness arises dependent on the eye and visible form."[15] More specifically, a moment of cognitive awareness *(vijñāna)* occurs when an object appears in its appropriate sense field, impinging upon its respective sense organ, and attention is present.

Note the syntax here. In contrast to most uses of the term, East or West, consciousness in these Buddhist formulations is not an active faculty. It is definitely *not*, as Bertrand Russell defines it, "the mental act of apprehending the thing."[16] As Vasubandhu explicitly states in his *Abhidharma-kośa*:

> The *Sūtra* teaches: "By reason of the organ of sight and of visible matter there arises the visual consciousness": there is not there either an organ that sees, or visible matter that is seen; there is not there any action of seeing, nor any agent that sees; this is only a play of cause and effect. In the light of [common] practice, one speaks, metaphorically, of this process: "The eye sees, and the consciousness discerns." But one should not cling to these metaphors.[17]

To cling to the "metaphors" of agents and actions—as if consciousness were an agent that acts rather than a process that happens—would miss the point. To interpret *vijñāna* as an *act* of cognition rather than an *occurrence* of cognitive awareness ignores the syntax of dependent arising, the mode of analyzing awareness favored by the Buddha and his Abhidharmic successors, including the Yogācārins with their concept of *ālaya-vijñāna,* as we shall see. While this is by no means the only kind of psychological discourse in Indian Buddhism, it was widely considered, in non-Mahāyāna circles at least, as the supreme or ultimate discourse (Skt. *paramārtha-satya;* Pāli *paramattha-desanā*) in contrast to which conventional talk of people, places, and things was considered expedient at best.[18]

The Buddhist dismissal of independent agents and autonomous selves is therefore not so much a proposition about the world as a consequence of its mode of analysis: How do things come to be? Conditioned by what does suffering arise? Conditioned by what does suffering cease?[19] This is all the more obvious when we consider a similar impersonal syntax, and its corollary eschewal of causal agents and experiencing subjects, in modern science.

Impersonal Discourse: Science

Despite the apparent opacity of this approach, we should note that most modern people already think in such impersonal terms in certain contexts: scientific accounts of causality eschew anthropomorphic agents as a matter of course. Pedagogy aside, phenomena that involve physics, chemistry, or even the biological reactions involved in digestion or perception are not analyzed in terms of active agents or directing subjects: masses do not decide to collide, molecules do not choose to cohere, and neural networks do not conspire to fire. Rather, these processes are understood as complex yet predictable results of interactions that occur naturally and automatically, by themselves.

One of the consequences of analyzing human beings in terms of impersonal causality is that it leads scientists to question the very notion of a "unified, freely acting agent."[20] Many cognitive scientists, such Lakoff and Johnson, reject the assumption that "there is always a Subject that is the locus of reason and that metaphorically has an existence independent of the body," on the grounds that "this contradicts the fundamental findings of cognitive science."[21] I have therefore found it expedient to use the perspectives, concepts, and syntax of science to convey Buddhist analyses of mind to modern audiences.[22] It is a ready-made bridge that avoids certain kinds of misunderstandings.

This "unified, freely acting agent," though, is not denied because it is difficult to detect, as if all we needed were better or more sensitive tools. It is rejected because it is both unnecessary to and incompatible with an analytical approach that asks *how* things come to be rather than *what* they are. That is, most current scientific approaches to mind, like those of most Buddhists, refrain from positing any central directing agency or experiencing subject, first, because the causal functions commonly attributed to it are considered sufficiently explained by naturally occurring causal patterns, and second, because unchanging or substantive selves cannot play any effective *causal* role within a syntax, an analytic discourse, that focuses upon occurrences rather than agents.[23]

These points are clearly seen in the arising of cognitive awareness, which occurs as a result of a multiplicity of conditions,[24] no single one of which has the capacity to either unilaterally determine or entirely encompass the form and range of such experience. The analysis of color perception well illustrates this interactionist approach. "Color concepts are 'interactional';" according to Lakoff and Johnson,

> they arise from the interactions of our bodies, our brains, the reflective properties of objects, and electromagnetic radiation. Colors are not objective; there is in the grass or the sky no greenness or blueness independent of retinas, color cones, neural circuitry, and brains. Nor are colors purely subjective; they are neither a figment of our imaginations nor spontaneous creations of our brains. . . . Rather, color is a function of the world and our biology interacting.[25]

This mode of analysis not only forsakes active agents. It also avoids both an uncritical realism which assumes an external world independent of an experiencing subject, as well as an idealistic subjectivism which assumes an internal subject independent of experienced objects. This approach, which sees the arising of phenomena as a result of the interaction of multiple conditions, comes surprisingly close to the Buddhist analysis of dependent arising.

This "phenomenological" approach also suggests that the discussion of whether or not there is a self in Indian Buddhism misses a crucial philosophical point: that an analysis of the interactive arising of experience precludes *by virtue of its syntax alone* any meaningful reference to an unchanging, substantive self.[26] Such a self is neither an object of experience nor an entity expressible in terms of dependent arising—since if it were *truly* unchanging it could neither act nor experience, which are temporal occurrences. And since this mode of analysis precludes any causal role for an unchanging, substantive self, to discuss such a self sidesteps the favored form of Indian Buddhist discourse, that of dependent arising.[27] And it is favored, we must add, for traditionally practical reasons: as Nāgārjuna explains, "whoever sees dependent arising also sees suffering and its arising and its cessation as well as the path."[28]

Exemplifying Dependent Arising: Ālaya-vijñāna

All this though is still propaedeutic, that is, it prepares the ground for more constructive proposals. It behooves us now to demonstrate how experience may be analyzed in such strictly impersonal terms. How, in other words, does our human experience, with all its personal, social, and cultural complexity, actually arise as the mere "play of cause and effect," bereft of any active agent or experiencing subject? As mentioned above, the favored method of analyzing mind, particularly in non-Mahāyāna Buddhism, was to specify the causes and conditions in dependence upon which consciousness and its associated processes occur. We suggest that it is precisely this *mode of analysis* that, as with our color example above, is able to encompass both the subjective and the objective, the individual and the social, without falling back upon the implicit subjectivism of much of modern psychology, on the one hand, nor negating the importance of living, human experience, on the other. As we shall see, this mode of analysis provided Indian Buddhists with the analytic ability to encompass ever enlarging circles of conditioning influences, while still retaining its originating inspiration: it is liberating to see things in terms of their conditioned arising, their impersonal "play of cause and effect."[29]

As we have seen, in this mode of analysis consciousness or cognitive awareness *(vijñāna)* is said to arise in concomitance with attention, an unimpaired faculty and its correlative object.[30] Cognitive awareness itself is thus neither an act nor a faculty that cognizes;[31] in Abhidharma terms it is a natural result *(vipāka)* which occurs depending upon appropriate conditions.

Although more active mental processes such as attention *(manasikāra)*, apperception or recognition *(saṃjñā)*, intention *(cetanā)*, feeling *(vedanā)*, etc. often accompany the arising of cognitive awareness,[32] they are not that awareness itself, they are only its concomitants. Moreover, as with the analysis of color above, cognitive awareness is neither purely subjective, for it always requires some kind of object, nor is it wholly determined by those objects, since it equally depends upon the specific faculties of a living organism. It is thus neither an exact reflection of objective reality, as realists contend, nor the unilateral projection of an independent "mind," as idealists assert. Rather, awareness is "a function of the world and our biology interacting," a correlation neatly captured in the expression "visible object." What else could we see? Cognitive awareness is thus a phenomenon that only arises at the *interface*, the concomitance, of a sense faculty and its correlative object.

This correlation between faculties and objects also underlies the basic understanding of the "world" *(loka)* in Indian Buddhism, which from early on was clearly conceived in relation to human activity, to karma.[33] As the Buddha states in several Pāli texts, "The world *(loka)* has arisen through the six senses [the five sense-modalities and mind]," and "it is in this fathom-long body with its perceptions and thoughts that there is the world, the origin of the world, the cessation of the world, and the path leading to the cessation of the world" [i.e. the four Noble Truths].[34] As with the arising of consciousness, a "world" is specifically defined in relation to the faculties and activities of the beings who live in it.[35] Like a visible object, the world we live in is an "experienceable world," inseparable from our experience of it.

This opens the door to a temporal dimension to the arising of the world: if a "world" is defined in relation to the faculties of living beings, then that world changes as those faculties change. And beings' faculties change and develop over time, like habits, through recurrent interaction with their physical and social environments. The "experienced world" then gradually develops, in both Buddhist and evolutionary thought, in correlation with the "circle of positive feedback" that occurs between forms of cognitive awareness and their accompanying feelings,[36] the afflictive activities (the karma) these feelings tend to elicit, and their accumulating psychological and physiological results.[37] As Vasubandhu states in the *Abhidharma-kośa*:

It was said[38] that the world *(loka)* in its variety arises from action *(karma)*. These actions accumulate by the power of the latent afflictions *(anuśaya)*; without the latent afflictions [actions] are not capable of giving rise to a new existence.[39]

In this perspective, our world arises in correlation with our gradually evolving capacities to experience it, which are in turn the result of reciprocally reinforcing patterns of interaction between a number of processes—actions, the afflictions, and their results[40]—not from the causal influences of any single factor.

Note that this analysis has not departed from the impersonal syntax of the dependent arising. It has merely added a temporal dimension by describing how specific "worlds" have come to be in correlation with the coming-to-be of specific kinds of beings. It suggests how the gradual building up of complex cognitive structures in relation to specific environments, giving rise to a specific world, can come about without reference to any truly independent agency, whether external or internal. It further adumbrates, as we shall see, how we could also conceive of the evolution of cognitively complex worlds, such as our distinctively human world which is dependent upon language and culture, without reference to any unilateral causal agency, whether social or genetic (and thereby avoiding two common forms of modern determinism).[41]

These extensions of dependent arising—the relation between forms of cognitive awareness and their correlative worlds, and the gradual evolution of these worlds through processes of circular causality—enabled Indian Buddhists to analyze some of the deepest conditions of human experience without positing substantive experiencing subjects or autonomous active agents. It thus avoids many of the problems plaguing modern thinking, with its vestiges of substances, selves, and essences still entrenched in everyday language.

These points are epitomized in the arising of subliminal awareness *(ālaya-vijñāna)*.[42] Although it appears to depart from earlier Buddhist ideas, it is no more an experiencer, agent, or substantive subject than cognitive awareness is in other Buddhist models. In fact, this *"ālaya"* awareness retains all the characteristics of *vijñāna* mentioned above, while adding several others: (1) it is still a resultant *(vipāka)* awareness that (2) "develops and increases" through the accumulating processes of cyclic causality; yet (3) it arises subliminally, that is, below the threshold of conscious awareness,

(4) occurring "continuously in a stream of instants"[43] (5) depending upon two traditional conditions, the sense faculties and their correlative sense objects, (6) which are now explicitly augmented by the influences of linguistic and cultural experience; and (7) dependent upon these subtle conditioning factors, it arises in regard to a new kind of correlative object: as "an outward perception of the receptacle world whose aspects are indistinct" *(bahirdhā-aparicchinnākāra-bhājana-vijñapti).*[44]

Most of these characteristics are summarized in a short passage from the *Saṃdhinirmocana Sūtra,* an important text from the second to third centuries C.E.:

> In cyclic existence with its six destinies *(gati),* such and such beings are born as such and such a type of being. They come into existence *(abhinirvṛtti)* and arise *(utpadyante)* in the womb of beings. . . .
>
> There, at first, the mind with all the seeds *(sarvabījakaṃ cittam,* a synonym of *ālaya-vijñāna)* matures, congeals, grows, develops, and increases[45] based upon the two-fold substratum *(upādāna),* that is,
>
> (1) the substratum of the material sense faculties along with their supports *(sādhisthāna-rūpīndriya-upādāna),*
>
> (2) and the substratum which consists of the predispositions toward conceptual proliferation in terms of conventional usage of images, names, and conceptualizations.[46]

In short, this form of "subtle" *(sūkṣma)* cognitive awareness *(ālaya-vijñāna)* continuously arises based upon both the living sense faculties and the predispositions or impressions instilled by past linguistic experience, conceptualization, naming, and the like, in correlation with an "indistinct external world." All of this, however, occurs outside of or below the threshold of conscious awareness, that is, subliminally. *Ālaya* awareness represents, in short, a fully developed yet still deeply impersonal mode of unconscious mentality, based upon which all conscious processes arise.[47]

Language and Consciousness

This inclusion of the influences of language at the subliminal basis of human awareness opens this mode of analysis to influences from our wider social and cultural worlds, that is, to an unbounded arena of intersubjectivity without, we must stress, abrogating the syntax of dependent arising. This intersubjective yet unconscious "arising of the world" comes into being through the interaction of living beings in conjunction with their physical and social environments.

Commenting on the expression "predispositions of speech" *(abhilāpa-vāsanā),* the commentator to Asanga's fifth-century C.E., Yogācāra text, the *Mahāyāna-saṃgraha,* explains that conscious awareness *(vijñāna)* arises in regard to expressions of selves *(ātman)* and phenomena *(dharma)* due to the special power *(śakti-viśeṣa)* of the predispositions or impressions *(vāsanā)* of conventional expressions *(vyavahāra)*[48]—predispositions, we have seen, that are one of the conditions for the arising of unconscious awareness. (Notice that we do not say: "predispositions existing *within the* unconscious/ *ālaya-vijñāna,*" a spatial metaphor that is incommensurate with the dependent arising of *ālaya-vijñāna.*) In other words, the conventional expressions of everyday speech *(vyavahāra),* which delineate a "world" of endless objects and categories, subtly and similarly influence how conscious awareness of those objects and categories arises. They are subtle because the use of language relies upon gradually reinforced habits that, once acquired, operate primarily outside of conscious awareness. And they are similar because human consciousness is similarly influenced by similar linguistic categories—and language could not work if these influences were not similar, if we did not similarly understand words like "cup" or "Careful!" These linguistic influences, of course, only operate intersubjectively, at the interface between faces, since we only learn, use, and understand language through interaction with one another.[49]

The texts further suggest that insofar as unconscious awareness *(ālaya-vijñāna)* arises conditioned by the subtle yet common influences of language, then—since cognitive faculties and "worlds" are correlative—such awareness arises not only in regard to a world whose "aspects are indistinct," but also to a world that we largely share in common. Accordingly, Asanga states in the *Mahāyāna-saṃgraha* I.60:

> The common [dimension of unconscious awareness *(ālaya-vijñāna)*] is the seed of the shared-world *(bhājana-loka).* The uncommon [dimension of unconscious awareness] is the seed of the individual sense-spheres *(prātyātmikāyatana).*

The commentary elaborates:

[The statement:] "The common [dimension of unconscious aware-
ness] is the seed of the shared-world" means that it is the cause *(kāraṇ-
a-hetu)* of perceptions *(vijñapti)* which appear as the shared-world. It
is common because these perceptions appear similarly to all who experience them through the power for results *(vipāka)* in accordance with
their own similar karma.[50]

In short, just as the world *(loka)* in its variety arises in accordance with
the accumulated results of our activities, our *karma,* so our similar "shared
world" arises in accordance with the accumulated results of our similar activities, our similar karma.[51]

And what makes these activities similar? Actions that are informed and
instigated by similar conditions and similar intentions give rise, over the
long term, to similar results, similar faculties, and hence, similar worlds.
There would be no shared-world that beings experience similarly,[52] one of
the commentaries explains, without the similar conditions for such shared
experience subliminally influencing conscious awareness, conditions represented here by the metaphor of seeds and the substratum of linguistic dispositions. What the texts are suggesting is that language has the special
power *(śakti-viśeṣa)* to impart similar influences, due to which similar forms
of unconscious awareness *(ālaya-vijñāna)* arise, based upon which perceptions of our shared-world "appear similarly." In short, we all instinctively
jump when someone yells "Fire!" Yogācāra analyses of mind thus consider
the intersubjective yet subliminal influences of language as an inseparable
aspect, the common aspect, of the arising of our shared-world.

Because this conception uses the particular Buddhist mode of analysis,
in which consciousness results from the interaction of causes and conditions, this model of unconscious mentality is able to easily encompass the
influences of shared experiences such as language without recourse to such
question-begging expressions as to "internalize this," or to become "socialized into that"—expressions which imply that intersubjectivity occurs only
after the fact, only incidental to some aboriginally isolated entity.[53] But since
in this mode of analysis both interaction and (for humans) intersubjectivity are *constitutive of cognitive awareness in the first place,* language, culture,
and social life are readily, indeed already, included in the conditions for the

arising of consciousness. There is, in short, no subtle subject implicitly hiding in the shadows, hopelessly, solipsistically, sealed away and waiting, like Sleeping Beauty, for some Prince Charming to appear and waken her from her slumbers. The syntax of the dependent arising of subtle awareness suggests, by contrast, how enthralled we remain to the "ghost in the machine."

Syntactic Considerations

Yet one may reasonably object that there is still something missing here. And that, somehow, is the "subject" of samsara, maybe not a substantive subject of experience or a truly active agent of perception, but the subject as the totality of the person, what Indian Buddhists call the "mental stream" *(santāna)*, which is thought to continue throughout this lifetime and into the next. Without reference to this larger frame—wherein identifiable "persons" are indeed stuck in samsara, actually do practice the *pāramitās*, and occasionally experience awakening—this acclaimed impersonal analysis of mind would be devoid of direction, meaning, or purpose. And *this*, it seems, marks the boundary of useful comparisons between Indian Buddhism and cognitive science. For while their modes of analysis and causal syntax may similarly preclude the postulation of substantive selves or souls, Buddhist analysis at least must still serve its larger soteriological goals.[54] For all the appeal and analytic power of its impersonal discourse, Buddhist analysis cannot exclude more personalist discourse altogether without simultaneously undermining the very aim of that analysis: the liberation of beings from the repetitive behavioral cycles called samsara.[55] Personalist discourse, in other words, however otherwise anathema to orthodox Buddhism, provides the indispensable context and articulates the underlying rationale for its impersonal, ultimate discourse, despite their apparent incommensurability.[56] This tension is reflected in the continuing Western debates over the role of self in Buddhism, epitomized in Jack Engler's now classic quip: "you have to be somebody before you can be nobody."[57]

This appeal to personalist discourse does not, as I once imagined, stem primarily from ill-advised attempts by well-intentioned Westerners to look for Buddhist affirmations of selfhood where they cannot be found. Rather, it stems more deeply from the tensions between two equally essential ways of thinking about the relation between agency and causation. It reflects, in fact, much larger trends in classical Indian thought that articulate two diametrically opposed orientations: impersonal versus personal causal models and their corresponding forms of ideal syntax, philosophical justifications, and theological ramifications. I will only briefly outline these two trends, these two orientations, setting them in stark contrast. Such contrasts shed interesting light, I believe, on the ongoing dialogue between Indian Buddhist traditions and Western ways of using and adapting these traditions of understanding and working with mind.

The Sanskritist Edwin Gerow outlines the development of these alternative approaches within the grammatical, philosophical, and religious traditions of India in a densely detailed article entitled "What Is Karma (Kim Karmeti): An Exercise in Philosophical Semantics."[58] He begins, of course, with Panini:

> For reasons that are never announced, but seem embedded in the syntactic possibilities of Sanskrit, not only are verbal ideas invariably twofold (semantically) but in any given sentence, one or the other must be given <<prominence>> (assertive or topical primordinacy). . . . We call these assertional alternatives active and passive voice. . . . neither is inherently primary in Pāṇinian syntax.[59]

This "delicate optionality" gradually disappeared, Gerow avers,[60] as the evolving grammatical and philosophical schools took one or the other of these alternatives, the active or passive voice, as paradigmatic of Sanskrit sentences in particular and, by extension, of the structure of reality in general.

The influential school that coalesced around the newer ideas of Bhartṛhari (sixth century, C.E.) advocated the primacy of a very unusual grammatical paradigm, one that combined *both* the passive voice, in which the direct object (called the *karman* in Sanskrit grammar) replaces the active agent (the *kartṛ*) and appears in its stead in the nominative case (e.g., "the rice is cooked by Tanaka"), *and* the intransitive sentence, in which the direct object disappears altogether and its traditional role of marking the result *(phala)* of an action[61] is subsumed by the verbal process *(vyāpāra)* itself[62] (e.g., in "it rains" or "it happens," "rains" or "happens" represent both the activity itself and its result).[63] These two grammatical forms are combined in the form of passive intransitive sentences where both the agent and the direct object are subsumed within the verbal process alone. The resulting sentences (and for Buddhists, nouns as well)[64] replace active agents with dummy agents, as in "it rains,"[65] and then drop the subject/agent altogether, yielding the nearly unspeakable: "[it] happens." In this way, Gerow concludes, "activity *(kriyā)*, which is [equated with the object] karman, and not kartṛ [the agent], is given the status of independent or first principle."[66] For Bhartṛhari's school then, "the <<passive>> impersonal has now become the normative mode of expression."[67] And making the short leap, for Sanskritists, from grammar to worldview, Gerow concludes that "the [religious] notion of karma itself is indeed an inescapable function (and *result*) of the passivization or impersonalization of the Sanskrit sentence."[68] The sentence, like reality, paradigmatically focuses on active processes alone, free of both agents and objects.

In Gerow's analysis, these developments are exemplified by two Indian philosophical traditions in particular. The Advaita school, of which Bhartṛhari was an early proponent (a *śabdādvaita*), attributes our samsaric bondage to "an ontological confusion" which identifies worldly agency with ultimate consciousness. To overcome this false identity and thereby become liberated, one must philosophically "disassociate consciousness and agency," extracting, as it were, the ultimately real agency (e.g., consciousness or *ātman*) from the merely apparent, worldly agency *(prakṛti)*. As a result "[g]rammatically speaking, simple assertive propositions involving [real] personal agents are no longer possible" since "it is precisely the [real] <<agency>> of such propositions that has disappeared."[69] What remain are either transitive sentences that lack real subjects, but are replaced by "dummy subjects,"[70] as in "*it* is raining," or intransitive sentences that designate only verbal processes, yielding "[it] happens." In effect, "the <<grammatical>> problem for Advaita is neatly solved by making all sentences with real content <<passive>> *(karmaṇi/bhāve)*, in fact <<impersonal>>."[71]

Pride of place for this "impersonalization of the Sanskrit sentence" is, as we would presume, preserved for the Buddhists:

> It is likely the Bauddha śāstra that provides us with the most logically satisfying philosophy—one that is in complete accord with the new <<language>>. And this is done by simply . . . denying the need for any <<active>> sentence at all. . . . [since] for the Bauddha, there is *no agent.*[72]

Gerow thus concludes, "This, it seems to me, is nearly an exact replica (in <<philosophical>> or <<metaphysical>> terms) of the position attributed to the grammarians and to Bhartṛhari," who therefore "appears once again more kin to the Bauddha, than in fact to the standard (Hinduized) Advaita."[73] In short, the impersonal causal discourse favored by the Buddhists represents an ideal expression of a systematically articulated grammatical/philosophical world view.

The Śaivite scholar David Lawrence, on the other hand, argues that this represents the extreme end of a broad range of Sanskritic grammatical-religious traditions.[74] He shows how the Kashmiri Śaivite traditions centered around the eleventh-century figure Abhinavagupta exemplify exactly the "opposite of the direction of thinking observed by Gerow," in that they extol the agent at the expense of the object. This is expressed in a thoroughgoing idealism that, for its part, subsumes all the grammatical cases into that of the agent: "The Śaivas' basic strategy is to reduce all the other categories . . . to the process *(vyāpāra)* of self-recognition internal to the subject/agent," in this case the absolute agent, Śiva. Thus, in sharp contrast to Gerow's Advaitan and Buddhist examples, "Abhinava states that some believe that the expression that does not mention the object is the most proper one."[75]

We have, then, two diametrically opposed ideal grammatical/philosophical discourses which underlie and inform radically divergent religious world-views:[76] one in which action subsumes agency and, at times, even objects, and the other in which agency subsumes objects and, at times, even action.[77] Truly, as Gerow observes, echoing Wittgenstein: "we speak our philosophies along with our grammars."[78]

A Middle Way?

The existence of such extreme, and opposite, grammatical/philosophical discourses within Indian culture throws the varieties of Buddhist, scientific, and psychological discourses we have been discussing into some kind of relief. Indian Buddhist discussions of selves, like most scientific treatments, strongly favor impersonal discourse. This stems, perhaps, from a search for causal regularities in the world that, to be dependable and predictable, must operate universally, irrespective of differences in time, place, or person. An early *sutta*, for example, declares, "Whether Tathāgatas appear or do not appear, this nature of things continues, this relatedness of phenomena, this regularity of phenomena, this law of conditionality."[79] But this is problematic because it requires us to use impersonal modes of analysis to understand, explain, and transform what appear to be personal modes of experience. For such modes of analysis to apply to our experience *as* persons, however, they have to be related to what (we at least imagine) we experience *as* persons. And even if this sense of personhood is ultimately unfounded, as the Buddhists and the cognitive scientists claim, it still remains one of our deepest dispositions and therefore needs to be acknowledged, worked with and understood.

This is one of the major problems with the current state of most cognitive science: it has not yet forged a language, a set of concepts with its associated causal syntax, that can successfully bridge these two distinct kinds of discourse.[80] Perhaps it will not be able to. Perhaps the constraints of its impersonal causal syntax require that scientists continue to talk about the regularities of human behavior in ways that systematically exclude the dimension of personal experience, as if we indeed functioned like animals or, worse, like machines or computers.[81] Most reductive explanations of human experience and culture, whether economic, scientific, sociological, or biological, eliminate the subject in a similarly systemic way, such that experience is not so much explained as explained away. We seem to face an unbridgeable gulf between the explanatory and interpretive disciplines.

The Buddhist mode of analysis couched in the syntax of dependent arising avoids these problems, in my estimation, precisely because its discourse is neither purely subjective nor wholly objective, but focuses rather upon awareness as a process of interaction: the consciousness that we directly experience arises with the coming together of the sense faculties *and* their correlative sense objects. The basic unit of Buddhist analysis, consciousness, thus *already* bridges what we typically call the subject and object, whose extreme separation results, among other things, in the opposite forms of discourse designated above as personal and impersonal. By literally changing the terms of the debate, Buddhist discourse suggests one possible way out of these conundrums.

This does not settle the complex question of the status of the self in Buddhism. It does suggest, though, that our questions about the relation between causality and human experience could be usefully couched in different ways. For, it is said, syntax speaks louder than words.

6

Transcendence and Immanence:
Buddhism and Psychotherapy in Japan

TARUTANI SHIGEHIRO

U NLIKE EUROPE, where psychotherapy emerged within a long evolutionary history of intellectual and social development, in Japan it came
into being as a rather sudden addition or overlay to the preexisting culture.
That does not mean that psychotherapy had no foundations upon which to
build. Indigenous spiritual and religious culture and its belief in the soul
(tamashii) no doubt helped to shape the emergence of a distinctive therapeutic environment in Japan. Buddhism, imported into Japan in the sixth
century, also has a long tradition of psychologically oriented thinking and
practice.

At the same time, the continued development of an industrial and postin-
dustrial high-tech and information-intensive society has tended to quickly
erode the influence of premodern religious culture. Within its short history,
Japanese psychotherapy is already facing a critical period of rethinking its
past influences and future development. The relevance of religious culture
too is being continually questioned. This essay seeks to identify and examine key themes in the interface between Japanese religion and psychotherapy in the Japanese context. Hopefully, this will be of relevance not only for
scholars and practitioners in Japan but also for audiences in the West, where
there is a burgeoning interest in the intersection of Buddhism and psychotherapy. Although historically distinct, the development of Buddhism
and psychotherapy in Japan may provide insights for both Japanese and
Westerners.

In particular, I examine the relation between religious transcendence and
life in the secular world within Japanese religion (Buddhism in particular) and
Japanese psychotherapy. The first section takes up the notorious case of Asahara Shōkō and the Aum Shinrikyō as a misguided attempt at transcendence

and as symptomatic of larger spiritual and psychological ills in contemporary Japanese society. The second section explores the premodern relation between transcendence and secularity out of which modern and postmodern Japanese culture arose. The case of Suzuki Shōsan (1579–1655), Zen priest and advocate of the Pure Land practice of intoning the *nembutsu,* or Name of Amida Buddha, and that of the so-called *myōkōnin,* the "wondrous persons" of the Shin sect of Pure Land faith, are compared in order to examine how premodern Japanese religious life has unfolded. In the third section I use Cicely Saunders's four dimensions of hospice care—mental, physical, social, and spiritual—to further differentiate the relationship between secularity and transcendence, returning to the case of Asahara and the Aum Shinrikyō. I then explore Freud's notion of "evenly suspended attention" and Jung's psychological view of the trickster figure as particularly useful for enunciating themes broadly applicable to the interface of religion and psychotherapy in the twenty-first century. Finally, the fourth section takes up the case of Hara Inashiro (1830–1906), a nineteenth-century Shin follower who offers important insights for our consideration of religious transcendence and the need for grounding it in the web of social and natural relations.

Asahara Shōkō and Aum Shinrikyō: A Case of Mistaken Transcendence

In 1995, the New Age religion Aum Shinrikyō, led by Asahara Shōkō, received worldwide attention as the perpetrators of the sarin gas incident in the Tōkyō subway in which scores of passengers were poisoned, and in which many died. Although the media made much of the cultic nature of Asahara's leadership and his group, there was little examination of the Buddhist influences in his religion. Drawing upon his own quasi-mystical experiences in another "new religion," the Agonshū, as well as his own appropriation of Tibetan Buddhist Vajrayāna, Asahara built up a reasonably systematic basis for his "Buddhist" religion and practice. As Shimazono Susumu notes, "there is a consistent thread in his thinking" and "a relatively sophisticated logical system."[1] Asahara and his group were also influenced by the recent boom in pop psychology and *seishinsekai* (literally, spirit world), a Japanese New Age movement that appeals to a blend of mysticism, occultism, and this-worldly benefits. The choice of Tibetan Buddhist thought was no accident, since

Evans-Wentz's *Tibetan Book of the Book of the Dead* had been translated into Japanese in 1974, and self-made Japanese spiritual gurus often appropriated it along with these other elements in the creation of new religions. In many ways Aum was a child of the wedding of pop psychology and Buddhism. It gained considerable legitimacy when Nakazawa Shin'ichi, a scholar of religious studies and Buddhist writer who had undertaken substantial Tibetan Buddhist practice in Nepal for over two years, began making favorable references to the use of esoteric Tibetan Buddhism by new religious movements.

As Shimazono indicates, the younger generation in Japan in particular was attracted by Asahara's rhetoric of transcendence rendered in a language that was culturally current and removed from the stale air of their parents' religions.[2] This represented a new direction in Japanese religiosity; traditionally, Japanese Buddhism as well as Shintō had a strong this-worldly orientation, emphasizing closeness to nature and the importance of a cohesive social fabric. As new religions began to emerge in the late nineteenth and early twentieth centuries, this trend continued with their emphasis on this-worldly benefits, such as good health and overcoming poverty. The spiritual basis for these benefits was often described in psychologistic terms, such as *konjō naoshi* (getting the spirit right) and *kokoro naoshi* (setting right the mind). But these terms were used in a communal context where setting the mind or spirit right meant that one understood the importance or significance of contributing to the communal good, of "helping each other out." The "new new religions" that began to emerge in the last quarter-century, including Aum Shinrikyō, then, represented a marked departure in this regard, taking instead the direction of the psychological privatization of transcendence.[3]

From around 1992, criticisms of Aum Shinrikyō began to increase, but there was still substantial support among intellectuals for its quasi-renunciant rhetoric of transcendence. As Shimazono notes, at some level these intellectuals, influenced by imported Western notions of rational, autonomous selfhood, were looking for religious movements that embodied in Asian or Japanese form a mode of selfhood that could rationally tackle the problem of evil.[4] Japanese intellectuals, heavily influenced by Western developments, had both valorized rationality as well as critiqued it. On the one hand, the modern notion of an individualistic self based on enlightenment rationality still carried considerable force. On the other, just as in the

West, postmodern intellectuals since the 1970s came to view the simplistic, linear-progress view of modern rationalism as a mere mask for a more deeply seated evil. They began deconstructing the optimistic modern worldview in order to unmask its violent authoritarianism. Traditional religion was often identified as the Japanese counterpart to traditional Western religion and its power structures, and the leaders of traditional Buddhist sects and Shinto shrines themselves seemed unable to respond to these criticisms. In such a milieu, the transcendent vision of a foreign religion (Tibetan Buddhism) untainted by Japanese Buddhism's corrupt past became a magnet for attracting Generation Xers.

The Japanese Cultural Milieu and the Relation between Transcendence and Secularity

Much has been made of the fact that there are few outward signs of Japanese religiosity. Japanese do not go to church on Sundays, and most do not engage much in the way of religious austerities or go on retreats. As reported by Ishii Kenji, according to several surveys "Japanese religiosity has been gradually waning since the end of the Pacific War."[5] Even before the end of the war, D. T. Suzuki lamented that many Japanese did not even know what sect of Buddhism their families belonged to until the funeral of a family member.[6]

According to Ama Toshimaro, however, one must look more carefully at the ways that the Japanese express their spirituality.[7] Until now, almost every family has had a religious shrine or altar in their own home for devotion to buddhas, *kami* (indigenous gods), and ancestors. There are many elements of nature worship in the annual cycle of festivals and memorial services celebrating nature, propitiating spirits, or commemorating the dead, and these practices have helped to engender a sense of community. Although the vitality of nature worship has lessened through a process of routinization in modernity and postmodernity, one can still find regions with remarkable spiritual vitality. According to Ama, Japanese have tended to stay away from the close study of the complex doctrines and ritual practices associated with the founding figures of religions like Buddhism. Nevertheless, many Japanese have tended to identify founder-based religions with sophisticated doctrines as full-fledged "religions" *(shūkyō)* but not the nature worship found in indigenous culture. Yet, one of the attractions of New Age religions such as Aum Shinrikyō has been their incorporation of elements of both founder-based and nature-based religions.

Even ascetic leaders have enjoyed widespread popularity in Japanese religious history, as found in the case of the wandering holy men *(hijiri)* of medieval Japan, including the Pure Land Buddhist figures of Kōya, Shinran, and Ippen, who reached out to the oppressed and braved charges of heresy. As Ama notes, in the sixteenth and seventeenth centuries there was something akin to the emergence of a Protestant work ethic. In particular, he identifies as a turning point the thought of the Zen priest Suzuki Shōsan (1579–1655) who advocated among the laity the Pure Land practice of intoning the Name of Amida Buddha. Suzuki was the first prominent priest to equate daily work and vocation as a civil servant with religious practice. Unlike Ama who saw in Suzuki Shōsan the loss of religious transcendence, D. T. Suzuki (no relation) saw in Shōsan a spirituality deeply grounded in daily life, and especially in the Great Earth worked by peasant farmers.[8]

Although Ama and D. T. Suzuki took diametrically opposed views of Suzuki Shōsan, they surprisingly agree on their positive valuations of the *myōkōnin*, the "wondrous persons" of the Pure Land faith, rustic lay figures who exhibited a remarkable religious genius in their simple, down-to-earth ways. Both agree that many of these "wondrous persons" were able to overcome the hardships of poverty and lack of social status by achieving spiritual liberation. In effect, they did not need to renounce worldly status, possessions, or knowledge, as monks of aristocratic upbringing did, because they did not possess these things from the beginning. Rather than become embittered by their hardships, they instead found an inner freedom through Shin Pure Land faith. D. T. Suzuki saw something quite similar in Suzuki Shōsan, whereas Ama saw in him a problematic assimilation into the dominant social and economic structures.

What is partly at stake in these differing interpretations of Suzuki Shōsan is what might be characterized as, following William James, the religion of the "healthy-minded" versus the religion of the "twice-born."[9] In the case of the "wondrous persons," often there were critical turning points in their religious lives, points that marked an awakening out of deep darkness (cf. James's references to the "sick-souled") into the illumination of Amida Buddha, a kind of spiritual rebirth. In the work-oriented religion of Suzuki Shōsan, one sees more of a healthy-minded affirmation of the world as it is. While there are important insights offered by Ama's view that Suzuki's religion was more susceptible to co-optation by the dominant sociopolitical forces in Japanese society, the idea that religious figures should openly oppose the autocratic, nationalistic agenda of the government and dominant social forces may be a case of a forced reading of modern Westernized notions of selfhood and individual autonomy back into the Japanese past. In the communal, agrarian local culture that dominated the premodern world of Suzuki Shōsan, religious awakening, while not quite "healthy-minded," tended to emerge gradually over an extended period of cultivation, just like the fields that required continual tending. Most followers of Shin Buddhism, as was the case with other sects, did not experience dramatic moments of "sudden enlightenment" but matured over time, like the plants growing around them. Religious transcendence, then, was usually not a sudden impulse that announced itself boldly. Rather, it was realized close to the earth, better described, perhaps, as an endless deepening rather than a clear-cut transcendence. Thus, Takeuchi Yoshinori uses the term "transdescendence" to describe Shin religious awakening.

Certainly, for the peasants constituting a large portion of the Japanese populace in premodern Japan, life was no easy matter. Many experienced deep socioeconomic suffering, for which religion was often the only balm available. But the healing of their suffering was effected for the most part not through becoming a monk or a nun or a religious hermit but by being soothed by the healing powers of a boundless compassion that embraced them in their daily lives of worship. In the case of Pure Land Shin faith, this occurred through repeatedly intoning the Name of Amida Buddha, Namu Amida Butsu.

Holistic Healing in Psychotherapy and Religion

Healing, etymologically related to "holy" and "whole," ultimately involves the whole subjectivity of the person at the level of holy or sacred existence. This subjectivity ultimately involves the entire life-environment or world of which one is a part, so that "whole subjectivity" must take into account the world as a living extension of any given person. Four aspects of Cicely Saunders's hospice care—physical, mental, social, and spiritual—may be helpful for understanding the ramifications of defining subjectivity in this way. For our purposes, the spiritual dimension is most important, but we must begin with the mental horizon of the individual. We are beings with mutable physical bodies that are limited by time and space, but with the mental dimension where the consciousness of pain and therefore of healing begins.

According to Saunders, the mental dimension must be addressed first in hospice work because the crisis facing the dying person usually begins there. That is because such a person faces above all else the loss of meaning, or more precisely the loss of the mentally constructed world which one has come to take for granted—health, career, family, material possessions, and the like. That is, the whole of one's world, however it is conceived, is called into question. The breakdown of the mental world reverberates through the physical and social dimensions of the person, such that everything one had taken to be part of oneself or one's world suddenly appears as other. It is as if a wall were suddenly erected between oneself and the world, and one has the strange feeling that one's own body, mind, and heart are on the other side, isolating one in a meaningless vacuum, a world fallen into chaos. It is only when faced with such an existential deadlock that the spiritual dimension becomes a pressing issue for the individual. This sets up a dynamism between mental, physical, and social chaos on the one hand and the need for a spiritual cosmos on the other. When and if this spiritual cosmos is realized within, the prior chaos is not merely forgotten and left behind, as it had a role in the spiritual rebirth of the individual. Chaos and a more harmonious cosmos become the polar pairs of a dynamic unfolding that may repeat itself over and over.

In Buddhism from its very beginnings, this awareness of spiritual chaos and cosmos has been actively cultivated through formal meditation on the impurity of the body and on skeletal remains. The Contemplation of the Nine Aspects of Death *(kusōgan)*, involving progressive stages of the decay of a corpse, is just one example of this type of meditation. Another example is the practice of breaking down attachment to the Four Conceptual Abodes *(shinenjo)* of purity, ease, permanence, and self. The Four Practices *(shigyō)* attributed to Bodhidharma—enduring hardships by seeing them as karmic retribution for past actions; practicing in accordance with a given situation, painful or not, with full knowledge of karmic causation; practice without attachment; and practice in accordance with emptiness—are similarly designed to lead one to awareness of one's attachments and to release from them.[10] Such practices are designed to lead one to an awareness of emptiness, the oneness of all sentient beings, the equality of all things, the communion of all beings, and the sharing of suffering. However, the ultimate realization is not of leaving behind attached, deluded consciousness in favor of pure, awakened consciousness; in true emptiness, both delusion and enlightenment are embraced, the distinction between them transcended in their dynamic mutuality and interpenetration.

When *satori,* or enlightenment, is viewed in a static, intellectual manner as happened with Asahara and the Aum Shinrikyō, the assumed superiority of the adept can even be used to justify murder, because from such a stance, respect for the autonomy of the other and thus a true encounter with the other is impossible. According to Shimazono, Asahara actually incorporated Buddhist meditations on impurity, specifically those of the Four Conceptual Abodes, into the foundational practices of his community.[11] However, he perverted this practice by attempting to isolate himself (and his followers) in an altered state of consciousness, sealed off against the threat of impurity infiltrating from without. He thus failed to engage in the dynamic of nirvana and samsara encompassed in emptiness. He called this altered state *sei-mutonjaku,* "holy carefreeness," a distortion of the Buddhist "mind of equality" *(byōdōshin).* Asahara's desire for freedom from suffering was well founded, for he had experienced poverty, discrimination because of his disability (blindness), academic failure, social insecurity, and so on,[12] but his attempt to overcome his suffering was misguided, to say the least. What he came to call his version of "Vajrayāna" was designed to create an armor against the suffering of the world rather than open his and his followers' hearts to compassion for and with the suffering world.

Although Asahara and the Aum Shinrikyō represent an extreme case, his and his group's attitude toward the world typifies one aspect of the postmodern turn in consciousness. It is a world fragmented, flooded with information, and denied access to any sort of broader truth. The past (especially past religion) and other human beings are seen as oppressive; in response to an undesirable, controlled world, one may attempt to control one's mind, and the minds of others, in a self-isolating manner. In this reliance on "mental" control, there is no openness to others or to the world.

Returning to Saunders's four dimensions, it becomes clear that Asahara attempted to go directly from the mental to the spiritual without any real connection to the physical and social. On the one hand, these four dimensions are mutually interrelated and ultimately inseparable. On the other, each dimension can operate with relative autonomy. This often gives rise to polarized approaches to the same kinds of problems. At one extreme, much of current psychiatric practice in both the United States and Japan is overly reliant on the pharmaceutical treatment of mental disorders; at the other extreme, New Thought (what William James called the "religion of the healthy-minded," which presaged what is now known as New Age) approaches tend to reduce everything to a problem of mental attitude adjustment. Yet, we know that even placebos rely on the interrelation and interdependence of body, mind, and the social influence of physicians and medical institutions and their perceived authority.[13] These miscellaneous elements act like a goblin that circumvents and upsets our conscious intention.

This brings us to the true spiritual dimension, the only dimension in which each of the other dimensions can be seen from a holistic perspective. Only within a holistic awareness can the dynamic relation between chaos and cosmos unfold unhindered by the distortions of fixed, static viewpoints.

There is a theoretical problem that is common to both Buddhism and psychotherapy, of how to understand the nature of the self and of the mind in relation to suffering in Buddhism, and various clinical pathologies in psychotherapy. Each school has its own distinct theory of human nature and methods of practice. Thus, despite the identification of a common base of problems and claims concerning universal theories of truth, the different schools in each field have difficulty agreeing about the specifics of the problems, general theories, and methods of liberation or cure. I would like to suggest, however, that two notions, Freud's "evenly suspended attention" and Jung's view that "the soul should be seen as a trickster" are particularly resonant with both the religious and psychotherapeutic needs of our time. Although there are significant differences, the former overlaps with Krishnamurti's "choiceless awareness" and Buddhist *śamatha*, or "equilibrium," in which the usual judgments and control of discursive consciousness are released to enable deeper levels of awareness to emerge. The trickster element is especially important in an age where there is so much perversion and inversion of the spiritual life. The depths of the mind or psyche must find a way to unmask and overturn the overwhelming influence of self-deceptive rhetoric and images that dominate popular culture. In effect, it must "trick" the conscious mind or insinuate itself so that one can become open to the chaos/cosmos dynamic.

Freud used his "evenly suspended attention" closely in tandem with his method of free association to expose the contents of the unconscious and to correct the self-deception of his clients. His psychodynamic approach differs significantly from Buddhist *śamatha*, as the former remains within a discursive framework. Unlike the discursive objectivism of natural science, however, Freud's method of unmasking self-deception through uncovering defense mechanisms relies on the perspective of an altered state of awareness, the so-called "evenly suspended attention." It led him to mobilize levels of awareness deeper than the merely theoretical, levels that might in contrast be called existential.

As a manifestation or voice of the deepest levels of the unconscious, Jung's trickster spirit likewise functioned to expose and critique the self-deceptions of ego-consciousness. Jung makes it clear that there is a level of the unconscious that is spiritual and beyond the grasp of discursive consciousness, a level in which the boundaries between all dichotomies begin to dissolve. The trickster, reflecting the movements of the unconscious as well as the dynamic between consciousness and the unconscious, is never a static entity but rather constantly in motion. On the one hand, the trickster facilitates the creative dynamism between unconscious and consciousness, cosmos and chaos; on the other, it is necessarily susceptible to the distortions and instability of the consciousness that it partly inhabits. There are numerous examples of tricksterlike figures in Buddhist history who are both unpredictable and fallible, constantly upsetting the apple cart of consciousness and willingly taking on the defilements of samsara. There are legendary figures like the layman Vimalakīrti, who willingly takes on the ills of sentient beings and becomes ill himself; historical figures like the Korean master Wonhyo, "the little layman" who wanders through the red-light district; and Saichi, the "wondrous person" of Japanese Pure Land, the simple maker of wooden clogs who unmasks the pretensions of the learned. All of these figures seem to have operated within something like an evenly suspended attention that enabled them to manifest the holistic, sacred dimension of the spiritual in full recognition of the interrelation between the mental, physical, and social worlds.

We now turn to the case of a Japanese Pure Land adherent, Hara Inashiro, who outwardly was rather ordinary if devout, but in whom deep attentiveness and the appearance of trickster figures in dreams led to the spiritual healing of the chaos/cosmos dynamic.

The Case of a Pure Land Practitioner—Hara Inashiro

Hara Inashiro (1830–1906) was a Pure Land Buddhist practitioner of the late nineteenth century, a follower of the Shin sect. His case is instructive insofar as it illustrates a life that is open to the dimensions of religious and social awareness within an incipient modern consciousness. Okuwa Hitoshi, a historian of Japanese religion, has analyzed consciousness as a complex accumulation of layers and dimensions unfolding within an open yet contoured sense of *topos,* consciousness-as-place.[14] Okuwa weds his concept of *topos*-consciousness with an examination of Hara's life history in order to provide an insightful view into the latter's psyche and religious life. According to Okuwa, Hara was particularly influenced by the conventional ethics of his day, by Kokugaku, a movement in Japanese ethics and social attitudes founded on classical Japanese literature, and the Pure Land faith of the Shin tradition.

Inashiro was born into a household that for generations had been the regional head of an area in Owari known to be a stronghold of Shin Pure Land faith. Frequenting the Shin temples in the area during his childhood, Inashiro was influenced by the spiritual culture around him, but any impulse toward transcendence remained dormant. Of course, he was also shaped by the conventional mores of the area. Influenced by his father, he also studied Kokugaku, and this study served as a catalyst in his attempts to contribute to local revitalization. As we shall see, however, the influence of Kokugaku would wane over time.

When Inashiro was twenty-three his father died, after which he experienced himself as "destined for hell," according to the Shin view of the self as inescapably mired in karmic evil. Because Inashiro was now the village headman, his family was the recipient of *mitsugimono* (tribute) from the local populace, but Inashiro was ashamed to benefit at what he regarded as others' expense. This awakening to a larger social and ethical reality might be attributed to the influence of the ethico-religious worldview of his Shin upbringing, but at this point at least, this incipient awareness did not develop into a transcendent realization of the religious. Instead, Inashiro, informed by conventional social mores, sought to overcome his sense of shame by attempting to assist the downtrodden. For example, he went all the way to Edo (present-day Tokyo) in order to appeal on behalf of peasants who were having difficulty with the fiefdom of Owari concerning water rights.

Inashiro began with an attempt to provide a model of moral behavior by overcoming his own excessive drinking. Through repeated failures to swear off alcohol, however, he only drove himself further into despair. Nevertheless, from an external perspective one begins to see emerging therein the dynamic tension between religious transcendence and secular immanence. As Inashiro continued to attempt to reform himself through conventional ethics, his behavior actually worsened, but this in itself helped to propel him toward the Shin awakening to *ga,* the ego or limited self. Only by seeing himself illuminated as absolutely worthless in the light of emptiness, illuminated by the boundless compassion of Amida Buddha, did the virtuous qualities of a true village headman eventually begin to appear in Inashiro's character. Conversely, he became aware of the self-destructiveness of believing himself to be somehow honest and merciful.

It was 1867, at the age of thirty-eight, when this deeper Shin awareness broke through the shell of his ego-consciousness. This coincided with the beginning of the Eejanaika movement, a popular uprising of free-spirited pilgrims who distributed paper amulets. These amulets symbolized the presence and saving grace of the *kami,* the indigenous local gods of Japan. The affluent households where the amulets fell were supposed to treat people who chanted "Eejanaika" ("Hey, it's all swell") to food and drink. At first Inashiro was critical of the movement, regarding it as instigated by rabble-rousers, but soon, caught up in the energy of the moment, he began to pick up these amulets himself and hoped that the gods would favor him by raining the amulets down on his own house.

When the amulets failed to materialize, he began to feel sorry for himself. One night, in a dream, a voice spoke to him: "The buddhas and the *kami* are one; since Amida Buddha resides in your home, the paper amulets are unnecessary." When even this dream did not settle his mind, his brother appeared in another dream to pick up the amulets for him. When Inashiro went to receive the amulet from his brother, it disintegrated in his hands. He looked closer to see what happened, whereupon the figure of his mother appeared. She was intoning the Name of Amida Buddha, "Namu Amida Butsu," and the Buddha appeared from out of her mouth. A voice told him that the Buddha would lead him to birth in the Pure Land.

This was a turning point for Inashiro who is said to have gained the "diamondlike faith" *(kongōshin)* of non-retrogression *(futaiten).* At forty-four he had another dream in which he was being led by Amida Buddha from the nearby Zenkōji temple. After a near-death experience later in the same year, he believed that he had visited the Pure Land of Amida and that all his karmic sins had been expiated. Thenceforward, he lived a life of deep gratitude in the *nembutsu,* intoning the Name of Amida. As a village leader, a lay officiant of the Shin temples, and a calligraphy teacher, he was especially admired by the local youths and finished out his life as a respected elder.

The Eejanaika movement arose under the influence of the Meiji Restoration and its nationalist sentiment and agenda. The documents left behind by Inashiro, including essays and letters, show that he never pursued a fuller understanding of the movement and failed to understand its political implications. He expresses no expectation of social reform or antigovernment sentiments typical of the movement. Okuwa concludes that Inashiro's initial sympathy for the movement arose not with any strong identification with its nationalist themes but rather with the spiritual urges and longings of the local populace. More importantly, the release of emotions and spirit he experienced in the movement mediated his larger religious awareness of Shin Buddhism.[15]

Shin Buddhism represents the lay-oriented egalitarianism so prominent in Japanese Buddhism, in which a kind of "evenly suspended attention" enables boundless compassion to break through to consciousness. In this awareness, transcendent awakening to no-self and impermanence emerges as a positive force within lay life, immanent to society, grounded in the Great Earth. In the process of Inashiro's spiritual development, one can see the mediating functions played by Kokugaku, conventional ethics, and the nonlinear appearance of dreams, through which he opens up to his deeper self as well as to the reality of others' lives.

As Okuwa notes, the self that reemerged on the plane of Inashiro's conventional social existence was not the self-enclosed ego of modernity but an interdependent subjectivity that was deeply connected to other people and beings.[16] Such a subjectivity is more a field of awareness than a discrete entity. It is the opposite of the modern egotism embodied by someone like Aum Shinrikyō's Asahara, who attempted to go in the direction of a self-deceived spirituality by way of an intellectual transcendence in which he remained closed off from others and society. Although Asahara seems to have attained some sort of altered consciousness that gave him the charisma to attract followers, it is a far cry from the kind of evenly suspended attention that allows the Buddhist practitioner to open up to the world around one. Asahara was merely lost in a fanatical narcissism.

The de-centered self of postmodernity with its multiple nodes of subjectivity superficially resembles the supple awakened self of Buddhism that flows through the web of interdependence, but the postmodern self is too often little more than a fractured, fragmented extension of the self-enclosed modern ego. In Japan the ego-self, whether regarded as modern or postmodern, is increasingly losing touch with the Great Earth that has grounded and mediated its realization of the true self or awakening to buddha-nature. Particularly alarming is the rapidly rising rate of violent juvenile crime and the inability of educators to adequately address the question, "Why is it wrong to kill someone?" These problems point to the failure of conventional ethics and the disintegration of communal cohesion and the family unit. No matter how severe the problem, it was long assumed that the unbreakable physical and emotional bond of parent and child would serve as the final bulwark against psychological and spiritual disintegration. It is true that, without going through the body, the psyche and spirit cannot be healed. In its present state, however, even the parent-child bond seems increasingly unable to mediate the healing process.

In such an environment, a kind of evenly suspended attention and the spirit of the trickster are necessary to unmask, expose, and overturn the self-enclosed ego-consciousness of modernity and postmodernity and open the self to the world. This awareness and trickster spirit deeply resonate with both Buddhistic religion and psychotherapy. These virtues and attitudes lack substantial content in and of themselves and only gain force by harnessing the concrete flow of history and culture within each locality within global culture. Conversely, the depth of any particular religious or psychotherapeutic approach can be tested against its own openness to the rhythms of the spirit vibrating beyond the bounds of a self-enclosed local ethos and culture. Whether working within a religious or a psychotherapeutic framework, we are given, each of us, the task of digesting the particularities of our own life, history, and culture, and we continue to encounter the limits of our spirit and psyche until we are enfolded in the dynamic rhythm of a cosmic transcendence that continues to unfold endlessly.

PART II

CREATIVE POSSIBILITIES:
PSYCHOTHERAPY AND BUDDHISM
IN MUTUAL ENCOUNTER

7

Psychotherapy and Buddhism: Attending to Sand

OKADA YASUNOBU

I HAVE MADE A CAREER out of attending to sand as a Sandplay therapist, and sand also has a special place in Buddhism. Thus, I would like to turn our attention to the significance of sand as a possible portal to the encounter of psychotherapy and Buddhism. In Japanese, there are two different Sino-Japanese characters used to depict sand, both read the same way, *"suna."* One uses the radical for "stone" *(ishi),* and the other for "water" *(sanzui).* The latter character is a popularization that also means "fine" or "tiny," hence its association with sand. The medieval Japanese Buddhist monk Myōe Kōben (1173–1232) wrote extensively about the use of sand in the ritual of the Mantra of Light (Jpn. Kōmyō Shingon), and he used the latter character. He writes about the significance of sand at a very subtle level, where the power of the Mantra of Light begins to flow through the sand like the waters of the ocean: "The nature of the mantra is like the ocean water. The addition of the mystic power to the sand is like wetting the sand and hardening it. Then, its becoming one with sentient beings, extinguishing sins, and producing good is like using salt as a spice for harmonizing the flavor of soup. This salt[-like sand] is nondual with and indistinguishable from the ocean water. Since the substance of the mantra is the realm of the tathāgatas' realization, it is like ocean water that has been made fresh and gentle for the sake of ordinary people."[1] In terms of Buddhist practice, then, the sand functions as a form of *upaya* (Jpn. *hōben)* or skillful means of liberation used to lead the devotee into the waters of *samādhi* or deep meditation. Psychologically, one might say that in Sandplay therapy sand functions to open consciousness to the deep waters of the unconscious.

Sand is generally composed of tiny grains of stone from about an eighth of a millimeter to two millimeters. Any smaller, and it tends to become dirt, *tsuchi.* Sandplay therapy originated in the West. When it was introduced into Japan, it came to be called "Hakoniwa ryōhō," or literally, "Boxed-garden therapy." In Japan there is a long tradition of children playing in boxes of sand and dirt, so it was natural to associate this "boxed-garden" play with Sandplay therapy, which also takes place in a box. The Japanese also have various traditions of landscaping with dirt, sand, and stone.

According to the *Kōjien* dictionary, dirt, *tsuchi,* can mean (1) soil, earth, (2) the earth as in "heaven and earth," or (3) worthless.[2] Sand, *suna,* can mean (1) small grains of stone, (2) worthless as in "turned to sand," or (3) to exploit, take for a fool. In Sumō wrestling, one is "besmirched with dirt" when one loses. One is said to "bite sand" when something is tasteless or bland.

Thus, there have traditionally been these two contradictory senses of sand and dirt, the one as valuable in play and in landscaping, the other as worthless or useless. In both Buddhism and Sandplay therapy, these apparently contradictory definitions are brought together: the value or significance of sand lies precisely in its being useless or valueless. It corresponds to the fact that emptiness in Mahāyāna Buddhism is used as an antidote to the "inverted views" of conventional social values. This paper will explore the paradoxical character of sand at the intersection of Buddhism and psychotherapy.

Earth, of course, is essential to growing crops. I recall a symposium at which the scholar Kyūma Kazutake gave a paper entitled "Is Soilless Agriculture Possible?" He showed that with proper irrigation, light, and nutrients in a computer-controlled climate, one can artificially cultivate plants. However, the costs would be prohibitive. The earth provides ideal conditions for plant growth at no cost, he said. The earth provides nourishment, holds moisture and warmth, and provides the bed for scattered seeds to germinate and sprout. With minimal human intervention, the earth becomes a source of agricultural riches. Listening to his presentation, I was struck by the great power of dirt, sand, and earth. On another occasion, someone said, "Three years after burying our pet in the yard, the skeletal remains had turned to fine sand, and out of the sand bloomed beautiful purple chrysanthemums. All of our children were moved by what they saw as the vivid life of their pet blossoming forth in the chrysanthemum." The natural process of purification that gave rise to the sand also gave birth to new life. The person reported, "Dirt and sand are fragile and easily lose their form but also serve as the powerful vessel for new life."

In East Asian Buddhism, one often sees the five-story pagoda that symbolizes the five great elements beginning with earth at the bottom and ascending to water, fire, wind, and air (see fig. 1 below). Earth forms the base that supports all of the others. In Indian Buddhism, one finds the expression "the sands of the Ganges," signifying an astronomically large number, innumerable. In the *Amida Sūtra* (Smaller Sutra of Eternal Life), a scripture of Pure Land Buddhism, one finds the expression "buddhas as innumerable as the grains of sand in the Ganges."[3] It refers to the idea that each being is protected by and the recipient of the great compassion of innumerable buddhas. According to the *Amida Sūtra*, the sands of the Ganges have two meanings worth mentioning here: first, the innumerable grains of dirt and sand are where the buddhas were born, where they live, and where they travel; and second, the innumerable grains of dirt and sand have the power to purify sentient beings of their sins and defilement, like the waters of a great river. The monk Myōe placed particular emphasis on the second of these meanings, which I would like to delve into in further detail.

FIGURE I. THE FIVE-STORY PAGODA

Myōe and the Sand of the Mantra of Light

Myōe Kōben, a monk of the Shingon or Esoteric sect of Japanese Buddhism, was responsible for interpreting and propagating what became one of the most important practices of his sect, the Mantra of Light. In his *Recommending Faith in the Sand of the Mantra of Light*, Myōe states,

If the mantra is used to augment the mystic power of the sand, this sand becomes transformed into each of the mantra's syllables, becomes replete with the significance of each character, and fulfills the meaning of the phrase.

If this sand is sprinkled on the corpse or grave of the deceased, then, even if the deceased had committed grave sins throughout her life, had failed to cultivate the slightest good, and had fallen into the Avīci Hell, the sand will immediately release the light of the mantra and reach the place of sin and suffering. The sin will dissipate spontaneously, and the deceased will attain birth in the Land of Bliss.

Of interest for us is that statement that due to the power of the sand, "sin will dissipate spontaneously, and the deceased will attain birth in the Land of Bliss." Of course, this is not any old sand, but sand empowered by the Mantra of Light, called "incantatory sand": "The sand gains the mystic power of the mantra and immediately becomes replete with the virtue of the mantra." This sand can be sprinkled on the corpse or even on the grave after the deceased has already been buried as well as used for those who are still living. "The sand blown by the wind can be understood to be like the clouds and mist which refract and reveal the radiance. Again, the many [grains of sand] point to the immeasurable radiance of the tathāgatas. Thus, when the radiance of the fivefold wisdom of all of the tathāgatas is to be revealed, sand should be used as the object of correlation." This passage shows not only the dynamic relation between sand and wind but also between the grains of sand and the innumerable buddhas. It expresses the infinite power of the sand-buddhas' radiance that emanates from the infinite store of sand.

Myōe gives one definition of sand that is similar to that which I gave above: "[The various grains] of sand differ in color, being blue, yellow, and so on; likewise, they differ in shape, being rectangular, round, and so on. [Together] they form a mass of tiny, hard [particles]. This is called 'sand.'" He further states, "Earthen sand is not a treasure and fills the whole earth."

When the wisdom of the buddhas is added to the sand of foolish beings, the sand radiates light by taking on the wisdom of the buddhas. This is the meaning of mystic power.

There is likewise a deep significance to each of the remaining phrases. This is thoroughly attained by the practitioners of yoga. The sand already contains innumerable meanings and principles, and when the power of the buddhas and dharma are added on top of this, how can anything prove too difficult for the understanding, no matter how miraculous things [may appear to] be.

Setting aside for the moment the theoretical complexities of Myōe's Buddhist thought, one gains from these passages the sense of cosmic scale and power conveyed through the sand. Yet, Myōe tells us that it is not anything inherent in the sand itself that has this effect but the power of the buddhas as conveyed through the mantra master: "There is no deep efficacy to the sand of itself. Truly, the sand becomes what it is by [the hand of] the mantra master because it is the esoteric sand that receives the mystic power of the mantra master."

My view of the sand as used in Sandplay therapy differs from Myōe's view insofar as I believe that there is something special about the physical qualities of the sand. However, there is a certain parallel with Myōe's attribution of power to the mantra master since the efficacy of Sandplay depends upon the therapist providing a safe environment. That is, the sand becomes the medium through which the protective and therapeutic environment created by the therapist is conveyed or mediated to the client. In addition, I believe that there are characteristics to the sand, such as its warmth and associated maternal qualities, that lend it mystic power, themes to which I will return later in this chapter.

Sandplay Therapy

Sandplay therapy was originated in Switzerland by Dora M. Kalff as a means of helping children. In 1965 Kawai Hayao introduced it to Japan where it has become one of the major forms of psychotherapy for both children and adults. It is one of the fastest growing forms of psychotherapy in the world and has been effectively used to address all kinds of conditions ranging from eating disorders to dissociative identity disorder. Figure 2 shows the setting and implements of Sandplay therapy including the toys that are used.

Kalff regarded the Sandplay compositions created by her clients as expressions of the unconscious. Some have referred to them as "worlds." In fact, Sandplay therapy is the result of Kalff applying the principles of C. G. Jung's analytical psychology to the Lowenfeld World Technique. In Japan this was further influenced by indigenous traditions of "boxed-garden" *(hakoniwa)* play and sand and stone landscaping. Thus, it is not surprising that Sandplay therapy has received such widespread acceptance in Japan.

FIGURE 2. IMPLEMENTS OF SANDPLAY THERAPY

There are a number of factors that make Sandplay therapy distinctive. While depth psychology and in particular Freudian psychoanalysis began as the "talking cure," Sandplay emphasizes forms of communication other than the verbal. Not only does it appeal to the visual senses of both client and therapist, it also makes use of subtle non-verbal communication through shared space and body language. That is, as the client creates the Sandplay composition, both client and therapist may be silent for extended periods of time, during which subtle cues of body position and body language may be conveyed. This is particularly significant in working with children who often find it easier to depict their state of mind than to describe it verbally. This nonverbal dimension is especially prominent in Japanese Sandplay where very few words may be exchanged in any particular session or even the whole course of therapy. In addition Sandplay is simultaneously diagnostic and therapeutic. The therapist may see both the problem or themes facing the client in the compostion as well as the unfolding healing process, often in the same Sandplay scene. Finally, the vast majority of therapists are women, perhaps because they tend to be more culturally at home in the nonverbal, maternal environment of Sandplay.

Although there is not space here to give further explanation of this form of therapy, three aspects that Kalff emphasized are pertinent to our discussion: a free and safe environment; a therapist-client relationship that can be described as a mother-child identification; and symbolic overtones to both the individual elements of the Sandplay composition and the composition as a whole. Kalff's emphasis on the mother-child relationship resonates with the important idea in Japanese social psychology that one always returns to the maternal as the foundation of security and of starting anything new. Further, she described a progression from an animal/vegetative stage to a confrontational stage and finally an adaptive stage, each of which is seen as a symbol of self-expression. The client is said to mature through this process.

The Implements of Sandplay Therapy

The most distinctive feature of Sandplay therapy lies in its implements, specifically the sand and a sandbox measuring 57 cm x 72 cm. The box is associated with maternal qualities; Bower has shown that the M (empathy) response in the Rorschach test correlates closely with the way that the client uses sand in Sandplay.[4] Bower indicated that the sympathetic and maternal characteristics of the M response were closely allied to qualities found in Sandplay. In clinical practice, clients with problematic relationships with their mother regularly fail to touch the sand, but when the relationship improves, they often begin working the sand directly with their hands. Although one's attention is understandably drawn to the toys and implements placed on the sand, it is the sand that forms the foundation or Mother Earth. The surface underneath the sand is painted blue so that it is like finding water at the bottom of a well when one moves the sand aside. This strengthens even further the association with Mother Earth.

The box forms a boundary framework. The composition is made inside the box, and going outside the box can be interpreted as "acting out." The box is not only restrictive but, as pointed out earlier, also protective. The client feels safe in expressing her or his unconscious precisely because of the protective framework provided by the box.

The toys have the benefit of easily drawing out the clients' interest and curiosity. This is true for both children and adults. Youths at risk may initially refuse to play with "mere toys," but they usually end up unable to resist putting their hands on them. Also, even though toys are not exact reproductions of objects from the social world, they often function as miniaturized representations. The three-dimensional aspect of Sandplay also sets it apart from other therapeutic media. Clients add or project their own meanings and symbolic significance from multiple perspectives.

The Significance of Sand in Case Studies

Although sand is basic to all Sandplay, there are cases in which the sand becomes particularly prominent. Rather than using the sand primarily as a base upon which to place toys, some clients work primarily with the sand, burying toys in the sand, excavating the sand, and so on. Here I would like to focus on a case where the client uses virtually no toys and works almost exclusively with the sand. A therapist presents the case of a fourteen-year-old girl with anorexia and complaints of depression.[5] She had a troubled older brother who required constant management while she herself was responsible and well behaved. Her mother reported that she did not need much directing. Academically, she was at the top of her class, and she was also a star athlete. However, she began to diet in order to develop her physique; she lost strength as a result, and she began to lose matches. This in turn led to a further loss of appetite, starting a vicious cycle. During her therapy she created forty-two Sandplay compositions consisting almost exclusively of sand. Figure 3 shows one example.

According to the therapist, she "let her hands go where they would, and the composition seemed to emerge spontaneously." "The self-expression and surface of the sand unfolded like water flowing quietly. There was a powerful sense of intensity and transparency to the composition, yet the meaning remained unclear." "There was also a lack of purposefulness and a sense of impermanence not unlike that found in the sand paintings of Tibetan Buddhist mandalas." The sense of impermanence does not conclude with a lack of purpose. Rather, as in the case of the Tibetan sand mandalas, there is paradoxically an accrual that accompanies the impermanence. Just as Buddhist wisdom and virtue is cultivated in the very context of impermanence, the healing powers of the unconscious are untapped and begin to replenish the psyche of the client as she creates the Sandplay composition. The therapist also noted that the sand compositions often "resembled internal organs"

FIGURE 3. A SANDPLAY COMPOSITION

such as the lungs, stomach, or uterus. Figure 4 depicts one such composition that appears to show a lung-shape being pierced by a foreign object from below. Interestingly, the client subsequently was stricken with a case of pulmonary inflammation that required hospitalization. Figure 5 shows a mandala-like configuration depicting a human form.

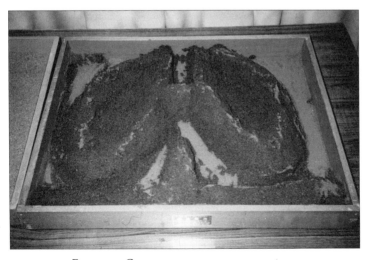

FIGURE 4. COMPOSITION RESEMBLING LUNGS

When asked by her therapist why she made compositions solely out of sand, she replied, "I have the feeling that it would lose its overall coherence if I used the toys." This conveys a sense of obsession and a desire to express her exact thoughts through the composition. It also seems to express her feeling that a composition of only sand is more complete. The therapist interprets her compositions within a religious framework, saying that her work seems almost like a religious practice in which the sacred is distilled from the profane. Initially, it is as though the client immerses herself in the sand and dirt of her own unconscious messiness but thereby also connects with her body and Mother Earth. Although she experiences further illness along the way (lung inflammation), this begins a process of sacred purification, and eventually she did overcome her anorexia and gain a new healthy diet and a more balanced view of food as nourishment and enjoyment rather than something to be avoided.

FIGURE 5. COMPOSITION DEPICTING A HUMAN FORM

Another therapist, Yokoyama Takashi, presents a case of a seven-year-old boy with localized mutism.[6] He points out that the therapeutic process suggests a reconstitution of the boy's inner cosmology: "Within the transformations of just the sand, one begins to see the rhythmic movement of the sand and the accompanying snakelike 'dance' of the client." Along the way there are numerous points at which the client's self-expression using just the sand indicates turning points in his inner reconstruction. This accords with Yamanaka Yasuhiro's comment: "There seemed to be an especially critical turning point in the therapeutic process when the client began to use only sand in his compositions,"[7] that is, without the use of toys. What this suggests is that the sand became the basis or foundation for the client's own recuperation and transformation. In a similar case study, titled "This Isn't Old Dirt That I'm Playing In—This Is New Earth," Peter P. Heidenrich notes that the client found a new basis for his life in the earth or sand of Sandplay.[8] In this way, the sand becomes Mother Earth or Daichi, Great Earth. Takuma Yukiko reports two cases in which the therapist provides the framework within which the energy flowing through the sand and the body of the client takes shape in Sandplay.[9]

Sandplay Therapy and the Self

The ultimate goal of the Shingon teachings is to realize the oneness of self and cosmos through the realization of their mutuality. From the devotional intoning of mantras to the most complex visualizations, the practitioner seeks to embody the wisdom and compassion of the Buddha as the ultimate embodiment of the cosmos. This is similar, though of course not identical, to Jung's idea of the Self understood as the totality and center of consciousness and the unconscious taken together. According to Dora Kalff, the client's first composition in Sandplay therapy also represents the initial image of the Self, and the process of integration develops from there on. Figure 6 shows the self-image at the conclusion of a course of therapy. It is a composition by a woman suggesting an image of self based on her body.

FIGURE 6. SANDPLAY COMPOSITION BASED ON THE BODY

One of the methods employed in the training of Sandplay therapists in Japan is to have them select toys that represent the past self, present self, and future self. One example of this can be seen in Figure 7.

FIGURE 7. TOYS REPRESENTING THE SELF

Psychotherapy and Sand

Sand is found not only in Sandplay, one of the fastest growing forms of psychotherapy in the world, but also in other forms and arenas of therapy such as play therapy and training analysis.

Play Therapy and Sand

Sandboxes, containers of sand, and sand used as "cooking dough" are ways in which one finds sand in play therapy; sand play can be related to a life-seeking impetus, which can mean the life of the psyche as well as biological life. It is interesting to watch children dig up the sand in a sandbox looking for water. Children also make mountains out of sand and then tunnel through them, perhaps looking to "get through" something. Of course, there are also cases where they seem to be just digging down, perhaps looking for something, perhaps not, maybe some physical object, maybe something in the unconscious. There are times when children will find the most unexpected things in the sand, and they might ask to take the object home. As a rule, one cannot remove objects from playrooms or play areas. This can pose a problem since a "found treasure" can have important meaning in the therapeutic process. However, I often regard whatever children find as belonging to them and allow them to take it home.

There are also children who wish to bury objects in the sand, and therapists will even set up "treasure hunts" by burying specific items such as marbles. Once the children find them, they tend to treat them as treasures in the play therapy. Children sometimes spray sand around the room in an apparent act of aggression, perhaps intentionally to upset the therapist, who will have to clean up afterward. Some even throw sand directly on the therapist. Although one seeks to give clients as much free rein as possible, at some point there must be a limit. One of the important challenges for the therapist is to creatively and appropriately set limits.

Family life can be reflected in the sandbox when children topple houses in an avalanche of sand and say, "Look! The house is being crushed!" or when they bury homes in sand. Sand can be fashioned into balls of rice or servings of pudding and might reflect a nourishing attitude or the attempt to acquire nourishment or energy. Children can refine their technique by creating sand dumplings (Jpn. *suna dango*). They make a ball of sand by adding water, then sprinkle more sand on it—only fine sand sticks to the wet surface. They repeat this process until they have a large ball of fine sand. It is often unclear whether they are preparing a make-believe meal or just enjoying the texture of an abstract process. We began to call this "fine-sand making." Wet sand like this can take on the texture of feces, and children with encopresis (inappropriate excretion) have been found to be playing with sand as though handling feces.

While this discussion of sand in play therapy does not bear directly on the relation between Buddhism and psychotherapy, it helps us to see the various qualities of sand observed in therapeutic settings that are related to the qualities identified by such figures as Myōe in his use of sand.

Sand and the Training of Psychotherapists

As part of the training for psychotherapists in our area in Japan, we have recently introduced the creation of colored sand "mandalas." "Mandala" here is used in a rather general sense of a circular diagram that, in this context, is expressive of the self beyond the usual boundaries of consciousness. The creation of these mandalas helps in the diagnosis and development of qualities crucial for skilled therapists: overall sensitivity to and awareness of emotional tones, inner self-awareness, overall self-knowledge, a balance of feminine and masculine, and maternal and paternal, qualities and virtues. The actual methods employed are as follows.

First, seven colors of sand are prepared, plus a bucketful of other sand (such as that used for Sandplay) in case the allotment of colored sand is exhausted. Approximately ten people can make mandalas from a box holding about half a pound of sand. In addition, a white cloth, measuring about thirty inches square, is used by each person to create their compositions on. Each is allowed approximately one hour, after which no further work can take place even if incomplete. Then each presents her or his work, and the others offer comments and questions. At the end of the discussion, a Polaroid photo is given to each mandala maker. Finally, each person empties the sand from the mandala into a container (plastic bag, can, vase) by lifting the cloth from one end. The swirling pattern exhibits the dynamism of the sand and reminds participants of the impermanence or emptiness of their expressions. The sand can then be reused, although not as individual colors. Even when compositions are incomplete or do not take the traditional form of a circular diagram, they present aspects of the trainee's self that might go unexplored through the usual course of training analysis and supervision. Figure 8 is just one example of a mandala created within the training context.

FIGURE 8. SAND MANDALA

Sand as a Literary Motif

By examining the role of sand in fiction, one can see that themes earlier identified in Buddhist literature find counterparts in modern fiction: purity and defilement, sense of dynamic flow, and the questioning and subversion of hierarchies.

Perhaps the most famous novel involving sand is Abe Kōbō's *Woman in the Dunes (Suna no onna)*,[10] eventually made into an internationally acclaimed film. An entomologist seeks out a species of fly that can live in desert conditions. This takes him to a village literally carved out of the dunes. As night falls, and he finds himself unprepared for camping, he seeks shelter. He is introduced to a woman living in a house buried in the sand dunes, one of several such dwellings. Someone comes and steals his three-wheeled motorbike, and he has no means to return home. He mostly sleeps during the day. When awake, he begins to explore the sand and finds out that it is quite moist and sticky. The moisture has penetrated the wooden structure of the house, which has started to rot. Passing empty days in succession, he dreams of escaping but fails in his attempts. He eventually figures out a way to gather water from the sand. He begins a strange affair with the young woman of the house. She becomes pregnant and falls ill. Fearing the loss of the baby, she is sent to the hospital, and he is unable to accompany her. Back in the city where he came from, however, a nondescript public notice of his disappearance is posted. The novel ends there.

A narrative of the protagonist's thoughts and his conversations with the woman drives the plot. However, it is the sand that bears the emotional and symbolic significance of the film with its ever-flowing, unpredictable, dynamic, and destructive rhythms. We human beings tend to believe that we are in control of our environment in our daily existence: We go to sit at a restaurant and order food, and then we walk through a park, believing that we have made the decision to do these things all on our own. Yet, when we look more closely at the currents of life that carry us along, it might be said that we are all like the entomologist trapped in the sand, the forces of life overtaking us from within even as we are outwardly complacent. The sand, symbolic of the raw power of life and nature, unmasks and exposes our empty social pretensions.

Another example of the literary use of sand is Matsumoto Seichō's mystery novel *Sand Vessel (Suna no utsuwa)*.[11] The novel traces a series of deaths that begin with the murder of a patrolman named Miki Ken'ichi at the national railway station at Urata. Detective Imanishi Eitarō takes fragmentary evidence and begins to put the pieces of the puzzle together. The murderer, Waga Hideyoshi, is a member of an avant-garde art group. The key to solving the murder lies in Waga's childhood background. As a child he and his father, who had Hansen's disease (leprosy), used to wander around on the seashore (sand) and in the mountains (rocks). As an adult he hid his family secret and gained recognition in the world of politics by marrying Kazuko, the daughter of a former cabinet member. Eventually the secret of his father's stigmatized leprosy is found out and Waga's life crumbles around him. "Sand" in the title of the novel has to do with the unreliable basis of the protagonist's career and life as a whole. The container of his life is made of sand, unreliable and subject to erosion in much the way one speaks of "feet of clay." In psychotherapy the container or vessel of therapy is essential to healing and growth. The alchemy of psychotherapy has been likened to a chemical reaction taking place in a flask. Although the flask is made of glass, it can hold the powerful energies being released because it has gone through a tempering process. Similarly, the therapeutic setting provides a channel for the client's psychic energies because it has been shaped by the therapist's power of constellation. Perhaps it can be likened to the sand spoken of by Myōe, that has been energized by the mystic power of cosmic buddhas.

A third example comes from the genre of children's fiction. Edith Nesbit's *Five Children and It* features a sand fairy.[12] Due the centrality of this creature, the Japanese translation is entitled *Suna no yōsei* (Sand fairy). The book is a coming-of-age story involving three boys (Robert, Cyril, and "Baby"), two girls (Anthea and Jane), and "It" (the sand fairy, named Psammead).

The children encounter Psammead at the coast where the fairy appears out of the sand (fig. 9). Psammead tells them that it will fulfill one of their wishes per day. That seems like a wonderful thing, but it doesn't always work out. For example, when they request a mountain of money, it turns out to be old, useless currency. They get hungry and end up stealing food. One evening, they land on the roof of a church after acquiring the ability to fly, but the spell disappears after sunset, they lose their wings, and they are unable to descend. Through these experiences the children live and learn. Psammead is a trickster figure who turns out to be a catalyst that mediates the growth and maturation of the children. It is significant that Psammead is a sand spirit rather than a forest spirit as is so often the case in fairy tales. It is almost as though the children are digging into their own unconscious to uncover untapped potential, but this potential is a double-edged sword. They must learn to respect and appropriately channel the powers of the sand or the unconscious. Similarly, the cultivation of Buddhist awakening is often likened to a digging down, through which the waters of *samādhi,* of meditative oneness, are released; just as it was important for the children to encounter Psammead, the power of *samādhi* must not be used carelessly, and one learns to direct it appropriately through trial and error.

FIGURE 9. THE SAND FAIRY PSAMMEAD

As these three stories illustrate, sand can be barren and destructive but also nurturing and filled with untapped potential.

As we have seen, sand occupies a central role in the psychotherapy of Sandplay as well as in the Buddhist practice of the Mantra of Light. For Myōe, sand has the ability to embody the power of emptiness—useless to human beings' social hierarchy of selfish desires, but thereby able to effectuate a purification of those desires. The sand, acting somewhat like a transitional object, can be used to enlighten the living as well as serve as a bridge to the dying and deceased. The virtue or *virtus* of the sand is similarly effective in

Sandplay. Like the mantra master who conveys the power of *samādhi* to the sand, the therapist mediates the power of the sand to create a safe environment for self-realization to the client.

Using another metaphor, the sand can be compared to medicine that must be taken in the right amounts and in the right way. Taking the qualities inherent in the sand, the therapist and the client must work together to find the appropriate amount and time frame for the application of sand. In fact, Myōe himself likens the sand of the Mantra of Light to medicinal or intoxicating mushrooms: "The sand is like the mushrooms. . . . Sentient beings believing [in the sand] is as though they eat the mushrooms. To believe, accept, and obtain virtue is like becoming intoxicated with the mushrooms."[13] The mushrooms or medicine must be accepted in the right way—too much, and it becomes poisonous, too little, and it will not work.

Whether in Buddhism or in therapy, when the sand hits the mark, it activates a process of transformation in the client's or practitioner's inner world, in the psyche or inner cosmos. Just as the Mantra of Light releases its power of *samādhi* only through repetitive practice, Sandplay therapy works only through the repeated creation of sand compositions.

8

The Borderline Between Buddhism and Psychotherapy

MARK UNNO

"Master, how do you teach your disciples?"
"It's like the blind leading the blind."
—ZEN PROVERB

Formal texts . . . and lectures portray therapy as precise
and systematic, with carefully delineated stages, strategic
technical interventions, . . . and a careful, rational program
of insight-offering interpretations. Yet I believe deeply that when
no one is looking, the therapist throws in the "real thing."
—IRVIN D. YALOM

Deep Questioning, Deep Hearing

IN ALBERT CAMUS'S NOVEL *The Plague,* the learned priest Father Pan-
eloux delivers a sermon at the height of the epidemic, railing against his
fellow Algerians and telling them that the plague is an illness sent by God
as a lesson for their sinful ways, and that they should not resent the plague
but repent their sins.[1] The protagonist, Dr. Rieux, is an atheist who has no
time for theological abstractions; instead, he is fully immersed in the day-
to-day work of alleviating the pain of dying patients and of seeking some
kind of relief against the onslaught of the epidemic. It is not that Rieux fails
to find any moral or philosophical significance in the plague. As he himself
states, "What's true of all the evils in the world is true of the plague as well.
It helps men to rise above themselves." That is, trials challenge people to dig
deep and find a more sustaining, authentic basis for their lives than the usual
search for pleasure. Yet, he quickly follows this with his insistence that when
evil (illness) strikes, the first priority must be to alleviate the pain: "All the
same, when you see the misery it brings, you'd need to be a madman, or a
coward, or stone blind, to give in tamely to the plague" and accept it as a

lesson. Rieux goes on to elaborate on what he sees as any larger philosophical or cosmic *meaning* attributed abstractly to the evil plague in contrast to
his concrete *need* to address human suffering:[2]

> "Do you believe in God, doctor?"
> Again the question was put in an ordinary tone. But this time Rieux
> took longer to find his answer.
> "No—but what does that really mean? I'm fumbling in the dark,
> struggling to make something out. But I've long ceased finding that
> original."
> "Isn't that it—the gulf between Paneloux and you?"
> "I doubt it. Paneloux is a man of learning, a scholar. He hasn't come
> in contact with death; that's why he can speak with such assurance of
> the truth—with a capital T. But every country priest who visits his
> parishioners and has heard a man gasping for breath on his deathbed
> thinks as I do. He'd try to relieve human suffering before trying to
> point out its excellence."

Rieux is an atheistic existentialist, the character from *The Plague* most often
associated with Camus himself. Yet Camus rejected both "atheist" and "existentialist" as labels applied to himself, and he would most likely have rejected
them for Rieux. When examined closely, one sees that Rieux is a complex
character, "fumbling in the dark," in process, not believing in God but
admiring of country priests. Indeed, a little-known fact about *The Plague* is
that it was inspired by Camus's experience with devout Christians. During
World War II Camus took refuge in a small town in the south of France
named Le Chambon, founded and inhabited by Protestants, a group of
Huguenots. Having suffered persecution at the hands of the majority, the
citizens of this humble town were sympathetic to the plight of French Jews,
taking them in and hiding them at the risk of their lives at a time when few
others would. It was in Le Chambon, in 1942, that Camus wrote of Algiers,
likely alluding to his local situation: "For those of our townsfolk who risked
their lives in this predicament the issue was whether or not plague was in
their midst and whether or not they must fight against it. The essential thing
was to save the greatest possible number of persons from dying. And to do
this there was only one resource: to fight the plague. There was nothing
admirable about this attitude; it was merely logical."[3]

One might say that Camus's objections were not to Christianity itself or to belief or devotion to a higher or greater reality. He knew that the Huguenots would not have responded the way they did without their simple but committed community of faith. Rather, his objections were to a rationalized faith—in any system—that failed to hear the voices of suffering and that made claims on a cosmic scale that could never be proven or justified. Digging even deeper, one finds that the issues are even more complex. Camus did not deny the significance of larger questions, theological or philosophical. Rather, he did not believe that they could be resolved in the abstract. Whatever was of moral, philosophical, or religious significance had to be responsive to the actual conditions of human life. Conversely, one's deeper philosophical or theological commitments and assumptions would inevitably surface in one's actions in daily life. Thus Camus offers insight into the tension between *deeper significance* and *immediate practical need.* The two are interrelated, and their effective interrelation requires both the right kind of relation (deeper truths *lived* out rather than merely *thought* out) and the appropriate proportionality (larger truths in balance with the details of life).

The Buddha's Ability to Bridge the Gap

In Buddhism, the well-known story of Kisa Gotami illustrates this tension and relation between deeper significance and practical need. Kisa Gotami, a poor woman who faced many hardships during her life, reached the end of her rope. Over time she lost all her family members including her only son, an infant who succumbed to illness. In her overwhelming grief, she simply could not accept that her son was dead. When she heard that the great healer Śākyamuni Buddha was to give a sermon nearby, she went to see him. At the end of the sermon, none of which she really listened to, she approached the Buddha and said to him, "I have heard that you are a great healer and that you can cure any illness. As you can see, my baby boy is very sick. Can you help me?"[4]

If the Buddha were only concerned with the deeper significance of his religious mission, he might have trotted out the Four Noble Truths, the Three Marks of Existence, and so on, and given her a catechism on suffering, impermanence, and no-self. Yet, because he recognized the immediate practical need, he responded by saying, "Of course, I can cure him," knowing full well that the baby was dead.

This calls to mind a Buddhist teacher with whom I studied once. A lay couple he had known for several years came to him one day with the good news that, after a long time, they had finally been able to conceive. They shared their joy, and the teacher looked forward to the birth of the couple's baby together with them. As the baby grew, however, the parents became overwrought with grief; the boy turned out to be autistic. When they went to see the teacher, they clung to the hope that somehow he could fix the situation. Seeing this, the only response the teacher could muster was to offer the services of a good medical doctor that he knew (in those days there were few therapeutic options in Japan for autism). The couple was too distraught to even consider that an autistic child could potentially lead a fulfilling life in his own way. The couple went home clinging to a thread of hope that the doctor could tell them something. In this case, as in the case of Kisa Gotami, it would have been useless to give a sermon on suffering and attachment. The Buddhist teacher did the best that he could to simply meet them where they were and hoped that they might later reflect on their situation and find deeper meaning.

Of course, the two episodes are quite different because the story of Kisa Gotami does not end with the Buddha's promise of a cure. He continued by saying that he could cure the boy with proper medicine. He had all the necessary ingredients to make the medicine on the spot except for mustard seed. Since the boy was very ill, he told the mother, the medicine had to be especially good, and for that he would need very pure mustard seed, so pure that it had to come from a family that had known no death. Kisa Gotami ran to her village to collect the mustard seed, but every home she visited had known the death of a relative at some point, be it a grandmother, father, sister, uncle, or someone else. By the time Kisa Gotami reached the last house in the village, she understood the real meaning of the mustard seed—spiritual medicine to teach her the deeper meaning of suffering and compassion. She also came to see her deceased son as her teacher, more alive to her spiritually than when he had been alive biologically. Kisa Gotami, now alone but spiritually awakened, entered the Sangha as a nun and was recognized by the Buddha as an *arhat*, a fully enlightened person. She came to be known as the Great Compassionate One.

In contrast to a doctrinaire Buddhist sermonizer who might have only made Kisa Gotami fall into deeper despair at her inability to grasp abstract religious ideas, the Buddha was able to lead her to a profound realization by addressing her immediate practical need. In contrast to the contemporary Buddhist teacher who tried to meet the parents of the autistic child at their point of need but failed to address the deeper level of religious understanding, the Buddha saw in Kisa Gotami's immediate plight the portal to boundless compassion. The remarkable insight of the Buddha is displayed in his ability to intuitively and creatively bridge this gap between deeper religious significance and immediate practical need at their very point of intersection in the here and now.

Rule-Breaking Psychotherapists

In psychoanalysis and psychotherapy generally, there has also been a creative tension between, on the one hand, the larger worldview and corresponding psychotherapeutic method and, on the other, the immediate clinical demands of the here and now. C. G. Jung often stated that each case was so unique as to demand an entirely new therapy; yet this all took place within a framework of depth psychology, archetypes, and personality types that remained remarkably consistent throughout much of his career. Conversely, Freud wrote at length on the qualifications and strict boundaries governing the therapist-client relationship, but it is well known that he broke some of his strictest rules, such as not analyzing a relative (he analyzed his own daughter, Anna, who became one of his leading disciples) and not seeing clients outside of the professional analytic setting (he had dinner and socialized with clients during their periods of analysis with him). Do Jung, Freud, and others' actions merely contradict or negate their larger analytic or therapeutic frameworks and principles, or is there a creative element in their rule breaking and contradictions that shows a responsiveness to the immediate needs of the client? This raises questions too involved to fully explore here, but some analysts have focused on this very issue and made it a point to show the dangers of becoming too ensconced in an objective analytic method. James Hillman, for example, has made a career of debunking therapeutic method, not in order to debunk therapy per se as others have done, but to dislodge what he perceives to be the ossified practices of the therapeutic establishment and to energize a therapy that is responsive to the client beyond dogmatic frameworks.

Milton Erickson, known as a pioneer in the fields of family therapy, hypnotherapy, and brief therapy, was an unconventional therapist who adapted his practice in all manner of ways: "One of Erickson's characteristics is his willingness to be flexible in every aspect of his therapy. Not only is he willing to see patients in the office, in the home, or in their place of business, but he is also willing to have short sessions or interviews lasting several hours. He might use hypnosis, or he might not. . . . [H]e is also willing to have a session in the form of a social call."[5] No matter what the setting, Erickson often seemed to do, or direct the patient to do, the most unexpected things.

The following is the case of a young woman, severely depressed and with no social life, who threatened suicide unless Erickson was able to help her within three months. She was attracted to a young man at work, and he seemed to show some interest in her, but she was unable to act on her impulses in any way. Her parents were dead, she was alone, and she felt completely isolated:

> The young woman was pretty, but she managed to make herself unattractive [with her unkempt hair and unflattering outfits]. . . . Her main physical defect, according to her, was a gap between her front teeth. [Yet] the gap was only about one-eighth of an inch. . . . Generally, this was a girl going downhill, heading for suicide, . . . and resisting any acts that would help her achieve her [stated] goal of getting married and having children.
>
> Erickson approached this problem with two major interventions. He proposed to the girl that she have one last fling [spending her savings on herself, at the clothing store and the beauty salon]. . . . The woman was willing to accept the idea, since it was *not* a way of improving herself but part of going downhill and merely having a last fling.
>
> Then Erickson gave her a [second] task. She was to go home and in the privacy of her bathroom practice squirting water through the gap between her front teeth until she could achieve a distance of six feet with accuracy. She thought this was silly, but it was partly the absurdity of it that made her go home and practice. . . .
>
> When the girl was dressed properly, looking attractive, and skillful at squirting water through the gap in her teeth, Erickson made a suggestion to her . . . [to play] a practical joke. When that young man appeared at the water fountain at the same time she did, she was to take a mouthful of water and squirt it at him. Then she was to turn and run, but not merely run; she was to start to run toward the young man and then turn and "run like hell down the corridor."

The girl rejected this idea as impossible. Then she thought of it as a somewhat amusing but crude fantasy. . . . She was in a mood for a last fling anyhow.

On Monday, . . . [meeting the young man at the water fountain,] she filled her mouth with water and squirted it on him. The young man said something like "You damn bitch." This made her laugh as she ran, and the young man took after her and caught her. To her consternation, he grabbed her and kissed her.

The next day the young lady approached the water fountain with some trepidation, and the young man sprang out from behind a telephone booth and sprayed her with a water pistol. The next day they went out to dinner together. . . . Within a few months she sent Erickson a newspaper clipping reporting her marriage to the young man, and a year later a picture of her new baby.[6]

Although the account is somewhat humorous, the young woman's inner condition was quite serious, serious enough that no amount of direct counseling would have worked. While there are major differences between the case of Kisa Gotami and this young woman, in both cases the teacher/therapist meets the supplicant/client at her point of greatest need in the here and now and turns what had seemed to be a great negative into the very thing that becomes the positive force for religious/therapeutic transformation.

The following, another case from Erickson's files, shows how a double load of suffering is transformed into multiple occasions for happiness. It is important to keep in mind that the case comes from the 1950s, a time when public attitudes about sexual orientation were very different from those of our time.

A psychiatric resident in training with me was treating a hospital employee, and he came to me in distress; he said his patient was a homosexual, but he wanted to get married. He asked how to find a girl who would marry him for appearance's sake . . .

The resident didn't know it, but I was seeing a girl who worked in the hospital and was a lesbian. She had a similar desire to have a husband for appearance's sake.

I said to the resident, "Suppose you tell your patient to walk along the sidewalk behind the hospital at four o'clock in the afternoon. Tell him that somewhere along the sidewalk he'll meet what he needs."

Then I told the young woman that on the same day at four o'clock she was to walk behind the hospital in the opposite direction. I told her she would know what to do.

They were to look for something on that walk, but they didn't know what. . . The woman was sharper than the man. She came to me and said, "You arranged that, didn't you?" I said, "Yes." She told me, "I knew when I saw him that he was a homosexual, and I frankly told him so. He was so elated. Should I tell him that you know?" I said, "It might be well, in case the two of you want further advice."

They married and lived respectably. . . . After about a year they got a job offer at a hospital in another state. . . . I knew a physician there, and I wrote to him and said, "Mr. so-and-so and his wife are coming. . . . They will need protection and guidance and a cover."

They went to him when they moved, and he told them he'd had a letter from me telling him they were coming, but without saying why. [He said to them,] "I think he expected you to tell me why." They sighed with relief—they had the chance to tell him [themselves].

They got a four-bedroom home. They often entertained friends. He slept in his room and she in hers, and the other rooms were sometimes filled with friends.

This illustrates again how Erickson was able to meet the clients at their greatest point of need in a transformative manner. Highly significant is the fact that Erickson allows the couple to tell his colleague on their own about their sexual orientations and situations. They are empowered by giving voice to their own realities. The case also shows how progressive his thinking was for a therapist of his time. (It is worth noting that Erickson sometimes interpreted apparent instances of homosexuality as suppressed or distorted heterosexuality and treated them accordingly.)

Shin Buddhism

The Shin tradition of Pure Land Buddhism is based on the path of the *nembutsu*, or invoking the Name of Amida Buddha, as found in the six-syllable phrase "Namu Amida Butsu." In terms of the twofold truth of Mahāyāna Buddhism, *Namu*, meaning "the one who entrusts," corresponds to form, or more precisely to the foolish being (Skt. *pṛthagjana*) attached to form. *Amida Buddha*, the Buddha of Infinite Light, corresponds to emptiness, or the illuminating power of emptiness manifest in the human realm of samsara. The accompanying table shows the correspondences.

form	emptiness
distinctions	beyond distinctions
blind passion	boundless compassion
attachment to fixed objects of desire	release into emptiness
foolish being	Amida Buddha
Namu	*Amida Butsu*
samsara	nirvana
karmically defiled world	Pure Land beyond form

That is the doctrinal explanation. Practically speaking, as in the foregoing cases of the Buddha and Erickson, there is in Shin Buddhism a focus on meeting the needs of the Pure Land follower in the concrete circumstances of the here and now.

Gutoku Shinran (1173–1262), regarded as the founder of the tradition, felt it was particularly important for the teacher to pay compassionate attention to the needs of his followers or students, rather than to take care of those needs. For this reason, he refused to take the mantel of institutional leader, leaving behind his own community to live out his last thirty years writing and reflecting while residing in his brother's house until he died at the age of ninety. When his followers journeyed hundreds of miles on foot to ask him to clarify their doubts, he told them straight away, "As for myself, Shinran, I do not have a single disciple. If I could make others say the Name of Amida Buddha through my own devices, they would be my disciples. But how arrogant to claim as disciples those who live the *nembutsu* through the sole working of Amida's compassion [the liberating power of formless compassion, of emptiness]."[7] Thus he called fellow Shin Buddhists "my honored fellow practitioners, my honored friends" *(ondōbō ondōgyō)*.

As an extension of this disavowal, he proclaimed himself "neither monk nor layman" *(hisō hizoku)*, a renegade priest who openly married, refused to take up residence in a temple, renounced personal ambition in both the lay and ecclesiastical realms, and lived outside the usual boundaries of society. In the end, he declared, "When I consider the compassionate vow of Amida (the unfolding of formless compassion) . . . I realize that it was for myself, Shinran, alone."[8] That is to say, regardless of whether others considered him to be a teacher or not, despite whatever effect he may have had on others, at the deepest level, he saw himself as the recipient of the gift of the dharma rather than its dispenser. His true Buddhist identity came effectively into relief only in the solitary light of his own self-awareness. The truth of the self can only truly be seen when one is alone with the universe.

One of the effects of this spiritual egalitarianism has been the lay-centered approach of the Shin path in which there is a great deal of emphasis placed on listening to *(chōmon)* and hearing the dharma *(monpō)*. The priest and congregants listen together to the call of formless compassion, the voiceless voice of Amida; and the priest listens to the needs of fellow practitioners as one who is also in need. While there are priests, then, the emphasis is on modeling deep listening, deep hearing, so that all followers of the Shin path listen for and to the voice of boundless reality calling out to meet their needs. As the Shin teacher Kai Wariko states in her poem:

> *Mihotoke no na wo yobu waga koe wa*
> *Mihotoke no ware wo yobimasu mikoe narikeri*

> The voice with which I call Amida Buddha
> Is the voice with which Amida Buddha calls to me.

Thus, whether one is outwardly a teacher or a follower, Shinran makes explicit that all followers of the Shin path are equally followers, equally foolish in their attachments, and therefore also equally the recipients of boundless compassion that comes to meet them at the point of greatest need.

A Contemporary Illustration

Early in my career, I had an opportunity to develop a course on women and religion, in part because a position for which I had applied included a job description for someone who could teach courses on women and Buddhism. Thinking in my own feeble way to follow Shinran's admonition to see one's own truth illuminated from beyond the narrow confines of my own foolishness, I organized an experiment: I planned to have the mostly female student body of the class show me how to teach a course on women and religion. I planned to observe and learn from the way that they approached the subject matter. It turned out to be a wonderful experience, and I continued to teach a similar course as I moved on.

During my next appointment as an assistant professor at another institution, I taught this course under the same title as before, "Women's Spiritual Journeys East and West." After the first of two exams, one of the students came to my office and asked if she could speak with me. I invited her to come in and sit down, and asked how I might help her. She told me that she was concerned about the poor grade she had received on the first exam, an "F." She explained that she had spent the previous term in a non-traditional learning environment and that she had not yet adjusted back into the academic rhythm on campus. I sensed that she wanted to somehow improve upon her situation by retaking the exam or doing an extra assignment. As the teacher, however, I needed to treat everyone fairly, so I told her that she didn't need to worry so much as the exam represented only ten percent of the grade and she could still excel in the class. She responded by saying that she could see the exam as a learning experience; she was used to doing well, and this gave her an opportunity to better understand others who had difficulty taking standardized tests. I did not think that she was entirely sincere, but I felt that she put a good face on what for her was a bad situation. We ended the meeting cordially, and sure enough, she improved her performance, receiving a course grade of "B+."

At this college there is a custom after commencement of greeting students and their relatives on the campus commons. As I strolled and greeted students, I noticed this student out of the corner of my eye, and I went over to congratulate her. As soon as I approached her, she said, "Mark, I want to introduce you to my mother." Her mother responded, "So you're Mark Unno. She often talks about your class. She says that the 'B+' from your course was the most important grade she received in her four years at Carleton." I mumbled something or other, trying to take it all in. It was especially surprising, given that, out of a graduating class of several hundred, my student was one of seven or eight to receive academic honors as *summa cum laude*. For her to have received such high honors, she would have had to have virtually straight "A"s due to my having given her a "B+". As I pondered this, she said to me, "Mark, I want you to meet someone else. This is my brother." I shook his hand, and as we began to converse, I realized that he had a learning disability. Then, it finally dawned on me, that what she had said back at my office was not a face-saving remark at all but had been offered in all sincerity. For her, always the perfectionist, receiving an "F" on the exam was a failure; yet this "failure" enabled her to see the world through her brother's eyes for the first time.

Through her "F," life had met her at her point of greatest need, and she had graciously received it as an invitation to a greater world of understanding. I, on the other hand, had lost my way somewhere along the path. Earlier, I had begun with the good intention of having my students unmask my male chauvinist assumptions and teach me the way to enter the world of women and religion. Yet by the time I was teaching the course at another school, I had become the "expert," reading my female students' minds at a "deeper level." In the terms of Shin Buddhism, my student arrived in my class like the extension of Amida's compassionate hand, illuminating my foolishness at the point of greatest need. I thought I was listening to her in my office, but then learned that it was boundless life itself that was listening to my needs so that I might hear the call of limitless compassion.

Listening to Psychotherapy at Kyoto University

In the fall of 2003 I had the great fortune to spend a semester as a visiting assistant professor of psychology and religion in the psychotherapy program at Kyoto University. As part of the experience, I was invited to attend the annual meeting of the Association of Japanese Clinical Psychology that was being hosted by Kyoto University that year. The conference took place in early September before the beginning of the term. I had never been to this event before, and I was astonished to find over eight thousand people in attendance at the conference, having previously gone only to the annual meeting of the Japanese Association for the Study of Religion, attended by a mere few hundred scholars and graduate students. I was asked to be a respondent for a panel of three doctoral student case studies.

As I listened intently to the presentations, several things stood out in my mind. First, I noticed that all of the case studies involved profound issues of pathology and/or disability. Second, all of the cases revealed levels of significance that might be characterized as spiritual or religious due to their all-encompassing, life-and-death seriousness. Third, all three doctoral students, who already had significant clinical experience, reported in detail on the process undergone or undertaken by their clients, but they

said very little about their own methods or theories. What follows is a summary of just one of these cases presented by Suruchi Mayumi, a doctoral
student and counselor:

> This is the case of a young woman of junior high school age. She is a
> talented musician and aspires to a life of music. However, there are sev-
> eral relatives who have been stricken with genetic hearing loss. She
> decides to undergo genetic screening to see if she might also be stricken
> with hearing loss. The test proves positive, indicating one-hundred
> percent certainty of [future] hearing loss. Upon learning of the results
> the girl tells her therapist: "I died when I received the test results." A
> long period of depression ensues, and the therapist reports that she
> continues to listen closely to her client's communications. After sev-
> eral weeks, the girl states that she is going to visit the graves of her rel-
> atives, of her great aunts, grandmother, and others who had the same
> hearing loss. After returning from her various visits, she reports to the
> therapist, "As I asked my [deceased] relatives what they had experi-
> enced and reflected on how they must have suffered, I began to con-
> nect with them in a way I never had before. I became aware of the deep
> life connection *(inochi no kizuna)* I had with them, and this gave new
> meaning to my life. Now I am ready to go on although I don't know
> what the future will bring."

Ironically, the only thing that Suruchi reported doing as a therapist was
to listen to her client, a client who was losing her own hearing. Listening in
this context, of course, is not limited to the ordinary hearing of the physical ears. Rather, it is a wholehearted listening that comes from beyond the
level of individual existence, and it helped this remarkable young woman
find her own deeper hearing, unlimited by her physiology; through being
deeply heard by her therapist, she was able to hear the call of life itself coming through the voices of her deceased relatives. In the midst of deep listening and deep hearing, the unspoken religious significance of life was heard
calling out to her from beyond the ordinary distinctions of life and death,
meeting her at her point of greatest need.

Although the graduate students at Kyoto University undertake a thorough
study of the various theoretical approaches to psychotherapy—Freud, Jung,
Adler, Rogers, Lacan, Winnicott, and so forth—I noticed in my seminar that

they tended not to respond to questions regarding theory. In one response paper for the seminar, a student wrote, "Here in Kyoto, we are above all taught to listen, to listen in class, and to listen to our clients. That is one reason why I sometimes find it difficult to interact in a rapid-fire discussion. It is not that I am uninterested or that I have not studied the theories. But I always think that I need to listen further in order to glean the deeper meaning. Perhaps, though, we also need to learn to interact more discursively."

It struck me that this emphasis on deep listening with one's whole being might be a point of resonance between Shin Buddhism and psychotherapy as it was practiced at Kyoto University.

In reality, the attempt to hear deeply does not always lead to such a seamless interface between deeper religious questions and the immediate needs of the present. Often the gap between human neediness and a deeper or wider awareness seems insurmountable. Yet, that very thought comes from one who perhaps does not listen deeply enough to the intimate coming together of teacher and follower, therapist and client, in which it is often difficult to know which is which. For ultimately, at least from a Buddhist perspective, deeper questions and surface realities, emptiness and form, boundless compassion and blind passion, are nothing more than two sides of the same coin.

A Widening Gap?

Turning this conclusion upside down, one might equally say: Although ultimately form and emptiness, or blind passions and boundless compassion, are two sides of the same coin, from the human perspective of form—from the side of form, that of the individual seeker—it is difficult to realize the kind of deep hearing and reflection that enables one to appreciate the significance of the larger whole. In order to explore this, I am about to make a problematic generalization, hoping that you will see the point as we continue: Generally speaking, Buddhist institutions tend to establish and maintain orthopraxy through protecting the traditional boundaries of ritual practices, while psychotherapists, in particular as found in American culture, tend to sustain their practice by quickly adapting to the changing social and cultural landscape. Or, stated another way, Buddhists, especially in Asia, tend to be more traditional and leery of adapting too quickly to contemporary trends, while psychotherapists almost necessarily place a premium on staying close to changes in pathology and new methods and perspectives to meet them.

In terms of the previous discussion on deeper questions and immediate practical needs, this means that Buddhists tend to focus on deeply hearing a dharma unfolding in the present but anchored in the past, and therapists tend to focus on meeting the needs of the client immediately in the present and anticipating the future. At some level, however, one must address past, present, and future all at once in the melding together in the present moment.

In our era of rapid change, a religion that holds too closely to the past comes to be seen as antiquated and anachronistic. Many Japanese, especially in the younger generations (forty and under), regard Buddhism as at best a quaint repository of the past and at worst a stale house of corruption. A psychotherapeutic culture that assimilates into the culture of the DSM and HMOs becomes itself reduced to little more than a commodity-dispensing psychobabble that is little able to resist the fragmenting tide of a postmodern economy.[9]

It is within this midst that Buddhism and psychotherapy have somehow found each other's company, at times comforting and at others discomfiting. And although the mutual interest and discussion inaugurated by such figures as D. T. Suzuki, C. G. Jung, and Erich Fromm nearly three-quarters of a century ago have developed into a much more sophisticated and steady stream of practice and discourse, it flows forth through uneasy byways and articulations, not just because of qualities inherent to these two fields but just as much because of the difficulties inherent in the global culture of the twenty-first century.

Within the confluence of these two fields, Japan and the United States together are uniquely situated to further the discussion and interaction between them. They are the two largest psychotherapeutic cultures in the world, a fact that is both promising and troubling. It is promising because Japan and the United States provide some of the best psychotherapy in a world that increasingly needs psychotherapy. It is troubling because the scale of psychotherapy reflects both the intensive and extensive nature of psychopathology in the two cultures. Twenty years ago it was said new pathologies that became widespread in the United States appeared in Japan ten years later. These included school absenteeism, borderline personality disorder, and eating disorders. More recently, such pathologies as dissociative identity disorder (formerly "multiple personality disorder") have begun to appear just five years after they become prominent in the United States. While all of these disorders are found in other cultures, in particular in the so-called advanced industrial nations, most of them appear with greatest frequency in the United States and Japan.

In the postwar period Japan has had a complex relationship with other Asian nations. On the one hand, unresolved issues surrounding war crimes and atrocities remain to be addressed. On the other, Japan, as the first country to "succeed" as a modern industrialized society, is a model for many other Asian countries. This has gone beyond industry and commerce. Whether it is Korea or China, in such areas as pop music, television dramas, and animation, Asian cultures have tended to emulate and adapt Japanese expressions as, in a way, predigested for Asian tastes, rather than look to their origins in Europe and the United States. Now as modern and postmodern psychopathologies are appearing with increasing frequency in these cultures, again it is to Japan and not the West that they turn for models. Thus Korean and Chinese representatives of these countries' associations for clinical psychology attend the annual meetings in Japan, and the Japanese have begun to attend the meetings in these countries. Although Western representation in the other cultures is not entirely absent, if past and present trends continue, Japan will serve as an important bridge for pan-Asian psychotherapeutic understanding.

Japan also has the largest Buddhist institutions in Asia as well as the academic resources in Buddhist studies to engage in cultural interchange. Of non-Asian cultures, the United States has the largest, most rapidly growing Buddhist culture and academic Buddhist studies programs, though still quite young by Asian standards. Yet, both Buddhism and psychotherapy have their own distinct characteristics and trends in Japan and the United States, and there is great potential for creative cross-fertilization involving all permutations of Asian Buddhism, Asian psychotherapy, Western Buddhism, and Western psychotherapy. In order to be truly effective, the resources of these cultures must be mobilized in the service of a truly diverse global understanding, willing to learn from all kinds of different perspectives and to transcend narrow sectarian and ethnic self-interest.

The Borderline of the Global Economy

Among the psychopathologies that have come to the forefront in both the United States and Japan is borderline personality disorder. Although a complex phenomenon that continues to be debated, there are some areas of broad agreement. It receives its nomenclature from the fact that those who are afflicted are seen to be on the borderline between neuroses and psychoses. Neurotic clients are defined as those in need of clinical care but are sufficiently integrated psychically to function in their day-to-day lives; neuroses include moderate depression, phobias, and bipolar disorder. Psychotic patients are not able to function normally from day to day and require periods of hospitalization or other intensive care; the most well-known psychosis is schizophrenia. The borderline patient is subject to depression, is often emotionally starved, and is prone to episodic breaks with socially accepted definitions of reality. At the same time, the borderline personality is often intellectually highly capable, is able to read others' emotions, and is highly manipulative. The combination of emotional starvation, lack of socially acceptable realism, high intellectual ability, and manipulative personality makes the borderline personality especially difficult to treat. Unlike both many neurotics and psychotics, an overtly sympathetic approach clinically not only fails to ameliorate the condition but often aggravates the disorder greatly. Not only that, the inexperienced therapist can become entangled in the client's self-created soap opera to such an extent that the former's personal life is disrupted. Having to work with a borderline personality can be a difficult rite of passage for therapists in training.

The emergence of borderline personality disorder in the current state of the global economy and culture is no accident. Affective manipulation through highly sophisticated media of communication that commodifies the culture wholesale, promises everything but delivers nothing, and leaves the individual (now redefined in his or her totality as a consumer) emotionally vacant: these are prominent features of a global economy undergoing intensive commodification. While it might not be right to label society as such with a psychopathology, and the majority of the population does not exhibit the extreme characteristics of the borderline personality, there is a striking correspondence between global cultural trends (dominated by the U.S. economy) and the prominence of the borderline personality.

Although this is purely anecdotal, it was telling to see a segment on an evening news journal about younger, more affluent members of Indian society who were entering the workforce in call centers being outsourced from the United States. These young Indians often left behind the traditional village life of the extended family to live in an urban apartment; they bought American goods such as jeans and MP3 music players and aspired to live the life of the postmodern consumer. In a living-room discussion with their parents, the parents lamented that whereas their own role models are the Hindu *guruji* or holy man, their children aspire to be like Bill Gates. When queried as to the accuracy of such a description, the young woman in the interview replied, "Yes, we have our own ideas, we are our own generation. Our guru is Bill Gates." Such is the transformation within a single generation.

In Japan, consumerization and commodification have already had far-reaching effects. In my psychology and religion seminar of fourteen students at Kyoto University, I asked how many have parents who have Buddhist altars or Shinto shrines in their homes. Eleven answered in the affirmative. Then, I asked how many of the students currently have or plan to have in their own home a family altar or shrine. Only four students answered affirmatively to this latter question. Although the family altar is no great indicator of deep religiousness, it still forms a crucial link to a lived sense of religion, and for centuries it was the one element that passed unchanged down through the generations. Now, it is quite likely that it will largely disappear from the cultural and religious life of the Japanese within one or two generations. Taking the place of the family altar and the village priest, already long faded in the background, are electronic media such as television, video games, and the culture of pop idols. Just as in the United States, movie stars, pro athletes, and billboard artists have become the dominant cultural icons.

Because of the very nature of their field, psychotherapists may be better equipped to track and understand emergent social trends and psychopathologies, while traditional Buddhist monks, nuns, and priests—especially those who pursue some kind of intensive practice—may be better connected to their spiritual ground. There may also be a wide gray area in between, where no one has a firm footing because the gap between an understanding of deeper questions and immediate practical (clinical) needs stretches out like an abyss.

For too many, it is the human heart, torn asunder, that occupies this abyss. Caught between the body as the necessary ground of the religious life and a mind of entitlement that churns headlong into the dream of consumer stardom, the heart, unable to hold the body and mind together, often falls into depression or erupts in anger at being torn asunder. This has given rise to some notable phenomena in modern Buddhist life, especially in the West. Although I know of no formal studies that have been carried out, I have spoken with Buddhist teachers who report that students who engage in intensive retreats not infrequently have difficulty readjusting to post-retreat social life and can become quite angry. Another observation that I have heard voiced is that students may achieve considerable levels of calm but have difficulty connecting with a deeply sustaining sense of compassion.

Just as the borderline personality is often intractable and resists a movement toward realism and deep emotional connection, the culture at large often has an isolating effect on individuals who seek deeper spiritual connection. For this reason religious communities play an important role in mediating the religious life of the individual and that of society, but Buddhist communities in both Japan and the United States have to their detriment been caught in the cultural interstices between religious callings and a commodified society.

Who Is Raising These Questions?

When someone is overly optimistic, there is a suspicion of one-sided extremes, of what Buddhists call eternalism, or the belief that everything good will last forever. When someone is overly pessimistic, there is a suspicion of the extreme of nihilism. The midpoint, the middle way, is neither particularly optimistic nor pessimistic but realistic in a quiet, deeply felt manner, and in the case of the Mahāyāna, riding the wave of the bodhisattva vow to liberate all beings.

Questions about the state of the human heart, and the relation between Buddhism and psychotherapy, are generally questions raised by human beings on the stage of history. The middle way, however, finds its center not on the temporal stage of human history but in the cosmic time of vast emptiness. Early Indian Buddhists expressed this by relativizing human beings within the larger framework of their cosmology. Human beings belong to the realm of desire, the least evolved of the three realms of desire, form, and formlessness. More evolved beings in other world systems inhabit higher realms; they have merely to inhale the scent of enlightenment to achieve realization and then enjoy the fruits of buddhahood for long periods. This was not a pessimism about human beings but a realism that expresses a sentiment that arose from beyond human boundaries. Paradoxically, it is within the capacity of human beings to rise above being merely human and to be imbued with an awareness of the profound oneness of all beings and things while fully sharing and suffering the foibles, tragedy, and foolishness that are so distinctly human.

So who is raising all of these questions, questions about human history and Buddhist cosmos? It is essential for me to connect them to the human heart in the here and now, so that I remember that they are about the depths of my own existence and not mere speculations about something "out there." This brief exploration of the borderlines of Buddhism and psychotherapy will have more than fulfilled its purpose if it stimulates reflection within the reader's own human heart and mind.

9

Naikan Therapy and Shin Buddhism[1]

TAITETSU UNNO

I

W HEN I FIRST WENT TO JAPAN to study Buddhism soon after graduating from the University of California, Berkeley, I visited D. T.
Suzuki at his home in the compound of Engakuji, the well-known Rinzai
Zen monastery in Kamakura. I asked him a question about the difference
between Rinzai Zen and Jōdo Shinshū or Shin Buddhism, knowing that he
grew up in Kanazawa, a stronghold of Shin, and having read about his own
mother's involvement with Shin practice.

At that time Suzuki was already in his early eighties and had devoted
much of his later years to writing about Shin Buddhism. I was curious concerning his view of Zen, described by Pure Land followers as the way of self-
power, and the Shin path that claimed to be the way of other-power. He
answered by giving an example of a toddler just learning how to walk.

Zen practice, he said, is like a baby struggling to walk toward his waiting
father. When the baby reaches the father and jumps into his lap, everyone
applauds.[2] This may be repeated several times. Suzuki then compared this
to Shin practice, which he said is not a "practice" in the traditional sense
but rather a "process" of awakening. He likened this to a baby walking
toward the father, but every time he gets close, the father takes a few steps
back. This process is repeated several times, the baby moving forward but
never reaching the father. But soon the baby becomes strong enough to walk
on its own, neither prompted nor supported from the outside.

Suzuki also used to say that although the Pure Land path is said to be
easy, there is nothing more difficult; hence, the scriptures say, "The path is
easy, but there is no one to walk it." He frequently quoted the poem by
Saichi, the Shin devotee and woodworker, who said, "There is no self-power;

there is no other-power; all is Other Power," the boundless life itself that sustains all existence.

I did not fully understand Suzuki's explanation at that time, but later I realized that this is akin to what Shinran (1173–1263), the founder of Shin Buddhism, once said to his followers regarding Buddhist "practice" and his view of what constitutes the "good": "The saying of the *nembutsu* (Name of Buddha) is neither a religious practice nor a good act. Since it is a practice without any calculation, it is 'non-practice.' Since it is also not a good created by my calculation, it is 'non-good.' Since it is nothing but Other Power, completely free of self-power, it is neither a religious practice nor a good act on the part of the practitioner."[3]

Does this means that a Shin follower never engages in religious "practice," such as meditation, nor in any so-called "good" acts? How can the Shin path be called Buddhist when it rejects religious practice and negates the good? The answer is the working of the Primal Vow of Amida Buddha that nullifies all self-centered human endeavors, religious or ethical, for transcendence. In fact, any transcendence of samsaric life can be effective only insofar as its source comes from beyond the conventional self and embodies the working of the Buddha. The efforts of finite human beings, however expended, are inherently limited.

This truth is articulated in the mythic story of Dharmākara Bodhisattva attaining supreme enlightenment as Amida Buddha in the *Larger Sukhā-vatīvyūha Sutra*. The Great Compassion of the Buddha embraces and transforms all life, including even that of *icchantika* (beings lacking buddha-nature) to realize Buddhahood. This is called Great Practice, the adjective "great" denoting that it is not the activity of humans but of the Buddha. Thus, the Primal Vow contains the power that enables each person to realize the truth of the buddha-dharma for ultimate liberation *(mokṣa)* and peace (nirvana), while living in the midst of a turbulent samsaric life. The Primal Vow fully realizes the reason for its being when it is fully realized in each person.

In order to properly appreciate the buddha-dharma, it is essential to clearly distinguish the practical, utility-value of religion and its truth-value.[4] The utility-value of religion is sought by many people for immediate material and psychological benefits, such as faith that promises happiness, peace of mind, good health, prosperity, and longevity. In contrast, the truth-value of religion focuses on the elemental question, Why do we exist at all?

The distinction between the truth-value and utility-value of religion is not obvious on the superficial level, because for most people both pursuits are seen as one and the same. But does that mean that when we are unhappy, lack peace of mind, have poor health or limited physical capacity, and so on life is not worth living? In fact, the opposite may be true: when we know that so-called worldly benefits can no longer meet our deepest needs, we experience a real hunger for meaning.

This contrast between the truth-value and utility-value of religion was played out in the history of Shin Buddhism in the unfolding of orthodox and heterodox movements in its history from the time of Shinran himself in the thirteenth century to the present. Orthodox movements are those based on truth-value, whereas heterodox ones are grounded in utility-value. One such heterodox movement is the Shin cultic practice followed by D. T. Suzuki's mother,[5] and another is the self-examination *(mi-shirabe)* procedure that is the original source of Naikan therapy.[6]

II

Among modern Japanese therapies, Naikan, meaning "introspection," is closely related to the traditional teaching of Shin Buddhism, because it began with the practice of self-examination undertaken by some Shin Buddhists in the past.[7] Naikan and Shin Buddhism, however, are fundamentally different in orientation, for the latter is a religious path directed to realizing the truth of buddha-dharma, whereas the former originally developed as a program to rehabilitate incarcerated inmates.

Naikan therapy was founded in 1941 by a Buddhist layman, Yoshimoto Ishin (1916–88), who grew up in a devout Shin family and who underwent many sessions of *mi-shirabe,* based on the twofold realization central to Shin teaching: "First, the limitless compassion that is bestowed upon us by life; second, the inherent self-centeredness that permeates our actions and thoughts."[8] This is a paraphrase of the two basic pillars of Pure Land Buddhism, first formulated by Shandao (613–81) in seventh-century China.

Yoshimoto originally sought to help juvenile delinquents in a prison in Nara, Japan, to develop socially acceptable behavior. Based on his own reflections as a Shin Buddhist, he devised a method of self-analysis that he formulated into three interrelated questions: What has one received from others, beginning with one's own mother and father? What has one done for others? and, What troubles and worries has one created for others? The focus is not on motives or feelings but on concrete responses or actions. Even a cursory self-reflection will show that the list of names for the first question becomes extremely long in contrast to the limited number of names on the second list. Even those who have had great difficulty in life, when led to reflect on how many people were involved, for example, in their birth and in the delivery of meals to their dinner table, eventually come to see that the forces sustaining their lives completely overwhelm what they, as a single individual, might have done for others.

Although Naikan therapy was first used in working with juvenile delinquents, it was soon expanded to help incarcerated inmates, people with marital difficulties, alcohol dependency, school truancy, and other social problems requiring the intervention of mental health professionals, social workers, guidance counselors, priests and ministers, personnel managers, and others. Its aim is self-transformation within the human nexus, beginning with family members and expanding it to include increasingly larger social units. In this process one realizes the extent to which one has been dependent on others to fulfill one's needs and as a consequence to gradually decrease self-centeredness. This self-examination is undertaken continuously in isolation, usually for a period of one week, beginning at 7 a.m. and continuing all day until bedtime. With intense self-reflection a meltdown occurs, while the circle of interaction with others is gradually widened. This process of self-questioning is exhausting, both emotionally and physically, guided and prompted by a Naikan counselor who visits the client once every hour or two to make sure that progress is being made in self-analysis.

Unlike other forms of psychotherapy, Naikan is concerned with concrete interpersonal behavior. The emphasis is on the here and now, and how one relates to others. As one develops in Naikan introspection, a deep sense of gratitude for the sacrifices and efforts of others should naturally grow. Rather than being obsessed with oneself exclusively, social awareness is cultivated in an ever-widening circle. The value of this therapy has many possibilities, including appreciation of others and their contributions to one's well-being, responding to the needs of others instead of just finding faults, undertaking self-reflection and admitting to one's limitations, and embracing life as a gift instead of being simply self-absorbed. In brief, the Naikan approach aims to change behavior in relation to other people and society. The success or failure of this enterprise rests solely with the individual, although trained professionals provide guidance. In brief, a systematic and thoroughgoing self-examination is crucial for Naikan therapy to be effective.

Naikan differentiates itself from any religious or spiritual path; it delegates responsibility to each person to discover his or her own religious path. Its aim is to develop a well-adjusted member of society, leaving the choice of a religion to the individual.

III

In contrast to Naikan self-examination pursued within a given structure in a prescribed time frame with a set procedure, the Shin Buddhist approach speaks of 84,000 paths to liberation and freedom. While the approach is open ended, the focus is on the truth-value of religion, on uncovering the meaning of life and death, and not on the utility-value of religion, whether it be cultivating peace of mind, finding solace in times of distress, resolving interpersonal conflicts, or contributing to social harmony.

As we have noted, a form of self-analysis has always been integral to the Shin Buddhist path in the practice of *mi-shirabe*. It is based on a process of reflecting critically on the assumption of being a "good" person—an unquestioned belief that never acknowledges that one may be good or bad, or even evil, depending on the circumstances.

Self-reflection, however, can have more than ethical or moral implications; this self-reflection constitutes a critical component in religious awakening itself, including the realization that one is a limited, finite being living within the light of the unlimited, boundless compassion that is Amida Buddha. This illumination can lead to the experience of one as foolish *(oroka)*, unworthy *(tsumaranai)*, shallow *(asamashii)*, arrogant *(gōman)*, willful *(wagamama)*, shameless *(hazukashii)*, evil *(akunin)*, and so on.

These are realizations that emerge from being awakened to reality as it is—the working of infinite compassion permeating life—that makes possible the interaction between limited karmic beings and unlimited compassion. This interrelationship also exists between the dualities of absolute and relative, good and evil, light and darkness. This is formulated in the Tendai school of Buddhism as the mutual interpenetration of good and evil, doctrinally expressed by recourse to the notion of the ten realms: hellish existence, hungry ghosts, beasts, fighting demons, human beings, heavenly beings, disciples, solitary awakened ones, bodhisattvas, and buddhas. Within each realm, be it a hell realm or the abode of buddhas, the other nine are found.

In Pure Land Buddhism this basic structure of interpenetration remains to form the basis for the unitary vision of limited karmic beings working within unlimited compassion. Among the many religious poems by Shinran is the following:

> Extremely difficult is it to put an end to our evil nature;
> The mind is like a venomous snake or scorpion,
> Our performance of good acts is also poisonous.
> Hence, it is called false and empty practice.

Yet this penetrating insight into the delusory self is simultaneously realized as the awakening to boundless compassion that transforms it:

> Although I am without shame and self-reproach
> And lack the mind of truth and sincerity,
> Because the Name is directed by Amida,
> Its virtue fills the ten quarters.[9]

Here we see the convergence of relative being (the evildoer) and absolute compassion (Amida Buddha). The simultaneous realization is compressed into the Name, Namu Amida Butsu, which symbolizes the unity of limited karmic being (Namu) and boundless compassion (Amida Butsu).

In short, Shin Buddhism recognizes the reality of human nature, variously described as karmic evil, blind passion, and delusory ignorance as well as its radical transformation into the highest good—awakening, enlightenment, buddhahood:

> One grain of elixir transforms iron into gold;
> One word of truth transforms evil karma into good.[10]

IV

The Shin religious life may be further clarified by turning to the teaching of Rennyo (1415–99), who was the driving force in turning an obscure movement maintained by the descendants of Shinran into the largest denomination in Japanese Buddhism.[11] In order to succeed in his mission Rennyo simplified Shinran's teaching while maintaining its focus on truth-value as a liberating power. In making the teaching available to a wider public, he had to contend with conflicting practices and interpretations of Shinran's teaching, including the practice of self-examination.

Rennyo explicitly asserted that religious awakening cannot be programmed or structured to be pursued within a given time frame; one also cannot become dependent upon a teacher to guide one. The Buddhist approach has always recognized that people have different karmic histories and diverse interests that demand appropriate religious guidance. Thus Rennyo likened some people to flowers that bloom in the sun, while others are like flowers that grow in the shade or are slower to bloom, all depending on circumstances. Diversity in growth is also due to the different kinds of karmic seeds planted and nurtured. "In the growing of good seed sown in past life, some are slow to grow and bloom. Hence, we speak of past, present and future births (in the Pure Land)." Whether entrusting ourselves to this process or not, he teaches that we must always devote ourselves to deep hearing of the buddha-dharma.[12] This requires constant effort, the effort likened to the steady drops of water that eventually make grooves even in a huge boulder. Only by such a process can the truly religious life be cultivated.

In addition to individual variations in awakening to the truth-value of the teaching, a power beyond the conventional self is acknowledged as crucial. Rennyo compares this power to the warm rays of the sun that are beyond human control but can effect transformation. It resembles the sun-rays that gradually dry some cloth hanging on a clothesline. This is a natural process also found in the deepening of religious life and insight. There occurs a settling of mind and body ultimately determined not by human calculation but this power beyond the self. Shin Buddhists refers to this as the working of other-power.[13]

When we become aware of such a power or force, our view of what constitutes good and evil is radically transformed. In ordinary discourse good and evil are sharply differentiated, but in religious experience they are realities to be simultaneously affirmed. "There are people who quote one passage or one word of the teaching and talk as if they understand fully," Rennyo wrote. "Based on true entrusting, however, one sees oneself as being both evil *and* good. Thus, one speaks with a deep sense of thankfulness."[14] As pointed out earlier, Tendai Buddhism also teaches the interpenetration of good and evil based on emptiness (Skt. *śūnyatā*) that is central to Shin Buddhist experience. In brief, good and evil are not in a horizontal, progressive relationship with absolute, boundless compassion as the culmination (evil ⅋ good ⅋ boundless compassion) but in a vertical relationship, such that the working of boundless compassion transforms evil into good. That is, both relative good and relative evil, based in ego-centered thinking, are transformed into the absolute good of boundless compassion.

This dynamic relationship between good and evil is also understood by the metaphor of "mending" *(shitsurau)*, whereby the good mind of Amida Buddha overlays and mends the deluded mind of a foolish being. "It is not that Amida will have our mind totally replaced, taking us in, but that our mind will be mended by the wisdom of the Enlightened One."[15] Contained in this so-called "mending" of our everyday mind is the ultimate "transformation of evil into good" that is the goal of Buddhist life.

This transformation of evil into good is described by Shinran as a natural, spontaneous occurrence: "Without the practicer's calculation in any way whatsoever all the practicer's past, present, and future evil karma are transformed into the highest good. 'To be transformed' means that evil karma without being nullified or eradicated is made into the highest good, just as all river waters, upon entering the great ocean, immediately become ocean water."[16] He compares this radical transformation to the natural process of ice (delusion) melting into water (wisdom):

> Obstructions of karmic evil turn into virtues.
> It is like the relationship of ice turning into water.
> The more the ice, the more the water.
> The more the obstructions, the more the virtues.[17]

The truly religious life liberates a finite, relative being to become a "rare and excellent person" naturally and spontaneously.[18] As imperfect humans, we are bound by our karmic limitations, but that poses no hindrance for reflecting the boundless life and light of the Buddha. It is not the case that everything that karmic evil connotes, including human foolishness, frailties, and failures, completely vanish but that the overwhelming working of compassion nullifies their negative karmic impact, enabling limited beings to make unlimited contributions to the well-being of all life.

This ultimate realization is expressed in everyday language by countless

Shin Buddhists, such as the followers revered as *myōkōnin* (wonderful people) or *nembutsu* faithfuls, who blossom like lotus flowers. One of the most famous was Saichi, who made wooden clogs and wrote thousands of poems on wood chips and shavings in his workshop. Here is one that shows the unity of karmic being (Namu) and boundless compassion (Amida Butsu):[19]

> How wretched!
> And how joyous!
> They are one.
> In Namu Amida Butsu.[20]

This unity of light and darkness is universally realized, covering the horizon of human experience. Utilizing symbolic language, Saichi writes,

> I may possess eighty-four thousand evil passions,
> But Amida too is eighty-four thousand.
> This is the meaning of the oneness of Namu Amida Butsu.[21]

Here the cardinal virtue of gratitude on the horizontal plane is completely negated but simultaneously affirmed in the realization of Namu Amida Butsu:

> To be grateful is all a lie,
> The truth is—there is nothing the matter;
> And beyond this there is no peace of mind—
> Namu Amida Butsu, Namu Amida Butsu
> Namu Amida Butsu!
> (With this peacefully I retire.)[22]

V

An interesting dialogue took place more than half a century ago between D. T. Suzuki and Kaneko Daiei, a Shin Buddhist scholar, when both were colleagues teaching at Otani University in Kyoto.[23] According to Kaneko, Suzuki once asked him about his age, and when he replied that he had just turned sixty, Suzuki mumbled to himself, "At that age, you can't really understand what life is all about." Ten years later Kaneko mentioned that conversation to Suzuki, who then said, "That's true, but at age seventy you really don't understand fully either and that's true even at eighty!"

Kaneko reminisces, "What I felt was that here is a seeker who is never satisfied with himself in embodying the buddha-dharma. He echoes the sentiment of Shinran, who said, 'In the person of *nembutsu* opens up the great path of unobstructed freedom' (*Tannisho* VIII)."[24] This freedom from complacency is also suggested in Suzuki's description of the Shin path as a never-ending process, comparable to the baby moving forward but never reaching the waiting father. Ultimately, however, the toddler becomes strong enough to walk on its own two feet, freely with "unobstructed freedom." It is descriptive of the Shin path, as well as Suzuki's own creative life. He died at the age of ninety-six in 1966.

The power of the Primal Vow, that sheer life force, natural and spontaneous, sustains all existence when it is fully actualized in the person of *nembutsu*. Suzuki frequently said, "We talk about Amida's Vow, but it has to become the deep vow of each of us." In his own way he was the living embodiment of the working of the Primal Vow.

10

Psychology, the Sacred, and Energetic Sensing

ANNE CAROLYN KLEIN

What nine months of attention does for an embryo
Forty early mornings will do
For your gradually growing wholeness.
—RUMI

BUDDHIST TEXTS, philosophies, and contemplative practices all move
from a conviction that human beings have much to discover about
being.[1] This conviction is also present in other wisdom traditions, that
is, those that see gnosis as fundamental to this discovery. Their path is
not psychological exploration as modern Western paradigms generally
understand, though it does look at similar material. The horizons toward
which modern psychology and Buddhist practices move, however, are
clearly quite different. Historical and cultural reasons for this are many.
Western psychology is, above all, both a product and an exponent of the
European Enlightenment. Buddhist and Hindu mythos are rooted in a
different matrix, including a different mapping of mind, body, and subjective states.

Much has been written about these differences. What I am interested in
here is what a psychology of the sacred transcendent might look like, how
it functionally differs from certain classic Western assumptions about the
psyche, and what types of knowledge would invite it in for cultivation. Most
important, I am concerned with the nature and function of energy as that
which permeates the psychophysical spectrum and thus offers a bridge to
current psychological theory.

Toward a Psychology of the Sacred

What does a psychology in service of the sacred even mean? Countless poets and mystics from Rumi to Theresa of Avila, the Indian *bhaktas* or *gopi* devotees to Krishna, and the tantrikas of Tibet have devoted themselves to the divine or the real as to a lover. What if we were to take seriously—as have countless contemplatives around the world—that the drive toward a reality that is construed as some kind of divinely unbounded wholeness[2] is as powerful as the drive for love, sex, power, or all of the things that psychology generally regards as motivating human behavior, consciously and unconsciously. What kind of theories of perception and other crucial elements of a worldview might inform such a vision of inter- and intra-human dynamics? And most compelling of all: how will the picture look if we explicitly understand human beings, not only as psychological and conceptual beings, but as energetically sensitive and deeply impacted by their own and others' energies, an understanding quite common in Asian and many other non-Euro-American traditions? To speak of human beings in this way is at the very least heuristically useful as we consider connections between psychological processes and the kind of sacred seeking discussed in Buddhist, Hindu, Christian, Sufi and other mystically oriented traditions. It is also therapeutically useful, as we will touch on later.

Freud understood human process as a dynamic unfolding. Eros, thwarted or enacted, is the dynamism that sets in motion key stages of development including the anal and the Oedipal. Freud and those after him, however, tended to emphasize more the patterning of pathologies and complexes, and the recognition of unconscious material, rather than the movement of energy per se; the focus on dynamism or energy as such has largely receded.[3] Currently, object-relations theory provides a narrative helpful for understanding developmental issues: a child begins to experience himself or herself as a self when there is a "good enough" parent to provide enough holding in the environment for that identity to emerge. In this way we can understand important stages in how the psychological self unfolds. When it comes to juxtaposing this with Buddhist theory, it is very useful, as Harvey Aronson has observed, to make a distinction between the psychological and ontological selves.[4] Buddhism affirms the psychological self at a conventional level and rejects any fixed, permanent self at the ontological level. The energetic dynamic of selfhood is a middle ground because it encompasses both the conventional, empirical self, and the ultimate metaphysical self. At the same time, unlike conventional psychological understandings of self even in terms of the energies of the libido, this is a metaphysics of utter boundlessness. For, from the most ultimate perspective, one's being, actual nature, soul or spirit is without margin, center, or reifiable qualities of any kind. Such a metaphysic or perspective purposefully undermines any attempt to grasp this heart-essence of one's being conceptually. At the same time, that essential nature is presented as positive, energetic, an open awareness.

For anyone seeking to benefit from the insights of both psychotherapy and contemplative practice, as is increasingly the case today in the West, it is crucial to find an accessible and experiential link between them. Energy awareness is certainly such a link. In this context what I mean by energy is, very generally, what the Tibetan tantric and medical traditions refer to as the "inner winds" *(rlung).* This corresponds in virtually all ways with what Indian Hindu as well as Indian Buddhist traditions refer to as *prāṇa* and the Chinese as *qi.*[5] All perception, all mental, emotional, or any kind of cognitive functioning, including what the West calls psychological, is always, in these views, accompanied by some movement of the inner currents of energy. When these currents run wild, the mind does also.[6] By bringing such energetic processes into our discussion, we find a category of human experience that speaks to psychological as well as contemplative experience, though it itself is neither. For our purposes here, we simply suggest that a psychophysical awareness of these currents in one's body and, especially, sensitivity to how they reveal and impact one's experience of self, is a central part of contemplative practice. Awareness of energetic currents is, therefore, of potential significance in a psychology that not only takes the possibility and power of contemplation into clear account but also sees that subtle or rarefied energetic experiences correspond in many ways to common descriptions of "the sacred." These dimensions, rather than afflictive responses, however deeply engrained, are the most fundamental structures of the self. The rich sense of multidimensional wholeness that characterizes rarefied contemplative experience, including the sense of a movement beyond ordinary conventions and restrictions, can be understood as a function of an energetic shift, or the result of psychological reorientation. The two perspectives enhance rather than limit each other. However, a perspective inclusive of the energetic component helps enormously in making sense of such experience, and is consonant with the possibility of a psychology whose fundamental premise is that humans seek above all else to experience their nature and that their nature is not, or not only, a set of psychological complexes.

In ancient India, meditative experiences and experiments with wind practices laid the foundation for later medical developments.[7] The divide between science and religion characteristic of Western modes of thought, including Freudian-based psychodynamic theory, was not a driving factor, and even in modern Asia the religious language of liberation and the scientific discourse of objective knowledge coexist without much tension. I believe that taking account of the place of the energetic in human experience and development offers a creative field of discourse in which psychological thinking and contemplative reflection can beneficially interact. This conversation has actually already begun in some quarters, for example, in the somatic therapies developed at Esalen, or the Mind-Science seminars in which scientists, including cognitive psychologists, gather for in-depth conversations with the Dalai Lama.

Thus far, the discussion of how psychological understanding relates to the transcendent sacred and to the energetic currents of embodiment has not taken any clear shape or direction. This chapter represents an attempt to provide outlines of a systematic reflection on energetic sensing of the transcendental sacred and its relation to psychology and psychotherapy. The energy described here is not merely a metaphor for understanding human religious experience but is an empirical reality that is subject to experiential inquiry as well as logical analysis. It is something palpable that can be investigated, just as psychological pain is palpable to the subject experiencing it, and can be fruitfully investigated. Articulating the energetic element in meditation and in psychological processing offers us a fresh vantage point on the nature of the self, including the relationship between being someone and being no one (Skt. *anātman*), for both can be read and experienced in energetic terms.

One of the most crucial differences between a sacred or transcendent perspective and Western psychology as typically practiced is the sense of an absolute, a divine, or an ultimate with which one can utterly identify and unite. Buddhist tantric practice, Advaita Vedānta, early Christian Gnosticism, and certain forms of Sufism all articulate dissolution into and union with just such a primordial state of identity. In most Freudian-based psychotherapy the dynamics of instinctual drives and relationships are explored without a larger matrix of universal holding that one should either encounter or enter. Jungian and transpersonal psychologies are in some ways closer to the mode of a sacred psychology, though the horizons are different.[8]

Psychotherapy is focused on this life. Buddhism, like Hinduism, sees its benefits extending not only into the one-stop hereafter of Christianity or Islam but into the infinitely alterable future. Despite this radically different framework, psychotherapy and Buddhism are each keenly aware of how a person's relationship to mortality profoundly affects this life. Both Buddhist practice and psychotherapy move toward great introspective understanding and have well-theorized accounts of why and how we fail to gain the understanding that we need.

Psychotherapy, as framed in many Freudian traditions, sees movement toward any womb as retrograde and infantile.[9] Buddhist practice, as framed in many Tibetan traditions, takes one to the metaphysical womb that is the matrix of reality, and with which one comes to wholly identify in holy identity. This dimension, the dharma-realm of unbounded wholeness (Skt. *dharma dhātu;* Tib. *thig le nyag gcig*), is the expansive wellspring of everything, and at the same time our most intimate nature. There can be no more joyous, fulfilling, constant, and mature union than with it, no more enlightening realization than to experience this undifferentiated oneness. It is all too easy, and very common, to confuse one's yearning for such union with the more infantile longings of which Freud and the entire psychoanalytic tradition is so wary. The crucial difference a sacred psychology provides is the semantic, epistemological, and contemplative space for the two trajectories—infantile longing to merge with the familial maternal and transcendent aspiration to realize the cosmic maternal as the embodiment of enlightenment—without collapsing or reducing them into one or the other. The urge for wholeness can remain distinct from, even when emotionally homologous with, the urge fueled by memory of the maternal. Moreover, longings for womb-safety in infancy and childhood as well as adulthood are read not as end points of analysis but rather as expressions of the actually much more powerful, though inchoate, longing for divine oneness. In a sense, the distinguishing feature of a sacred psychology is precisely this longing for ultimate identity, true and simple being—it is the force that drives all others, not the other way around. In other words, *contra* classic Freudian and Freudian-based perspectives, the religious quest for an ultimate is *not* fueled by a wish to return to the womb; rather, our nostalgia for the womb bespeaks our profound yearning for that greater holding called, variously, enlightenment, Christ nature, atman, soul, essential nature, and so on. Love, after all, can be among the most regressive of emotions, and as well most profoundly mature and enriching. Psychology is not at all irrelevant here. But it might be limiting.

In practical terms, it is not easy to distinguish these two yearnings. Knowing that they are different, however, alters what one is capable of noticing about oneself. And being aware of the different feel of energies that express, or resist, either of these yearnings, can be mind opening.

Risking oversimplification for the sake of emphasis, I will use selected Buddhist and Freudian reflections on "womb" to distill many of the elements relevant to distinguishing a sacred from a conventional psychology. Entering the path to enlightenment, especially the Tantric path, is often explicitly depicted as a rebirth; to be enlightened is to be born into the Buddha Family. The womb is always the same, what changes is one's understanding of and relation to it, including the ability to distinguish it from the more regressive type of womb-longing. Exploring the meaning of this can help us understand spiritual rebirth as, to a very large extent, an energetic process in both its transcendent and more conventionally psychological dimensions.

Spiritual rebirth, meditative insight, and other path-based wisdoms are neither a function of mind alone, of analysis, nor even of the deepest introspection in psychological terms. The importance of recognizing contemplative *and* psychological practices as "whole body" experiences cannot be overestimated. To fail in this is to be locked into conceptual trajectories, which, although absolutely important, cannot—as every experienced contemplative and psychologist knows all too well—hold the full dimension of human being.

In both psychological and contemplative systems, one comes to divest oneself of deeply held self-representations. This is a profound commonality. It is also why energetic sensing, present in both, also bridges these two endeavors. In both systems one seeks a kind of wholeness, a kind of integration. What is the relationship between "negative" emotions and the maternal womb? And what is the relationship between those psychodynamics and the sacred matrix? Most succinctly, what is the relationship between knowing and not knowing? What is the path from the former to the latter?

The path does not open through mind alone. If we are to consider a sacred psychology we must include among our methods something akin to what Aristotle called *energeia,* something equally akin to what in Buddhist traditions runs through the body as breath and more subtly through major and secondary channels such as *prāna, rlung,* and *qi,* as found in India, Tibet, and China, respectively. To recognize awareness of energetic functioning as an element in spiritual or therapeutic work provides an additional channel that can be utilized for either. Moreover, since both conventionally therapeutic and traditional religious practices are ways of shifting energy, even when they are not explicitly articulated as such, the category of energy awareness provides an important bridge between conventional and sacred processes. It is the contention of most Asian traditions, and a common experience among contemplatives, that if one pays attention, every self-representation is also, literally, a way of "holding" the self, and is associated with certain types of energetic patterns that can be brought to awareness and shifted.

In this regard I think it is no accident that in Sanskrit, Pāli, and Tibetan Buddhist literature, what one seeks to overcome is, literally, the "grasping" or "holding" of a self (Skt. *ātma-grāha,* Tib. *bdag 'dzin*). The Sanskrit *grāha* is apparently cognate with the English "grab" or "grasp" and is translated literally into Tibetan as *'dzin.* Clearly these terms are describing something that is not merely conceptual but embedded in the dynamics of the mind-body process. As such, grasping cannot be overcome by cognitive reflection alone, important though this may be. The existence of Tantric practice is powerful evidence that a wide swath of Asian traditions address the question of self-representation energetically as well as cognitively and, in a certain sense, psychologically. Indeed, many types of religious practice in traditions around the world—speaking in tongues, visionary ecstasies, appearance of stigmata—can also be understood as intentional or unintentional reorientations of energy. If we observe closely, however, we can see that even much less dramatic practices also are energetic in nature. The practices of mindfulness, widespread throughout Buddhist traditions, begin with well-known instructions on posture, and the type of vipassana practice discussed in sections of the *Path of Purification (Visuddhimagga),* or made widespread by Sri Satyanarian Goenka, are also energetic practices, though they do not announce themselves as such. To sit and observe one's breath, to take the most classic example, is also to calm the breath, the body, and all the subtle currents moving through it. Here, as in Tantra, as in Zen, it is clear that these kinds of practices will not lead to enlightenment—in fact, cannot even be engaged—unless one has a body. This is not a second-order issue; it is of primary significance. We will return to this below.

Perspectives of the Sacred

What factors might distinguish a sacred from a more conventional process of personal development? We have spoken already of the dissolution of *any* holding to self as such; a particular kind of transparency seems crucial as well as a concomitant ability to be fully reflexive: awareness swimming in its own clear awareness. Jack Engler refers to both these points in his discussion on no-self,[10] and the question of reflexivity has for centuries been a central debate among Indian and Tibetan-based traditions, especially the Cittamātrins and Prāsaṅgikas; it is also a central assumption of more esoteric traditions such as Dzogchen in Tibetan Buddhism. Reflexivity alone does not fully articulate the distinguishing characteristics of a sacred or transcendent psychology, but it is a necessary part of that whole.

Nonduality of Opposites

In a sacred psychology, as in Buddhist practice, the choice is not really between being somebody and being nobody. The choice, or possibility, is between being encrusted with a false self-representation or being authentic. Psychology has much to say about false representation, being focused on the cure or elimination of pathology. In sacred perspectives, there is no "dead" space—an absence of thought or of specific representational material does not mean an absence of awareness; an expanse unbroken by form does not mean lack of potential. There is no absolute nobody. Like the *brahman* of Advaita Vedānta, the matrix-womb (Skt. *dhātu;* Tib. *dbyings*) through which everything arises in Dzogchen is sometimes described as a vast pure expanse, filled with potency. In the end, the most primordial awareness is a reflexivity that finds itself at one with that expanse. This is also one possible meaning of the Vedic *tat tvam asi,* "thou art that," referring to the union of *ātman* and *brahman.*[11] Only the *ātman* cleared of veils can nakedly experience this union. In Buddhism this vast horizon is expressed as the union of emptiness and the wisdom in sutra, the union of the pledge and wisdom beings in Tantric practice, or the union of open awareness and the expanse brimming with potent emptiness in Dzogchen. All of these are experienced and, ideally, cognitively understood as well, in energetic terms, certainly not in cognitive or psychological terms alone.

Knowing and Being

In short, a crucial element of the sacred is the dissolution of any divide between epistemology and ontology. Knowing and being are intimately connected. Many Buddhist texts on path structure make this clear—awareness of certain ontological truths are available only in certain epistemological states. (One well-known example: without cultivation of the calm state [Skt. *śamatha;* Tib. *gzhi gnas*], emptiness cannot be directly cognized.) But even beyond this kind of profound connection, in the end, especially in more esoteric systems like Dzogchen, they are one. Being is not to be known, it is what one is. And being is, intrinsically, aware of being. This is why the question of reflexivity, mentioned briefly above, is so important. And why discursive or analytic cognitive insight, which by definition can never be fully reflexive to itself (because thought is always excluding something as it includes its particular object of focus), is an inadequate model for human processes of becoming. The energetic dynamic, however, is intrinsically capable of reflexivity; just as water is always wet and never apart from its wetness, so energy as such is always alive to itself.

Unknowing and Mystery

Another element of the sacred perspective is an acknowledgment of ultimate unknowing and mystery. Certainty expands into awe. Knowing dissolves into space.

To understand and to cultivate these aspects of the sacred thus invites recognition of their energetic dimension. As an epistemological category, and as a process, energy sensing also serves to bridge these aspects with more conventional perspectives, including the psychological. This is important. Psychological issues must also be addressed before esoteric orientations can evolve. For all these reasons, it is vital to include, as a well-formed category, a distinctly energetic element in the account of human transformation, whether psychotherapeutic, spiritual, or a combination of both.

What might this look like? What might we gain thereby? And what will this have to do with juxtaposing womb theory in Buddhist or Freudian contexts? And, even more fundamentally, what might it have to do with the way we hide from our knowing? Or with the simple unavailability of certain types of knowing—certain memories, understandings, integrative connections? Freudian traditions certainly recognize that these limitations are not a matter of cognitive functioning or will alone; they identify unconscious material as often impervious to conscious will or intellect. Indeed, the id and other drives of which Freud speaks are also a kind of energy. Yet analysis does not typically focus on energy awareness as such, nor on the information it carries.[12] Will making such a sensibility conceptually significant enrich our understanding of the epistemology of transformation? Will it be a trope that can incorporate unknowing without dissolving into disarray because of it? And what does womb symbolism have to do with it?

We have already touched on the significance of the energetic dynamic in contemplative practice and its affinity for reflexivity, a topic Engler aptly introduces in his reprise of the somebody-nobody issue.[13] In fact, Buddhist teachings do not move from a state of being *somebody* to a state of being *nobody;* they move from a recognition that the somebody we thought we were is absent (and indeed everyone has some such self-representation). That absence is understood differently in different traditions: a fusion with divinity, a mere spaciousness, a spaciousness redolent with incandescent qualities, for example. How does this movement occur? Being somebody and being nobody each involve distinctive psychodynamics and distinctive energetic dynamics. While psychotherapy offers a rich set of narratives regarding such movement, it is not the only narrative. Its embeddedness in the culture, sciences, and intellectual history of Western modernity has allowed it to offer many insights into contemplative practices rooted in Asia, but has also given us some significant blind spots. Energetic sensing is a category that maps easily onto psychological states, since every state has its own distinctive dynamic. At the same time, energy, subtle flows within the mind-body complex, is a category native to Asian and contemplative traditions, and therefore a vital category of analysis for us. It is a dynamic that extends all the way from the most concrete sense of self to the most mysterious and unbounded dimension of freedom from that self.

Tibetan esoteric and tantric traditions are famous for their explicit incorporation of the body's energies in practice. But in fact, as we have said, religious practice of all kinds works energetically. This means that cultivation of the Buddhist path (and many other paths) necessarily involves energetic learning. And unless we can name this learning and understand what it is, Buddhist practice—especially those practices that at first seem not to involve the body, such as visualization or analysis—is likely to become a desiccated shell rather than a supportive structure for real growth. There is then the potential for unknowing the bounded self of a false somebody and entering the dynamic state of sheer being, confidently known and yet ever mysterious.[14]

Womb: Primitive and Transcendent

This point relates to the perplexing connection between being someone and being no one. I would suggest that energetic being of any kind—somebody, nobody, everybody—is a one that is whole. We can understand this better after we explore further the significance of energy, energetic sensing, and the type of information that energy carries. Then it will become clearer how the sacredly transcendent is intimately connected with an expansive, metaphysical womb with which one ultimately seeks to identify, and why most Freudian-based perspectives associate the womb primarily with regression, darkness, a place to move out of. In this regard, a key difference between sacred and conventional therapeutic perspectives is that in the latter a rarefied metaphysical womb is theorized as actually pointing to that more primitive womb space, much as spiritualized love is interpreted as libido sublimation. As we have observed, in a sacred perspective yearning for the ultimate is primary, and all other yearnings, including that for a lesser womb, are but a shadow or distortion of this seeking.

So now, going back to some of those elements that seem central to a sacredly transcendent perspective on human being, how does our articulation of an energetic dynamic enrich this picture? And how does energetic sensing attend to the relationship between being somebody and being nobody?

Self-knowing and Consciousness

The question of how consciousness ultimately relates to itself is central here. Can it know itself? Is it like an ocean that flows through itself easily, or is it rather like a knife that cannot cut itself? This has long been an important debate across Buddhist traditions. Among exoteric or sutra-related perspectives, the Mind Only school, Cittamātra, maintains that self-knowing (Tib. *rang rig*) is indeed possible. The mind's contents are the objects of *rang rig*, but *rang rig* itself is always and only a subject. Otherwise, they argue, memory of one's own previous intentions would be impossible. For many of us, such a view seems plausible on the basis of common sense. Prāsaṅgika, however, says that this is an unnecessary reification; memory operates without any such substantiation of agency being necessary. In either case, insofar as memory is a matter of recalling some particular kind of image or self-representation, this does not speak to the matter of transcending any such imaging. This is not, in short, really the kind of reflexivity we are inquiring into.

Dzogchen and Open Awareness

Nonetheless, the above is relevant insofar as we can use the Cittamātrin position as a steppingstone to a more subtle position that does address the question of nonconceptual reflexivity. Dzogchen, the Great Completeness, places great importance on what it also calls a self-knower, *rang rig*, or sometimes simply *rig pa*, open awareness. This open awareness is the ultimate, uncontrived, and natural state. It is the ground or matrix for all other processes. This is what the practitioner seeks to identify, experience, and dwell in. What this open awareness knows is neither conceptual thought nor recalled images but literally itself. And "itself" is synonymous with what Dzogchen calls unbounded wholeness *(thig le nyag gcig)*, inclusive of everything without limit.

The crucial point, of course, is that the kind of knowing envisioned here is utterly without an object, much less a concept or image; it is an awareness that is fully open, unified, and yet endlessly variable. It is in several respects different from any other type of perception. Thus, for example, in his *Treatise on the Mother Tantra*,[15] Lopon Tenzin Namdak maintains that although open awareness is a type of direct perception, it is not found among the classic categories of direct perception discussed in sutra vehicle literature, especially that associated with the Sautrāntika and Cittamātra systems *(mdo sems thun mong ba)*.[16]

These four are well known: sensory direct perception *(dbang po'i mngon sum, indriya-pratyakṣa)*; mental direct perception *(yid gyi mngon sum, mānasa-pratyakṣa)*; and two categories seemingly most compatible with Dzogchen discussions: yogic direct perception *(rnal 'byor mngon sum, yogi-pratyakṣa)* and self-awareness direct perception *(rang rig mngon sum, svasaṃvedana-pratyakṣa)*. Lopon's point is that Dzogchen's self-knowing open awareness is none of these. Neither sensory nor mental direct perception are true open awareness, writes Lopon, because they do not observe their own natural state.[17] Such perception lacks the meditative stabilization of open awareness, and open awareness is not, like these, induced by an immediately prior condition *(de ma thag rkyen).*

We note here the assumption of a natural state—something called into question by Stephen Mitchell.[18] This is an important issue interwoven with the question of reflexivity; we will return to it in a moment. First let us see what one important voice from the tradition has to say about it.

In his *Commentary on the Mother Tantra,* Lopon Tenzin Namdak, widely acknowledged as the foremost scholar and master of the Bön Dzogchen tradition, writes, "Once one has completed familiarization with the primordial wisdom, the spontaneously occurring mind, thoughts, and desires no longer dwell or form within the continuum of that person. They are finished, just as some oily husks placed in fire will burn without residue. In this way, primordial wisdom has the capacity to overcome the faults in this person's continuum because that primordial wisdom is the open awareness which realizes the final abiding condition of all knowables."[19] This state of open awareness is a more natural or genuine state than conceptual functioning because it is without any effort whatsoever. As the *Scripture of the Blissful Samantabhadra* states:

> Unless one realizes that there is primordially Buddha,
> How could the fruit be found through temporary effort?[20]

Primordial Purity and Effortlessness

All conceptualization, even subtle imaging, is understood to require effort. Thus, we can understand that in part the difference between the optimum, naturally transcendent state and our usual one has very much to do with how we use and distribute energy across our system. This is why in Chan/Son/Zen, as in Dzogchen, effort is counterindicated. Effort always has something to do with a subject and an object. It has also to do with a goal and thus with an absence of being present to that goal-accomplished self. This effort that a subject makes in relation to its object or goal is an implicit yet powerful acknowledgment that the currently performing self is in fact an absence of certain salient characteristics. As such, it seems incapable of being fully present to itself and subtly disassociated from the wellspring of wholeness that gives rise to both subject and object. Yet no such disassociation can possibly occur. This principle is often discussed in

Buddhist traditions in terms of the inviolability of one's buddha-nature or primordial purity. It is, as we have said, a crucial element of any sacred psychology.[21]

There can be no thought without effort, energetically speaking. This gives significance to the description of great yogis as utterly at rest. In the *Heart Essence, of the Vast Expanse* tradition's cultivation of *bodhicitta* (the aspiration for enlightenment), one explicitly practices so that all beings may "rest in the clear light of their own open awareness." This is the ultimate cradling mother-womb. The principle of the inviolability of buddha-nature or primordial wisdom, combined with its assured potential for recognizing itself as such, is a central factor distinguishing a sacredly transcendent from other therapeutic perspectives. It is, in short, the kind of description of ultimate being that classical psychoanalysis tends to distrust, eschew, or explicitly undermine. The transpersonal schools embrace it, but they do not necessarily see it as their task to provide people with the means to actualize it as the central fact of their identity, even if they posit it as the ultimate goal.

If we can acknowledge the theoretical and experiential possibility of such a state, it makes sense to direct attention toward it. From this perspective, which has resonances in many wisdom traditions, any intervention that does not have this realization as its ultimate goal or, at the very least, as an important part of the larger picture, does not provide a full picture of what it means to be human.

Spontaneity and Unbounded Wholeness

Every human being has access to what A. H. Almaas refers to as *Being*, and which I understand as functionally homologous to buddha-nature, variously defined, or to Dzogchen's unbounded wholeness.[22] In each case we speak of an energetically dynamic yet wholly unbounded state that is only obscured when one mistakenly becomes identified with something less than it. The link with psychology comes because, in Almaas's words, One's work on oneself must lead to accessing the realm of Being for it is the alienation from Being that is the fundamental cause underlying egoic experience. While psychological processing is a necessary part of the work, no amount of psychological processing can release the soul from ego fixation."[23]

This is not unrelated to Herbert Fingarette's astute point, engaged by Engler, that "anxiety calls the self into being."[24] In both Fingarette and esoteric Buddhism, the conventional self is a kind of smallness experienced as a fortification against something too threateningly expansive to simply stand by and let be. Such anxiety can be a response to the womb itself, threatening to smother and contain, or to the vastness of the universe. It takes effort—even if a deeply ingrained, even irrepressible thwarting of available energies to fend off this wholeness. Buddhas, we are told, are capable of infinite discrimination, but have no conceptual thought. This makes sense only if we understand energy systems as carrying immediate knowing. Psychoanalysis works similarly when it succeeds in shifting and expanding not ideas but energies. Early in his career, Freud spoke of catharsis and abreaction, both descriptions of an energetic dynamic. There can be complementary energetic and psychodynamic explanations as to why any particular effortful, discursive habit arises.[25] The classic Prāsaṅgika-Madhyamaka position is that the senses are simply set up in such a way that things look as if they exist independently "out there" and are thus separate from us. This gives the appearance that they are more self-sufficient and real than they actually are; conscious effort arises as an attempt to bridge what turns out to be an illusory gulf. Dzogchen offers precisely calibrated descriptions of how the world arises from its own unbounded matrix.[26] This does not happen through effort but occurs spontaneously *(hlun grub)*. Simply through its intrinsic dynamism *(rtsal)* and playfulness *(rol ba),* unbounded wholeness naturally gives rise to myriad expressions of itself. In their self-proliferation, there can arise a dissociative forgetting of that originary, unbroken wholeness. We can look at this forgetting in psychological terms as well. To paraphrase Almaas, things inevitably arise in the life of a child that cause some type of wounding or loss, which in turn bring about some type of compensatory withdrawal, defending, and concomitant limitations in the types of responses that remain accessible to the self.[27] Any such limitation or fixation becomes the impetus and axis of ego-formation. Such an ego is, by definition, a perspective that obscures the wholistic sensibility of Being itself, of human being.

Access to unbounded wholeness or its functional analogues will most likely (at least in the West) require psychological work, but uncontrived wholeness does not really make sense unless human beings are understood as energetically constituted, that is, as a kind of open, unbounded field of energy. This does not mean that the self is beyond conceptualization or cannot be understood as constituted psychodynamically. However, it presents the reality of the self in such a way that it cannot be completely integrated on the finite terms of classical psychoanalysis.

The Wound and the Nectar: A Case Study

An example Almaas gives is also typical of my own, our students', and many others' experience in which a subtle sensing of one's own energetic dynamic brings forward information and functions as a medium by which experience is transformed. In the following case, a student is exploring a particular wounding in connection with her mother:

> Part of the reason I sell myself short is to try desperately to get her [my mother's] love; she did not want me to be me and do well. Another is the terror of losing her and really seeing that she never loved me; she hated me.
>
> I felt a large gaping hole around my heart and lungs as you [Almaas] spoke [in the retreat]. I kept trying to fill it in various ways, one of which is trying to be my mom. When she is sick and upset, I get sick. I worked on the hole in a private teaching session before. I have a gigantic wound where my mother continued to emotionally stab me as an infant every time my strength and love came out to her. I believe subconsciously that I am her, and I believe she has the love and warmth, and I am nothing without her.
>
> As we worked Saturday night I felt at some point a juicy, honey-like feeling or presence in my chest, where the wound is. It was sweet and warm and like nectar.[28]

There is much that could be said about this psychodynamically. I want simply to point to the inner sensing that allowed this student to palpably experience her own wounded state as well as a shifting of energies so that that same area of her body was now experienced as juicy, like honey, and sweet. Such shifts come through understanding and observation—and through it the body is experienced as a vessel for and communicator of information. Buddhist practice also relies to a significant degree on such a sensibility. For example, in Tibetan traditions, the more refined, secret, and esoteric the stage of Tantra, the more emphasis on increasingly subtle energetic awareness. Enlightenment is finally simply a matter of the inner winds coursing through the very center of the body, instead of on either side of one's center. In Dzogchen, unbounded wholeness is the deep nature at our center, physically and metaphysically.[29]

Four Characteristics of Unbounded Wholeness

And what exactly is this state of unbounded wholeness? Lopon Tenzin Namdak names four central characteristics, of which the first two are:

1. It is unconditioned because it is permanent.
2. It is unchanging because it is not produced through causes and conditions.

Clearly, the self that we ordinarily cling to is neither of these. Being "somebody" in any ordinary sense involves being conditioned and, therefore, affected by causes and conditions. Dzogchen does not really use the vocabulary of self and selflessness, but rather emphasizes the movement from a state of unawareness *(ma rig pa)* to full and open awareness *(rig pa)*. There is really no possibility to be utterly and completely nobody. *Feeling* like nobody is a different matter. But the base and its innate dynamism are ever present. Still, absent a fully manifest, open awareness, there will always be effortful thought, including the conceptual holding to self, until awareness frees one from this error.

> Not recognizing just as it is
> The mind's real nature
> Is delusion
> Lost in enormous, elemental darkness
> Endlessly a wanderer, endlessly in circles.[30]

Escape from the endless cycle of samsara thus cannot come through discursive effort, and it cannot come about through conceptual processing, which is also based on a reified goal, according to Dzogchen. This is why reality is inconceivable and inexpressible (yet logically articulate) and why one cannot think, or psychoanalyze, one's way to enlightenment. While enlightenment thus will not yield to linear effort *(rtsol ba)*, artful endeavor *('bad pa)* requiring tremendous aspiration is nevertheless indispensable.

While there is more to be said about this than we have space for, at the very least we can see that the type of energetic approach one brings to the path makes all the difference between moving toward full open awareness

and remaining unaware. And it is not only the esoteric systems that emphasize effortlessness—the same effortlessness is also, classically, a characteristic of full accomplishment of the calm state, *śamatha,* which is distinguished
from the previous eight states leading to it by being utterly effortless from
inception to conclusion of the session, even if the session lasts for days.
Energy matters, the information it carries matters, and its pliability and
ease of transformation also matter. Enlightenment is thus not so much a
question of being either somebody or nobody, but of shifting into a qualitatively different dynamic by which one moves in the world. Instead of
being effortful and unaware, there is a spontaneously responsive and wide-
open awareness.

Energy: Like Water, Nectar, Light, Wind

It is not uncommon, as in Almaas's vignette above, for an extremely painful
self-representation to yield to a much more positive one in the course of a
few minutes. Energy, like water and unlike ice, has this capacity of swift
transformation. Similarly, energy experienced through inner awareness as
specific images or patterns of light is an important medium for traditional
Buddhist practice and for mystical experiences of many kinds. Once one
has moved from a wounded sensibility to a nectar-light sensibility, it is possible to open into wholeness. In more traditional Tantric paradigms, once
one has been able to experience one's entire being as divine light, one can
dissolve into spaciousness in a way that physical bodies or tightly held ideas
or emotions cannot. It is actually the inner wind supporting such minds or
perceptions that dissolves. For this inner wind is famously compared to a
horse on which the perspicacious but lame mind rides. Practice, from the
initial states of calm to the most esoteric Tantric or Dzogchen, aims at taming these winds; a more subtle wind carries a subtler mind. Release of erroneous holding allows the natural dynamism *(rtsal)* of unbounded wholeness
to express itself in a way that maintains, rather than obscures, reflexive open
awareness of its actual, infinitely expressive nature. Most Buddhist traditions
find it crucial or at least beneficial to gain conceptual compass of the tradition in which one practices, but in the cultural context of all these traditions,
whether South, North, Southeast, or East Asian, human beings are also
understood as functioning through an energetic dynamic that is at least as
important as—and intimately a part of—other styles of perception. As
Buddhism comes West, it is for the very first time entering a cultural system

that does not already have this dynamic as a well-established perspective, as a category naturally folded into other types of analysis.

This is especially important to keep in mind as we consider the question of being somebody and being nobody in the context of a sacred psychology that is energetically sensitive and assumes the presence of something like an unbounded wholeness. Such wholeness is, by definition, unconditioned and uncaused. Being "nobody" in a nihilistic sense might *feel like* an unconditioned, uncaused state but would lack the next two, equally vital, qualities noted by Lopon. For unbounded wholeness is also a changeless ceaseless dimension *(g.yung drung gi sku)*, for two reasons:

3. It is the base and support for the many exalted qualities *(yon ldan)* that rely on it.
4. Its own essence *(ngo bo)* is unchanging.

Dissolving the boundary between self and no self, this state is ultimate because it is the ground of all other states. Innumerable practitioners have described their experience in these terms. We do not need to make claims for its objective validity here; we can simply say that there is an empirical state that in powerful ways *feels like* the effortless, uncontrived, natural and wholly integrated ground of all other experience. Moreover, once experienced and thoroughly cultivated, it reorients one's worldview in a way concordant with Buddhist ethical, metaphysical, and other principles. Taking our inspiration from D. W. Winnicott, a founding figure in object-relations psychology, we could call this a "good-enough ultimacy." It is powerful and available enough for us to take it seriously as a possibility in the human condition without needing to objectify it or seek some kind of apodictic certainty.

Engler and even more pointedly Mitchell raise the question of why such a state should be preferable to other states. From a Buddhist perspective, it is preferable because of its effect on others and its impact on one's own experience. Across the Tibetan traditions we find claims that understanding the ultimate occurs only when there is a strong enough ethical basis for it, hence the importance of maintaining the precepts and undertaking many practices of purification—such as the Foundational Practices *(sngon 'gro)* of Dzogchen. Moreover, knowing the ultimate gives rise to even greater compassion and provides a powerful inspiration to help others gain that same understanding. This knowing is also an avenue to bliss. Such bliss is the fourth characteristic intrinsic to unbounded wholeness. Lopon writes that such wholeness is great bliss because its essence is uncontaminated by an accumulation of poisonous bon, and because it is the final abiding condition. Moreover, because unbounded wholeness is free of all extremes, it is "the abiding condition of all knowable phenomena."[31]

Now we see further the value of such an attainment. This state is, in and of itself, not only free from suffering but intrinsically blissful. Such is the fabric of reality touched on through the ages. The vast literature containing firsthand reports of such experiences, across mystical traditions, constitutes what we might call "living proof."[32] This is not double-blind scientific proof, yet it has its own power.

Self As One and Many

There is one final point to make. This has to do with the question of self as singular or multiple. While these two options are logically and conceptually in opposition, energy is a medium in which there is no conflict between them; it can hold, for example, love and hate simultaneously, like water can be a medium for sharks and dolphins simultaneously. Thus the complete self is both unified as one and at the same time multiple. This compatibility is in fact a hallmark of unbounded wholeness—its unchangeable essence is singular, whereas the dynamic displays for which it is the all-pervasive ground are infinite, multifarious. Matter cannot function in this way, nor linear logic, but energy does. Its unity cannot be compromised, just as the ocean cannot be fractured, even by tsunami waves and hurricane-force winds. Thus, in contrast to the dyad Engler offers of self as "multiple and discontinuous" or "integral and continuous," we have a manifoldly expressive and continuous energetic display that becomes the basis for the illusory designation of "self."

The *Mirror of Mindnature Treasure (Sems nyid me long gi mdzod phug)*, a Dzogchen work from the Buddhist-related Bön tradition, states that unbounded wholeness cannot be fractured by contradictions or multiplicities.[33] To the contrary, emphasizing its multitudinous character is precisely what enables us to appreciate its spaciously open nature, an ambiance innocent of limits, one well-rounded "whole" *(thig le).*[34]

This kind of description, central to Dzogchen understandings of unbounded wholeness, speaks to the self-as-one-or-many conundrum to which Engler refers. As an unspecified essence, it is constant; yet it is the nature of that dynamic essence to constantly express itself in infinite ways.

The early Tibetan Bön-Buddhist tradition displays the intimate connection between a traditional metaphysical and more contemporary psychological perspective:

> Once hatred is renounced, love cannot be revealed
> The single nature of the mind renounces nothing.
> Once unawareness is renounced, wisdom cannot be revealed.
> The single nature of the mind renounces nothing.
> Once desire is renounced, generosity cannot be revealed
> The single nature of the mind renounces nothing.[35]

This unified nature is the particular and very subtle energetics of unbounded wholeness. It is present in all subjective states, loving and hateful alike. One reason why it has been difficult to get past dualistic paradigms such as "self" and "no self" is that ideas of unity and wholeness have been too reified and even idealized; they are no longer dynamic and are thus incompatible with change and instability. The energetic dimension is, by contrast, simultaneously fluid, multiple, and whole.

By taking this fluidly organic component of human being as a crucial medium of practice, by understanding ourselves not only in psychological and cognitive terms but also energetically, we gain a different vantage point on what practice is, and on how psychology and practice might speak to each other.[36]

The dynamic of the energy is arguably itself more like the reality Buddhists describe than any of the other constituents of self—mind alone has no dynamism; the body disintegrates; discrimination and consciousness are typically conceptual and based on a linear view of effort. But the dynamics of energy—which includes the dynamism intrinsic to the subtlest state of open awareness—is itself, like reality, instantaneously responsive, infinitely interconnected and expansive, and, above all, the resonant matrix in and through which all other experiences unfold. It is the womb one never leaves, but to which one must open one's eyes to be reborn.

Indeed, we could take a step further and, with the Sufis, state that the root of all longings is nothing other than the wish to reconnect with this all-encompassing womb-nature, the heart of one's heart. All other love is but a shadow of this one, including the regressive desire to return to the much more constraining maternal womb.

This is the love of which all other loves, including mother love, is a reflection. This primordial yearning is expressed in innumerable ways— Christian mystics speak of the bride of Christ, Rumi of the friend and the hidden beauty, Tibetan Buddhism of yearning for the Lama in Guru Yoga. Though often expressed in sexual terms, and sometimes even involving sexual practices, this yearning is not reducible to sexual desire; it expresses the irrepressible urge of reality, one's deepest nature, to make itself known, and one's own wish to know it.

Tibetan Buddhist traditions indicate this powerfully by their emphasis on the bliss intrinsic to this state, and the oft-repeated observation that all beings seek happiness. Reality in the form of the primordial Buddha Samantabhadra itself calls out encouragement. As the *Secret Scripture Collection (mDo lung gsang ba)* states,

> Nothing, not even one thing,
> Does not arise from me.
> Nothing, not even one thing,
> Dwells not within me.
> Everything, just everything,
> Emanates from me.
> Thus am I only one,
> Knowing me is knowing all—
> Great bliss.[37]

A sacred psychology would similarly assume that, despite many appearances to the contrary, the most profound human urge is in fact the wish to reaffirm through direct experience that primordial, expansive, and thoroughly enlightened awareness. It is easily confused with more primitive and infantile urges to merge with mother, but they are not the same thing.[38] Rumi himself, in the verse cited at the opening of this chapter and again below makes an implicit connection between these two kinds of womb-longing. Perhaps its meaning is for us clearer now, so we listen again:

> What nine months of attention does for an embryo
> Forty early mornings will do
> For your gradually growing wholeness.[39]

Sacred Journeys to the Womb of Reality

A sacred journey becomes possible when there is a sacred destination. The sacred destination is, like the river sought by the Lama in Rudyard Kipling's *Kim*, already at our feet but temporarily hidden from view. Such a destination can be reached through subtle energetic reorientation; it cannot be reached through the efforts of the ego, driven by awe and fear of the superego, or by the activity of clinging to certain limited forms and vilifying those who have other forms or none. The sacred energies are the medium through which the kind of womb-matrix enjoyed by the mystics can actually be accessed. Not only this, but it can readily be seen that the self *as currently construed*—with all its erroneous assumptions, unwholesome inclinations, and so on—possesses a sensitivity to energies which, even in their cruder form, already partake of many of the qualities of the ultimate. The same could not be said of conceptual thought. The limitations of thought and speech are keenly felt across mystic traditions. As Rumi writes:

> Language does not touch the one
> who lives in each of us.[40]

Energy intrinsically shares in the immediacy, the feeling of presence, and the intimate resonance with a wider field that characterizes gnostic realities such as unbounded wholeness. It shares this in a way that is impossible for thought to emulate. Even if, psychologically or conceptually, we are unable to resonate with the more expansive and elusive womb of reality, we are energetically already in some congruity with it. Recognizing this makes the mystic's purpose—and hence the metaphysical, metamystical womb—more available than if we see ourselves only as a whorl of drives, instincts, object relations, and other psychological dynamics. It has been A. H. Almaas's great insight to engage these same psychodynamics to better understand what patterns will govern a practitioner's approach to the reality-matrix. Those wounded by the flesh-and-blood mother from whose womb they came, or by any mother figure, will also fear wounding by the womb which is reality. This is also where we came from. However, unless psychotherapeutic principles maintain this more expansive reality on their horizon, they tend to form a closed system. Such a closed system is incommensurable with human potential. The energetic dimension, and thus the energetic sensing that is part of every living being, is never a closed system.[41] To the extent that psychotherapy itself defines its boundaries to address only the human dilemmas it so skillfully addresses, it remains limited. We also require, and have real potential for, access to a quite different dimension. At this point in history, the unprecedented, unfolding conversation between Buddhism and psychotherapy seems ready to open toward the integration of therapeutic insight with the even more expansive perspective of the womb-matrix that is the sacred mother of all wombs.

PART III

DEATH AND DYING
IN PURE LAND BUDDHISM

11

Shandao's Verses on Guiding Others and Healing the Heart

JULIE HANADA-LEE

H EARING OF ANOTHER PERSON'S PAIN evokes sympathy. We hear of someone's mother dying, and our affinity and association to their loss and grief develops. If death has touched our home, and it probably has, we begin to remember our own experiences. Hearing another person share the pain evokes even stronger emotions. We not only remember the facts of our own experience, we begin to remember how we felt, and we hurt all over again.

It is easier for us to talk to others about another person's losses. It is easier for me to call friends to tell them that John's mother died than to get up the courage to go visit John. It is easier for me to help John plan his mother's funeral than it is for me to hear John talk about his feelings of losing his mother. This is aptly illustrated by the case of Kisa Gotami, a poor woman living in India at the time of the historical Buddha Śākyamuni.[1] Because she could not face her infant son's death, the Buddha told her to go find some mustard seed so that he could make medicine for her. He told her that the seeds must come from a family that had not known death. By the time she arrived at the door of the last house in her village, she realized that the mustard seed, although not in hand, was a great spiritual medicine for her. By means of the mustard seed, the Buddha had taught her that all people suffer loss and death, and this led Kisa Gotami to the deeper realization of boundless compassion. But this story is not just about her journey; it is also about others' willingness to listen to her. How many people would rather go look for mustard seed for Kisa Gotami than listen to her lament the loss of her child?

This chapter will address the process of learning to be with people during their crises and listening to their laments, and teaching students to do the same. It will consider how the heart that is not at ease, in a state of being in "dis-ease,"[2] becomes transformed. How do we live in ease while at the same time experiencing the difficulties we face in life? In other words, how does Buddhism heal our heart? My focus here is on religious educators and their impact on students whose ministry is being with people experiencing loss and grief.

I will share from my own experience as a supervisor-in-training with the Clinical Pastoral Education Program. CPE is an educational program providing clinical educational methods to spiritual caregivers of all faiths to improve the quality of their ministry and pastoral care. The Association for Clinical Pastoral Education (ACPE) is an international organization that monitors the accreditation of CPE centers and the certification of supervisors.

How We Learn to Cope

Pain, sorrow, anger, despair, loneliness, and fear are experiences that arise in our lives. They emerge in times of crisis and continue long after, returning to us like waves that sometimes lap softly at the shores of our hearts and at other times fiercely pound us.

When we look back, we can see that how our families cope at times of crisis conditions us in our attempts to cope with crises. We might learn to "look on the bright side," "stop crying (or I'll give you something to cry about)," "just get over it," "keep on keepin' on," or "take an aspirin and go to bed." Our families may have instilled in us phrases such as "But we have so much to be grateful for," "If you just stay busy . . . ," "Be happy, they are in the Pure Land/heaven/with Mom and Dad," "This will build character," and "You'll be much stronger after this."[3]

Some of the coping behaviors we have learned include avoiding, medicating, managing, meditating, and seeking counsel and support. We learn what is acceptable and what works for us. That information becomes a blueprint, informing and guiding us as to how to respond when someone seeks our counsel and support in their crises.

For those choosing a lifestyle that brings them to be a part of another's crisis, hearing another's pain is their ministry. What is essential for those doing this work is the ability to heal the heart.

Mentoring and Learning

I believe that the extent to which we are able to be with others in their crisis and dis-ease is limited by how we are able to face and cope with our own adversity. I suggest that healing the heart must begin with oneself. Or stated another way, my ability to hear another is limited to my willingness to listen to myself.

The challenge of guiding others and of realizing the profound healing power of compassion is aptly captured in the following verses by the Chinese Pure Land master Shandao (613–81), cited by Shinran in the chapter on *shinjin* (true entrusting) in his central work, the *Kyōgyōshinshō (The True Teaching, Practice, and Realization)*:

> Extremely difficult is it to encounter an age in which the Buddha
>   appears,
> And difficult indeed for a person to realize the wisdom of *shinjin*.
> To come to hear the dharma rarely met with
> Is again among all things most difficult.
>
> To realize *shinjin* oneself and to guide others to *shinjin*
> Is among difficult things yet even more difficult.
> To awaken beings everywhere to great compassion
> Is truly to respond in gratitude to the Buddha's benevolence.[4]

Within these verses, I hear Shandao acknowledging how extraordinary it is for ordinary people with limitations to experience the Buddha's compassion. Even with that experience, how complicated it is to facilitate someone else's experience of the Buddha's compassion.

I am suggesting that what occurs between teacher and student can repeat itself in the relationship between student and patient. The converse is also true. What takes place between patient and student can repeat itself in the relationship between student and teacher. It is a chain reaction that can occur from the top down and from the bottom up. In essence, it is a systemic process that can have both negative and positive results. Because of this, it becomes important to monitor and assess the clinical relationship. Although I am referring to the clinical environment in this chapter, what I say can be applied to different environments. In the temple environment a parallel process can be explored in the relationships between a minister, parent/sangha member, and child, or between a board of directors, minister, and sangha member. The same process may also be explored in the home environment in the relationships between ancestor, parent, and child.

Grief and Loss

I view end-of-life care as one aspect of samsara, the continuous cycle of birth and death. In the story of Kisa Gotami, for example, the focus was not on the death of the child, but the experience of loss and grief felt by the mother. Death and dying are aspects of loss and grief. Caregivers struggle with their own mortality especially when they work with patients of their own age or younger or with patients suffering from diseases that have caused pain and death in their own families. Moreover, patients and their families share the difficulties they have had with past life events and losses. When we deal with another's loss and grief, our own experiences of loss and grief are called forth.

Supportive Statements

Several years ago I began to study the art of pastoral care as a chaplain in a nursing home, an addiction treatment center, as well as acute care environments such as hospitals. I have been a chaplain for the past four years. For the past three years I have worked concurrently as a supervisor-in-training who educates both ordained clergy and those planning on becoming either ordained clergy or certified chaplains in pastoral care. As a chaplain my focus has been to sit with those in dis-ease, listening to their laments, angers, worries, and pains. I assess their spiritual needs and offer the spiritual support they want and ask for. As an educator, my focus is to work with those who have dedicated their life to being with others in their grief and loss.

As I mentioned, my ability to listen to another is limited by my ability to listen to myself. Whenever I sit on my own issues that I do not want to face, I collude with that part of us all that refuses to speak the truth and seeks to avoid dis-ease. We help each other keep secrets from ourselves. Therefore, honesty is important in these exchanges. I facilitate and model for students how to be honest with themselves. I cannot educate without learning to sit with those in dis-ease, and I cannot sit with those in dis-ease until I have learned that I need to be willing to sit and accept my own dis-ease. I have relied on the buddha-dharma to continually heal my heart, as I continue to do this ministry.

In other words, according to this model, ministry is not merely about attending to others but requires self-ministry. Shinran modeled this with his follower Yuien by bringing himself into the latter's situation. The following dialogue was initiated by Yuien, who had doubts about his own understanding:

> "Although I say the *nembutsu*, the feeling of dancing with joy is faint within me, and I have no thought of wanting to go to the Pure Land quickly. How should it be [for a person of *nembutsu*]?"
>
> When I asked the Master this, he answered, "I, too, have had this question, and the same thought occurs to you, Yuien-bō!"[5]

I now offer my own experience and journey in how healing my heart has provided for me the impetus to work and minister to others.

My Experience

Leaving temple ministry was a difficult and painful process. I enjoyed many aspects of this type of ministry. Physically being in the temple and caring for the religious articles was nurturing for me. It was gratifying when people would connect with the buddha-dharma with "aha!" moments of intellectual understanding as well as "ahh" intuitive ones. I was honored to participate and officiate at sacred rites of passage. Despite this, however, there were circumstances in my situation that I felt prevented me from growing and developing spiritually. Although I tried to overcome these difficulties, I came to understand that I could not do this in the same environment where I was experiencing these difficulties. I was presented with the opportunity to explore chaplaincy and accepted a one-year residency at the Clinical Pastoral Education Program of the Portland Veterans Administration Hospital.

My hope at that time was that CPE would provide an environment where I would feel supported and nurtured; this would allow me to reflect on how I responded to situations in the broader clinical situation and also help me to integrate the buddha-dharma in my ministry. I was excited and grateful for the new environment, which stimulated me to grow and develop as a minister. Within a month a peer encouraged me to explore my grief about leaving temple ministry. I was not ready. I spoke only of my excitement and appreciation for the program. At the conclusion of my residency year I decided to enter supervisory training. There were no positions available in the Portland area so I pursued a position that required relocation. I was accepted as a supervisor-in-training in Redwood City, California. Accepting the position would mean living apart from Alan, my husband of eighteen years, and our dog, Botai.

Although many sacrifices have to be made to pursue a new course in life, it is not unusual for students to relocate for CPE residencies. Sometimes there is a change in their life that prompts them to enter chaplaincy and the training process or to seek other forms of ministry among CPE students and supervisors. What I did was not unique.

In helping me to make my decision, Alan, who is ever supportive of my career and religious growth, encouraged me to take the position. Once the decision was made I moved in with my brother and his family in San Jose, just a couple of miles from my parents and where I was raised. In the high-rent Bay Area, I was grateful for the hospitality and generosity of my brother and his wife. With my stipend I could still commute home to Portland every third weekend. So I was fortunate.

Although a colleague had suggested that I get in touch with my grief at having left temple ministry, I could not think about what I had lost when others were sacrificing so much for me. Yet, I was grieving many losses. This became apparent to me when I attended the religious services at the San Jose Buddhist Temple. I found myself in tears, hearing the chanting of the sutras and listening to the minister share the dharma message my first weekend in San Jose. I realized that I missed throwing my voice into the sangha to chant the sutras; I missed the community and my role within it, and I missed the temple. Of course I was also homesick for Alan, Botai, and my home. Despite all the symptoms of being in dis-ease, I chose to ignore this and focused all my energies on my new position and all that helped make it happen.

In my first year of supervisory training I was determined to be successful. I was grateful and lucky to be where I was, that "everything had fallen in place." Knowing there were those who were disappointed and even angered by my decision to leave temple ministry, proving I had made the right decision was important to me. I would not permit myself to acknowledge my losses or listen to my own grief. Needless to say, I encouraged my students to also express their excitement and gratitude for this new phase and venture in their life. Just as there are losses that accompany any new endeavor, my students had their share. I cannot say how they were experiencing grief. I did not hear it. I could not hear it.

In assessing the students' work, however, I became aware that they did not pick up on their patients' loss and grief. Their inclination to move the patient from "sad" to "happy" or "grateful" was too quick. They were impatient with expressions of sadness, anger, loneliness, and hopelessness. They were too quick to follow a patient's comment of appreciation for their care or support from family and friends. In essence, they were doing with their patients exactly what I was doing with them.

The situation with my students reminded me of my colleague's suggestion early in my career as a chaplain. I began to touch on my losses and grief. I made an effort to listen to myself as I spoke to my therapist and consulted with friends and colleagues. I admitted my loneliness, sadness, frustration, and anger. I acknowledged my losses and how I was impacted by my choices. I tended to my grief and gave voice to it.

I listened to the buddha-dharma and heard the compassionate voice of the Buddha through the sutras, chanting, and readings. Shandao's story of the traveler in "The Two Rivers and the White Path" became my story and brought me solace on my journey.[6] I sought community by participating in the activities at the San Jose temple and began *zazen* meditation practice with a People of Color group at the San Francisco Zen Center.

I began to notice the losses of my students and encouraged them to seek support with therapists, spiritual directors, friends, and peers. As they did, they became more sensitive to hearing patients talk about their losses and being with them in their grief.

Every choice comes with costs and benefits. When we only focus on the benefit, we lose half of the experience. It seems that Shin ministers in the United States, including myself, emphasize gratitude and appreciation to the detriment of lament, loss, grief, and anger—what are often considered negative emotions. How does one experience the boundless compassion of Amida as realized in the saying of the Name, Namu Amida Butsu, when there is such an imbalance? If there is an emphasis on Amida Butsu (Amida Buddha), then where is the experience of Namu (the practitioner as foolish being)?[7]

Four Noble Truths

The Four Noble Truths have been a guide and outline for healing my heart and have helped me to develop a way of working with patients and students. The Four Noble Truths can be paraphrased as follows:

The Truth of Dis-ease: acknowledgment and awareness that dis-ease is being experienced. In the language of the Buddha, the term *dukkha* is used, which refers to the hub of a wheel being off-center. What is off-center in the person's experience, or in other words, what is the dis-ease? Is it experiencing anxiety, anger, sadness, grief, and the like?

Truth of the Cause of Dis-ease: identification of the source, cause, or basis of the dis-ease. In sharing their personal histories, attitudes, values, and assumptions, people reveal life lessons, and family of origin messages.[8] The Buddha identified the major causes of dis-ease as the three poisons: greed, anger, and ignorance. The three poisons naturally arise and are part of the human condition and experience. Correspondingly, I understand them to be forces that impact a person's relationship with others. When people experience the dis-ease of greed, they are self-absorbed and use energy to pull things or people toward them. The actions they display are based on attachment. When anger arises, energy is used to push away; actions are based in aversion. If we are ignorant, or choose to ignore experience, we consume energy to remain distracted.

Shinran called these energies *blind passions* (Jpn. *bonnō*), because they are based on a misperception of reality. Blind passions inhibit or interfere with a person's ability to be aware of the compassionate, embracing nature of the Buddha in their life. Awareness, on the other hand, is experienced when the person becomes conscious of their motivations and energies through reflection and/or feedback from others.

Another cause of dis-ease is dualistic thinking: good–bad, right–wrong, me–you, birth–death. In this kind of polarized thinking there is a favoring of one side and a disregard or distrust of the other. This increases separation and alienation from others.

Although everyone has the capacity to experience all three poisons, the tendency is to prefer one more than the others. Understanding our dualistic way of thinking helps to clarify our preferred poison. Thus it is a matter not of elimination but of seeing clearly when we are stuck, and of taking action to realign the hubs in the wheels of our hearts, minds, and our very being.

Truth of the Extinction of Dis-ease: potentiality of future story. Buddhism is a religion of unlimited, infinite potential. Based on the Buddhist principle of attaining nirvana, ultimate repose, the Buddha taught that dis-ease could be extinguished. Because all beings have buddha-nature, they have the potential to re-center their wheel. "Nirvana" means to "blow out" and refers to eliminating the three poisons. Shin Buddhism interprets this to mean transformation rather than extinction. It focuses on the limitedness or finite state of human beings. In this state we are not able to extinguish blind passions, but these blind passions can be transformed; the experience of transformation is expressed by the phrase "blind passions are none other than (the source of) enlightenment" (Jpn. *bonnō soku bodai*). One seeks not the elimination of blind passions but their transformation into an essential component of enlightenment.

Transformation takes place by embracing the blind passions and karmic conditions of others and working with them, rather than trying to eliminate them. Transformation is movement from duality to oneness and unfolds when two conflicting and contrasting qualities become one experience. It is movement beyond duality toward potentiality and is experienced as a personal growth process.

Truth of the Way: methodology to move from dis-ease to peace. The Buddha outlined the Eightfold Path as a guide to identify what needs to be done, adjusted, changed, or accepted when dis-ease arises. The Eightfold Path (appropriate views, thoughts, speech, conduct, livelihood, effort, mindfulness, and meditation) directs a person to develop awareness of their senses and their internal and external relationships.[9] I use the Eightfold Path as a source of methods and aids to help the individual to expand into the fullness of their potential. Buddhism is about becoming a buddha, an awakened being, seeing oneself as one is. This means seeing oneself perfectly rather than becoming perfect. My experience in Buddhism, and particularly Shin Buddhism, is that there is an emphasis on awareness and being able to see oneself clearly.

Using the Four Noble Truths

I will now illustrate the process using the personal example I began this chapter with. Additionally, I will discuss how I work with students. My role is to partner with the other person to identify their dis-ease, become aware of the cause, imagine the possibilities and potential outline of their goals, and develop a methodology for personal and professional development.

The Truth of Dis-ease. In the autobiographical vignette recounted above, I initially avoided acknowledging my losses and facing my grief. At that point my dis-ease was avoidance, the poison ignorance. Eventually I acknowledged my grief. I identified the losses I was experiencing: not being in the temple and doing all the things that made ministry so important for me, being physically away from Alan and Botai, and not living in my own home. Of course, I was experiencing dis-ease before I was aware of it. In retrospect, I can identify how I was ambivalent. I was choosing to ignore my sadness and masked it with outward expressions of gratitude and excitement. Yet my sadness could not be consoled by appreciative thoughts or self-motivation. As time passed, the energy of swinging between sadness and gratitude became stronger. Because I knew some people were against or disappointed with my decision to leave temple ministry, I felt compelled to express excitement and to suppress my sadness. Needless to say, I could not begin to consider any anger that I had with regards to my decision.

The Truth of the Cause of Dis-ease. In consultation with friends and in therapy I shared my story and described how I found myself in my current situation. This process required me to explore, examine, and critique my journey and decisions. I explored the greed and anger that had been a part of my story. I saw how I blamed others and pushed them away, how I held on to beliefs or tried to pull people to take my side. It was humbling to see my role in all this.

In exploring our personal stories, our personal and spiritual journeys, we find the causes of dis-ease, causes from their family of origin, previous life experiences, and religious understanding. Students are asked to remember "what I learned in my family," what they promised themselves "if I ever find myself in this situation again," and what they were told to believe.

My students were avoiding addressing their own grief as well as that of their patients; I could see that they were avoiding their patients' grief, but I could not see their avoidance of their own because I was avoiding my own. Even though I was aware that my students were not addressing grief issues with their patients, I could not understand why. I was limited by my own dis-ease. As I began to identify and acknowledge my own grief, I began to hear the students' grief. As they began to hear their own grief, they were more willing to engage their patients' grief.

Students shared how they found their way, how they learned to cope in their families of origin, and how their attitudes, values, and assumptions developed. Their supervisor and peers encouraged them to hear themselves and gave them feedback regarding consistencies and inconsistencies with their personal past and their aspirations for ministry and pastoral care. When issues from their personal past needed to be worked through, they were often referred to individual counseling or psychotherapy so that they could address internal issues.

The Truth of the Extinction of Dis-ease. Embracing the blind passions and karmic conditions of self and others frees one to imagine a future story and to work toward the fulfillment of a new potential. Potentials and future stories are as individual as our personal pasts. Exploring such possibilities is not the same as exploring a predetermined set of solutions to predefined, objective problems.

In the experience I shared, exploring possibilities meant exploring emotions other than excitement and appreciation. It was scary. I began to explore my sadness and anger. My reaction was to think I had made the wrong decision. From my dualistic perspective I could be happy only if I had made the right decision, or sad only if I had made the wrong decision. Transformation came when I could feel both gratitude and grief, and accept both the benefits and consequences. I then understood that I would always miss many aspects of temple ministry. This grief is part of my future story. Embracing the whole of my experience became the experience of Namu Amida Butsu.

Working with students from different religious traditions means assisting them to incorporate their religious beliefs and understandings into their experience. I frequently ask students what their theology says about polarities, how they experience God's grace, whom they identify with in their scriptures, and how that informs them as ministers. Sometimes a student's understanding or experience of their theology will amplify their dis-ease. Then, it becomes necessary to return to the Truth of the Cause of Dis-ease.

Truth of the Way. Transformation does not mean elimination. It means an awareness of the potential to move from dis-ease to peace. The Eightfold Path of transformation harnesses sense experience as well as internal and external relationships. Through applying the Eightfold Path, I am able to explore what is "appropriate" for my grief at this time. I consider my perspective, thoughts, words, language, behavior, lifestyle, energy, mindfulness, and meditative practices. In addition to internal reflection, consultation with others about my experience helps me to monitor my ongoing dis-ease. Is how I am handling my grief appropriate or am I off-center, and are new forms of dis-ease arising?

In the CPE program students learn to develop clinical methods of learning that will support them after they complete the program. Addressing experiences of dis-ease will not prevent them from arising again. However, the tools they learn to use in the program will help them to address future problems more effectively.

Healing the Heart

The Four Noble Truths have provided a method for my interior work in facing my dis-ease. They have also enabled me to support my students in working with their dis-ease. It is not just the personal work that transforms our lives but also the interpersonal relationships.

> Extremely difficult is it to encounter an age in which a Buddha
>   appears,
> And difficult indeed for a person to realize the wisdom of *shinjin*.
> To come to hear the dharma rarely met with
> Is again among all things most difficult.
>
> To realize *shinjin* (true entrusting) oneself and to guide others to
>   *shinjin*
> Is among difficult things yet even more difficult.
> To awaken beings everywhere to great compassion
> Is truly to respond in gratitude to the Buddha's benevolence.

These words of Shandao impact me as I work with others, in relationships and community, both in an earthly sense and in a cosmic sense. To truly relate to another is to encounter each person, each being at the level of true entrusting, listening deeply to their suffering and joy, to my own suffering and joy. My work in the CPE program challenges me to be sincere in my experience of the buddha-dharma and to deepen and open my heart as I supervise students. I offer one last vignette about how Shandao's statement is a lesson about healing the heart, healing relationships, and building community.

The CPE academic year consists of four units. At the conclusion of each unit, students (and the supervisor-in-training) write final self-evaluations, and the supervisor writes a final evaluation for each student. For a variety of reasons I did not finish my final self-evaluation at the end of a unit. Because of my dis-ease of guilt and shame I began to avoid my supervisor. The cause of my dis-ease was my self-expectation. Finally, I could avoid her no longer and so confessed what she already knew, that I had not yet finished my evaluation. She responded by saying, "You've been busy." I was touched by her compassion. She opened up another way of seeing the reality of the situation as I explored the appropriateness of my dis-ease. I *had been* busy, busy coming to grips with my inner life.

A few weeks later a student had a personal crisis. She sobbed out her story filled with self-blame, shame, and failure as a mother. "You need to go home," I said. Her response, "I can do that?" indicated that she had not expected compassion, compassion that truly helped her.

I know that, had my supervisor had been rigid with me, I would have found it more difficult to be compassionate with my student. How difficult it is to offer a compassionate heart if it has not been modeled for us, if we ourselves have not received it. My heart was healed by the compassion of my supervisor, and my student's heart was also healed my mine. I trust that this student will be able to listen with more compassion when a patient expresses feelings of guilt, shame, and failure in a family crisis. My heart was also healed by offering compassion to my student. This is what it means to respond in gratitude to the Buddha's benevolence.

12

Shin Buddhist Ministry: Working with Issues of Death and Dying

SEIGEN H. YAMAOKA

As a Shin Buddhist minister in America, one of the critical issues that I face is how to work with those who are confronted by the reality of death and dying. When I first faced this issue, I tried to find some guidance within the context of my studies but found it lacking.

The difficulty arose because there was no systematic pastoral tradition or education within Shin Buddhism (Jōdo Shinshū) during the early stages of my ministry. This is somewhat ironic given the deeply pastoral nature of the life of Shinran, the founding figure of the Shin tradition, which is lay oriented. Due to its historical roots, pastoral care, especially with regards to death and dying, has been integral to the work of Shin ministers down through the centuries. There are, however, some doctrinal and institutional reasons why the pastoral tradition has not been fully articulated.

As Shin grew into one of the largest sects of Japanese Buddhism, at Honganji, the center of institutional power, there was an increasing focus on theological issues concerning doctrinal orthodoxy, and the importance of pastoral care receded even as it was integral to the work of the ministers. The aspiration to "awaken all beings," a basic theme of Mahāyāna Buddhism generally and a clearly pastoral mission, is also central to Shin as articulated by Shinran. However, this dimension eventually faded into the background and became subsumed under the doctrine of other-power *(tariki)*, whereby faith or true entrusting in the other-power of Amida Buddha tended to absorb all other concerns. This in turn had a negative effect on Shin ministry, and there arose a gap between dharma and person.

This became a particular problem for Shin ministers in the West. In the Japanese context, pastoral care evolved organically even if it was not always adequately addressed institutionally. However, the same practices could not be applied in the Western context, and there was not a sufficiently developed official program either. As Shin Buddhism spreads in the West, there is an increasing need to formulate and articulate an appropriate approach to pastoral care. I have been working on a program called the Six Aspects in order to help Shin ministers formulate an approach that can work in the Western context. Drawing on three case studies to illustrate the application of the Six Aspects, this paper focuses on Shin pastoral care in relation to issues of death and dying.

Core Issue

As a Shin Buddhist minister within the Western context, I was at a loss in working with members facing critical matters of illness, suffering, and death. If we are to follow the absolute doctrinal position that everything is due to other-power, what is the role of a Shin Buddhist minister in a pastoral care situation? No doubt the central doctrine of other-power is well grounded, but how does a minister work with the numerous critical issues of those who are facing the reality of death?

Shinran himself understood that there were two approaches to the Buddhist teachings. First is the one vehicle path *(ichjōdō)* of "sudden awakening" *(tongyō)* wherein the all-embracing compassion of Amida Buddha is realized all at once in the saying of the Name, Namu Amida Butsu. Second is the "gradual process" *(zengyō)* which means to teach depending on the capacity of the practitioner. From the perspective of Shin Buddhism, the former is the focus of doctrinal studies *(kyōgaku)*, based on Shinran's words identifying the *Larger Sutra of Eternal Life* as "the ultimate teaching of the one vehicle."[1] The latter reflects the practical spirit of Shinran as found in the *Kyōgyōshinshō (The True Teaching, Practice, and Realization)*, which can be said to have a pastoral and educational approach. With the above in mind, I would like to relate one example based on the second approach.

Case Study 1: Sachiko[2]

Sachiko was a wife and mother of four. She was a devout Buddhist, a dharma school (Buddhist Sunday school) teacher for twenty years who was very active in her temple. One day she took a physical examination and was told she had cancer. She asked the extent of her illness. The doctor was surprised at her strength and openness.

I went to see her in the early stages of her cancer. She commented how grateful she was to be a Buddhist because the teaching of impermanence made it easier for her to accept her situation. At that time I mentioned the emotional ups and downs that she would face. As her illness progressed, and the possibility of death neared, her initial resolve faltered, and she said, "I don't know what to do! I don't want to die! I am afraid! Please help me!" Her first question to me was, "Please tell me what *shinjin* is, what true entrusting means." I responded, "Entrust yourself to the pure mind of Amida's wisdom and compassion, just as you are, and experience the sense of utmost gratitude."

Shinjin, the core realization of religious awareness in Shin Buddhism, has sometimes been rendered as "faith." However, "true entrusting" represents the etymological and philosophical meaning more accurately. The practitioner entrusts herself to Amida's other-power, so called because the power is "other than ego" and Amida is the infinite light of the deepest truest self. Insofar as *shinjin* is the power of Amida Buddha embracing the Shin follower, true entrusting ultimately comes from Amida. Being embraced by Amida, the Shin Buddhist is able to entrust herself to Amida as her deepest reality. Released from the confines of the rigid ego, gratitude naturally arises in the heart of religious awareness.

In continuing our conversation Sachiko asked, "What happened to my *shinjin?* Why can't I feel gratitude? Why is this happening to me? What did I do?" I replied, "Sachiko, it is too late for whys and whats. The answer is already clear!"

She thought for a moment, and with great strength and composure said, "It's all so simple. I guess I lost the feeling of gratitude because I became attached to living and hoped that things would go well. I became so obsessed that I lost sight of the truth of my life. My life is not a life full of questions; it is based on a simple fact. I have cancer, and I will die. Even the question of *shinjin* is not a question. Embracing me just as I am, the wisdom and compassion of Amida constantly works to reawaken me to the joys of gratitude. It is the only way I can live with meaning. It is all so simple." And she cried softly.

A transformation occurred, but as to its depth I could not know. As a Shin Buddhist minister, I was given the privilege of knowing Sachiko, sharing that moment and also learning of the inconceivable way in which the dharma works. Sachiko passed away after a few months, but I heard wonderful stories about how she made life meaningful for her family and friends. In her short life of true entrusting, she became a dharma light, showing the reality of the truth of life in its hardship, pain, and suffering, but also the beauty of a life transformed, which became the source of comfort and truth for those she left behind. She lived the life of gratitude in *nembutsu*, the saying of the Name of Amida, Namu Amida Butsu, and shared it with all who came near.

Her final note to family and friends read, "They've all done so much. After all these wonderful gifts of life what more can there be? Friends! Friends scattered far and wide all over who have shown their concern. My true-blue friends, thanks so much. There is no more that can be said, but done is done. *Arigatō*, thank you in deepest gratitude. Namu Amida Butsu. May peace, harmony, and love be with you always."

Discussion

The approach that I took as a Shin minister might not be considered proper from a psychological perspective. As a minister, however, I am often faced with critical life-and-death issues. At such a time, how does one respond? With Sachiko, for example, I could have gone into the description of Amida's Pure Land or the doctrinal meaning of the Eighteenth Vow, the central vow of Amida's forty-eight vows made while still a bodhisattva. But Sachiko was not asking about abstract doctrines. I tried to respond to her concretely, to her need. The Shin Buddhist life that she had led but temporarily lost came back to her in full force. What happened in that singular moment?

A Shin Buddhist minister is a fellow follower of the way as well as a religious teacher who will provide answers and guidance for the patient. At the same time, the minister is a fellow seeker. In this light the minister must reflect on the innermost question that he (or she) has. That is, if he faces the instantaneous life-and-death moment, what is it that is desired, how does one find meaning in life? The truthful or honest response of the teacher is required in that moment. Thus, when the patient asks the question, it is mirrored within the innermost heart of the minister as a fellow seeker, and the response comes forth as the minister's words. It is as if the patient's question draws out the response in a unique, uncontrived moment, both patient and minister being embraced in the compassion of the Buddha.

Based on such experiences as a Shin Buddhist minister, I began to wonder how the transformation came about within the context of Shinran's thought. Thus, I began the task of putting together something I call MAP (Meaning and Process), at the core of which lie the Six Aspects discussed below; I wanted to see for myself how the dharma and person become one. It is an educational tool to see how the dharma moves and works within the life process of a person. Before getting into the specifics, however, we need to see how Shin Buddhist pastoral ministry evolved within the context of Shinran's teaching, following that of the historical Buddha.

Śākyamuni Buddha, Shinran, and the Development of Pastoral Ministry

Śākyamuni Buddha taught the truth that all things are dependently originated or interrelated in a constant process of change or impermanence. The Mahāyāna philosopher Nāgārjuna expressed this in terms of emptiness (Skt. śūnyatā) as the reality of life, embodied in the awakened one as wisdom and compassion. Wisdom shines as the light enabling us to see the totality of interrelationships that we are in, and the life of compassion enables us to find meaning even though interrelationships are constantly changing. Śākyamuni had great concern for the householder who could not engage in monastic practices such as intensive meditation or renunciation.

The *Larger Sutra of Eternal Life,* a key Pure Land scripture of early Mahāyāna, expresses the way of Amida Buddha. "Amida" is a transliteration of the Sanskrit *Amitābha* and *Amitāyus,* meaning respectively "infinite light-wisdom" and "infinite life-compassion." Amida is the Buddha of Wisdom-Light and Compassion-Life, manifesting enlightenment itself. Shinran identifies the Buddhist concept of emptiness as having two aspects, dharmakāya-as-suchness and dharmakāya-as-compassion.[3] Dharmakāya-as-suchness is none other than emptiness and has neither color nor form; thus the mind cannot grasp it nor words describe it. From this oneness was manifested form, called dharmakāya-as-compassion or Amida Buddha, emptiness as the activity of compassion.[4] Realizing the complexity of the human life process, Shinran focuses on the dynamic movement of dharmakāya-as-compassion. Realizing that householders do not have the capacity to directly understand or experience dharmakāya-as-suchness in their lives, Shinran states, "In order to make us realize that the true Buddhahood is without form, it is expressly called Amida Buddha."[5] How is the house-holder connected to Amida? The householder, caught in the web of foolish attachment, is nevertheless able to hear the call of reality, emptiness, Amida, and thereby entrust in the Name of Amida. This is the great compassionate work of Amida, who calls to all householders to awaken to *shinjin,* true entrusting. To hear the Name as the embodiment of Amida's other-power is the key. *Shinjin* is the critical door through which the dharma constantly enters the householder's life, and it is also the door through which the house-holder can enter the true experience of life and of the self. It is that moment which brings together the dharma and the person as one.

Householders' lives tend to be fraught with the anxiety of being trapped in the ego. As Jack Engler says, "When I take myself to be that separate, ongoing 'entity residing within,' that singular self with which I identify so profoundly, any realization of that self's inherent emptiness as a represen-tation, a moment-to-moment construction only, can only be profoundly disturbing."[6] The other side of the coin of the seeming vacuum of empti-ness turns out to be the profound oneness of life. The Buddha's teaching is based on the dynamic movement of wisdom and compassion coming through him or her to awaken all beings to this profound connection; this is the essence of Buddhism.

Recently, I spoke to another woman who was dying of cancer. She said, "I know I am dying, and I am not afraid. I am so happy that I have the opportunity to express my gratitude to my family. *Sensei* (dear teacher), life is so simple, but we make it so complicated." In Shinran's terms she was able to see and experience the full simplicity of life coming down to an expres-sion of gratitude to everything that made her life possible. The polar events of life and death merged into the single profound feeling of the meaning of life as gratitude. Her transformation was made possible by the very thing that she initially wanted to avoid, her own death.

Rennyo, the second great teacher in the Shin tradition, points out that "rather than pouring the water [of enlightenment] into the basket [of the ego]," one should "put the basket in the water."[7] In this way, Shinran's focus is on the working of Great Compassion *(daihi),* which awakens householders bound to their karmic influences and who do not have the capacity to elim-inate their passions and desires by their own efforts. For the householder, the task is not one of "transcending worldly experiences but rather one of finding a wiser way of living within it."[8] Because of some of the issues discussed above,

Shin Buddhism, nurtured in the Asian context, needs to be clarified for the context of the West.

Again, taking a cue from Engler, for Shin Buddhists in the West, "there is a need to reclaim and develop a healthy sense of self and self-esteem, a capacity for intimacy, and a creative way to live in a world with full commitment cannot and should not be separated from Western spiritual practice."[9] Yet this represents a great challenge, as such a self may not easily blend with the Shin teachings of self-effacement and simple gratitude.

Working with people suffering in various stages of cancer, I noticed a transformation occurring in patients who went from the dire depths of agonizing suffering to a sense of spiritual peace in the realistic knowledge of what they were facing. What made the transformation possible in the death and dying experience? How did patients go from despair to a sense of grateful peace, despite the life-and-death situation facing them?

The challenge for me as a Shin Buddhist minister was to develop some framework within which we can see the whole picture of the relationship of the dharma and the person as one within the Western context.[10] I was able to share with each of the cancer patients their emotional turmoil. It meant the end of everything that they held dear. In that process there is the uncertainty of approaching death, physical and mental pain, and the question of "Why me?" The mind is filled with anxiety. At times there is the lament regarding one's misfortune, depression in the realization that no one can help, and the pain of being alone. There is fear, anger, frustration, and desperation in the aloneness of that moment when one is overwhelmed with the fear and finality of a life seemingly devoid of meaning.

Yet, in that very moment of meaninglessness and powerlessness of the self, I saw a transformation occurring in many patients. In that instant, it is as if that person encounters a word or a thought that resonates in his or her mind. The patient deeply reflects and feels that they are not alone. They realize that many support them. The unhappiness they previously felt turns to happiness, and they begin to express their thankfulness to all those around them. Their lives are transformed into happiness, and they come to realize the value of life. At that point they come to realize the meaning of life. As Engler states, "The point is to loosen the anxious grip we have on ourselves and initiate the mourning and grief work that will finally allow life and experience to flow unimpeded by maladaptive fixations about who 'I' am."[11]

I saw this happening time and time again as I worked with cancer patients. There is a transformation from the depths of self-despair and the fear of death to one of not fearing death and finding the meaning of life for whatever time is left.

As a Shin Buddhist minister, I felt a need to understand the process that evolves within the context of Shin Buddhism. How can we systematically articulate the dynamic movement of the dharma in the human life process that leads to the coming together of the dharma and person in the moment of transformation?

Six Aspects

In attempting to work out the process I began with the focal point of Shin Buddhism, which is *shinjin*. In Shin Buddhism *shinjin*, or true entrusting, is the critical reference point that unifies dharma and person. Drawing upon the experience of cancer patients, we worked out what we call the Six Aspects of *shinjin:* (1) an expansion of life into its deeper dimensions, which occurs as the teachings open up to us and permeate our lives, leads to (2) self-reflection in the light of (3) Amida's Great Compassion and gives rise to (4) great joy and (5) gratitude, ultimately leading to (6) a life of spiritual growth and meaning in the awareness of interdependence and interrelation—a life of *shinjin* and *nembutsu*. Here the Six Aspects are presented in a linear fashion, but it can work from any one of the aspects as the starting point. All six are nothing more than the content of the singular experience of *shinjin*.

In terms of Shinran's thought, the Six Aspects can be understood as follows:

Expansion. In the "Chapter on True Teaching" of the *Kyōgyōshinshō*, Shinran states, "Amida raised the unsurpassed Vow and opened wide the dharma-store."[12] "To open wide the dharma-store" means that the teaching of Great Compassion permeates the universe to awaken all beings, and flows into every pore of suffering.

Self-Reflection. Shinran's depth of self-reflection within Great Compassion can be found in the *Shōzōmatsu Wasan* (Hymns on the Three Ages) when he says, "How shameless and unrepentant I am."[13] Also, in the "Chapter on True Faith" he writes, "Truly, I know. Sad is it that I, Gutoku Ran, sunk in the vast sea of lust and lost in the great mountain of fame and profit, do not rejoice in joining the group of the Rightly Established State. . . .

What shame! What sorrow!"[14] This sense of shame is not self-punishing; rather, it unfolds in the illumination of limitless compassion.

Great Compassion. In the chapter "Practice" in the *Kyōgyōshinshō*,[15] Shinran says that the saving action of all beings originates from the Seventeenth Vow, which guarantees that all Buddhas of the ten quarters shall praise Amida's Name. Thus, Shinran calls it the Vow of Great Compassion.[16] This is a way of expressing the unifying power of compassion.

Great Joy. In the chapter "True Faith" Shinran says, "As I contemplate the True Serene Faith, there is the one thought in the Serene Faith. One thought reveals the moment of the awakened Serene Faith, and it expresses the great and inconceivable Joyful Mind."[17] This is based on the *Larger Sutra* section on the fulfillment of the Primal Vow, which says, "If all sentient beings, hearing the Name, . . . have joy in Faith," they will realize the land of true fulfillment. Yet he also says in the chapter "Transformed Buddha and Land," "What a joy it is that I place my mind in the soil of the Buddha's Universal Vow and I let my thoughts flow in the sea of the Inconceivable Dharma. I deeply acknowledge the Tathāgata's Compassion and sincerely appreciate the master's benevolence in instructing me."[18] These ideas together express the coming together of the finite mind of the practitioner and the nurturing embrace of infinite compassion.

Gratitude. In the *Shōshinge* (Gathas on True Entrusting), Shinran states, "When the continuant Faith in Amida's Primal Vow is awakened, in that very instant we spontaneously enter the Truly Assured State. Uttering the Tathāgata's Name always, we should express our gratitude for the Great Compassionate Vow."[19]

Life of Growth and Meaning. The *Larger Sutra* in essence reveals the life of spiritual growth for the householders. Even though they are caught in the bonds of human existence, they will attain birth in the Pure Land through the endowed *shinjin*. For this reason Shinran calls this sutra the "ultimate teaching of the One Vehicle."[20]

The Six Aspects describe not only the working of *shinjin* but also all of the content, context, and function of the dharma's movement to enlighten sentient beings. With the inclusion of the Six Aspects, we can see how the dharma through *shinjin* awakens us or connects us to enlightenment, wisdom and compassion, Amida Buddha, and Śākyamuni Buddha; and how Great Compassion dynamically works to awaken us to the truth of our lives.

How is the householder connected to Amida? According to the *Larger*

Sutra, Śākyamuni said to entrust oneself to the Name of Amida and say his Name. In the world of the householders, a name identifies any important relationship that they may have. Therefore, the Buddha urges the entrusting of the self to the Name of Amida. But, what is the human condition in which the Name is heard and has meaning? How does *shinjin* or Amida's Great Compassion work in the householder's life?

Three Conditions in the Human Life Process

Elsewhere, I have delineated Six Characteristics of human life in addition to the Six Aspects outlined above.[21] Together, these characteristics and aspects provide a fuller view of life processes that become especially concentrated at the time of death and dying. Here, however, I would like to focus on three conditions that precipitate the religious search that becomes most intense as one nears death: (1) polar events in life, (2) karmic influences, and (3) personal and spiritual shortcomings. These conditions lead one to recognize the limits of one's ability to achieve happiness through the relative, finite terms of human desire. This recognition, in turn, opens up the possibility of going beyond our preconceived notions about life and fulfillment.

Polar Events in Life. Our lives contain challenges of negotiating such polar opposites as life–death, happiness–sorrow, success–failure, victory–defeat, gain–loss. At any one time we may be grappling with several of these polarities, making life complex. Since everything is always in flux and in interrelation, we cannot rest easy in dealing with any of these polarities; they constantly shift from one extreme to the other. Thus we are caught in the constant struggle to find meaning in change. We try to make permanent that which is impermanent. We suffer because we are caught in situations that are difficult to understand. Rather than seeking permanence in an inherently impermanent world, we can find a more effective basis for our lives by coming to understand the patterns—both binding and liberating—of the flow of karmic circumstances. Problems arise most often when we fail to see how our actions have been shaped by binding karmic patterns of behavior.

Karmic Influences. Our life experience is influenced by both what we inherit from the past and how we act. When we look deeply into our own karma, we see more clearly the scope of our own lives and actions. Karmic influences include all our past and present attitudes, perceptions, tendencies, prejudices, hopes, fears, and habits, which constantly shift and change as they give rise to our actions. Shinran identified his own personal karmic life as "karmic evils and blind passions;"[22] he took ultimate responsibility for the karma of all beings as inextricably intertwined with his own.

Shortcomings. In reflecting on the outcome of our actions, our karmic circumstances, we inevitably become aware of our shortcomings as finite beings. We make selections as to what is desirable, important, and significant for us personally at every moment; these choices are necessarily tainted by self-centeredness, no matter how noble they may seem in a relative sense. There is attachment to that which is self-satisfying and a casting off of other possibilities. Therefore, when we are forced to determine which of the extreme poles to select, we choose life over death, happiness over sorrow, victory over defeat, and success over failure. We make moral and ethical judgments regarding events and situations affecting us. This in turn causes us to become caught up in the question of our own self-worth. Because we want life to fit our preconceived picture of it and it never quite does, we cause pain and suffering for ourselves and those around us.

The usual meaning in life that we find is temporary. Depending on circumstances, events, and conditions, it can be turned upside down. The turmoil often comes from the very areas that we have tried to negate or eliminate—death, sorrow, failure, and defeat. This is the struggle within the self that causes its own suffering and pain. We try to maintain the measure of self-worth that we have arbitrarily decided for ourselves. If we fail we may resign ourselves to an inability do anything, or we may struggle to the point of hopelessness after attacking everything in sight. Yet, this very struggle and failure can become the entry point into an educational process that leads to realizing a greater wholeness and a release from continual fragmentation.

The problem with the human condition is that we are heavily influenced by our karmic past and its ego-centered trajectory. Thus, we struggle with the issue of attachment, ignorant of potential meanings, and attempt to rationalize our needs and wants. We lose sight of our true nature in a constantly changing world and seek to make permanent our pleasurable experiences, possessions, views, and beliefs. Unfortunately, we all experience defeat, failure, evil, material loss, illness, sorrow, and countless other conditions that diminish our happiness and meaning in life, and ultimately we all experience death. We live in a constant cycle of hope turning to disillusionment, happiness to sorrow, success into failure, and so on. It is precisely this human experience with its karmic limitations, however, that is the necessary ground of enlightenment and the dynamic working of wisdom and compassion, understood by Shinran as Amida's Great Compassion. In *shinjin*, there is self-reflection within Great Compassion that bestows on us great joy, gratitude, and a life of meaning and growth. Through *shinjin* we are given the opportunity to experience life not only from the perspective of our own ego and desires but also from the perspective of living within the Great Compassion of Amida Buddha. This does not mean that our karmic influences are erased. We must still live with happiness and sorrow, life and death, and so on, but the fundamental difference will be that through endowed *shinjin* we will find meaning in life and death, happiness and sorrow, and the like.

When we become mired in ego-centered thinking, we often go around in circles, unaware that we are trapped in a prison of the mind's own creation. There is no way for us to break out of that situation or work toward growth and deepening meaning. Yet, the wisdom and compassion of Amida enable a person to realize how we have created our own karmic hell and simultaneously release us into a sustaining web of interrelationship. This becomes our life of *shinjin/nembutsu*, the ultimate life of meaning for the householder Buddhist, unfolding in the midst of manifold karmic influences.

Case Study 2: Ken

As a Shin Buddhist minister in the Buddhist Churches of America, I have been privileged to share the lives of many wonderful people who struggled to find meaning as they faced death. In working with them, I noticed a distinctive process that could benefit all of us in understanding the Shin Buddhist way of life.

Ken was examined by a doctor who told him that he had cancer. He was devastated by the news. The cancer progressed despite treatment, and he went into a severe depression. When he entered the hospital, he constantly yelled at the doctors and nurses. He vented his anger at them, which made his stay in the hospital unpleasant for all concerned. He even vented his anger at his family.

"No one cares about me!" was a theme that frequently punctuated his conversation.

I was approached by his younger brother to see if there was anything that could be done to help Ken. I was asked to talk to him and perhaps help him accept the reality of his situation.

When I visited Ken at the hospital, I was greeted with a sarcastic, "What are you doing here? If you are here to talk about religion, Amida Buddha, *nembutsu*, I don't want to hear it. Religion is worthless!"

I listened to him and tried to calm him down. His voice was getting louder and louder. I tried to explain that he was in the hospital and that he should have consideration for the other patients. He told me to leave because I did not understand what he was going through. I left with a promise to return.

His anger grew worse, and his loved ones, friends, and nurses found it difficult to work with and visit him. My second visit was no better than the first. In fact, it was worse. He began with verbal abuse.

"I don't want to see you! Go home! You can't do anything for me. You are worthless!"

I tried to calm him down by telling him that I would like to help. This made him even angrier. He screamed, "If you want to help me, tell me what I want to hear! Can you do that?"

I sensed that he wanted me to affirm something, which was very dear to him, that is, his life. I asked, "You want me to tell you that you will not die. Is that it?"

"Yes, can you do that?" he asked.

"I cannot," I replied.

"See, you are worthless. You can't help me! No one can. I am all alone. No one cares," he yelled.

Stunned, I fell silent, but then something came to my mind. It was something he had told me about his mother quite a while ago. I replied, "There is someone who cares. She is no longer living, but she was always concerned about you. You told me that she always worried about you, but you, being a bad son, never listened to what she had to say. She cares for you even now. It's your mother."

Ken became silent for the first time. He was in deep thought. Slowly, he began to speak as if to himself.

"Yes, she always worried about me. I was not a good son, but she never stopped worrying about me." He expressed his gratitude to her and deeply felt that even though she was not living, her concern for him was still there. Through his mother's love, he began to be freed from his own self-centered thoughts and found himself being expanded to self-reflection within Great

Compassion. His transformation was brought about by a moment of other-centered reflection free from his own attachments.

Ken thanked me and asked me to leave so that he could think about his own feelings.

From that day on, Ken changed. He began to express his appreciation to the doctors, nurses, friends, and family. People were shocked to see how his relationship with others changed.

My role in this process was merely a facilitator of spiritual growth. Unlike monastic traditions in which the teacher or master is regarded as the equivalent of the Buddha, in the Shin tradition, much of a minister's work involves simply being with the person in need. Yet, by bringing the teachings to the attention of a person like Ken, when karmic conditions ripen, great changes can take place although very little may have been done in an overt sense. Without being conscious of it, Ken had greatly benefited from the deep spiritual life of his religious community and his family, in particular his mother. Now, in his moment of greatest need, all of these positive karmic influences were triggered and brought to life.

Discussion

As time went on, Ken's illness continued to get worse. Yet, from that experience of recalling his mother, he seemed to go beyond the mother and began to express his life in terms of Amida's Great Compassion. He began to utter the *nembutsu* of gratitude, saying Namu Amida Butsu spontaneously. Ken passed away in this feeling of oneness with Amida. How was this remarkable transformation possible? Is there something that we can learn from Ken's experience or any experience that a person undergoes? What is there in human life that interrelates with the wisdom and compassion of Amida? What is the content of *shinjin* that interrelates with the human life process?

Ken had sought to find the meaning of life in success, winning, and the self-satisfaction that came through his own efforts. However, when he encountered his approaching death, everything changed. His self-centered thoughts, filled with attachment, led him to lash out, hoping against hope that this might prolong his life. He wanted to deny the death he feared. He was afraid to accept death because it meant that everything that he had worked for would vanish. More important, he was afraid of what would happen to him, and he was unsure who he was. He lashed out at everyone. In anger and fear, he attacked those around him because he was hurting. He felt terribly alone. In ignorance of his impermanence in an ever-changing world, goaded by his karmic influences, an angry fear overcame him. In desperation he clung to his anger in hopes of finding answers to his loneliness. He was trapped in his own karmic evil and blind passion.

When his mother was mentioned, however, it was as if a warm light was turned on and broke through the hard, cold shell of his own making. He encountered the loving warmth of his mother's memory coming into his life of stark desperation and found himself basking in her embrace. Because of this loving warmth, he was able to entrust himself to the love that she exemplified. Enveloped in her love, he reflected on its ultimate depths and further expanded to self-reflection within Great Compassion. He saw himself as a son who continually disappointed his mother. A sense of unworthiness flooded his mind. Yet, he felt her warmth, and he was no longer alone. Following the words of Shinran, he reflected, "How shameless a person am I and without a heart of truth and sincerity, but because [the power of] the Name is transferred by Amida, its virtues pervade the ten directions."[23] He felt great joy and gratitude. From that point on, despite the reality of his impending death, he found a life of meaning and growth.

Despite this spiritual transformation, being human, he continued to have his ups and downs. At times he lapsed into anger, but after a personal bout with self-pity he commented with deep conviction, "It's my karma." With that realization he continued on. He could not control his ups and downs. Nevertheless, he found himself in the greater world of the religious life. As his awareness deepened, his ups and downs affected him less. They became like waves on the surface of the ocean that are embraced by and dissolve back into the deep flow. In the language of Shin Buddhism, this is the great ocean of Amida's boundless compassion. As we learn to entrust ourselves to the ocean's warm embrace, we realize that the true entrusting or *shinjin* endowed to us by the ocean itself is the causal key to our realization of our spiritual birth in Amida's Pure Land of enlightenment.

Case Study 3: Alexander

Alexander, twelve years old, passed away after over two and a half years of battling cancer. Alexander was kind, considerate, and loving despite his personal struggle. His parents and two brothers supported him through all of his ups and downs. Beyond all of this, there was something special about Alexander.

Late one evening, I checked my e-mail and found a short note from Dora that said, "Sensei, Alexander is asking about dying and what it is like to die. Can you come and speak to him?"

I went the following morning. Our conversation was awkward in the beginning because it was hard to bring up the subject. But his mother, who held nothing back, opened it up. Alexander asked, "Sensei, what's it like to die?"

"Alexander," I said, "in Buddhism we talk about life and death as a natural process, but death is not a subject we can know completely. Death is a truth that all of us experience, but no one knows when or how it will happen. In a sense, we have no control over death or dying. Rather than worrying and fearing something you cannot control, isn't there something that you can control and take charge of?"

Alexander thought for a moment and said, "My Life right now! I will take charge of my life and every moment that I can!" In that moment, it seems, Alexander merged the polar events of life and death into one. He did not fear death. Instead he used it as a catalyst to live meaningfully within the time frame that he had. In that moment, it is as if his life was expanded and self-reflection took place within Great Compassion. Death became a compassionate friend that helped him direct his life with a deep feeling of gratitude to all around him. Again, my own role was minimal, like that of a midwife to Alexander's spiritual birth. One cannot overestimate the positive influence of spiritual traditions surrounding temple and family and handed down through the generations. With very little coaxing, Alexander instinctually found his way.

"There will be times when you are not feeling well; when that happens, tell your parents. Help them to help you. At other times, when things are not going well, a doctor may give you the choice of trying something new. You will be asked to make a choice. It may help you, but it may not. If you choose to try, it may not work for you. But it may help others."

Alexander nodded in agreement.

His mother wasn't quite sure if Alexander really understood, so she asked, "Alexander, do you know what sensei is telling you?"

"I know, Mom. I can't waste time worrying about something that I can't control; death will come when it comes. I know that I'm alive now, so I have to concentrate on that alone," Alexander replied.

"I heard that you wanted to sleep in bed with your parents so that you would not be alone if you should die in your sleep," I said. "That's okay, but if you thank everyone before you go to sleep, then you will know you took care of everything and won't feel uncertain. We feel uncertain because we didn't take care of the important things."

"That's a good idea, I'll do that," said Alexander.

At eleven years of age, Alexander took charge of his life as he knew it. He did not fear death or dying. His heart and mind were open to everything he experienced. He lived with gratitude and found peace of mind and heart. During his last two and a half years he created a lifetime of memories for himself and for those around him. He learned from heartaches and the pains as well as joys and laughter. His heart was open and filled with love for his parents, brothers, and all who came to know him.

Once Alexander said, " I want to go to the Buddhist church and say *Namu Amida Butsu.* I miss going to church."

After many ups and downs, he came to church on October 28, 2001. It happened to be Halloween party day at our Dharma School. It would be the last service he could attend. During the service I saw his smiling face as he sat next to his parents. When the service was concluded I greeted the students as they left the temple, as I have always done. Alexander whizzed by me without saying hello. I called out, "Alexander!" He stopped, came back, gave me a short hug, and went downstairs. He was anxious to take part in the party. He took part in everything. It was amazing. He truly enjoyed that day.

He loved the church, and knowing this, the family felt that his last service would be at church, surrounding by family, friends, and, most important, Amida Buddha. We will all miss Alexander, but we are grateful for the great lesson of life and death that he left with each of us. His life was short, but he taught many of us the true meaning of life.

Discussion

In the beginning, I am sure, Alexander had great difficulty in dealing with the challenge of death. But he had to face up to his cancer in order to start with his treatments. He wanted to live no matter what.

It was not easy; the ups and downs were huge. The medication made him sick, and he could not keep down his food. No one can know the suffering that he was going through. Through it all he remained positive. He felt that he was sustained by the unseen interrelationships in his life. He was appreciative of any help, concern, and love that he received, even though he was going through hell. He always encouraged and expressed concern for those around him.

He was aware of death in his battle for life; eventually, he realized that things were not going well, and he was afraid to die. In my conversation with him at that critical time of his life, he chose not to fear death but rather to work with what he had. He decided to live to the fullest for himself and also those around him.

What struck me most were the bedtime conversations that he had with his mother. In her letter of appreciation to our church members she recalled those special moments. "Every night," she wrote, "we would go through this ritual of telling each other how much we loved each other. I would tell him that I loved him all the way around the world and back. He would tell me that he loved me all the way around the universe (or to infinity) and back. Then, we would laugh and snuggle together and go to sleep happy." Alexander's words still echo in her heart and give her the strength to continue with her life.

It seemed to me, after the simple discussion that Alexander and I had, that he was living out the Six Aspects (see terms in *italics* that follow). He *reflected* deeply within *Great Compassion* and thereby experienced *expansion* to realize *great joy, gratitude,* and a *life of meaning and growth.* Within the short life that he had left, he lived with Great Compassion and gave meaning to all those around him, so that they too could face life's challenges courageously.

In my own counseling sessions, the Six Aspects help me to see the overall picture of the workings of dharma. In Shin Buddhism it is clear that the self-in-interrelation unfolds in the light of the deep truth of life and death. It is only through the working of Great Compassion that our finite lives are expanded to encompass and affirm all dimensions of life: youth and old age, highs and lows, music, drama, stories, death—and the meaning that they constitute in our lives.

At present, we are introducing this unfolding process of understanding to our dharma school teachers so that they can be creative in teaching their students and in their own development as human beings.

As a Shin Buddhist minister working with death and dying, it was imperative for me to see the content, context, and function of how the dharma and the person become interrelated. Only then can we begin to understand what each person must go through to find meaning in life and meet its challenges. In the Western context, I am constantly challenged to be creative and speak to the needs of our people. The pastoral area is a critical one, but equally important is an educational process that supports pastoral work. Working with one person at a time may be slow, but it can bring about the realization of the inconceivable and dynamic work of wisdom and compassion, embodied as Amida.

13

A Buddhist Perspective on Death and Compassion: End-of-Life Care in Japanese Pure Land Buddhism

NABESHIMA NAOKI

Caring for the sick is no different from caring for oneself.
—ŚĀKYAMUNI BUDDHA

As both favorable and adverse causes are not fruitless, we can all meet as
friends in the same Buddha's Pure Land.
—HŌNEN

WHEN ONE GOES THROUGH the final separation from loved ones or
has a presentiment of one's own death, one realizes the preciousness
of life. But how should one deal with the suffering and wishes of others, of
patients confronting their deaths, or the sadness of their families? Recalling the Latin phrase *memento mori*, Buddhism also teaches that one should
always live in awareness of death, as seen in the Zen expression "live at the
moment of great death" *(taishi ichiban)*, or the Pure Land admonishment
to realize "the essential matter of the afterlife" *(goshō no ichidaiji)*. When
we think about the end of life, we naturally seek to find out the meaning
of life.

Kamei Katsuichirō (1907–66), who studied the history of Japanese spirituality, had this to say about the significance of contemplating death:

> In our everyday lives, even between friends or husband and wife, we
> often hate each other, fight, and do not always live peacefully. Love
> always comes hand in hand with jealousy or hateful feelings. However,
> when loved ones or friends die, how do we feel about them? We usu-
> ally forget our hateful feelings for them or their shortcomings in every-
> day life, and each one of their traits turns into cherished memories.
> We may rethink our past experiences with them, even quarrels. In

death, for the first time we realize the significance of a person's many aspirations, actions, and works. A person's death tells his or her life completely. Through death, it becomes clear what kind of a person he or she was, and we shed tears of love. But if there is one kind of love that we might call the most profound love in this world, it is this: While we feel deep love for a person who has died, if we can feel that kind of love for the person while he or she is still alive, that must be the most profound love.[1]

In this way, death provides us with an opportunity to reflect on the meaning of our own lives and to realize true kindness and compassion. This chapter examines death and dying in Japanese Pure Land Buddhism, in particular the relationship between end-of-life care and the cultivation of heart and mind in Shin Buddhism. The chapter begins with an overview of recent developments in end-of-life care including hospices and a Buddhist program called Vihara Care. It then provides historical background on death and dying in Pure Land Buddhism. Next it explores current practices in the light of some case studies.

Recent Developments in End-of-Life Care

Though the media always reports dramatic instances of death, in recent decades, especially since the 1970s, the Japanese have tended to increasingly put off thinking about their own deaths or the death of loved ones. At least three changes lie in the background of this transformation of Japanese consciousness about death.

First, in 2002 the life expectancy of the Japanese rose to seventy-eight for men and eighty-five for women, making Japan the country with the longest life expectancy in the world. This change is due to declining mortality rates of newborns and patients with acute illness.[2] Second, the nuclear family has taken firm root in Japanese society, displacing the extended family, and more people live separately from their parents and grandparents.[3] Third, 80 percent of people are now expected to die in the hospital.[4] This contrasts to the 1950s, when 90 percent of Japanese died in their own homes.

Because people die not in their own houses but in hospitals or care centers for senior citizens, there are few opportunities to encounter the process of death in an everyday setting. In the twenty-first century, with the expansion of nuclear families in which both husband and wife work, the younger generations of Japanese have lost the luxury of caring for their own family members, whether young children, the elderly, or the sick.

Hospice and Palliative Care in Japan

In response to the aging of the population, Japanese interest in hospice care has been growing each year. Efforts to start hospice care began in the early 1980s. In 1990 the Ministry of Health and Welfare certified the hospice program led by Kashiwagi Tetsuo at Yodogawa Christian Hospital in Osaka as a palliative care facility, as well as the hospice care facilities started by Drs. Hara Yoshio and Chihara Satoshi at Seirei Mikatagahara Hospital in Hamamatsu and Tsuboi Hospital in Fukushima.

According to the National Council of Hospice and Palliative Care Facilities, as of June 2003 in Japan there are 117 facilities with 2,229 beds certified as palliative care facilities. The National Council of Hospice and Palliative Care Facilities explains hospice care as follows:

> We consider it important that all members of the hospice staff understand your situation and share it with you. We assist you in alleviating your physical pain and reducing your psychological anxieties, we aid in your everyday life, and also provide assistance to your family members who share the pain with you. Together as a team, in discussion with you and your family, we consider how to support you so that you may live just as you wish within your limited time. Hospice care provides assistance to each person to live out their life just as they wish.[5]

Hospices in their early development were considered to be facilities for patients who had given up on medical treatment and simply waited for a peaceful death. For many Japanese patients and their families, the practice of hospice care was not easily acceptable. However, gradually, hospice care came to be understood as a program for supporting patients to live as normally as possible until the last moment of their lives by providing holistic remedies to alleviate pain and, on a case-by-case basis, medical treatment. As a result, the necessity of palliative care is beginning to be recognized by patients and their families.

Buddhist Vihara Care in Japan

In accordance with hospice care in Japan, Buddhists started modern Vihara Care. The Sanskrit word *vihāra* means "temple" or "monastery," as well as "peace of body and mind," and "an infirmary, a place for practicing asceticism and resting." The concept of Vihara Care is based on the Buddhist view of life, of interdependence, in which one realizes that one supports one's own life but also that one's life is supported by all living beings and things in the universe. All beings and all things are mutually connected beyond time and space. The sense of interdependence brings people to critically reflect on their egotism and engenders compassion for all other beings. Through the realization of interdependence, Buddhists have found a way to approach people's sorrows and sufferings.

The modern Vihara movement, initiated by Tamiya Masashi in 1984, was created through the teamwork of specialists in Buddhism, medical care, and social welfare. Learning from the spirit of Christian care, the Vihara movement was established through the creation of "end-of-life care facilities with a Buddhist background."

The first Vihara Care program in Japan was established in 1993 as the Vihara Care Unit, a twenty-two-bed facility in Nagaoka Nishi Hospital. The ideals of the unit are as follows:

1. This is a place for people who have been told that they do not have long to live, so that they may reflect upon themselves quietly and be watched and cared for.
2. It is a place in which care and medical treatment are given primarily according to the wishes of the patients themselves. For this reason it is necessary that the Vihara be directly connected with a medical facility where complete medical services are available.
3. It is a small community founded upon the Buddhist teaching in which people who have realized the preciousness of life have gathered together. (However, patients and their families are free to hold any religious beliefs.)

This ideal of Vihara Care, in response to the universal problems of birth, aging, sickness, and death, conforms to the wish of Buddhists to act responsibly together with medical and social welfare specialists.

In 1987 Jōdo Shinshū Hongwanji-ha released the following statement about the Vihara movement:

This Vihara movement is created by Buddhists through the teamwork of specialists in Buddhism, medical care, and social welfare, so that people who seek assistance will not to be left by themselves, and so that we may empathize with their anxieties and alleviate their suffering even a small amount. We ourselves also aspire to develop a mindful relationship that transcends death by viewing suffering and sorrow as a chance to reflect on the meaning of our own lives. The Vihara movement is a holistic system of care provided to those who embrace the suffering and sorrow of "birth, aging, sickness, and death" and is a community of people who realize the preciousness of human life.[6]

Since the 1980s, similar Vihara movements have been established by various Buddhist denominations, including the Jōdo-shu, Sōtō-shū, Rinzai-shū, Tendai-shū, Shingon-shū, and Nichiren-shū, providing care at hospitals and nursing homes.

Vihara Care starts by communicating with patients and their families with love and respect and sincerely listening to their voices. It is a movement that aims to link people's hearts and minds beyond the suffering of death. Participants in the Vihara listen to patients and their families to understand their thoughts on the meaning of death and dying, love and care of others, and the meaning of their own lives.

Hospice care or palliative care aims to care for and support patients and their families with compassion until the patient dies. Vihara care shares this same goal but also seeks to care for and support bereaved families during their grief after a loved one's death. The Vihara movement aims to link grieving people with deceased loved ones through memories even after death.

The History of Death and Dying in Japanese Pure Land Buddhism

Interdependence, or in Buddhist doctrine, interdependent co-origination (engi), means that all beings depend on one another to live, but also that death is dependent upon life, and life is dependent on death. Buddhism aspires to peace among all living beings and aims for mature human growth, with the understanding that death is inevitable. Accepting the inevitable does not mean that one simply gives up. Illness, for example, is neither to be cured by magic or divination, nor simply given up on as fate. Buddhists understand that diseases are to be diagnosed by medical doctors and hope to alleviate them by appropriate medical treatment.

Śākyamuni Buddha and Caring for Others

In the Buddhist scriptures, the Buddha is often referred as the "Great Excellent Physician" and "Great Doctor King." The teaching of the Buddha is likened to medicine that relieves our suffering and brings peace to body and mind. In this spirit of healing, monks were taught to care for one another:

> The Buddha told the monks, "Since the time you all became monks, we have all been equal friends, just as water and milk mix together. However, we have not cared for each other when we are sick. From now on, we shall help each other when we are sick. If a sick monk does not have a disciple to care for him, other monks should take turns to watch him. This is because there is no more blissful practice than the care of the sick. Caring for the sick is no different from caring for oneself."[7]

Buddhism teaches that one who cares for a sick person, without consciously intending it, learns the importance of life from the sick person through that act of one's caring.

Since the time of the early Buddhism in India down through the development of the Pure Land teaching in China and Japan, Buddhists have provided compassionate care for the sick as an integral component of their cultivation of the path of the buddha-dharma.

Genshin and Death Bed Rituals

In tenth-century Japan the Buddhist monk Genshin (942–1017) wrote the *Essentials for Attaining Birth (Ōjōyōshū)* and established Pure Land Buddhist care for death and dying. Following methods for caring for the sick prescribed in Chinese Pure Land texts from the fifth century, many Buddhists aspired to attain birth in the Pure Land, a world of ideal practice and awakening. The first movement of methodical care for the dying in Japan was the fraternity of the Twenty-five Samadhi *(Nijūgozanmai-e)* at Shuryōgon Temple at Mt. Hiei based on Genshin's *Essentials.*[8]

Genshin begins with an apocryphal reference to practices during the time of the historical Buddha. According to him, there is a practice that originated at the Jeta Grove monastery in India; many people visited the "Imperma-nence Hall" there, but only a few came back. In this hall, the sick person single-mindedly contemplated the buddha-dharma. The statue of Amida Buddha faced the sick person, and to the statue's left hand was tied a five-colored long banner that reached the floor. The sick person was given the other end of the banner, which he or she held while aspiring to be born in Amida Buddha's Land of Bliss. The nursing attendants burnt incense and scattered flowers to adorn the room of the sick person. They were also there to clean up the sick person's feces, urine, vomit, and saliva. It is said that Genshin himself died while holding a cord of five-colored threads that would be used to pull him into Amida's Pure Land. The number twenty-five refers to a gathering of twenty-five monks who supported one another through illness and death.

Noteworthy in this account is the way that people care for one another through providing group support, attending to the physical needs of the ill and dying, and establishing a contemplative environment and ritual setting to ease the hearts and minds of those about to depart. In the *Essentials for Attaining Birth*, Genshin goes on to cite the section on "Entering the med-itation hall and the method of caring for the sick" from Shandao's *Method of Contemplation on Amida Buddha (Kannen bōmon):*[9]

1. When you are about to die, whether due to illness or not, follow the method of the *samādhi* for recollecting the Buddha.

2. Turn your face to the west, and, with concentrated mind, focus your thought on Amida Buddha. Harmonizing both your mental and oral acts, recite (the Name) uninterruptedly, and resolutely think of attaining birth in the Pure Land and of the bodhisattvas sitting on lotus-daises coming to receive you.

3. If the sick person feels that the Buddha's coming is close at hand, he should relate his psychological state, and the attendant should record his story.

4. If the sick person cannot speak, the attendant should question him about what kind of phenomena he has seen.

5. If he tells of visions of karmic evil or hell, the attendant should himself recite the Name [of Amida Buddha] and repent in order to help the sick man repent, to help clean away his karmic evils. If the karmic evils have been extinguished, he may see the sages on

lotus-daises appear before him. At that time, record his psychological state as prescribed above.

6. When the aspirant's relatives and kinsmen come to nurse him, do let not those who have drunk wine or eaten meat or any of the five pungent foods (leek, onion, garlic, shallot, and ginger) enter (the room). If such a person comes alone to go to the sick man's bedside, the sick man may lose his tranquillity of mind, be confounded by spirits, and, after having died in a state of madness, fall into the three evil realms.

7. *Nembutsu* reciters attending the sick person should consider themselves to be just like the sick person, uphold the Buddha's teachings, and perform the causal practice for seeing the Buddha [namely, chanting the Name, Namu Amida Butsu].

As one nears death, it is common to be overwhelmed by fearful or disturbing thoughts, images, and feelings. From early on, Buddhists understood that the opportunity to share one's fears and openly confess matters hidden in one's heart could provide great mental, emotional, and even physical relief. Furthermore, as noted above, the practices surrounding death could just as well make life more meaningful for everyone's daily life.

Hōnen and the Rejection of Ritualized Practice

In the twelfth century, during the Kamakura period, collections of stories of birth in the Pure Land *(ōjōden)* were compiled, and the practice of deathbed rituals became very popular. However, there were people who paid too much attention to the form of practice and peaceful death, and, in extreme cases, some chose to end their own lives dramatically by self-immolation or drowning. The Pure Land Buddhist monk Hōnen (1133–1212), who lived during this difficult period in history, was not concerned with the form of practice, although he respected the practice of deathbed rituals.[10] Hōnen proposed that no matter how one died, one could attain birth in the Pure Land simply by reciting the name of Amida Buddha in everyday life, which insured that Buddha would come to welcome you at the moment of death:

In the teachings of our virtuous predecessors, at the moment of one's death, one should place a statue of Amida Buddha by the western wall in the room, lay the sick person facing to the west, and a good spiritual friend *(zenchishiki)* should encourage him to recite the name of Amida Buddha. This is certainly the ideal situation. However, the occasion of one's death does not always proceed the way one hopes it would, and you never know when you may suddenly drop dead in the middle of the street. You may even die on the toilet. Because of unavoidable karmic causes, one may be slain by the sword, burned to death, or drawn. There are many who have lost their lives like that. However, whatever happens to you, if you recite the name of Amida Buddha daily and aspire to be born to the Pure Land, at the moment of your last breath, Amida Buddha, Avalokiteśvara Bodhisattva, and Mahāsthāmaprāpta Bodhisattva will appear to welcome you. You must believe in this teaching.[11]

This exposition shows that while Hōnen was well aware of the reality of death, he believed—in contrast to his contemporaries—that, no matter how one dies, if one recites the name of Amida Buddha daily, one will be welcomed by the Buddha.

In fact, Hōnen faced his own death without holding the five-colored strings described by Genshin. "Again, his disciples tied the five-colored strings to the hand of the Buddha and counseled him (Hōnen) to hold them. But he did not take the strings and said, 'That is the protocol for ordinary people. It does not necessarily apply to me,' and he would not take them."[12] Hōnen also said: "As both favorable and adverse causes are not fruitless, we can all meet as friends in the same Buddha's Pure Land."[13] This means, no matter how we die, there are no meaningless deaths. Certainly, we will all become equal in Amida Buddha's Pure Land. Though death is sorrowful, it is also venerable.

Hōnen's understanding thus differs from Genshin's understanding of the meaning of Amida Buddha's welcoming. Genshin's understanding was that the Buddha's welcoming will happen after the dying person's mind is tranquilly settled with right mindfulness at the moment of death. Hōnen taught that if one simply recites the Name daily, Amida Buddha will appear at the moment of one's death, and then naturally one will settle in true mindfulness and attain birth in the Pure Land. Traditionally, the Pure Land was described as a jeweled paradise, and practitioners engaged in elaborate practices to visualize it. For Hōnen, however, the Pure Land is the flow of oneness that permeates everything, although most people fail to recognize this while alive: "Even if one is able to see the jeweled trees [of the Pure Land], they could not be more beautiful than the blossoms and fruit of plum and peach trees [found in this world]."[14]

Shinran's Perspectives on Death and Compassion

The Pure Land priest Shinran (1173–1262) received and accepted Hōnen's teaching, but he also had his own interpretation. Shinran said this about the death of his follower Kakushin-bō: "Regarding Kakushin-bō, I was deeply saddened by his death, but also felt great esteem for him, for he never deviated from *shinjin* (true entrusting). . . . At the point of death he uttered Namu Amida Butsu, Namu Mugekō Nyorai, Namu Fukashigikō Nyorai (Tathāgata of light that surpasses understanding), and putting his hands together, quietly met his end."[15] This letter expresses how Shinran embraced the reality of death both in its sadness and its sublimity. Kakushin-bō, who met his death while reciting the *nembutsu* with gratitude, demonstrates the significance of the *nembutsu* practice.

Shinran, who often wrote letters to those facing the end, wrote about his own imminent death in this way: "My life has now reached the fullness of its years. It is certain that I will go to birth in the Pure Land before you, so without fail I will await you there."[16] This letter shows Shinran's belief that death is not the end of life, because it means one will be born in the Pure Land (of oneness beyond life and death). That is, the Pure Land is a realm in which we can meet people who have been separated from us by death ("meeting together in one place" [*kue isshō*]) in the samadhi of the Buddha's boundless compassion. To give people an answer that goes beyond life and death, Shinran used terms like the "Land of Peace and Bliss" (Annyō) and the "Land of Immeasurable Light"; he taught that death is not necessarily an unhappy occasion, and that the place beyond death is filled with the light of the Buddha's oneness.

What enabled Shinran to be so certain about the afterlife was his realization of oneness beyond all distinctions in the present moment of life: "The practicer of true *shinjin*, however, abides in the stage of the truly settled, for he or she has already been grasped [by the hand of compassion], never to be abandoned. There is no need to wait in anticipation for the moment of death, no need to rely on Amida's coming."[17] In fact, one cannot be certain about the future moment of death. People die under all kinds of circumstances such as famine or epidemics, common occurrences in medieval Japanese society. One may die a peaceful or agonizing death due to circumstances beyond one's control. Thus, he accepted death as filled with pain and sadness as well as a wonderful occasion:[18]

> It is saddening that so many people, both young and old, men and women, have died this year and last. But the Tathāgata taught the truth of life's impermanence for us fully, so you must not be distressed by it.
>
> I, for my own part, attach no significance to the condition, good or bad, of people in their final moments. People in whom *shinjin* is determined do not doubt, and so abide among the truly settled. For this reason their end also—even for those ignorant and foolish and lacking in wisdom—is a happy one.
>
> You have been explaining to people that one attains birth through the Tathāgata's working; it is in no way otherwise.[19]

Here, Shinran demonstrates that by reciting the *nembutsu* and entrusting and following Amida's Vow, which is beyond human calculation, one's birth in the Pure Land is settled. According to Shinran, one's birth is not determined by the state of mind of the person at the moment of death. Rather one goes to birth in the Pure Land by the working of the Tathāgata, the unfolding of reality as such *(shinnyo;* Skt. *tathatā).*

Ultimately, as approaching death forces one to release the ego's illusory grip on life, one is inevitably enveloped by compassion. Thus, according to Shinran, the Buddha also embraces those sentient beings who cannot accept the reality of death: "Truly, how powerful our blind passions are! But though we feel reluctant to part from this world, at the moment our karmic bonds to this Saha world run out and helplessly we die, we shall go to that land. Amida pities especially the person who has no thought of wanting to go to the Pure Land quickly. Reflecting on this, we feel the Great Vow of great compassion to be all the more trustworthy and realize that our birth is settled."[20]

Accepting death is very difficult for most of us. But that is fine. Without lying to oneself, still holding on to the anxieties and loneliness that remain until the moment of death, one can be saved by the Buddha. This is because the Buddha embraces precisely those who are in the depths of delusion, and his compassion penetrates the body and mind of delusion.

No matter how well you prepare for the final moments, no matter how hard you try to discipline your own mind, there is no guarantee that you will meet a peaceful death. Therefore, Shinran taught not to recite the *nembutsu* with our own calculations at the moment of death, and not to anticipate the welcoming of the Buddha. Instead, he recommended that one trust in and rely on the unfailing compassion of Amida Buddha in the present moment, here and now. In fact, by letting go of future expectations and fears and concentrating on the present, one actually maximizes the possibility that, when the end does come, one will be fully prepared. This is because the Pure Land cannot be realized apart from the present moment, whose depths go beyond life and death. That is the path to "attain birth in the Pure Land by becoming a foolish being."[21]

But even "birth" or realization of the Pure Land is not the ultimate goal. Rather, one immediately returns to this world to help other suffering beings as a bodhisattva, to guide people out of delusion into enlightenment. This is termed the "thought of the directing of virtue in the returning aspect" *(gensō ekō)* that expresses the great compassion and the working of the Buddha continuing beyond death. "Whether one is left behind or goes before, it is surely a sorrowful thing to be parted by death. But the one who first attains nirvana vows without fail to save those who were close to him first and leads those with whom he has been karmically bound, his relatives, and his friends."[22]

A loved one who has passed away becomes a guide for other family members. Shinran's wish was that *nembutsu* practicers live in both aspects of the journey to the Pure Land, going and returning, and that they realize Amida Buddha's liberating power so that all beings become teachers and disciples, mothers and fathers, brothers and sisters, in the flow of Life beyond life and death.

Case Studies: Stories of Life and Death on the Pure Land Path

According to reports by the World Health Organization, terminal patients have physical, mental, social, and spiritual pain, and their sufferings from these kinds of pain are related one another.[23] Here spiritual pain is sometimes also termed existential pain, referring to "patients' efforts to seek the meaning of life and to reflect on the significance of their own existence when facing their own death. They may repent past sins or express gratitude to people who have cared for them, or for life itself. They may seek reconciliation with family or friends. In their suffering, they seek spiritual ease through God's love or the Buddha's compassion."

As Sawada Aiko, who has been promoting palliative care in Japan, says, "Dying people, without exception, are seeking for truly human encounters and relationships. In front of them, false friendships or self-centered relationships fall through. Only true relationships can survive for them."[24]

Case 1. Letter from a Dying Father

The following letter written by a male patient to his son provides a glimpse into the human mind facing death and contemplating family relationships.

> When people face the inescapable reality of death, what do you think they will do? Some people may become depressed and cry all day long. Some may lose the power to live.[25]
>
> But your father [the letter's author] did not think like that at all. I wanted to extend my life as long as possible so I could have more time to live with you, your sister, and your mother. Everyone, at some time and in some place, has to realize something. What is needed for that realization is not superficial niceness, but recognizing everything that is true, even things that are really tough. That's what I think. And I wanted you to know that, too.
>
> I am wondering when are you going to read this letter. I am sure it won't be long now. And you will read this as my last letter to you. I decided to give this letter to your sister. I am sure she will keep her promise and keep this letter in a safe place until the time comes.
>
> Whenever I think that my death might ruin your future dreams, it stabs my heart. Please forgive me. But I will do my best to extend my life to live with you whom I love most. I hope you'll see that your father is fighting the best fight of his life. And whenever you face difficulties in your life, please remember that my blood also runs in your body.
>
> I just peeked at your sleeping faces. I really wanted to see them because this could be the last opportunity to do so. Please forgive me for sneaking in, but you looked so beautiful.
>
> When I looked at you, I understood how much I love you. And I also understand why I am not afraid of the reality that I may die. I love you so much that I do not worry about my own life. And I also feel that you love me as much as I love you.

Now I know, it is not because of courage that people can overcome death. It is because of the unfolding compassion and the truth that they love someone. When they feel that they are loved by someone, all fear disappears. Some day, you will understand this, too.

I had hoped to stay longer, but I need to get ready for my trip. I need to prepare for my last fight. So I will finish my letter now. But before I finish, I have one last thing I need to tell you. Perhaps you are not ready for this, but I need to tell you because you are a man. Please take good care of your sister and your mother.

Your father loves you all from the bottom of his heart.

Good-bye.
Father

As expressed in this letter, people who are very close to death often seek to have sincere, truthful relationships. For patients in the terminal stages of illness, when they discover that they love someone and realize that someone also loves them, this relationship can give them the strength to live longer. Acceptance of death is not their goal. Their aspiration is to live with their loved ones as best as they can within their limited time.

Human beings have the capacity to grow through suffering. Mahāyāna Buddhism teaches that "blind passions are none other than enlightenment" *(bonnō soku bodai)* and "samsara is [in its depths] nirvana" *(shōji soku nehan);* consequently, it is possible for human beings to find the meaning of their lives in suffering. Embraced by the Buddha's compassion, one's blind passions are transformed into the truth of enlightenment. In this sense, what is needed when attending to a dying person is both an easing of the patient's pain and an understanding of the hopes and truths that patients may discover through their suffering.

Generally, those who are aware of their own deaths have three aspirations. The first is the extension of everyday life. Patients wish for the easing of their physical pain and improvement of their condition even a little bit so they can continue living their modest everyday life. For example, they hope to be able to talk about their memories, and reaffirm with their family that they have had a good time. They want to stay in their own room in their own house, eat in their own dining room with their family, get out of the hospital to take a walk on the street as they used to. They would like to do something good for family or children, even the giving of small gifts. These aspirations may not seem grand, but most patients, through their experience of sickness, become aware of the preciousness of ordinary everyday life.

The second aspiration is for the "existence of their wishes." People facing death hold on to open-ended dreams or aspirations to the very end. In that sense, it is desirable that family members or relatives who attend to them make sure to accept their love and aspirations. If those who attend the patient can tell him or her, "I promise to carry out your wishes as best as I can," the bond between them may even transcend death.

Third is the "hope for reunion." A hope that arises within dying patients is to be reunited with people they love. Though they recognize that in reality they cannot meet again in this life, patients nevertheless hope to meet the people they love again in the hereafter. The important thing is that this wish to meet again implies a transformation in the quality of human hope. That is, instead of wishing for this-worldly achievements like honor or wealth, they seek for true love beyond death.

Śākyamuni Buddha, when his death was drawing near, said this to his disciples: "No one can avoid the reality of death. The truth of impermanence is absolute. However, what is dying is this, my physical body. It is supposed to decay eventually. The true life, however, is the timeless dharma I have discovered and taught you. If people realize this, and practice according to the teaching, then I am living. That is eternal life."[26]

In Pure Land Buddhism, it is taught that even people separated by death can meet again in the Pure Land, and that the deceased will become a buddha who guides the surviving family and friends. The real feeling that the loved one will continue to live in people's hearts and even physical effects (home, photographs, gifts) eases the loneliness of the patient and links the hearts and bodies of patient and family together.

Death opens a new perspective on infinite life as a realm that transcends everyday life. Finite life is the impermanent and irreplaceable life possessed by each one of us. However, by realizing the limitations of this finite life, we can discover the infinite life that is not subject to death.

Case 2. Suzuki Akiko:
After the Notification of My Cancer

Suzuki Akiko was the director of a preschool affiliated with a Buddhist temple. When she was notified that she had cancer, at first she was horrified and could not accept the reality. But, guided by her father, she realized that she was "a person who cannot be replaced by any other." She passed away at the age of forty-seven. Two months before her death, Suzuki Akiko presented her four children with the following poem.

> Now
> I,
> My husband,
> My children,
> In this living room
> Are talking and
> Laughing.
> It is a scene we have repeated here thousands of times but
> Now, it is very strange
> By tomorrow
> It may be destroyed
> So I want to hold on to it and never let go.[27]

This poem, titled "Now," demonstrates how it is precious for patients to spend their everyday life with their family. We can see that Akiko wishes to have "an extension of her everydayness." Here is another poem she composed for her children:

> Do not try to be a step ahead of everyone
> In this vain and impermanent world
> My children
> Please do not spend your lives
> No matter how far you go
> There will be no satisfaction
> Do not compete
> Do not compare
> Do not be envious
> Do not lament
> Do not belittle yourself
> Please let your own flowers bloom
> You are yourself and that is enough
> Just like the rose in the garden
> Just like the pine tree in the garden

Please let the flowers of your human accomplishment bloom
True satisfaction arises there[28]

This poem, titled "Satisfaction," expresses Suzuki's wishes as the mother of her children, wishes that are illuminated by her own self-reflection:

> I can only think of myself as having lived selfishly, but now since death has not come suddenly, I find I am given an opportunity to reflect upon my life and death, and I am very grateful that I was given this illness called cancer.[29]
>
> Sometimes I hear whispering voices that say, "you do not need to have an operation at this stage," or "you won't need to have to go through such a painful experience ever again." But as a mother facing terminal care treatment, this is a life I cannot throw away. I have come to believe that to continue to live in the preciousness of each day's life is the most meaningful way to live, and that there truly is nothing better.
>
> Simply guided by Namu Amida Butsu . . .[30]

To die peacefully was not her main concern. Rather, it was to live each day in the awareness of the preciousness of each moment.

Case 3. Hirano Keiko: Thank You, My Children

Hirano Keiko was the mother of three children, the wife of a Buddhist minister, and herself a devout Buddhist. In the winter of her thirty-ninth year while she was preparing for the New Year service at her temple, she was suddenly struck by a severe abdominal pain and discharged a significant amount of blood. She realized that she had a very serious illness. Bursting into tears, she thought, "This reality before me is not a dream or an illusion. This is an unmistakable reality and I cannot walk away from it. I have to look straight ahead and deal with it."[31] After learning that she had cancer, she thought about what she could possibly give her three children. Just before her death, she wrote to them,

> When I think about the terrible sadness and pain that my illness and eventually my death will bring to you, I can't forgive myself and I can only cry. But there is nothing I can do. Even though I am sick, the only

thing I can give to you is being your "mom" until the moment I die.

While I am still strong, I can make your meals and do the laundry and as much as possible just be a normal mother. And when I can't move, I'll ask for your help, and when I am in pain, I'll just suffer the pain. That is the best that I can do for you. And then, perhaps, death will be the last gift that I can give to you.

In life there is not a single thing that is a waste. Even my illness, even my death, should not be a waste or a loss to you. In sadness and pain, there is always hidden something that is just as unpleasant, and something that is much more happy and joyful. Children, please don't forget that.

For example, at that time, even when you are so sad that you can't take it anymore, at some point it will turn into happiness. Please don't forget that there is a world that you can know only by going through such deep sadness and pain. And please realize that there is a great place that supports you when you are sad or suffering. That is the wish from your mother's heart.

Thank you for being born as my children. Thank you, thank you, and thank you![32]

Although understanding the inevitability of death, she nevertheless wished to continue her everyday life, and even in her sadness she showed gratitude to her family. She also wrote that "even in great sadness deep happiness is hidden," revealing to her children the wondrous truth that springs from adversity.

Finally, before her death, she sent this letter to her children:

Yukino-chan, I am waiting for you in the Pure Land! When you have ended your precious life and thrown off your body of heavy karma, you and I will both become the wind and run around the mountainside. Maybe we can even shake the tree branches and sing together with the birds. . . .

I was born from the "limitless" world, and I will return to it because the "limitless" world is the "home of life" for all living things, and for your mom it is the only home to return to. I always think, when this life I have been given as "Hirano Keiko" has ended, I will joyously go back to the "home of my life." And I will become the air and dance in the sky. I will become the wind and run through the fields with you. I will become the green grass and trees and comfort you. I will become beautiful flowers and make you happy. And I will become water and run in the rivers, and become waves in the ocean and frolic with you. Sometimes I will be a fish, sometimes a bird, sometimes rain, and sometimes the snow.

"The limitless is life" means that it is a world of limitless aspiration. And all living things can only live by being supported by that deep "aspiration of life." That's why I have been near you all this time until now. Sad times, bitter times, happy times, whenever, all you have to do is listen. You'll be able to hear my voice. "Please live, please live." My hopes for you, my encouragement, will reach to the bottom of your heart.[33]

Her love for her children was without bounds, a pure love that transcended even death. The bonds of parent and child that transcend death expressed for her the path of the *nembutsu*, the Pure Land Way. She understood that the Pure Land is the true home of all beings, the limitless world. No one lives alone; all beings live by supporting one other. She realized this truth in facing death. Perhaps that is why she said that after her death her life would become one with the life of nature, become a limitless life, and that she would always live together with her children. Herein is expressed the view of life based on dependent co-origination, the core of Buddhist spirituality.

Approaches for Attending to the Dying

The most important thing in attending to dying patients is to be present, in the here and now, and to listen to the patient in an accepting, nonjudgmental manner. Based on Buddhist understanding, there are at least eight dimensions to this attending in the here and now.

Sharing the Truth of Impermanence

It is important to share the reality of the impermanence with patients, their families, and the medical staff. When they all share this truth together, they are able to have true conversations with each other. The concept of informed consent has finally taken root in Japan. By knowing the truth about their illnesses and talking openly about their true feelings, both patients and their families can relieve burdens from their minds.

Alleviating Pain in a Holistic Way

Reducing physical pain is more important than anything else. Unceasing pain can damage the mind of a patient. Patients usually feel more pain during the night than the day. By easing their physical pain, their psychological, social, and spiritual pains are often reduced as well. However, patients' physical pain is also a natural sign of trouble in the body. Nursing attendants should also not forget that there are some patients whose spiritual strength is firmly established even though they continue to have physical pain.

Assisting in the "Completion of Life"

Even when patients say they want to die, it is necessary to contemplate thoroughly the meaning behind their words. Statements like "I want to die" sometimes are simply expressions of other feelings, such as "I do not want to be a burden any longer" or "I do not like the situation I am in right now." It may also be a way of expressing the opposite feeling: that they want to live. The feelings or emotions of patients can change depending on the circumstances or their relationships with others. It is necessary for caregivers to know what the patients are hoping for.

On February 18, 2004, the Forum on Biomedical Ethics of the Japanese Association of Medical Doctors issued guidelines titled "Medical Practices and Biomedical Ethics." According to the guidelines, which were based on Buddhist attitudes toward life, medical doctors should adopt the following manner of responding to death and dying:

> When the fight with death is over, it is necessary to make efforts to assist patients to complete their lives in better circumstances, which is to make sure that they successfully complete their lives with dignity and prepare for death in their minds and hearts. This is part of our responsibility to the citizens of this country.

> An "advanced directive" [or living will] is a way of knowing the will of the patient at some earlier time. However, we must proceed with caution in judging whether the entire policy for terminal care has been

decided in such a document. In order to legalize the process, it is necessary to consider broader issues involved, including how to void it and what it requires. Since an advanced directive is not a final decision and must be confirmed repeatedly according to changing circumstances, the existence of such a directive can be a hindrance and may even go against the will of the patient when he or she actually enters into the process of terminal care.[34]

Easing physical pain and accelerating the process of death through euthanasia are two separate issues. As the end draws near, patients do not live in order to accept death. They live with endless hopes and dreams until the last moment. The work of clerics and doctors is not to assist patients in dying peacefully. It is more important to assist patients to fulfill their lives as they are until the last moment.

The Causes of Death Are Infinite, the Manner of Death Is Unimportant

End-of-life care exists for the sake of the patients themselves. In caring for the dying, sometimes the caregivers are too focused on external appearances, that is, how the family including the dying person appears to the outside. In their hearts, a peaceful death is not only something the patient hopes for but also a wish of the people providing care. Confusion over the concepts of an ideal death and euthanasia starts here. From the perspective of those who provide care to patients, it is painful to witness a loved one having to meet the moment of death full of pain, and because of that caregivers might even think subconsciously that euthanasia is desirable. Perhaps this arises out of egoistic hopes to idealize and control the process of the patient's death so that the caregivers can handle it more easily. Although they may appear to be concerned for the patient's peace and well-being, in many cases they are actually hoping to make things easier for themselves as caregivers.

According to the "Medical Practices and Biomedical Ethics" guidelines,

The concept of "death with dignity" *(songenshi)* aims at a peaceful death without pain and recognizes that people expect a peaceful death. However, as "the causes of death are infinite," people may meet their end unexpectedly in traffic accidents, natural disasters, or by acute illness. Therefore, in the history of Japan, no matter how unhappy the deaths that people have met, death has always been accepted with dignity, and people did not make the manner of death an important issue. Therefore, while doctors should remember that the best medical practice is to provide a peaceful death, they must also develop a deeper perspective on human life though which they can accept any death with dignity.[35]

There is no need to judge good or bad at the final moment of death. The way one dies is not important because the cause of death is unpredictable. The Buddhist Vihara movement, in accordance with Shinran's thought, does not merely aim to provide a peaceful death, nor does it try to determine the status of a person's salvation based on the manner of the event. The Vihara movement accepts each person's death as a unique individual death. In Buddhism, patients do not need to put on an outward show on their deathbed. All ways of death are sad and precious. Because everyone is embraced in the compassion of the Buddha, patients do not have to deceive themselves or others.[36]

Learning from Patients' Hearts and Minds

While attending to sick patients, caregivers also reflect upon themselves. They learn about suffering, people's aspirations, and the meaning of spiritual repose. In spiritual care, chaplains should not push their own thoughts on the patients or force them to accept their own religion or propagation. A strong religious belief or preaching from the caregiver may feel like a threat or scolding. A religious conversation can be started at any time in response to the wishes of patients and their families. The most important thing is to be aware that patients, families, and caregivers are all human beings with fragile lives and that they are all equally precious children of the Buddha or of whatever they take to be the ultimate truth of life.

Staying at the Patient's Side

People facing death take off the masks they have been wearing all their lives. Instead of flowery words, patients seek true understanding. This means that caregivers must be ready to stay at the patient's side with honesty, without putting up a front. Caregivers must listen to patients without thought of self-conceit or self-protection. Even though caregivers may not completely understand what the patient is trying to say, this is usually fine with the patient as long as the caregivers try to understand.

"Not doing but being" represents the ideal of palliative care. This phrase expresses the reality that, for people in despair, not doing anything but simply holding their hand or gently rubbing their shoulders will be supportive and appreciated, even if in a small way. The Sanskrit word *karuṇā*, "compassion," originally meant "groaning." The enlightened Buddha groans because he is always sharing the sufferings of human beings, guiding them to blissfulness without abandoning anybody.

According to David Eckel,[37] many great Buddhist teachers, including the Dalai Lama, emphasize the deep meaning of compassion. One of the Dalai Lama's favorite sources of meditation on compassion is the teaching about "exchanging self and other." Exchanging self and other signifies nondual compassion in which self and other relate equally in oneness rather than treating the other with subtly condescending pity. As the Buddha taught, "Your suffering is my suffering." However, it is difficult for human beings to exchange themselves with others. One wants to help loved ones, yet it is impossible to really help even a single person. Nevertheless, there is tremendous meaning in extending one's thoughts and feelings, by "groaning with others" in compassion. The greater the patients' suffering and the closer they come to their deaths, the more communication without words becomes important. We can learn many things from the Buddha's groaning. The manner of "being there" represents caregivers' courage and their sincerity not to abandon the suffering patients.

Reciting the Nembutsu

When people face the suffering of serious illness, they often lose their foundation for daily life. For Pure Land Buddhists, reciting the name of Amida Buddha offers a way of self-reflection in the embrace of Amida Buddha's deep compassion. Together with the patients, the caregivers may recite the *nembutsu*, Namu Amida Butsu. In everyday life until the moment of death, listening to the Buddhist teachings and reciting the *nembutsu* in gratitude for the Buddha's benevolence open up the path to go beyond the delusions of life and death and to be born in the Pure Land of infinite life. This can carry great meaning for both the dying and for those left behind.

As mentioned above, Kakushin-bō, a follower of Shinran, kept reciting the *nembutsu* on his deathbed. Reciting the *nembutsu* was the expression of his gratitude for meeting good people and the teaching of the Buddha. The tranquillity of mind brought to him through reciting the *nembutsu* shows that the boundless Primal Vow of the Buddha pervaded his limited life. Recitation of the *nembutsu* in this defiled world makes us aware that we are foolish beings filled with blind passions. In becoming aware of our foolishness, we are naturally led to repent our karmic evil, and this nurtures our gratitude toward the Buddha and loved ones.

Participating in the Mourning of the Surviving Family

Separation from a loved one usually brings deep sorrow. Such sorrow is a natural expression of the feelings of separation and loss. The grief caused by the separation of death can be very involved, depending on the person. It can include numbness, a sense of powerlessness, guilty conscience, self-reproach, anger, anxiety, fatigue, or even a sense of relief. Yet feelings of sorrow and even misgiving are themselves part of the process of healing the wounded heart. At the funeral or memorial services, shedding tears and sharing sorrow with others is the first step to recovery from sorrow.[38] Pure Land Buddhism teaches the concept of merit transference in the returning aspect *(gensō ekō)*. This means that the deceased is born in the Pure Land, becomes a buddha, and returns to this world of suffering to guide the family left behind. The deceased are not simply living in past memory. They continue to live in the present and future.[39] People left behind can perhaps see the separation brought by death as an opportunity to know and learn from the heart of the deceased.

When one becomes aware of death, one reflects upon the meaning of life and realizes true kindness and compassion. The examples of caregiving by Buddhists provide us with perspectives that go beyond medical treatments. There is an emphasis on the fact that all patients are embraced by the compassion of the Buddha and, without eliminating their fear of death, can realize limitless life. End-of-life care in Buddhism leads the patient's family and caregivers to learn from the deep aspirations that patients discover within themselves under the most adverse circumstances.

Appendix I

Illusions of the Self in Buddhism and Winnicott

FRANZ AUBREY METCALF

1. Introduction: Call and Response

THOUGH IT'S AN UNUSUAL REQUEST, I ask readers of this appendix to put it down and first read Jeremy Safran's and Jack Engler's contributions to *Psychoanalysis and Buddhism*.[1] Safran's introduction[2] and Engler's chapter, "Being Somebody and Being Nobody: A Reexamination of the Understanding of Self in Psychoanalysis and Buddhism"[3] are the calls to which this appendix is a response.[4] Your reading of this appendix will be grounded and immeasurably enriched by reading their work, first. I'll wait.

Excellent, now I can presume readers have a basic grasp of what Safran and especially Engler are attempting and we can proceed from there. Engler's piece in particular simply *cried out* for my critical and constructive response (or so I believed), and that's what I have given it. I present here, in response to Engler, my own vision of human development grounded both in D. W. Winnicott's psychology and in the lives of practitioners at the Zen Center of Los Angeles.

Call and response: that's the structure of this paper, and of most fruitful dialogue. As Safran and Engler called me, I hope my work provides a call for others. I also hope my response to Engler's chapter illustrates the care with which that conversation must move forward. We owe this care to each other and to the *vipassanā* and Zen practitioners we sometimes study and sometimes are.

2. My Call, Safran's Answer
2.1 The Need to Go Beyond "America" and "Buddhism"

In *Westward Dharma*[5] (at this writing the most detailed treatment of Buddhism in the West), I and other contributors explicitly criticize a contemporary tendency to take Buddhism out of context. I see danger in the deracination of Buddhism in America, especially as it is appropriated as a psychologically focused set of personal techniques. We see this appropriation particularly in *vipassanā* practice, but it exists in other schools, too. I find this a profound impoverishment of the richness of the Buddhist tradition. What is more, this impoverishment is a direct and unacknowledged reflection of 20th century Western—especially American—cultural preferences and needs. While I deeply respect the new Buddhisms of America, we cannot let ourselves believe they reflect or express all the buddha-dharma. This is why I both loved and was frustrated by Safran's introduction and why it makes a fit beginning for this appendix.

2.2 Going Beyond "America" and "Buddhism"

Safran gives much needed and long overdue attention to the cultural context of the psychological appropriation of Buddhism in America. He writes that the assimilation of Buddhist ideas into contemporary psychology "can be understood only if we know something about how this process of assimilation expresses contemporary cultural values, tensions, and problems."[6] Absolutely, and this requires understanding the origins of modern psychology, which arose as a kind of secularized mode of attaining salvation.

Safran looks into the tension of valuing freedom from religion and yet still needing the commitment and meaning traditionally supplied by religion. Without understanding the cultural needs, kept in tension in contemporary America, we cannot understand the ways in which our culture has assimilated Buddhism in psychology or any other sphere. To understand those needs, we need a clear sense of the religious, cultural, social, and psychological landscape of America, something well beyond the reach of any one scholar, and certainly any one book introduction. Still, Safran gamely lays out some basics and he does an excellent job.

As Safran's treatment of the rise of psychology and the assimilation of Buddhism is necessarily sketchy, my treatment of Safran here is even more so. I wish only to remind readers of the importance of the work that has been done (for example, on the rise of psychology, see the work of Homans,[7] Kirschner,[8] and Richard Payne's contribution to this volume), and the work remaining to be done. Any good work on the relationship of Buddhism and psychology can only be done in the context of this larger project.

If Safran points up the need for attending to cultural difference and development, surely we also need to attend to the diversity and specificity of Buddhisms and Buddhist practices in America. I find myself intensely annoyed when supposedly high level examinations of Buddhism and psychology fail to do this. Safran does not give this attention (nor could he be expected to) in his introduction. To find it we need to turn to Engler (and then beyond).

3. Finding and Using Each Other

"it is perhaps the greatest compliment we may receive if we are both found and used."[9]

It is a relief when we come to read Engler and find he does take care in detailing the psychological aspects of one Buddhist meditative system. That is what made his work such a leap forward, twenty years ago—that and his still useful dictum, "you have to be somebody before you can be nobody."[10] His work has remained at the forefront of this dialogue for decades because he gives us both nuanced detail and a great soundbite. I have truly learned from and long appreciated both.

Nevertheless, I want to critique Engler's work here on two levels. The first critique is brief and cautionary, on the narrowness of his apparent view of Buddhism and Buddhist practice. The second critique is central and constructive; it amounts less to a critique and more to a contribution, an answer to his call. In giving such a critique I am trying to give Engler what D. W. Winnicott calls "the greatest compliment." This is fitting because Jack Engler paved the way for my own work. He blazed a trail not only in his publications, but, before that, in the areas of Religion and Psychological Studies and History of Religions at the University of Chicago Divinity School. That was where he did his dissertation on *vipassanā* practice and object relations theory, thus opening the space for me to begin my own dissertation there, on American Zen practice and object relations, ten years later—and not only scholarly space, but the space to be personally engaged with Buddhism. I take great pleasure in being able to thank him in print.

I have quoted D. W. Winnicott once already, and I will quote him many more times in this appendix. He is my own psychoanalytic guiding light. About dialogue such as we are having, Winnicott wrote, "in any cultural field *it is not possible to be original except on a basis of tradition.*" This is "just one more example, and a very exciting one, of the interplay between separateness and union."[11] This interplay happens when a younger person learns to play with an older one, and the older one can withstand any aggression and still remain loving. In the family, this extends love to the next generation. In scholarship, it extends knowledge.

3.1 My Call, Engler's Answer

3.1.1 Going Beyond Schools

I concluded my chapter in *Westward Dharma*, by pronouncing:

> The academy's duty is to see that what passes for Buddhism in the West acknowledges that Buddhism—even each school of Buddhism—goes beyond the practices of any one therapist or dharma center or teacher. To preserve an authentic Buddhism, perhaps greater than the sum of its parts, individual teachers and promoters must acknowledge their inevitable partialness and the greater tradition's diverse fullness.[12]

We need to remember that our particular Buddhist traditions always remain fragmentary, interpretive, and constructed, not original, pure, or complete. And here we come to my first critique of Engler's work. Several times in *Psychoanalysis and Buddhism*, Engler appears to see his own particular meditation practice and theory (contemporary *vipassanā*, following the "Burmese Method") as normative for all Buddhists—more than that: normative for all "the enlightenment traditions."[13]

Engler describes the contemporary *vipassanā* meditation practice of retracing the processes of perception,[14] but then illustrates it with the example of the Hindu teacher, Sri Nisargadatta. I question Engler's implication that the good swami has achieved his experience of "Self" through the process of witnessing radical *anatta*. Indeed, I believe Nisargadatta's experience is quite different from Buddhist experience and any reference to "the no-self of the enlightenment traditions,"[15] collapses religious, cultural, and even perceptual distinctions. I question whether it makes sense to equate experiences of Hindu Self and Buddhist no-self, as Engler explicitly does.[16] Is Engler really claiming the experience of *tat tvam asi* is identical with the experience of *anatta*? If so, then either *ātman*/Brahman is empty—which reduces Hinduism to Buddhism—or *anatta* must be identical with *ātman*/Brahman—which reduces Buddhism to Hinduism.[17]

If Engler effaces the differences between *vipassanā* and Hinduism, he certainly effaces differences within Buddhism itself, taking the Burmese Method to be a kind of Platonic form of meditative practice, something all other forms approximate to their benefit.[18] But in contrast to Engler's description of Zen, kōan practice does not work along exactly the same lines as *vipassanā*. B, a dharma heir at Zen Center of Los Angeles (henceforward, ZCLA; note that for the sake of confidentiality, I use symbolic initials to refer to all my interpreters), said about kōan practice, "At a minimum you learn about Buddhism" because through kōan practice you embody aspects of the dharma, of awakening. Kōan practice puts the student into the position—sometimes literally—of the ancient teachers. It is truly embodied learning, a re-experiencing of the minds of the Buddha Ancestors. This simply does not parallel the quiet, mindful awareness of *vipassanā*. One might say similar things about other forms of Buddhist practice. Daniel Capper, for example, has written an entire book on the rich and sometimes emotional dynamics of Tibetan guru devotion in America.[19] It hardly resembles *vipassanā*.

Engler's meditational model, exceptionally valuable as it is, cannot be uncritically exported as the model for all Buddhism, let alone all "the enlightenment traditions." We need to help each other remember, again, that our provinces of Buddhism may be normative to us, but that the Buddhist "World is crazier and more of it than we think,/Incorrigibly plural."[20]

3.1.2 No-self in Self, Self in No-self

In 2002, I issued a challenge to myself and any others who might care: Those who would combine object relations and Buddhism must do so coherently. If they wish to set Buddhist *bhāvanā* in an object relations framework, then let them show why it's there and how its presence is expectable:

> it is one thing to claim that Buddhism carries object relations development beyond the self; it is another thing altogether to show, from the baseline of object relations, *why this should be so*. The burden of proof is on those of us, including myself, who claim meditative development continues object relations development.[21]

Remarkably—here is the engine that first got this appendix moving—Engler turns my call around. His own "crucial question" as he labels it,[22] is the mirror of mine. He speaks of the idea of the "self," the experience of a bounded ego, and asks "*Why* would we represent ourselves to ourselves in just this way if it only produces suffering, as Buddhism maintains?"[23]

I ask "Why have no-self if it's not part of any developmental line?" Engler asks "Why have self if it's so *dukkha*-inducing?" Together, I think these reflective questions (and their answers) contain the potential to put Buddhist psychology and contemporary Western psychology in genuinely fruitful dialogue. I claim serious observation of Zen practice coupled with nuanced use of object relations psychology, specifically the work of D. W. Winnicott, enables us to begin answering both these questions. A sketch of those answers forms the constructive part of this appendix.

3.2 Engler's Call, Engler's Answer

First, I want to remind us how Engler answers his own question. His answer is really my answer (and my answer is really his answer, to echo the Heart Sutra, which Engler appreciatively quotes). Engler asserts we will understand the self, with all its adaptive and maladaptive qualities if:

> we view the singular, constant, separate self of normal experience as a *compromise formation* in the psychodynamic sense: a psychological structure that emerges to confront a "danger situation" by binding anxiety and warding off unwanted and unwelcome knowledge and the aversive feelings that knowledge evokes.[24]

Engler is saying we create the self so we can avoid unwanted and unwelcome knowledge. I would add that we create the self to safeguard the biological unit and thus perpetuate the species. Engler then adds that the self betrays its origins, as all psychological defenses do, and thus continues the conflicts and sufferings it is intended to resolve. I agree entirely, but we need to go further.

3.3 Engler's Call, My Answer

Engler's explanation of why there's a self sounds vaguely Freudian, but Engler makes no effort to tie his description of the origin of the self to any particular psychological theory. Yet I believe it is exactly in pinning down pronouncements like this that we make progress in understanding. I'm now going to pin down Engler's answer—not, probably, in the way he would, but in the way I have already done without knowing I was doing so. It seems that, in the last ten years, as I've been pinning down my own answer, I've also been pinning down Engler's. I think I've done this carefully enough that my answer may be falsifiable. That makes it useful, whether it turns out to be false or true, because it moves us forward. So let's see that answer formulated, sprawling on a pin.

3.3.1 My Perplexity

I love Engler's work, but I think it's unfortunate he shows little interest in Winnicott. Unfortunate because Winnicott (at least through my own extension of his work) responds directly to Engler's main question: Why is there a self? Winnicott's answer lends developmental coherence to Engler's. They are fully in harmony.

Engler asserts that unselfconscious experiences have recently been labeled:

> "transitional" phenomena in Winnicott's sense. But these seem like default positions, attempts to incorporate a different mode of functioning within existing theory without recognizing its uniqueness. There is no natural place for this mode of self-organization in the standard model of psychological functioning. It does not inform the core of psychoanalytic thinking about the person.[25]

I'm not sure there even *is* a core of "general" psychoanalytic thinking about the person, but the core of Winnicott's psychoanalytic thinking is *exactly* this mode of unselfconscious functioning. Engler is talking about "the realm of cultural experience—play, creativity, art."[26] Excellent, this is Winnicott's focus and Engler appreciates this. Engler here labels unselfconscious experience as "transitional" phenomena. This does follow Winnicott's usage, but it troubles me because it reminds me of a fundamental error in reading and understanding Winnicott, one a shocking majority of nuanced psychological thinkers make. They understand Winnicott as speaking of "transitional phenomena" and "transitional objects" as if they led only to an autonomous self. In fact, Winnicott sees transitional experiences as the first movements toward play, the genuine play that exists before games and players, and exists beyond them, as well. Play, love, art, science, religion, when done unselfconsciously are not merely transitional in an infantile sense; they are *vital* and they take place in what Winnicott calls the *potential* space, never the "transitional space" (this latter term Winnicott does not employ). They contain the potential for everything worthwhile in life and are the heart of true experiencing. When we read Winnicott this way, we open ourselves to what he calls the "third area of experiencing,"[27] an experiencing larger than the autonomous self.

The heart of Engler's recent work may be his assertion[28] of four types of self experience. The first two are self-conscious and the province of psychology, but the last two go beyond a sense of the separate self and are the province of what Winnicott would call play. The third type Engler labels "unselfconscious experience," and I believe he would agree with me that Winnicott's psychology encompasses it. I want to suggest that Winnicott's "third area of experiencing" goes beyond that, to Engler's fourth type: no-self experience.

3.3.2 Going Beyond Engler

Engler sees no distinction between self and no-self, since all is empty. But Engler denies psychologists are able to go there with him, saying "the few psychoanalytic thinkers who have tried to incorporate this sense of nonbeing underlying existence into their theory" have only been able to conceptualize it as "catastrophe," "oblivion," "meaninglessness," "terror," "null," and "psychotic."[29] As you are no doubt expecting, I assert there is at least *one* exception: D. W. Winnicott. I will now detail his central incorporation of emptiness.

Winnicott famously wrote,[30] "there is no such thing as an infant because when we see an infant at this early stage we know that we will find infant-care with the infant as part of that infant-care." He meant this literally, at least on a developmental level. The infant is not a self. Indeed, we may well see the neonate's experience as no-self experience. The mother acts as the environment that holds the infant's life and self together; in her eyes the infant sees itself. Her "primary maternal preoccupation," her desire, like the infant's, is that it get what it wants, when it wants it.[31] In fact, there is essentially no "it" at all at this stage, without the mother to provide "its" continuity.[32]

The mother reflects back originally formless experience, allowing the infant to organize a self. "Formless" is not merely a "Buddhist" word; it is Winnicott's own psychological word, as we will see, below. Later, the therapist can do this reflecting. And, at ZCLA, I found Zen teachers and the holding environment provided by the center doing the same thing. Crucially, in all these

cases, formlessness becomes integrated into the person, but only in formlessness is there creativity. Hardly catastrophic or meaningless, formless experience is what makes life worth living.

For Winnicott, at bottom is chaos, what Engler calls "nonbeing," and
which the therapist allows, as well as the patient. Speaking of searching
within a therapeutic session, Winnicott writes:

> the searching can come only from desultory formless functioning, or
> perhaps from rudimentary playing, as if in a neutral zone. It is only
> here, in this unintegrated state of the personality, that that which we
> describe as creative can appear. This, if reflected back, *but only if
> reflected back*, becomes part of the organized individual personality.[33]

As I read this, Winnicott is saying formlessness or unintegration lies at
the heart of the creative and, with the help of mother/therapist/teacher is
incorporated into the individual. To again play on the Heart Sutra: a kind
of psychological emptiness within form.

From this basis, human development begins. The good enough mother
holds the formless experience of the infant. This forms the mother-infant
dyad, an achingly beautiful achievement. As the infant matures, mother
allows it to emerge from this undifferentiated continuum of experience. The
infant loses and mourns its felt non-duality with her. Facing this optimal
failure of the mother, the infant soothes and consoles itself through organ-
izing behavior into rituals symbolizing her. These often coalesce into one
object, the transitional object, that both joins (being regressive and soothing) and separates (being developmental and assertive) the infant and
mother. As Winnicott clarifies,

> It is not the object, of course, that is transitional. The object represents
> the infant's transition from a state of being merged with the mother
> to a state of being in relation to the mother as something outside and
> separate.[34]

The transitional object is found/created in the potential space that the
relationship with the mother has provided. This space is the capacity in
the infant for play. "The baby's separating-out of the world of objects
from the self is achieved only through the absence of a space between,

the potential space being filled in in the way that I am describing."[35] Thus, the potential space is empty only in the way my Zen interpreters describe the universe as empty. Both are an unlimited space "which the baby, child, adolescent, adult may creatively fill with playing, which in time becomes the enjoyment of the cultural heritage."[36] Note that this space is not an absence or void, but rather the very place of the most intimate connection. In fact, it is always full because it expands exactly as we are capable of filling it. E evokes this internal and external space and its dependence on relationship beautifully:

> "And—Rōshi is brilliant—he gave a talk on the moon, and in *doku-san* I said look how much *space* there is. (And you know the dokusan room is tiny.) He said 'No; *you've* given you all this space'."

This expanding emptiness, this potential space, begins in infancy, but does not end there. There is a direct development from transitional phenomena to playing, and from playing to shared playing, and from this to cultural experiences." In the potential space, the realm of experiencing "widens out into that of play, and of artistic creativity and appreciation, and of religious feeling, and of dreaming."[37] Winnicott devoted the last twenty-five years of his life to:

> studying the substance of *illusion*, that which is allowed to the infant, and which in adult life is inherent in art and religion. . . . We can share a respect for illusory experience, and if we wish we may collect together and form a group on the basis of the similarity of our illusory experiences. This is the natural root of grouping among human beings.[38]

Of course ZCLA and other Buddhist sanghas are examples of this kind of grouping based on shared illusions. Taking part in such illusions, we live creatively; for Winnicott only this is full life, something which goes far beyond mere health or sanity. Winnicott famously wrote, "we are poor indeed if we are only sane."[39] He meant, and he repeated throughout his work, that we must always remain rooted in illusion to be able to live creatively.

It is these cultural experiences that provide the continuity in the human race that transcends personal existence. I am assuming that cultural experiences are in direct continuity with play, the play of those who have not yet heard of games.[40]

As if he had himself read Engler's chapter, Winnicott critiques the too-solidified self whose "life is lived through the compliant false self, and the result clinically is a sense of unreality. Other writers have used the following term to describe similar states: Observing Ego."[41] Winnicott agrees with Engler that the observing ego self is both false and impoverishing. Clearly, Winnicott is not exalting this self as a final or even a fully effective construct. For Winnicott, as for Engler, it is a compromise function. What or who, then, experiences "full life"? How, if at all, does Winnicott's vision fulfill the final stage of Engler's vision of human development?

3.3.3 Going Beyond Winnicott

3.3.3.1 No-self in Winnicott's Object Relations

Having said all this, having answered Engler's central question with Winnicott's work, I am not satisfied, nor, I imagine, are many of you. Despite what I see as the fundamental emptiness of the self in Winnicott's theory and practice, he himself was never able to fully integrate it into his developmental model. He could never relinquish his notion of some kind of ultimately substantial "True Self." He wrote "Only the True Self can be creative and only the True Self can feel real,"[42] and implied that this self is somehow present from the beginning.

But what *is* this "True Self"? Winnicott continues, saying the True Self "does no more than collect together the details of the experience of aliveness."[43] If so, then I think it does no more than the Buddhist "self" does. In the end, both can be abandoned by practitioners and indeed by us. Practitioners can let go of selves, both true and false, in zazen and in other no-self experiences. We can see the True Self as an anachronistic holdover from Winnicott's earlier and less authentic theoretical perspective (here I am in agreement with Zen teacher and psychotherapist Joseph Bobrow[44]). This means, as I've tried to go beyond Engler's answer to his own question, I will now try to go beyond Winnicott's answer.

Here is my fundamental contention: the self is part of a developmental line of transitional behavior leading to full play in the potential space. This line begins before the self and extends beyond it. This makes sense precisely because *the self is itself a transitional object.* Seeing the self as a transitional object, as a necessary illusion, we can see it as something eventually to be decathected, to be diffused, both developmentally and ontologically. Yet— as with any transitional object—never fully abandoned, only held more lightly, even let go of.

Experiences of what Engler calls "unselfconscious experience" or "no-self experience" threaten the sense of being a personal self. This threat causes the experiencer of the personal self, whatever we label it, to react as the experiencer of the nursing couple self did when the mother optimally failed it. These selves are in analogously threatening situations and each clings to a soothing transitional object to console itself during the process of weaning from an outmoded experience of the self. The first transitional object was a symbol of the lost part of the illusory nursing experience: the mother/breast, and this symbol both joined and separated the new experiences of self and relation to mother. What was lost was preserved through the transitional object, the fundamental structure of personal experiencing.

Similarly, the new transitional object, the autonomous "self," or "ego," is a symbol of the lost part of the illusory adult experience: the reified sense of an individual consciousness. As the transitional object connected and separated the mother and infant, this new symbol connects and separates the evolving no-self and the coherently experienced ego. In this way, the first and last transitional objects are functionally parallel. The first facilitates the transition from an illusory sense of non-duality to seeming duality. The second facilitates the transition from an illusory sense of duality to seeming non-duality.[45]

Engler might object that most of us develop senses of self very early and without no-self incursions. I counter that we have no-self incursions all the time; we just very efficiently ignore or deny them. Certain love experiences, for instance, and—according to Tibetan claims—sneezes, orgasms, and falling asleep. Neurological studies, such as those described in James Austin's *Zen and the Brain*,[46] support this claim that no-self experience recurs in several common experiences, especially borderline states between sleep and waking. In *Psychoanalysis and Buddhism*, Jeffrey Rubin[47] and Joseph Bobrow[48] propose their own versions of the ongoing simultaneity or alternation of self and no-self experience. All these perspectives support viewing the development of a coherent self as a reaction to fragmenting no-self experience from early in life. We value and we strengthen our transitional object self as a matter of evolutionary adaptedness. We need to remember, though, that this transitional self is not only a haven from *threatening* no-self experience, it is also transitional to *liberating* no-self experience.

Using the transitional personal self to ease the transition, the no-self can begin to play in the potential space. Here it encounters other illusory selves with real mutuality, analogous to the precarious mutuality between mother and infant, supported by the ongoing existence of the first transitional object. Though this play is both threatening and liberating, given enough time and practice, the experiencer gives up or diffuses the last transitional object as he or she gave up or diffused the first.

3.3.3.2 No-self at the Zen Center of Los Angeles

The diffusion of the self happens with repeated immersion in the cultural deep end of the potential space. Most persons experience this in sharing the perspectives of others in art, in dialogue, and in relationships. Engler claims that a deeper diffusion can occur when a meditator experiences perceptions that transcend any personal perspective, and of course this has become a goal of much of American Buddhist practice.

In my dissertation[49] research at ZCLA, I saw how practice fostered no-self experience, despite the fact that becoming a no-self was not a goal of ZCLA practitioners. Their goal was closer to a continual erasing of limited roles or masks (and "role," even perhaps "mask," is after all, the root of the word, "person"). My observation and experience at ZCLA supports seeing the personal and the impersonal as simultaneous and reciprocal. I now want to give this very theoretical appendix a bit of energy with some living words from a few of my interpreters.

First, some comments on the role of the Zen teacher. (The material to follow comes from my interview transcriptions. Exact quotes are indicated by quotation marks. The remaining words are paraphrases usually written out the same day the interview took place.)

F said, "Rōshi, he was a gardener, he watched *how* you grew and responded. So my relationship with him—outside the tending I received from my mother—I've never experienced from a male that kind of true regard and respect." Maezumi Rōshi and his successors, like all good mothers and Zen teachers acted as what Winnicott called the "facilitating environment." In fact, most of my interpreters literally referred to coming to ZCLA as coming home, as these examples illustrate. F enthused "I got some instruction and as soon as I sat zazen I felt I was home." E's arrival "was sort of a coming home. That's a good expression for Zen." And K made an explicit parallel between her relationships with her mother and with Maezumi Rōshi, saying that relating to him gave her "a chance to work through this again."

This work is not necessarily easy; it leads out into formless relationship and formless experience:

R: "Rōshi was trying to make me see it for myself, put it in my words. Here's my teacher and he's giving me *nothing*!"

Me: "That sounds hard."

R: "Yeah! It was like torture, but that was the point. And he gave me so much nothing, nobody else could pick it up."

E described how her practice alone and with Maezumi Rōshi led to no-self experience:

E: "Rōshi always had a wonderful way of mind-to-mind transmission." He could speak to you as a patriarch but make it applicable to you.

Me: You mean be on his level but make it make sense on your level?

E: "No. I remember going in and I'd ask him something. The whole environment would change. I'd go bleaah [gesture of vomiting forth some blather]. And he'd speak softer and everything would shatter in my mind. And I'd ask him about it (as if *he* had done it) and he'd say no, it's *your* mind." This sort of experience, this shattering of mind, would happen during *dokusan* [meeting with the teacher] but also during *teishō* [teacher's dharma talk] and during zazen.

Many of my interpreters seemed to share the experience of a "shattering of mind," including every one of those who had been practicing for more than five years, though all described it differently. M, for example, said "Now I would say that increasingly I live less out of the mental picture or story that I'm telling and truly deeply from the texture of the moment." This sounds much less flashy than E's experience, but, given what I came to know of M, I would assert her living from the "texture of the moment" signifies a similar freedom from boundedness.

Following Sōtō tradition, ZCLA teachers often use the metaphor of opening. Unsurprisingly, it surfaced in interviews. E described her self-described quest for "enlightenment" this way: "What I thought it was, it turns out that it wasn't. That enlightenment doesn't come from outside us. You just keep going and something else opens up." F expressed a similar distance from "enlightenment":

> "People get stuck in the mystic experience, but the mystic experience will open them to that experience [of breaking down distinctions]. . . . I don't like to talk about it because for me this is natural for persons. . . . Every culture has always touched [mystical experiences] or pointed to them. It comes up over and over—but if we get a fixed idea of that then we've learned not to trust our own experience and nature. If you have a good guide you can learn to trust this life we're leading . . . If you let go of enlightenment—no enlightenment—then what?"

Then you return to the moment-to-moment experience of life. Opening up to and trusting this experience was a hallmark of the senior practitioners I came to know at ZCLA. Several remarked on a fearlessness that comes from letting go of the self and that, in turn, leads to wider experience. For F, to be fully human is "to include everything." She added, "I don't see myself as constructed because I'm deconstructed continually. I'm experiencing it now. I could name adjectives that describe the life I live, but they're just containers for something that cannot be contained." F is describing the self deconstructing to a point of effectively being no-self, and, as F implies, this deconstruction is not limited to times of meditation. P noted that it is "possible for a human being to drop away and the experience be of only zazen," but she also claimed that, at least at times, she had this kind of no-self experience *during our interviews.* Yet neither F or P lack personality. Quite the opposite; both are exceptionally interesting and individuated persons. They embody what we might call the not-two-ness of self and no-self.

In words and perhaps more powerfully in their relationships with each other and with me—in their sincerity and their compassion—senior students at ZCLA conveyed to me something of the results of their practice of opening to experience and liberating the self. As a participant-observer, one of my strongest impressions was the capacity of the most advanced practitioners to change personas in response to changing conditions. Each of the dharma heirs of Maezumi Rōshi displayed this ability, impossible to quantify and very hard to describe qualitatively, yet crucial in my evaluation of their development. They were able to let go of themselves, to be free *within, despite, and outside of* the particulars of their personalities. I propose this capacity is one index of the experience of no-self. Now I want to return, one last time, to Winnicott, to tie this capacity to what he calls the capacity for unintegration.

3.3.3.3 Unintegration and No-self

Winnicott once said, "the symbol of union gives a wider scope for human experience than union itself."[50] I take that to mean Winnicott felt we live more broadly and deeply in the symbolic world of the potential space than in the inner or outer worlds of fantasy or reality. Those two worlds depend on a perpetual distinction of self and other. The third realm of experiencing, the realm of shared illusion, allows experience that paradoxically both supports and transcends self and other and thus allows no-self experience. This realm is, in Zen, the realm of non-duality.

The term "no-self" does not appear in Winnicott's work, but this does not mean no analogous state or term exists. I suggest the closest analogue to "no-self" is Winnicott's idea of "unintegration." He discusses infantile unintegration positively in several papers, but to my knowledge the only paper in which he explores the possibility of unintegration as a positive experience for adults is "Ego Integration in Child Development."[51] Near the conclusion of this short paper Winnicott describes a situation in which adult persons can dispense with integration and experience a formlessness I see as equivalent to Engler's no-self experience. Achieving this unintegration, one is unbounded, undefended and yet unthreatened. ZCLA practitioners frequently described their most profound experiences in just these terms.

Whether or not we call this "no-self" experience, we are looking here at particularly deep experience of creative living in the potential space, a human achievement of free experimentation. This takes place in a personally and culturally constructed realm where persons share illusions, where the symbols and the scale of experience transcend the separate person. Continuing experience of this kind (in my data especially arising from *zazen*) allows continuing expansion into the potential space. Can we not here imagine an (un-)limiting case that uncovers the full no-self? It would take place in a third realm I look on as the psychological analogue of *samsara*, the Buddhist word for our illusory world. As with Winnicott's illusions, *samsara* is a real illusion,[52] at least when experienced from the viewpoint of *anātman*.[53] In this realm of illusion beyond sanity and health, human experience might move so far beyond the person that it embraces free play through the whole cosmos. Such play is the omega point of development, Winnicott's full "life," Engler's full no-self, and Buddhism's full awakening.

4. Conclusion: Going Beyond All of Us

4.1 Self is No-self, No-self is Self

As I mentioned, Engler quotes the Heart Sutra to good effect. He writes of the interplay of self and no-self, of how we only perceive no-self through experience of things, or rather of forms that are not ontologically separate from ourselves.[54] For Engler, and for me, this embodies the sutra's most famous line, "Form is exactly emptiness; emptiness is exactly form."

I suggest this admission calls into doubt the notion of no-self as something distinct from self. If we experience emptiness through form, surely we experience no-self through self. I believe this Buddhist view of human experience supports my view of psychological development, sketched above, and not only mine, but other views as well. Joseph Bobrow, for example, has written:

> Rather than having to construct a self before we can discover no-self, as Engler suggests, I think it takes a (distinctive, personal) self to fully embody our essential (no-self) nature.[55]

4.2 Seeing Through Each Other

Bobrow's defense of the need for the self to embody no-self strikes me as a more mainstream view of human (and Buddhist) experience than Engler's. I must also admit that it not only seems more mainstream to me, it also seems more Mahāyāna. I mention Bobrow and this Theravāda/Mahāyāna contrast as an opening onto the wider context of the dialogue between Buddhism and psychology.

Despite his extension of his model of practice to all "the enlightenment traditions,"[56] Engler remains rooted in Theravāda *abhidhamma*, in the foundational commentary of Buddhaghosa, and in one form of contemporary Theravāda meditative practice. It's no surprise that Bobrow and I, coming from a Zen background, should interpret no-self doctrine differently from Engler. This again should alert us to the need to speak not of "Buddhism," but of Buddhisms.

Further, Safran's and Engler's assertions about the theories and goals of object relations psychology differ from each other, and both differ from my own. There are points in my notes on their writings where I employ bold-face, italics, exclamation points, and outright invective to express my dismay at a few claims about object relations and the work of Winnicott. And yet these men's views on object relations are *at least* as educated as my own, as was demonstrated to me at the conference leading to the publication of this book. This, again, should alert us to the need for precision. As we must avoid talk of "Buddhism," so must we avoid talk of "psychology," or even "object relations."

This need for precision is why I've tried to try to conceive of no-self strictly through the theory of one variety of object relations thought. I see my work as merely one example of what I hope many thinkers will attempt. Only through multiple attempts will we gain a sense of which work better as bridges between Buddhist and psychological lifeworlds. With precision in these attempts comes at least a modicum of falsifiability, without which we have no chance to learn from each other's critique.

We are engaged in dialogue, which means thinking through words, ours and our partners'. When I think through Jack Engler's words I try, by extension, to think through Jack Engler himself, his mind, his experience. Thinking through Engler means, first of all, getting him right, as near as possible for me; it means also deconstructing his arguments and perspectives in ways he is not so well-situated to do, himself (here we find Winnicott's "use"); and it means seeing myself, my own arguments, from *his* perspective (this is a form of "play," a cultural encounter in the potential space where Engler and I are not separate from each other or each other's ideas). This perspective on thinking through another (or an "Other") comes from Richard Shweder's[57] method of doing cultural psychology (also see Harvey Aronson's chapter in this volume), though also shaped by my Winnicottian views. But this method goes beyond cultural psychology, applying to all forms of true dialogue and thus to the work of any functional scholarly community. We need to think through each other. If that strikes your ears as a way of working in harmony with *pratītya-samutpāda*, you're hearing it as I am.

I've given this close reading to Engler and Winnicott (and myself) because putting these perspectives together allows us to see through them all. Seeing through them all, I come back to the reciprocal questions Engler and I asked: *What is the reason the experience of self develops at all?* and *What is the developmental place or purpose for anything beyond the experience of* ātman? Asking these questions simultaneously forces us to deconstruct our own disciplinary paradigms for the sake of dialogue. Psychologists must release the reified and unquestioned self to answer Engler's question. Buddhists must release the reified and unquestioned no-self to answer mine. And not only must paradigms be questioned, but answers must be given in language consonant with the *other's* paradigms.

Engler and Winnicott offer preliminary answers to these questions, and I have struggled to discover language consonant with the paradigms of both. I am convinced these answers move the dialogue forward elegantly. Still, there remains an enormous amount of work to do, to either support these answers or begin to falsify them. By way of conclusion, let me think through where the dialogue might go.

4.3 "To Infinity and Beyond!"

✦ We need more clearly to illustrate the evolutionary adaptedness of the self. This kind of work might come from ethnology as well as human studies. We need to operationalize the self so we can study whether bounded self experience really helps the species or its coherent cultural subgroups to survive.

✦ We need to do the same for the evolutionary adaptedness of no-self. This task is mandatory and pressing, since no one in the harder regions of science, such as biology, neuropsychology, or even material anthropology, will take the notion of no-self seriously unless someone can demonstrate its development is beneficial for *Homo sapiens* as a species or for its subgroups. This work will involve operationalizing no-self and studying whether those operations lead to some kind of benefit.

This kind of study takes place on the border of the reductive—not surprisingly, as this is the burden of cutting edge research. As I say, dialogue across disciplines requires thinking through the perspective of the other, and this, in turn, requires accepting the language and paradigms of the other's methods. In this case, Buddhists and sympathetic psychological researchers would have to go back to Buddhist texts and traditions to find examples of no-self behaviors and persons. They would then need to show these things lead to results recognized as beneficial by hard science researchers.

+ We need to consider abandoning self/no-self language. During the Boston conference, in an evening conversation between Richard Payne, William Waldron, and myself, a rough consensus emerged that self/no-self discourse might not be our best language game to illuminate the practices of therapeutic and Buddhist cultivation. In cultivation, what is cultivated? A self? A person? A process? One reason I'm grateful to have participated in the conference is that it has spurred me toward the work of replacing the label "self" with more useful labels, such as "person" or even "experiencer."

As Waldron has labored to show (in this volume and elsewhere), Indian Buddhist language is neither personalized nor non-experiential. It avoids both distortions because it focuses on human experience without reifying its own metaphors. Its core is neither the naïve realist ego (of depth psychology), nor reductive material processes (of neurophysiology), but what we feel, what we think. And this experience is not reduced, but deconstructed. Future dialogue on Buddhism and psychology might take a cue from this middle way.

+ We need to do the work of falsification I've spoken of. My own conclusions from my research at ZCLA are nice, but my conclusions are only falsifiable if my quantitative and qualitative data is of sufficient richness that it can be reinterpreted by others using their own metaphors and paradigms. If their interpretations are more elegant (or less) than mine, then there's the possibility of falsifiability. All our field work should reach this level of depth and care.

+ We need to apply this paper's theoretical bridge (or any better ones) to practical work. That is, meditation teachers need to learn how their work parallels psychotherapeutic work, so that their students gain from their new knowledge. Psychotherapists need to do the same, *mutatis mutandis.* Beyond the *zendō* and the consulting room, projects like hospice work (as discussed in Naoki Nabeshima's chapter in this volume) need to be informed by such bridges. And human science researchers need to ground their upcoming studies in such bridging theories, so that further social welfare projects are made more effective.

All this seems to me perfectly obvious. I'm constantly surprised by the continued separation of areas of study within the fields of Buddhism and psychology. Though I'm certain my own work betrays this lack of connection, I'm glad to be offering it here. I've used the work of Engler and I know it is strong enough to withstand my challenges. Now I, too, recede, hoping my own work is also found and found useful.

Appendix II

Shinran's Thought Regarding Birth in the Pure Land

Significance of the Concept of Birth in the Pure Land

BUDDHISM IS A PATH to attain enlightenment by overturning delusions *(tenmei kaigo)*. Having originated in India, Buddhism spread into East Asia and developed into diverse forms of practice in response to differences in the ethnicity and culture of the people who accepted the teaching. Even within the single nation of Japan, the diverse development of Buddhist thought can be classified as the Buddhism of the Southern Capital (Nanto Bukkyō), Buddhism of the Heian period (Heian Bukkyō), and the new Buddhist movements of the Kamakura period (Kamakura Bukkyō). Although there are various different forms of practice in Buddhism, one point they all have in common is the claim that Buddhism offers the path to attain enlightenment by overturning delusions. For example, at first glance the doctrinal systems of the Pure Land Buddhist teachings and Zen Buddhism appear almost diametrically opposed. However, they agree on the main point that the current state of one's existence is delusion, and the state of existence that one should aim to attain is enlightenment.

Most of the diversity within Buddhist practice originates from the fact that the path from delusion to enlightenment is manifold. Although all kinds of Buddhism agree there is a path from delusion to enlightenment, the path in fact is not single but has various branches, mergers, and crossovers. Buddhism has developed according to how practitioners have chosen to follow the path. Birth in the Pure Land *(ōjō)* is one such concept that has developed among the diverse Buddhist traditions.

Birth in the Pure Land, in brief, means being born into the other world after completing life in this world. In the context of the path from delusion to enlightenment, the term *ōjō* (birth) means to be born into the Pure Land, which is the realm of enlightenment, after completing life in the *sahā* world (this world), which is the realm of delusion. Therefore, the various paths to enlightenment can be divided broadly into paths for attaining enlightenment in this world and paths for attaining enlightenment in the Pure Land.

Buddhism began with the teaching of Śākyamuni Buddha. Śākyamuni taught the path to enlightenment for we beings who continue to float in the ocean of the world of delusion. Śākyamuni could teach the path to enlightenment to others because he himself walked the path from delusion to enlightenment. In this sense, Śākyamuni is a being who guides us to enlightenment; he is both a teacher and a guide who has walked the path before us. Since Śākyamuni reached enlightenment in *this* world, and we are following the path he walked, it is natural for us to try to attain enlightenment in this world. When we look back over the history of Buddhism, it is undeniable that the path to enlightenment in this world is the main current of Buddhist practice. The difficulty of attaining enlightenment in this world, however, led to the goal of attaining enlightenment in the *other* world and the development of the concept of birth in the Pure Land.

There are two major causes that make it difficult to attain enlightenment in this world. One is an external cause, namely, the absence of the Buddha. A long time has passed since Śākyamuni attained enlightenment, guided people with his teaching, and passed away. When Śākyamuni was alive, people were able to receive appropriate instruction from him, but we live in an age in which it is very difficult even to follow the path toward enlightenment. The concept of the Last Dharma Age developed from this way of thinking.[1] The other major cause is an internal cause: our own inability to follow the path toward enlightenment.[2] No matter that the path to enlightenment has been shown to us right in front of our eyes, if we do not have the ability to follow the path, it is nothing but pie in the sky. The combination of these external and internal causes makes the attainment of enlightenment in this world very difficult—and the idea of enlightenment in another world, the Pure Land, very appealing.

Originally, Buddhist practices leading out of delusion to enlightenment, on the one hand, and the practices specific to Pure Land Buddhism for attaining birth in the Pure Land, on the other, only differed in their details. Both types of path required meditative practices as well as other practices such as following the precepts and mastery of various ritual and liturgical forms. The main difference was that the Pure Land practices, generally targeted towards those with inferior karma, led to birth in an ideal Pure Land and then shortly after enlightenment, rather than the attainment of nirvana and enlightenment in this life. Yet, the core of the Pure Land vision as articulated by Shinran turns this entire picture upside down and makes the foolish being who is wholly incapable of mastering any kind of practice the focus of Amida's Great Practice (Daigyō) of boundless compassion. Of course, the Pure Land practitioner still has to make great effort. Yet, it is precisely in the failure of self-power practice that Amida's other-power becomes manifest.

The idea of birth in a Pure Land is the path presented for beings who lack the ability to walk the path from delusion to enlightenment. Therefore, in order for them to be born in the Pure Land, it is necessary that the ability or power should come from another. If the Pure Land they aspire to be born into is the Pure Land of Amida Buddha, they need to rely on the other-power of Amida Buddha. This other-power is called the Power of the Primal Vow *(hongan riki)* because it is the power based on Amida Buddha's fundamental promise to save all living beings who suffer in this world of delusion—that is, his Primal Vow *(hongan)*, the Eighteenth Vow in the *Larger Sukhāvatīvyūha Sutra*. In the history of the tradition of the Pure Land teaching, the Eighteenth Vow is widely noted as the vow revealing the cause of birth in the Pure Land. The significance of the vow is understood to be that Amida will lead practitioners who recite the Name of Amida (the *myōgō*, Namu Amida Butsu) to be born into his Pure Land.[3] The tradition of the teaching of birth in the Pure Land through reciting the *nembutsu* was developed on this understanding. In Japan, Hōnen (1132–1212) established the teaching of birth through the *nembutsu* as the path of wholly entrusting the self to the vow.

One of the special characteristics of the concept of birth in the Pure Land is its emphasis on emotion. Originally, the fundamental principle of Mahāyāna Buddhism was to free oneself from attachments to fixed ideas. Some have questioned the aspiration to be born in the Pure Land as just another attachment or fixation. In short, the doctrine of birth in the Pure Land has been criticized as being contrary to the fundamental principles of Mahāyāna Buddhism.

In order to understand the Pure Land response to such questions which were raised in the development of the tradition, one must first examine the Mahāyāna view that delusion and enlightenment are seen as both nondual and dual simultaneously. Delusion and enlightenment are the same in emptiness and yet different in the realm of form. The nondual aspect is expressed by such phrases such as "blind passions are identical with enlightenment" *(bonnō soku bodai)* or "samsara is nirvana" *(shōji soku nehan)*. The aspect of duality is expressed by the phrase "cutting off delusions to realize the principle" *(danwaku shōri)*, that is, cutting off blind passions to realize enlightenment. On the one hand, delusions themselves are enlightenment. On the other hand, the extinction of delusions is the establishment of enlightenment. This relationship between delusion and enlightenment is often explained by the metaphor of ice and water.[4] Delusion is likened to ice, and enlightenment is likened to water. Although ice and water are made of the same material, their states of existence are different. The relationship between delusion and enlightenment can be understood in a similar manner. Since delusion and enlightenment are of the same nature, deluded beings can become enlightened buddhas. But since delusion and enlightenment are different states of existence, one cannot become a buddha unless one can transform the state of delusion into the state of enlightenment.

Although all Mahāyāna teachings agree on this point, their modes of instruction are different depending on which aspect they emphasize. If more emphasis is placed on the aspect of nonduality, one looks for the buddha within one's mind, and comes to regard this world itself as the Pure Land. On the contrary, if more emphasis is put on the aspect of duality, one recognizes a buddha as an existence different from oneself and aspires to attain birth in a Pure Land that is different from this world. The Pure Land doctrine of birth belongs to the latter.

The reason that Pure Land thought recognizes delusion and enlightenment as different—indeed, diametrically opposed—is that it targets beings who can only recognize all things as opposed to each other. For most people, the nonduality of delusion and enlightenment can be grasped intellectually but cannot be realized emotionally or somatically. By sticking to the standpoint of nonduality, ironically, one falls into an unrealistic idealism. Pure Land thought sees delusion and enlightenment as opposed to each other because this conforms to the facts of our experience, however deluded it may be. By seeing delusion and enlightenment as opposed to each other, the Pure Land practitioners aspire for the Pure Land as a world beyond this realm and view the Buddha affectionately as a savior filled with loving compassion.[5] This is the central religious feeling of Pure Land thought. Although quite different in terms of the dynamics of practice, this appeal to emotion is similar to the feeling of absolute reliance on a higher being defined by Schleiermacher as the core of religion.[6]

In the sutras, the Pure Land is depicted as a world with concrete form. The Chinese Pure Land master Tanluan explains how structural adornments are formed out of unknowing wisdom *(muchi)* and formlessness *(musō)*, expressed as the true wisdom of the unconditioned dharma-body (Jpn. *shinjitsu-chie mui-hossin)*. Later, this structure of the Pure Land was explained with the metaphor of the golden lion. According to this metaphor, the original nondiscriminating wisdom *(konpon-mufunbecchi)* of dharma-nature of ultimate tranquility *(jakumetsu hosshō)* is the gold that is used to make a golden lion, and the wisdom that discriminates *(funbecchi)* the forms of adornments *(usōshōgon)* is the form of the golden lion. The significance of this metaphor of the golden lion is that we do not need to melt the lion to obtain gold. The form of the lion is gold just as it is. The Pure Land in this way maintains its original nature as the dharma-nature of ultimate tranquility and equality *(jakumetsu byōdō)* while taking the distinctive forms of adornments such as the Buddha, bodhisattvas, palaces, and towers. Aspiring to be born in the Pure Land with distinctive forms of adornments is equal to aspiring to the dharma-nature of ultimate tranquility and equality. Aspiring to birth in the Pure Land with forms is therefore not contradictory to the fundamental principle of the Mahāyāna teaching of emptiness and selflessness, and such criticisms should be rejected. It should also be noted that because the Pure Land has forms of adornments, it stirs up a passionate grasping for the truth of salvation.

When Hōnen established the Pure Land teaching of birth through the *nembutsu,* it was enthusiastically accepted by ordinary people who could not do special Buddhist practices and who lacked the financial resources to nurture their roots of goodness by supporting the institutional development of Buddhism through the building of temple halls and towers. This teaching eventually developed into one strand of mainstream Buddhist thought and had a great impact on the later development of Buddhism in Japan. For ordinary people, a lofty ideal does not provide any help. And difficult practices that require a strong will were not for them either. The concept of birth in the Pure Land, which guaranteed that simply through the practice of *nembutsu* a Buddha filled with loving compassion would guide them to birth in his shining land, provided ordinary people with a spark of hope.

Shinran's Thought Regarding Birth in the Pure Land

The concept of birth in the Pure Land advocated by Shinran (1173–1262) was heir to Hōnen's idea of birth through *nembutsu*. Shinran, following his master's understanding that the Pure Land path of birth is opened for those who lack the ability to walk the difficult path to enlightenment, extended the reach of the *nembutsu* path not only to those who lack abilities but also to those who have no capability at all.[7] For Shinran, therefore, birth is not accomplished through a mutual cooperation between the savior and the saved; that is, salvation is not accomplished through any effort by those who are saved. Rather, salvation is accomplished totally through the power of Amida, who is the savior; this is the concept of the complete other-power *(zenbun tariki)*. Allowing for no power on the side of the saved means the power of the savior must be complete, and if the power of the savior is complete, the reality of salvation itself is also complete. If the reality of salvation itself is complete, the reality of birth does not simply mean a turning point in the path to enlightenment. It comes to mean the accomplishment of enlightenment itself. For Shinran, birth in the Pure Land itself means the accomplishment of enlightenment. This also means that those who are standing on the side to be saved are given the ability to save others.[8]

In Pure Land Buddhism before Shinran, birth in the Pure Land had been understood as a turning point in the path toward enlightenment. For example, birth meant forsaking this Buddha-less world to be born in the Pure Land with a presiding Buddha where practitioners can walk the path to enlightenment while receiving instruction from the Buddha.[9] Shinran shifted the focus of realization from birth into the Pure Land at the moment of physical death to the realization of *shinjin,* true entrusting, in every moment of life. Traditionally, those who attain birth in the Pure Land are all identified as beings at the bodhisattva stage of the truly settled *(shōjōju),* for whom enlightenment is assured. Shinran, however, asserts that attaining the stage of the truly settled occurs through true entrusting in this life rather than in the moment of birth into the Pure Land.

The nature of birth in the Pure Land is such that it is generally spoken of as occurring at the end of one's life in this world. Pure Land thought thus has a tendency to anticipate the future. In Shinran's understanding of Pure Land thought, however, the attainment of the stage of the truly settled is discussed in the context of one's life in this world, because he interprets the attainment of birth and the accomplishment of enlightenment in equal terms.[10] The possibility of our birth in the Pure Land in the future is not an issue for us to solve by ourselves at all. It is the problem of the working of the Buddha himself, who has pledged to save all living beings. The *Tannishō (A Record in Lament of Divergences)* records Shinran as saying, "I have no idea whether the *nembutsu* is truly the seed for my being born in the Pure Land or whether it is the karmic act for which I must fall into hell,"[11] which clearly reflects his understanding of the situation.

For Shinran, the accomplishment of salvation here and now means encountering the truth and being sustained and embraced by the truth. Salvation is accomplished when a being, who is nothing but delusion itself, encounters the truth from the other realm and is sustained and embraced by it. For Shinran, this encounter with truth means encountering the true teaching of the Primal Vow, which is an encounter with the Primal Vow itself. Being sustained and embraced by the truth is also the experience of being embraced by the light of the Buddha, or the feeling of being within the light and being protected by the light. This experience is something that happens here and now, not in the future. In this sense, Shinran's understanding of the concept of birth in the Pure Land is not future-oriented but locates it in the here and now.[12]

Although Shinran's concept of birth in the Pure Land focuses primarily on the present life, he does not neglect the future aspect. As discussed above, a major factor in the development of the concept of birth in the Pure Land was despair at not being able to reach enlightenment in this present life. The traditional Pure Land idea of birth is premised on the impossibility of fully attaining enlightenment here and now, thus shifting the focus to the future.

Shinran also discusses birth in the Pure Land in the context of the end-of-life experience. Although he emphasizes the accomplishment of salvation here and now, full attainment, including the ability to liberate others as a bodhisattva, is only fully realized at the moment of death, entering the Pure Land, and then returning to save all beings. For Shinran, the Pure Land to be born into at the end of life is called "the land of immeasurable light" (*muryō kōmyōdo*).[13]

The Pure Land is filled with light. Although virtually synonymous with emptiness, which is formless, odorless, and colorless, the foolish being lost in the darkness of ignorance experiences the *release* into emptiness as immeasurable light (Skt. *Amitābha*). The impetus to be born into the Pure

Land does not come from the practitioner's self-power (ego) but rather from emptiness itself, now manifested as Amida Buddha. Additionally, Shinran explains that, if the impetus for birth did come from the practitioners, they would all be born into different lands due to their diverse views of the ideal realm. For all beings to be released into the selfsame Pure Land, the impetus must emanate from the utter formlessness of the Pure Land/Amida Buddha.[14] It is Shinran's own realization of this that enables him to state, "Without fail I will await you there [the Pure Land]."[15] In another letter he says, "We will certainly go to the same place [the Pure Land]."[16]

There are people who maintain that since these statements are found only in Shinran's letters written for simple *nembutsu* practitioners, and do not appear in the *Kyōgyōshinshō* written for people with advanced knowledge of Buddhist doctrine, they do not represent his real intention but should be understood as skillful means to teach beginners. However, at the end of the *Hymns of the Dharma-ages* Shinran confesses that:

> While persons ignorant of even the characters for "good" and "evil"
> All possess a sincere mind,
> I make a display of knowing the words "good" and "evil";
> This is an expression of complete falsity.[17]

In this hymn, he recognizes that truth is present in people who do not know how to read characters, but that intellectual elites who manipulate words and characters are filled with falsity and delusion. And I would reiterate that Shinran clearly distinguishes the difference between truth and skillful means. Certainly, he considers the Buddha's skillful means that lead him to the truth as something one should appreciate with deep gratitude. But for Shinran, who recognizes that he himself is an ignorant being, it is impossible to apply effective skillful means to other people. He teaches by modeling this fact, that, wholly incapable himself, he relies on the other-power of Amida Buddha. Shinran made a special effort to use easier expressions for the simple *nembutsu* followers in Kanto, but this was not a compromise, for the essence of the teaching is simplicity itself.

The realization of birth in the Pure Land is the accomplishment of enlightenment, which also means that the saved will be equipped with the power to save others (the accomplishment of the ability to save others freely, as discussed above). Living in the world of delusion, we fetter ourselves with our own ignorant nature, like a silkworm entrapped in the thread it produces. The silkworm, however, has the power to rip open the cocoon and fly away. We do not possess such power and can do nothing but wholly rely on the power of the Buddha. The realization of birth in the Pure Land through the power of the Buddha means to be released from all the bondages of life, which in turn means the accomplishment of the power to save others freely.

In sum, for Shinran, the realization of birth is attainment of birth in the world filled with light. In that world we are released from the bonds of life and death and are able to meet those who have passed away before us.[18] The realization of birth is a natural result of the accomplishment of salvation here and now, and the accomplishment of salvation here and now means encountering the Primal Vow in the embrace of immeasurable light. In Shinran's idea of birth in the Pure Land, life in this world here and now is living within the light of the Buddha;[19] and when people end their lives in this world, they go to be born in the world filled with light, released from the bonds of delusion, and can expect to be reunited with people they have known.

We can conclude by saying that Shinran's thought on birth in the Pure Land is a mature expression of Mahāyāna Buddhism. His thought sets out the goal of the attainment of enlightenment for all living beings. Instead of falling into intellectual games that merely play with lofty ideals, it responds to the natural, everyday feelings of ordinary people who grow angry and fearful, who cry and laugh.

Appendix III

Key Terms: Shin Buddhism

MARK UNNO

Pure Land Buddhism and the Philosophy of Hōnen and Shinran

Pure Land school. Pure Land Buddhism originated in India around the beginning of the Common Era, at about the same time as the emergence of the Mahāyāna, or Great Vehicle. Advocates of the Pure Land teachings can be identified quite early in Chinese Buddhist history, but Pure Land Buddhism emerged as a major force in the Tang dynasty along with Chan/Zen. While both arose partially as a reaction against the perceived metaphysical excesses of the philosophical schools, Zen focused on awakening through monastic practice, while Pure Land focused on attaining birth in the Pure Land of the Buddha Amitābha through practices that were accessible to lay people.

The Three Pure Land Sutras. Three key sutras of Pure Land Buddhism were compiled in India: *The Larger Sutra of Eternal Life* (Skt. *Sukhāvatīvyūha Sūtra;* Ch. *Dawuliangshoujing;* Jpn. *Daimyryōjukyō*), the *Amida Sutra* (Ch. *Amitojing;* Jpn. *Amidakyō*), and the *Meditation Sutra* (Ch. *Guanwuliang-shoujing;* Jpn. *Kanmuryōjukyō*). Like many other Mahāyāna sutras such as the *Lotus (Saddharma-puṇḍarīka), Flower Ornament (Avataṃsaka),* and *Vimalakīrti,* these sutras were compiled near the beginning of the Common Era. At the center of the Pure Land sutras is the story of the Bodhisattva Dharmākara, a former king who decides to set out to seek enlightenment. In the process of doing so, he establishes the Western Pure Land. When sentient beings accumulate sufficient virtue, they are born there, and due to the ideal conditions, immediately attain enlightenment. In later developments, especially in Japan, the Pure Land becomes virtually synonymous with the highest truth, emptiness, nirvana.

Early practitioners aspiring to birth in the Pure Land visualized the jeweled paradise of the Buddha Amitābha, where the evil karma of his or her past was transformed into the Pure Land and the virtue of its Buddha. However, the ultimate goal of these visualizations was to transcend any visual Pure Land and realize the non-origination or emptiness of self and world.

Amitābha Buddha. Bodhisattva Dharmākara eventually becomes the Buddha Amitābha, the Buddha of Infinite Light. Amitābha is also known as Amitāyus, the Buddha of Eternal Life, hence the title of the *Larger Sutra.* In China and Japan these two names, sometimes referring to distinct Buddhas in the Indian context, are referred to singularly as A-mi-t'o in Chinese and Amida in Japanese. Furthermore, although male in the Indian context, Amitābha becomes increasingly referred to in female, maternal terms in East Asia. In Japanese Pure Land, the primary reference is "compassionate mother." The distinctive characteristic of Amitābha is compassion.

The Name of Amida Buddha. In the *Meditation Sutra* it is stated that, for those who are unable to achieve the meditative visualization of the Pure Land, the recitative invocation of Amitābha's name is sufficient to attain birth. In China and especially in Japan this becomes the most widespread form of practice, known as the *nembutsu,* in which the repetition of the name, "Namu Amida Butsu" (meaning "I take refuge in Amida Buddha"), is the very manifestation of Amida. Philosophically, to take refuge in Amida Buddha is to abandon ego-centered, attached thinking and to entrust oneself to the infinite wisdom (light) and infinite compassion (life) of Amida. Since the ultimate body, or *dharmakāya,* of Amida is formless, one attains formless reality through the name.

Hōnen (1133–1212). An exponent of Pure Land Buddhism, Hōnen broke with the traditional views of other Buddhists who looked to a variety of teachings and instead advocated the single-minded recitation of the *nembutsu,* Namu Amida Butsu. Hōnen was known for his broad and deep philosophical understanding, the purity of his observance of the precepts, and his ability to cultivate various states of meditation including visualizations.

Self-power and other-power. However, he abandoned ritual observance of all of these practices at the age of forty-three and turned his attention solely to the *nembutsu.* His conclusion was that, no matter how skillful he may have appeared outwardly, inwardly it was impossible to become free from thoughts of attachment, conceit, and insecurity. The failure of this self-effort or self-power *(jiriki)* opened up the realm of other-power *(tariki)*, the formless reality of the highest truth taking shape in the wisdom and compassion of boundless light, Amida Buddha, embodied in the name. The two ideas of self-power and other-power are complementary. Without seeing the one, the other cannot be seen; they are like the clouds and the sun that shines through them.

Foolish being. Hōnen states, "In the path of the Pure Land one attains birth by returning to an ignorant fool."[1] One aspect of this indicates the foolishness of sentient beings, the other aspect the wisdom of one who is aware of foolishness (i.e., one's blindness; one's limited, incomplete self), a kind of beginner's mind. Thus the same being who attains awareness of his or her foolishness is also regarded as "equal to the buddhas" (a limitless, complete self). There is some similarity between Shinran's notion of foolish being (Jpn. *bonbu*) and the Zen expression of beginner's mind (Jpn. *shoshin*). Only the one who knows his foolishness is open to the boundlessness of reality; only one who knows that she is a beginner can tap the vivid wisdom of emptiness unfolding in the here and now.

Pure Land beyond form. The Pure Land no longer refers to a jeweled paradise here; it refers to the realm of emptiness in which all beings and phenomena are grasped in their suchness. When a disciple asked Hōnen near the end of his life, "Master, what is the importance of visualizations?" Hōnen replied, "At first I, Hōnen, also engaged in such frivolities, but no longer. Now I simply say the *nembutsu* of entrusting." "Even if one is able to see the jeweled trees [of the Pure Land], they could not be more beautiful than the blossoms and fruit of plum and peach trees [found in this world]."[2]

The Pure Land can be understood to be the realm of emptiness. Hōnen taught that the unfolding of Amida's compassion and wisdom was felt in this life, but full birth in the Pure Land in the next. This parallels the relationship between nirvana and Parinirvana in the life of Śākyamuni. As long as one has attachments, it can be misleading and dangerous to say that emptiness is already present. However, at the very end of his life, when a disciple asked Hōnen if he would be born in the Pure Land, he replied, "Since I have always been in the Pure Land, that will not happen."[3]

Shinran (1173–1262). Shinran was an exponent of Pure Land Buddhism who studied with Hōnen. His form of Pure Land Buddhism is often referred to as Shin Buddhism, reflecting his expression "Jōdo-shinshū," the "true teaching" of the Pure Land. Like his teacher, he emphasizes the awareness of the foolish being who, endeavoring to free him- or herself from the cycle of ignorance and attachment, sees more and more clearly his or her own foolishness.

Shinjin. Like Hōnen, Shinran advocated the recitation of the *nembutsu.* Whereas Hōnen emphasized simply repeating the name constantly, Shinran emphasized the simultaneous awareness of foolishness and the awareness of boundless compassion. The term for this is *shinjin,* which is often rendered as "true entrusting," a letting go of all attachments enabling the natural unfolding of compassion and wisdom. One who attains the wisdom of true entrusting is regarded as the equal of buddhas. Since the heart of the *nembutsu,* as is the case in all forms of practice that are thought to embody highest truth, is beyond distinctions, Shinran states, "In the *nembutsu,* no meaning is the true meaning."[4] At the same time, Shinran cautions, "If you talk about [this] too much, then 'no meaning' will appear to have some kind of special meaning."[5]

Naturalness (jinen). The foolish being is always contriving or calculating to reach a goal dualistically, whether that goal is material, such as worldly success or health, or is spiritual, such as enlightenment or birth. The one who becomes aware of this foolishness and is receptive to the compassion of Amida is led beyond this contrivance to a realm of spontaneous freedom. This spontaneity, in contrast to the contrivance of the foolish being, is called *jinen hōni,* the suchness of spontaneity, or more simply, naturalness.

The Vow of Amida. Shinran understands Amida Buddha in terms of two aspects of the *dharmakāya,* or dharma-body: *dharmakāya*-as-suchness (emptiness) and *dharmakāya*-as-compassion. The awareness of *dharmakāya*-as-compassion leads to the realization of *dharmakāya*-as-suchness. The process of being led to the life of spontaneity through the *dharmakāya*-as-compassion is expressed as entrusting oneself to the Vow of Amida, the vow to lead all sentient beings to buddhahood by awakening them out of their foolishness.

Tannishō.[6] The *Tannishō* is a record of statements made by Shinran, the founder of Shin Buddhism, the largest movement of Japanese Pure Land Buddhism. Shinran abandoned the monastic life, lived among farmers and fishermen, and married and had a family. He lived the life of the *nembutsu,* the saying of the Name of Amida Buddha, Namu Amida Butsu.

The *Tannishō* is the most widely read work of Japanese Buddhism and also the most widely translated. It is written in two parts: The first ten sections are direct quotations from Shinran's own words communicated to his followers. The next eight sections plus the epilogue consist of commentary by Shinran's close follower Yuien; there are also several quotations of statements made by Shinran embedded in Yuien's commentary.

Key Terms in Mahāyāna Buddhism and Shin Buddhism

Pure Land Buddhism makes use of key terms in the two-fold truth scheme of Mahāyāna Buddhism in which all phenomena are seen in terms of two aspects: that of appearances, words, and distinctions, on the one hand; and that which is without form, inconceivable, and beyond distinctions, on the other. In addition to the usual terms of this two-fold truth as diagrammed below in two columns, Pure Land Buddhism uses close correlates such as foolish being/ Amida Buddha and defiled world/nirvana.

Suffering arises when one becomes attached to the conventional world of appearances, words, and distinctions and fails to realize their illusory, provisional nature. The form of appearances, such as the shape of a beautiful flower; words or ideas, involving friendship or material goods; or distinctions, as found in high/low, beautiful/ugly, by themselves entail no suffering. It is only when one becomes attached to them that they cause suffering. In the left hand column below, the terms above the lateral line denote the world of conventional truth which in itself does not bring about suffering. The terms below the line denote conventional truth accompanied by the attachments that cause suffering. Thus, attachment to a fixed idea of romantic love causes suffering, turns the world into samsara, defiled by the misperceptions of our skewed senses, resulting in blind passion, based on the self-enclosed narrow-mindedness of self-power, turning us into foolish beings, which, paradoxically, is none other than "Namu" the object of boundless compassion.

Conventional truth   Highest truth
Form   Emptiness

| Distinctions | No distinctions |
Words	Beyond words
suffering	liberation
samsara	nirvana
defiled world	Pure Land
blind passion	boundless compassion
self-power	other-power
foolish being	Amida Buddha
Namu	Amida Butsu

Some Expressions and Ideas for which Shinran Is Well Known

I really do not know whether the nembutsu may be the cause for my birth in the Pure Land, or the act that shall condemn me to hell. . . . Since I am absolutely incapable of any religious practice, hell is my only home. (*Tannishō*, sec. 3)

Even the good attain birth in the Pure Land, how much more so the evil person. (*Tannishō*, sec. 3)

I am neither monk nor layman. (*Kyōgyōshinshō*, afterword)

As for myself, Shinran, I do not have a single disciple. (*Tannishō*, sec. 6) [Shinran referred to his followers as *ondōbō, ondōgyō,* "fellow seekers, fellow practicers (of the *nembutsu*)," using the honorific prefix *on-* to relate to them.]

Amida's Primal Vow does not discriminate between young and old, good and evil—true entrusting (Jpn. *shinjin*) alone is essential. The reason is that the Vow is directed toward the person burdened with the flames of blind passion.

I, Shinran, have never even once uttered the *nembutsu* for the sake of my father and mother. The reason is that all beings have been fathers and mothers, brothers and sisters, in the timeless process of birth-and-death. (*Tannishō*, sec. 5)

When I ponder the compassionate vow of Amida, established through five aeons of profound thought, I realize it was for myself, Shinran, alone. (*Tannishō*, epilogue)

In the *nembutsu* no meaning is the true meaning; it is indescribable, ineffable, inconceivable. (*Tannishō*, sec. 10)

A Poem by a Modern Shin Teacher and Poet

Mihotoke no na wo yobu waga koe wa
Mihotoke no ware o yobimasu mikoe narikeri

The voice with which I call Amida Buddha
Is the voice with which Amida Buddha calls to me.

—Kai Wariko

"T." refers to the *Taishō shinshū daizōkyō* (full bibliographical information below). "P." refers to the Peking Tripitaka, and "D." refers to the Derge or Tibetan Tripitaka; in these cases, it is common practice to not provide full bibliography as the standard, classical collections are well-known and do not have the same kind of publication information as the Taishō or other modern collections.

Some individual works included in endnotes have been subsumed under the collections listed below so that they are not listed individually.

Premodern Works

Abhidharmakośabhāsyam. Ed. S. D. Shastri. Varanasi: Bauddha Bharati Series, 1981.

Dharmadharmatāvibhaṅga-vṛtti. By Vasubandhu. P.5529; D.4028, attributed to Maitreya.

Eshin Sōzu Zenshū. Ed. Eizan Gakuin. Kyoto: Shibunkaku, 1973.

Hōnen Shōnin zenshū. Kyoto: Heirakuji Shoten, 1987.

Jōdo Shinshū Seiten: Shichiso hen chūshaku ban. Kyoto: Hongwanji Shuppansha, 1988.

Kathavatthu. London: Pali Text Society, 1979.

Mahāyāna-saṅgraha. By Vasubandhu. T.1594; P.5549; D.4048.

Mahāyāna-saṅgraha-bhāsya. By Vasubandhu. Hsüan-tsang's Chinese tr., T.1597. and Tibetan tr., P.5551; D.4050.

Mahāyāna-saṅgraha-upanibandhana. By Asvabhava. T.1598. Tibetan trans. P.5552; D.4051.

Shinshū shōgyō zensho. Kyoto: Ōyagi Kōbundo, 1941.

Suttanipāta. London: Pali Text Society, 1948.

Taishō shinshū daizōkyō. Edited by Takakusu Junjirō and Watanabe Kaigyoku. 100 vols. Tokyo: Taishō Issaikyō Kankōkai, 1924–32.

Trimsika-bhāsya by *Sthiramati.* Paris: Sylvain Levi Librairie Ancienne Honoré Champion, 1925.

Yogācārabhūmi by *Asaṅga.* Ed. Bhattacharya. Calcutta: University of Calcutta, 1957.

Yogācārabhūmi. Trans. Hsüan Tsang. T.1579.

Modern Works

BOOKS

Almaas, A. H. *Diamond Heart, Book Three: Being and the Meaning of Life*. Berkeley, Diamond Books, 1990.

_____. *The Pearl Beyond Price*. Berkeley: Diamond Books, 1988.

_____. *The Point of Existence*. Berkeley: Diamond Books, 1996.

_____. *Self versus True Nature*, Talks on Tape. Berkeley: Almaas Publications, 1997.

_____. *Spacecruiser Inquiry*. Boston: Shambhala, 2002.

Ama Toshimaro. *Nihonjin wa naze mu-shūkyō nanoka*. Tokyo: Chikuma Shobō, 1996.

Aronson, Harvey B. *Buddhist Practice on Western Ground: Reconciling Eastern Ideals and Western Psychology*. Boston: Shambhala Publications, 2004.

_____. *Love and Sympathy in Theravada Buddhism*. Delhi: Motilal Banarsidassa, 1984.

Aronson, Nicholos D. *Being Interior: Autobiography and the Contradictions of Modernity in Seventeenth-Century France*. Philadelphia: University of Pennsylvania Press, 2001.

Austin, James H. *Zen and the Brain: Toward an Understanding of Meditation and Consciousness*. Cambridge, Massachusetts: M.I.T. Press, 1999.

Batchelor, Stephen. *Buddhism Without Beliefs*. New York: Riverhead Books, 1993.

_____, trans. *A Guide to the Bodhisattva's Way of Life*. Dharmasala, India: Library of Tibetan Works and Archives, 1979.

Bateson, Gregory. *Steps to an Ecology of Mind*. New York: Ballantine Books, 1972.

Bechert, Heinz. *Buddhismus, Staat und Gesellschaft in den Ländern des Theravāda-Buddhismus*, Vol. 1. Frankfurt am Main and Berlin: Alfred Metzner Verlag, 1966; Vol. 2. Wiesbaden: Otto Harrassowitz, 1967.

Bennett-Goleman, Tara. *Emotional Alchemy: How the Mind Can Heal the Heart*. New York: Harmony Books, 2001.

Benz, Ernst. *Buddhas Wiedekehr und die Zukunft Asiens*. Munich: Nymphenburger Verlagshandlung, 1963.

Bodhi, Bhikkhu. *A Comprehensive Manual of Abhidhamma*. Kandy, Sri Lanka: Buddhist Publication Society, 2000.

_____, trans. *The Connected Discourses of the Buddha*. Boston: Wisdom Publications, 2000.

Brassard, Francis. *The Concept of Bodhicitta in Śāntideva's Bodhicaryāvatāra*. Albany: State University of New York Press, 2000.

Broad, C. D. *The Mind and Its Place in Nature*. London: Routledge and Kegan Paul, 1925.

Buswell, Jr. Robert E. and Robert M. Gimello, eds. *Paths to Liberation: The Mārga and its Transformations in Buddhist Thought*. Kuroda Institute Studies in East Asian Buddhism, No. 7. Honolulu: University of Hawaii Press, 1992.

Camus, Albert. *The Plague*. Trans. Gilbert Stuart. New York: Vintage Press, 1972.

Capper, Daniel. *Guru Devotion and the American Buddhist Experience.* Lewiston, New York: Edwin Mellon Press, 2002.

Carrithers, Michael. *Why Humans Have Cultures.* New York: Oxford University Press, 1922.

Cary, Phillip. *Augustine's Invention of the Inner Self: The Legacy of a Christian Platonist.* Oxford: Oxford University Press, 2000.

Clarke, J. J. *Jung and Eastern Thought: A Dialogue with the Orient.* London and New York: Routledge, 1994.

Collins, Stephen. *Selfless Persons: Imagery and Thought in Theravāda Buddhism.* Cambridge: Cambridge University Press, 1982.

Comité de traduction Padmakara, trans. *Comprendre la Vacuité: Deux commentaires du chapitre IX de La Marche vers l'Eveil de Shantideva.* Saint-Léon-sur-Vézère, France: Editions Padmakara, 1993.

Crosby, Kate and Andrew Skilton, trans. *The Bodhicaryāvatāra.* Oxford: Oxford University Press, 1995.

Dalai Lama. *Transcendent Wisdom.* trans. and ed. B. Alan Wallace. Rev. ed. Ithaca, New York: Snow Lion, 1994.

_____. *A Flash of Lightning in the Dark of Night: A Guide to the Bodhisattva's Way of Life.* Trans. Padmakara Translation Group. Boston and London: Shambhala, 1994.

Danziger, Kurt. *Constructing the Subject: Historical Origins of Psychological Research.* Cambridge: Cambridge University Press, 1990.

Davis, Madeleine and David Wallbridge. *Boundary and Space: An Introduction to the Work of D. W. Winnicott.* New York: Brunner/Mazel, 1981.

Deacon, T. W. *The Symbolic Species: The Co-evolution of Language and the Brain.* New York: W. W. Norton & Co, 1977.

Deshung Rinpoche. *The Three Levels of Spiritual Perception.* Boston: Wisdom Publications, 1995.

Despeux, Catherine. *Le Chemin de l'Eveil.* Paris: l'Asiatheque, 1981.

Droit, Roger-Pol. *Le Culte du Néant: Les philosophes et le Bouddha.* Paris: Éditions du Seuil, 1997.

Edinger, Edward. *Ego and Archetype: Individuation and the Religious Function of the Psyche.* Baltimore: Penguin Books, 1974.

Edgerton, Franklin. *Buddhist Hybrid Sanskrit Grammar and Dictionary.* Reprint. Kyoto: Rinsen Book Co, 1985.

Epstein, Mark. *Thoughts Without a Thinker: Psychotherapy from a Buddhist Perspective.* New York: Basic Books, 1995.

Freud, Sigmund. *New Introductory Lectures to Psychoanalysis.* New York: W. W. Norton & Co., 1965.

Friedman, Milton and Rose Friedman. *Free to Choose.* New York: Harcourt, 1980.

Garfield, Jay, trans. with commentary. *The Fundamental Wisdom of the Middle Way.* New York: Oxford University Press, 1995.

Gearein-Tosh, Michael. *Living Proof: A Medical Mutiny.* New York: Simon & Schuster, 2002.

Gethin, R. M. L. *The Buddhist Path to Awakening.* Oxford: Oneworld Publications, 1992, reprint 2001.

Goodwin, Brian. *How the Leopard Changed its Spots: The Evolution of Complexity.* London: Phoenix Press, 1994.

Gregory, Richard, ed. *The Oxford Companion to the Mind.* Oxford: Oxford University Press, 1987.

Guenther, H. V. *Philosophy and Psychology in the Abhidharma.* Delhi: Motilal Banarsidassa, 1959.

Gyatso, Geshe Kelsang. *Meaningful to Behold: View, Meditation and Action in Mahayana Buddhism.* Ulverston, England: Wisdom Publications, 1980.

Haley, Jay. *Uncommon Therapy: The Psychiatric Techniques of Milton H. Erickson.* New York: Norton, 1986.

Hamilton, Sue. *Early Buddhism—A New Approach: the I of the Beholder.* Surrey: Curzon Press, 2000.

Hammer, Olav. *Claiming Knowledge: Strategies of Epistemology from Theosophy to the New Age.* Numen Book Series, Vol. XC. Leiden: Brill, 2001.

Hirano Keiko. *Kodomo tachi yo arigatō.* Kyoto: Hōzōkan, 1990.

Hirose Hirotada. *Kokoro no senzairyoku—placebo kōka.* Tokyo: Asahi Shinbunsha, 2001.

Hirota, Dennis, *et al,* trans. and ed. *Collected Works of Shinran, The.* Volumes I and II. Kyoto: Jōdo Shinshū Hongwanji-ha, 1997.

Hisamatsu Shin'ichi *et al,* ed. *Suzuki Daisetsu no Hito to Shisō.* Tokyo: Shunjūsha, 1961.

Homans, Peter. *The Ability to Mourn: Disillusionment and the Social Origins of Psychoanalysis.* Chicago: University of Chicago Press, 1989.

Horner, I. B., trans. *Majjhima Nikāya, Middle Length Saying.* London: Pali Text Society, 1954–59.

_____, trans. *Milinda's Questions.* London: Pali Text Society, 1963–64.

Inagaki Hisao, ed. *A Glossary of Zen Terms.* Kyoto: Nagata Bunshodō, 1996.

_____, trans. *Commentary on the Discourse on the Pure Land.* Kyoto: Nagata Bunshodō, 1998.

Ireland, John D. and Bhikkhu Nanananda, trans. *An Anthology from the Samyutta Nikāya,* Kandy: Buddhist Publication Society, 1981.

Ishida Mizumaro. *Nihon Jōdokyō no yoake.* Tokyo: Heibonsha, 1981.

Ishii Kenji. *Deeta bukku—gendai Nihonjin no shūkyō.* Tokyo: Shinyōsha, 1997.

Jackson, Roger. *Is Enlightenment Possible?* Ithaca: Snow Lion, 1993.

Jacoby, Mario. *Individuation and Narcissism: The Psychology of Self in Jung and Kohut.* Trans. Myron Gubitz and Françoise O'Kane. Reprint. New York: Brunner-Routledge, 2002.

James, William. *Varieties of Religious Experience.* New York: Collier Books, 1977.

Jayatilleke, K. N. *Early Buddhist Theory of Knowledge*. Delhi: Motilal Banarsidassa, 1963.

Johansson, R. E. A. *The Dynamic Psychology of Early Buddhism*. London: Curzon Press, 1979.

Jonas, Raymond. *France and the Cult of the Sacred Heart: An Epic Tale for Modern Times*. Berkeley, Los Angeles and London: University of California Press, 2000.

Jung, C. G. "The Psychology of the Transference" in *Collected Works of C. G. Jung*. Vol. 16. Princeton: Princeton University Press, 1946.

_____. "The Spirit Mercurius" in *Collected Work of C. G. Jung*. Princeton: Princeton University Press, 1943.

_____. Religion: West and East, trans. R. F. C. Hull. Bollingen Series, No. XX. Collected Works of C. G. Jung. Vol. 11. Princeton: Princeton University Press, 2nd ed., 1969.

Kalu Rinpoche. *Luminous Mind: The Way of the Buddha*. Boston: Wisdom Publications, 1997.

Kamei Katsuichirō, *Ai to inori ni tsuite*. Tokyo: Daiwa Shobō, 1967.

Kapleau, Phillip. *Zen Dawn in the West*. New York: Anchor Press/Doubleday, 1979.

Kawai, Hayao. *Buddhism and the Art of Psychotherapy*. College Station, Texas: Texas A & M University Press, 1996.

_____. *The Buddhist Priest Myōe: A Life of Dream*. Trans. Mark Unno. Venice, California: The Lapis Press, 1992.

Keown, Damien, ed. *Buddhist Studies from India to America: Essays in Honor of Charles S. Prebish*. London and New York: RoutledgeCurzon, 2006.

Kirschner, Suzanne. *The Religious and Romantic Origins of Psychoanalysis: Individuation and Integration in Post-Freudian Theory*. Cambridge: Cambridge University Press, 1996.

Klein, Anne C. *Meeting the Great Bliss Queen: Buddhists, Feminists, and the Art of the Self*. Boston: Beacon Press, 1995.

_____ and Geshe Tenzin Wangyal Rinpoche. *Unbounded Wholeness: Dzogchen, Bon and the Logic of the Nonconceptual*. New York: Oxford University Press, 2006.

Kohut, Heinz. *How Does Analysis Cure*. Chicago: University of Chicago Press, 1984.

_____. *The Analysis of the Self*. New York: International Universities Press, 1971.

Kornfield, Jack. *A Path with a Heart: A Guide Through the Perils and Promises of Spiritual Life*. New York: Bantam, 1993.

Kretch, Gregg. *Naikan: Gratitude, Grace, and the Japanese Art of Self-realization*. Berkeley: Stone Bridge Press, 2002.

Kuo Li-ying. *Confession et Contrition dans le Bouddhisme Chinois du Ve au Xe siècle*. Paris: École Française d'Extrême-Orient, 1994.

Lakoff, George and Mark Johnson. *Philosophy in the Flesh: The Embodied Mind and its Challenge to Western Thought*. New York: Basic Books, 1997.

La Vallée Poussin, Louis de, trans. *Abhidharmakośabhāṣyam by Vasubandhu*. Retranslated into English by Leo Pruden. Berkeley: Asian Humanities Press, 1990.

Lambert, Kenneth. *Analysis, Repair and Individuation*, The Library of Analytical Psychology, Vol. 5. London: Academic Press, 1981.

Lamotte, Etienne, ed. and trans. *Samdhinirmocana Sutra: L'Explication des Mysteres*. Louvain: Université de Louvain, 1935.

Lenoir, Frédéric. *La rencontre du bouddhisme de l'Occident*. Paris: Librarie Arthème Fayard, 1999.

Linehan, Marsha. *Cognitive-Behavioral Treatment of Borderline Personality Disorder*. New York: Guilford, 1993.

Longchen Yeshe Dorje. *Treasury of Precious Qualities*. Trans. Padmakara Translation Group. Boston: Shambhala Publications, 2001.

MacIntyre, Alasdair. *The Unconscious: A Conceptual Analysis*. London: Routledge Kegan Paul, 1958.

Malin, Shimon. *Nature Loves to Hide: Quantum Physics and the Nature of Reality, a Western Perspective*. Oxford: Oxford University Press, 2001.

Masterson, James F. *The Emerging Self*. New York: Basic Books, 1993.

Matics, Marion L., trans. *Entering the Path of Entering the Path of Enlightenment* by Śāntideva. New York: The Macmillan Co., 1970.

Maturana, Humberto and Francisco Varela. *Autopoiesis and Cognition: The Realization of the Living*. Dordrecht, Holland: D. Reidel Pub. Co., 1980.

Metcalf, Franz. "Why Do Americans Practice Zen Buddhism?" Ph.D. diss. Chicago: University of Chicago, 1997.

Michaels, Axel. *Hinduism: Past and Present*. Princeton and Oxford: Princeton University Press, 2004.

Molino, Anthony, ed. *The Couch and the Tree: Dialogues between Psychoanalysis and Buddhism*. San Francisco: North Point Press, 1999.

Murphy, Michael and Steven Donovan. *The Physical and Psychological Effects of Meditation: A Review of Contemporary Research with a Comprehensive Bibliography 1931–1936*. Sausalito: Institute of Noetic Sciences, 2nd ed., 1977.

Nagao, Gadjin. *Madhyamika and Yogacara*, trans. and ed. L. Kawamura. Albany: SUNY Press, 1991.

Nakamura Hajime. *Gotama Budda, bk. 1, Nakamura Hajime Senshū*. Vol. 11. Tokyo: Shunjūsha, 1992.

Needham, Joseph. *Science and Civilization in China, Vol. 2: History of Scientific Thought*. Cambridge: Cambridge University Press, 1969.

Nihon Ishikai Dai Hachiki Seimei Rinri Kondankai, *Iryō no jissen to seimei rinri ni tsuite no hōkoku*. http://www.med.or.jp/nichikara/seirin15.pdf. [February 18, 2004].

Nyanamoli, trans. *The Middle Length Discourses of the Buddha*. Boston: Wisdom Press, 1997.

_____. *Visuddhimagga: The Path of Purification* by Buddhaghosa. Berkeley: Shambhala, 1976.

Ohtani Kōshin. *Ashita niwa kōgan arite*. Tokyo: Kadokawa Shoten, 2003.

Olendzki, Andrew, trans. *Therigatha Atthakatha,* X.I. http://www.accesstoinsight.org/noncanon/comy/index.html [August 14, 2005].

Pabonka Rinpoche. *Liberation in the Palm of Your Hand.* Rev. ed. Boston: Wisdom Publications, 1993.

Padmakara Translation Group, trans. *The Way of the Bodhisattva: A Translation of the Bodhicaryāvatara.* Boston: Shambhala, 1997.

Pezzali, Amalia. *Śāntideva: Mystique Bouddhiste des VIIe et VIIIe Siècles.* Firenze: Vallecchi Editore, 1968.

Pitman, Don A. *Toward a Modern Chinese Buddhism: Taixu's Reforms.* Honolulu: University of Hawai'i Press, 2001.

Prebish, Charles S. and Martin Baumann, eds. *Westward Dharma: Buddhism beyond Asia.* Berkeley and Los Angeles: University of California Press, 2002.

Rahula, Walpola, trans. *Le Compendium de la Super-doctrine (Philosophie) (Abhidharmasamuccaya) d'Asanga.* Paris: Ecole Française d'Extrême Orient, 1980.

Restak, Richard M. *The Modular Brain: How New Discoveries in Neuroscience are Answering Age-old Questions about Memory, Free Will, Consciousness, and Personal Identity.* New York: Touchstone Books, 1994.

Reynolds, David. *Naikan Psychotherapy.* Chicago: University of Chicago Press, 1983.

Reynolds, John. *Self-liberation through Seeing with Naked Awareness.* Barrytown, New York: Station Hill Press, 1989.

Roland, Alan. *In Search of Self in India and Japan.* Princeton: Princeton University Press, 1989.

Rorty, Richard. *Philosophy and the Mirror of Nature.* Princeton: Princeton University Press, 1980.

Rubin, Jeffrey. *Psychotherapy and Buddhism: Toward an Integration.* New York: Plenum Press, 1996.

Rumi. *The Essential Rumi,* trans. Coleman Banks with John Moyne. San Francisco: Harper Collins, 1996.

Russell, Bertrand. *The Problems of Philosophy.* New York: Oxford University Press, 1959.

Safran, Jeremy D., ed. *Psychoanalysis and Buddhism: An Unfolding Dialogue.* Boston: Wisdom Publications, 2003.

Rhys-Davids, C. A. F., ed. *Compendium of Philosophy: Translation of Abhidhammattha Sangaha.* Originally trans. Aung Shwe Zang. London: Pali Text Society, 1979.

_____. and F. L. Woodward, trans. *Samyutta Nikāya: The Book of the Kindred Sayings.* London: Pali Text Society, 1917–30.

Saddhatissa, trans. *Suttanipata.* London: Curzon Press, 1985.

Sangharakshita. Ritual and Devotion in Buddhism: An Introduction. Birmingham, England: Windhorse Press, 2nd ed., 2000.

Sayadaw, Ledi. *Manual of Insight (Vipassana Dipani).* The Wheel Publication, No.31/32. Kandy, Sri Lanka: Buddhist Publication Society, 1961.

Schmithausen, Lambert. *Ālayavijñāna: On the Origin and the Early Development of a Central Concept of Yogacara Philosophy.* Tokyo International Institute for Buddhist Studies, 1987.

Shimada Hiromi. *Bukkyō wa naniwo sitekureruka.* Tokyo: Kōdansha, 1992.

Shimazono Susumu. *Gendai shūkyō no kanōsei.* Tokyo: Iwanami Shoten. 1997.

_____. *Postmodern no shin-shūkyo.* Tokyo: Tokyōdō Shuppan, 2001.

Shweder, Richard. *Thinking Through Cultures: Expeditions in Cultural Psychology.* Cambridge, MA: Harvard University Press, 1991.

Sparkes, A. W. *Talking Philosophy: a Wordbook.* London: Routledge, 1991.

Stein, Murray. *Jung's Map of the Soul: An Introduction.* Chicago and LaSalle: Open Court, 1998.

Stern, D. G. *Wittgenstein on Mind and Language.* New York: Oxford University Press. 1995.

Suryadas, Lama. *Eight Steps to Enlightenment: Awakening the Buddha Within.* New York: Broadway Books, 1997.

Suzuki Akiko, *Gan kokuchi no ato de.* Kyoto: Tankyūsha, 1989.

Suzuki D. T. *Nihonteki reisei.* Tokyo: Iwanami Shoten Bunkoban, 1977.

Taylor, Charles. *Sources of the Self: The Making of the Modern Identity.* Cambridge, Massachusetts: Harvard University Press, 1989.

Thera, Nyanaponika and Bhikkhu Bodhi. *Numerical Discourses of the Buddha: An Anthology of Suttas from the Anguttara Nikāya.* Walnut Creek, California: AltaMira Press, 1999.

Thompson, Leonard L. *The Book of Revelation: Apocalypse and Empire.* Oxford: Oxford University Press, 1990.

Tomasello, Michael. *The Cultural Origins of Human Cognition.* Cambridge: Harvard University Press, 1999.

Tsong-kha-pa, *The Great Treatise on the Stages to the Path to Enlightenment.* trans. Lamrim Chenmo Translation Committee, Joshua Cutler, Editor in Chief. Ithaca, New York: Snow Lion Publications, 2001.

Ueda, Yoshifumi. *Mahayana Buddhism: An Approach to Its Essence.* Los Angeles: Pure Land Publications, 1989.

Unno, Mark. *Shingon Refractions: Myōe and the Mantra of Light.* Boston: Wisdom Publications, 2004.

Unno, Taitetsu, trans. *Tannisho: A Shin Buddhist Classic.* Rev. ed. Honolulu: Buddhist Study Center Press, 1996.

Urban, Hugh. *Tantra: Sex, Secrecy, Politics, and Power in the Study of Religion.* Berkeley: University of California Press, 2003.

Varela, Francisco and Jonathan Shear, eds. *The View from Within: First-person Approach to the Study of Consciousness.* Exeter, UK: Imprint Academic, 1999.

Waldron, William S. *The Buddhist Unconscious: The Alaya-vijñana in the Context of Indian Buddhist Thought.* London: RoutledgeCurzon, 2002.

Wallace, Vesna and B. Alan Wallace, trans. *A Guide to the Bodhisattva Way of Life* Ithaca, New York: Snow Lion Publications, 1997.

Warren, Henry Clarke. *Buddhism in Translations.* New York: Atheneum, 1963.

Weber, Claudia. *Buddhistische Beichten in Indien und bei den Uiguren: Unter besonderer Berücksichtigung der uigurischen Laienbeichte und ihrer Beziehung zum Manichäismus.* Wiesbaden: Harrassovitz Verlag, 1999,

Welwood, John. *Toward a Psychology of Awakening: Buddhism, Psychotherapy, and the Path of Personal and Spiritual Transformation.* Boston: Shambhala Publications, 2000.

Wilber, Ken, Jack Engler, and Daniel P. Brown, eds. *Transformations of Consciousness: Conventional and Contemplative Perspectives on Development.* New Science Library. Boston: Shambhala Publications, 1986.

Williams, Bruce. *Mea Maxima Vikalpa: Repentance, Meditation, and the Dynamics of Liberation in Medieval Chinese Buddhism, 500–650 C.E..* Ph.D. diss. Berkley: University of California, Berkeley, 2002.

Winnicott, D. W. *Collected Papers: Through Paediatrics to Psycho-Analysis.* New York: Basic Books, 1958.

_____. *The Maturational Processes and the Facilitating Environment.* London: Hogarth Press and the Institute for Psycho-Analysis, 1965.

_____. *Playing and Reality.* London and New York: Routledge, 1971.

_____. *Psychoanalytic Explorations.* Ed. Clare Winnicott, Ray Shepherd, and Madeleine Davis. Cambridge: Harvard University Press, 1989.

Weber, Max. *Theory of Social and Economic Organization.* Glencoe: Free Press, 1964.

WHO, ed. *Gan no itami kara no kaihō to pariatibu kea.* Tokyo: Kanehara Shuppan, 1993.

WHO, ed. *Gan no itami kara no kaihō.* Tokyo: Kanehara Shuppan, 1996.

Whyte, Lancelot L. *The Unconscious Before Freud.* London: Julian Friedmann Publishers, 1978.

Williams, Paul. *Altruism and Reality: Studies in the Philosophy of the Bodhicaryāvatāra.* Richmond, England: Curzon Press, 1998.

_____. *Mahayana Buddhism.* London: Routledge, 1989.

_____. *The Reflexive Nature of Awareness: A Tibetan Madhyamaka Defence.* Richmond, England: Curzon Press, 1998.

Wolf, Ernest S. *Treating the Self.* New York: The Guilford Press, 1988.

Yamaoka, Haruo. *Awakening of Gratitude in Dying.* San Francisco: BCA Research and Educational Committee, 1978.

Yamaoka, Seigen H. *Jōdo Shinshū: An Introduction.* San Francisco: Buddhist Churches of America, 1989.

_____. *The Transmission of Shin Buddhism to the West.* San Francisco: Federation of Dharma School Teacher's League, 2005.

Yamazaki Fumio. *Byōin de shinu to iu koto.* Tokyo: Bunshun Bunkō, 1996.

Yanagida Seizan. *Zen shisō.* Tokyo: Chūōkōronsha, 1975.

Yoshimoto Ishin. *Naikanhō.* Tokyo: Shunjūsha, 1989.

Yuasa Yasuo. *Kodaijin no Seisinsekai.* Kyoto: Minerva Shobō. 1980.

_____. *Postmodern no shin-shūkyō.* Tokyo: Tokyōdō Shuppan, 2001.

Zenkoku hosupisu kanwa kea byōtō renraku kyōgikai, ed. *Hosupisu te nāni?* Tokyo: NHK Kōsei Bunka Jigyōdan, 2003.

Zotz, Volker. *Auf den Glückseligen Inseln: Buddhismus in der deutschen Kultur.* Berlin: Theseus Verlag, 2000.

ARTICLES

Asai Jōkai. "Shinran no shōji kan." *Nihon Bukkyō Gakkai-Bukkyō no shōji kan.* Kyoto: Heirakuji Shoten, 1981.

Atwood, George E. and Robert D. Stolorow. "Metapsychology, Reification and the Representational World of C.G. Jung." *International Review of Psychoanalysis,* 4 (1977): 197–214.

Bloom, Harold. "The Internalization of Quest-Romance." In *Romanticism and Consciousness: Essays in Criticism,* ed. Harold Bloom. New York and London: W.W. Norton, 1970.

Bobrow, Joseph. "The Fertile Mind." In *The Couch and the Tree: Dialogues between Psychoanalysis and Buddhism,* ed. Anthony Molino. San Francisco: North Point Press, 1999, 307–320.

_____. "Psychoanalysis, Mysticism, and the Incommunicado Core." *fort da* 8, no. 2 (2002): 62–71.

_____. "Moments of Truth, Truths of Moment." In *Psychoanalysis and Buddhism: An Unfolding Dialogue,* ed. Jeremy D. Safran. Boston: Wisdom Publications, 2003, 199–221.

Brown, Daniel and Jack Engler. "The Stages of Mindfulness Meditation: A Validation Study. Part I." In their *Transformation of Consciousness.* Boston: Shambhala, New Science Library, 1986.

Drefus, Georges. "Tibetan Scholastic Education and the Role of Soteriology." *Journal of the International Association for Buddhist Studies,* 20.1 (1995).

Eckel, Malcolm David. "Is There a Buddhist Philosophy of Nature?" In *Buddhism and Psychotherapy,* eds. Mary Evelyn Tucker and Duncan Ryuken Williams. Cambridge, Massachusetts: Harvard University CSHR Publications, 1997.

Engler, Jack. "The 1001 forms of self-grasping." *What is Enlightenment,* 17, in M. Friedman and R. Friedman, *Free to Choose.* New York: Harcourt, 1980.

_____. "Being Somebody and Being Nobody: A Reexamination of the Understanding of Self in Psychoanalysis and Buddhism," *Psychoanalysis and Buddhism: An Unfolding Dialogue,* ed. Jeremy Safran. Boston: Wisdom Publications, 2003.

_____. "Can We Say What the Self 'Really' Is?" In *Psychoanalysis and Buddhism: An Unfolding Dialogue,* ed. Jeremy D. Safran. Boston: Wisdom Publications, 2003, 86–95.

_____. "Therapeutic Aims in Psychotherapy and Meditation: Developmental Stages in the Representation of Self." In *Transformations of Consciousness: Conventional and Contemplative Perspectives on Development,* eds. Ken Wilber, Jack

Engler, and Daniel P. Brown. New Science Library. Boston and London: Shambhala Books Publications, 1986, 17–51.

Freud, Sigmund. "Ratscläge für den Arzt bei der psychoanalytischen Behandlung" (1912). *Gesammelte Werke 8*. Frankfurt am Main: S. Fischer Verlag, 1990.

Geertz, Clifford. "On the Nature of Anthropological Understanding." *American Scientist*, 63, 1975.

Gerow, Edwin. "What is Karma (Kim Karmeti): an Exercise in Philosophical Semantics." *Indological Taurinensia*, V. 10 (1982).

Greenblatt, Stephen. "Toward a Poetics of Culture." In *The New Historicism*, ed. H. Aran Veeser. New York and London: Routledge, 1989.

Hakamaya, Noriaki. "Araya-shiki sonzai no hachi-ronshu ni kansuru shobunken." *Kamazawa Daigaku Bukkyō-gakubu Kenkyū-kiyō*, 16.

_____. "Viniścarya saṁgraha ni okeru araya-shiki no kitei." *Tōyō bunka kenkyūjo kiyō*, 79: 1–79.

"Heisei 15 Kokumin seikatsu kisochōsa gaiyō." Tokyo: Kōsei rōdō shō, 2003. http://www.mhlw.go.jp/toukei/saikin/hw/k-tyosa/k-tyosa03/1-1.html [November 2004].

Hori, Victor Sōgen, Richard P. Hayes, and James Mark Shields, eds. In *Teaching Buddhism in the West: From the Wheel to the Web*. RoutledgeCurzon, 2002.

Jackson, David. "The *bTsan rim* ('Stages of the Doctrine') and Similar Graded Expositions of the Bodhisattva's Path." In *Tibetan Literature: Studies in Genre*. Eds. José Ignacio Cabezón and Roger R. Jackson. Ithaca, New York: Snow Lion, 1996.

Jaffe, Richard M. "Seeking Śākyamuni: Travel and the Reconstruction of Japanese Buddhism," *Journal of Japanese Studies*, 30.1, 2004.

Jōdo Shinshū Hongwanji-ha, Dendō Shakai-bu, "Vihara katsudō no rinen to hōkōsei." http://www2.hongwanji.or.jp/social/vihala/html/rinen.html [November 2004].

Kohut, Heinz and Ernest S. Wolf. "The Disorders of the Self and Their Treatment: An Outline." *International Journal of Psycho-Analysis*, 59 (1978).

Kokumin seikatsu kisochōsa gaiyō [Overview of Research on the Fundamentals of Citizens Living, 2003]. Kōsei rōdō shō, 2003. http://www.mhlw.go.jp/toukei/saikin/hw/k-tyosa/k-tyosa03/1-1.html. [November 2004].

Kōsei rōdō shō tōkeihyō deetabeesu. http://wwwdbtk.mhlw.go.jp/toukei/index.html [November 2004].

Lawrence, David. "The Mythico-Ritual Syntax of Omnipotence," *Philosophy East & West*, 48:4 (1998).

Markus, Hazel Rose and Shinobu Kitayama, "The Cultural Constructions of Self and Emotion: Implications for Social Behavior." *Emotion and Culture: Empirical Studies of Mutual Influence*, 1994.

Metcalf, Franz. "The Encounter of Buddhism and Psychology." In *Westward Dharma: Buddhism beyond Asia*, eds. Charles S. Prebish and Martin Baumann. Berkeley: University of California Press, 2002, 348–364.

_____. "An Object-Relations Psychology of Zen Practice." In *Buddhist Studies from India to America: Essays in Honor of Charles S. Prebish*, ed. Damien Keown. London and New York: Routledge/Curzon, 2006, 191–206.

Nabeshima Naoki. "Hōnen ni okeru shi to kanshi no mondai, 2." *Ryūkoku daigaku ronshū*, 436 (1990).

_____. "Shinran's Approaches towards Bereavement and Grief: Transcendence and Care for the Pain of Separating from Loved Ones in Shinran's Thought," CCSBS On-line Publication Series 3 Berkeley: Institute of Buddhist Studies, 2001. http://www.shin-ibs.edu/pdfs/NabeThree.pdf.

_____. "Shinran to sono montei ni okeru shi no chōkoku," *Shinshūgaku* 97 and 98, 1988.

"Nihonjin no heikin yomyō" (Life expectance of Japanese people). Kōsei rōdō shō tōkeijōhōbu, 2002. http://www.mhlw.go.jp/toukei/saikin/hw/life/life02/index. html [November 2004].

Ōkuwa Hitoshi. "Bakumatsu zaison chishikijin to Shinshu—Hara Inashiro ni okeru 'ga' no keisei." *Nihon shisōshigaku* 29. Sendai: Nihon Shisōshigakkai, 1997.

_____. "Aru Shinshūmonto no bakumatsu." *Nihon Bukkyō no Kinsei*. Kyoto: Hōzōkan, 2003.

Rubin, Jeffrey B. "A Well-lived Life: Psychoanalytic and Buddhist Contributions." In *Psychoanalysis and Buddhism: An Unfolding Dialogue*, ed. Jeremy D. Safran. Boston: Wisdom Publications, 2003, 387–410.

Safran, Jeremy D. "Introduction: Psychoanalysis and Buddhism as Cultural Institutions." In *Psychoanalysis and Buddhism: An Unfolding Dialogue*, ed. Jeremy D. Safran. Boston: Wisdom Publications, 2003, 1–34.

Sawada Aiko, "Shi to kodoku: Makki kanja no shinriteki kumon wo mitsumete." In *Sei to shi no kyōiku: Death Education no susume*, eds. Higuchi Kazuhiko and Hirayama Masami. Osaka: Sōgensha, 1984.

Shweder, Richard A. "You're Not Sick, You're Just in Love." In *The Nature of Emotions: Fundamental Questions*, eds. Paul Ekman and Richard J. Davidson. New York: Oxford University Press, 1994.

Spiegelman, J. Marvin. "The Oxherding Pictures of Zen Buddhism: A Commentary." In J. Marvin Spiegelman and Mokusen Miyuki, *Buddhism and Jungian Psychology*. Phoenix, Arizona: Falcon Press, 1987.

Suzuki, Daisetz T. "The Awakening of a New Consciousness in Zen." In *Man and Transformation*, ed. Joseph Campbell. Eranos Yearbooks, Vol. 5, Bollingen Series, No. XXX. Princeton: Princeton University Press, 1964.

Ulanov, Ann. "Jung and Religion: the opposing Self." In *The Cambridge Companion to Jung*, eds. Polly Young-Eisendrath and Terence Dawson. Cambridge: Cambridge University Press, 1997.

Waldron, William. "Beyond Nature/Nurture: Buddhism and Biology on Interdependence." *Contemporary Buddhism*, Vol.1, No. 2 (2000).

_____. "A Comparison of the *ālayavijñāna* with Freud's and Jung's Theories of the Unconscious." *Annual Memoirs of Otani University Shin Buddhist Research Institute*, 6:109 (1998).

Williams, Paul. "General Introduction: Śāntideva and his World." In Śāntideva, *The Bodhicaryāvatāra*, trans. Kate Crosby and Andrew Skilton. Oxford: Oxford University Press, 1995.

Winnicott, D. W. "Primitive Emotional Development." In *Collected Papers: Through Paediatrics to Psycho-Analysis*. New York: Basic Books, 1958, 145–156.

_____. "Transitional Objects and Transitional Phenomena." In *Playing and Reality*. London and New York: Routledge, 1971, 1–25.

_____. "Ideas and Definitions." In *Psycho-Analytic Explorations*, ed. Clare Winnicott, Ray Shepherd, and Madeleine Davis. Cambridge: Harvard University Press, 1989, 43–44.

_____. "Primary Maternal Preoccupation." In *Collected Papers: Through Paediatrics to Psycho-Analysis*. New York: Basic Books, 1958, 300–305.

_____. "The Fate of the Transitional Object." In *Psycho-Analytic Explorations*, eds. Clare Winnicott, Ray Shepherd, and Madeleine Davis. Cambridge: Harvard University Press, 1989 [1959], 53–58.

_____. "Ego Distortion in Terms of True and False Self." In *The Maturational Processes and the Facilitating Environment*. London: Hogarth Press and the Institute for Psycho-Analysis, 1965 [1960], 140–152.

_____. "Ego Integration in Child Development." In *The Maturational Processes and the Facilitating Environment*. London: Hogarth Press and the Institute for Psycho-Analysis, 1965 [1962], 56–63.

_____. "The Location of Cultural Experience." In *Playing and Reality*. London and New York: Routledge, 1971 [1967], 95–103.

_____. "On the Use of an Object, Parts II–VII; Part IV, The Use of the Word 'Use'." In *Psycho-Analytic Explorations*, eds. Clare Winnicott, Ray Shepherd, and Madeleine Davis. Cambridge: Harvard University Press, 1989 [1968], 233–235.

_____. "The Place where We Live." In *Playing and Reality*. London and New York: Routledge, 1971, 104–110.

_____. "Playing: Creative Activity and the Search for the Self." In *Playing and Reality*. London and New York: Routledge, 1971, 53–64.

Zysk, Kenneth G. "Science of Respiration and the Doctrine of Bodily Winds," *Journal of the American Oriental Society*, Vol. 113, No. 2:205.

Introduction

1. Jeremy Safran, "Introduction," in *Buddhism and Psychoanalysis*, ed. Safran (Boston: Wisdom Publications, 2003), 2–3.
2. Individuals have interacted, of course, traveling between Asia and the West, but organized events have been relatively few in number. The Eranos conference in Ascona, Switzerland, and the Mind and Life conferences of the Dalai Lama, which often include psychotherapists and psychotherapeutic themes, are two notable exceptions.
3. Jack Engler, "Being Somebody and Being Nobody: A Reexamination of the Understanding of Self in Psychoanalysis and Buddhism," in *Buddhism and Psychoanalysis: An Unfolding Dialogue*, ed. Jeremy Safran (Boston: Wisdom Publications, 2003), 35–79.
4. Suzanne R. Kirschner, *The Religious and Romantic Origins of Psychoanalysis: Individuation and Integration in Post-Freudian Theory* (Cambridge: Cambridge University Press, 1996).
5. For a translation see, for example, Vesna A. Wallace and B. Alan Wallace, trans., *A Guide to the Bodhisattva Way of Life* (Ithaca, N.Y.: Snow Lion Publications, 1997). Payne lists several other translations and studies in the endnotes to his article.
6. C. G. Jung, "Foreword to D. T. Suzuki's 'Introduction to Zen Buddhism,'" in *Self and Liberation: The Jung/Buddhism Dialogue*, ed. Daniel Meckel and Robert Moore (New York: Paulist Press, 1992), 23.
7. Safran, *Buddhism and Psychoanalysis*, 2–34.
8. For a more complete account of MAP including the Six Aspects, see Seigen H. Yamaoka, *The Transmission of Shin Buddhism to the West* (San Francisco: Federation of Dharma School Teacher's League, 2005).

Chapter 1

1. Robert Langs, *Rating Your Psychotherapist* (New York: Henry Holt, 1989).
2. Phillip Kapleau, *Zen Dawn in the West* (New York: Anchor Press/Doubleday, 1979).
3. Buddhaghosa, *The Path of Purification (Visuddhimagga)*, trans. Nyanamoli (Kandy, Sri Lanka: Buddhist Publication Society, 1975; Boulder, Colo.: Shambhala Publications, 1976).
4. Harvey Aronson, *Buddhist Practice on Western Ground: Reconciling Eastern Ideals and Western Psychotherapy* (Boston: Shambhala Publications, 2004), 56.

5. Jack Kornfield, *A Path with Heart,* (New York: Bantam Books, 1993), 249–50.
6. Karen Armstrong, *Buddha* (New York: Penguin Putnam, 2001).
7. See Kornfield, *Path with Heart,* 246.
8. Aronson, *Buddhist Practice,* 54.
9. Kornfield, *Path with Heart.*
10. John Suler, *Contemporary Psychoanalysis and Eastern Thought* (Albany: State University of New York Press, 1993).
11. Richard Clarke, trans., *Hsin Hsin Ming,* cited in Mu Soeng, *Trust in Mind* (Boston: Wisdom Publications, 2004), 15.
12. Robert Bly, *The Kabir Book* (New York: Beacon Press, 1997).
13. Aronson, *Buddhist Practice,* 57.
14. Kornfield, *Path with Heart,* 118.

Chapter 2

1. For a concise treatment of this view, known as "perennialism," see Olav Hammer, *Claiming Knowledge: Strategies of Epistemology from Theosophy to the New Age,* Numen Book Series, vol. 90 (Leiden: Brill, 2001), 170–76. I suspect that this view is so acceptable to religious liberals because it sounds very inclusive, very accepting of religious plurality.
2. Hugh B. Urban, *Tantra: Sex, Secrecy, Politics, and Power in the Study of Religion* (Berkeley and Los Angeles: University of California Press, 2003), 47.
3. It seems that even the conception of Buddhism as a single, unitary entity was created in this process. New opportunities for international contacts created in the nineteenth century, together with the goal to assert Buddhism's status as a "world religion" equal to Christianity, led to the formulation of a shared identity that had not existed previously. See Richard M. Jaffe, "Seeking Śākyamuni: Travel and the Reconstruction of Japanese Buddhism," *Journal of Japanese Studies,* 30, no. 1 (2004): 65–96.
4. The term "Buddhist modernism" was introduced by Heinz Bechert in his *Buddhismus, Staat und Gesellschaft in den Ländern des Theravāda-Buddhismus,* 2 vols. (vol. 1: Frankfurt am Main: Alfred Metzner Verlag, 1966; vol. 2: Wiesbaden: Otto Harrassowitz, 1967). See also Ernst Benz, *Buddhas Wiedekehr und die Zukunft Asiens* (Munich: Nymphenburger Verlagshandlung, 1963), and Don A. Pitman, *Toward a Modern Chinese Buddhism: Taixu's Reforms* (Honolulu: University of Hawai'i Press, 2001).
5. I prefer to avoid the term "soteriology" because of its own roots in salvation from sin-based models of religion that are inappropriate to Buddhism.
6. It should be noted that this is not a question unique to analytical psychology. As Kurt Danziger puts it,

> Although knowledge claims are generated in specific sociohistorical situations, it does not follow that they have no significance or validity beyond

those situations. There are two possibilities here. First, psychological knowledge may be generalizable to situations other than those in which it was generated. This is the question of applicability. More fundamentally, however, there is the possibility that psychological knowledge claims may be able to tap a level of "psychological reality" that is independent of the special conditions under which it is investigated. (Kurt Danziger, *Constructing the Subject: Historical Origins of Psychological Research* [Cambridge: Cambridge University Press, 1990], 179)

It seems clear that Jung considered individuation as an instance of the latter.

7. C. G. Jung, "Foreword to Suzuki's "Introduction to Zen Buddhism,'" in *Psychology and Religion: West and East*, trans. R. F. C. Hull, Bollingen Series, no. 20, Collected Works of C. G. Jung, vol. 11, 2nd ed. (Princeton: Princeton University Press, 1969), 556 (§906). Regarding the idea of analytical psychology as a metalanguage for the study of religion, in his "Psychology of the Transference" Jung in passing describes religions as psychotherapeutic systems. C. G. Jung, "The Psychology of the Transference, Interpreted in Conjunction with a Set of Alchemical Pictures," in *The Practice of Psychotherapy: Essays on the Psychology of the Transference and Other Subjects*, trans. R. F. C. Hull, Bollingen Series, no. 20, Collected Works of C. G. Jung, vol. 16, 2nd ed. (Princeton: Princeton University Press, 1966), 193 (§390).

8. J. J. Clarke, *Jung and Eastern Thought: A Dialogue with the Orient* (London: Routledge, 1994), 120.

9. Suzanne R. Kirschner, *The Religious and Romantic Origins of Psychoanalysis: Individuation and Integration in Post-Freudian Theory* (Cambridge: Cambridge University Press, 1996), 99.

10. Leonard L. Thompson, *The Book of Revelation: Apocalypse and Empire* (Oxford: Oxford University Press, 1990), 28.

11. See, for example, Martin Bickman, *American Romantic Psychology: Emerson, Poe, Whitman, Dickinson, Melville*, 2nd ed. (Dallas: Spring Publications, 1988); and Henri F. Ellenberger, *The Discovery of the Unconscious: The History and Evolution of Dynamic Psychiatry* (New York: Basic Books, 1970).

12. Kirschner, *Religious and Romantic Origins*.

13. Ibid., 94. The idealized past of the Romantic narrative is directly related to another tendency found within modern American religious culture, primitivism. This is the idea that the primitive—either in the past of our own society, or in the present of another—is in some way more authentic, spontaneous, natural, and happy. The idealized simplicity of agrarian (or pastoral) existence embodies the image of a simple people, living close to the earth, and being naturally and spontaneously religious in a way that those living in a modern, urban, industrial society cannot possibly be. The idealized primitive not only serves as a critique of our own condition but also offers an image of what we may potentially be—if only we can somehow find it within ourselves to give

up all the complexities and sophistications of our own present existence. The rhetoric of primitivism is frequently found in connection with fascism, and provides one of the bridges between Romanticism and fascism.

14. This latter is the atonement, which significantly is often glossed in contemporary American "New Age" folk religion as "at-one-ment," thus emphasizing the return to unity.

15. Raymond Jonas, *France and the Cult of the Sacred Heart: An Epic Tale for Modern Times* (Berkeley and Los Angeles: University of California Press, 2000), 200.

16. Kirschner, *Religious and Romantic Origins,* 96.

17. Ibid., 113. When Kirschner distinguishes between psychology and psychoanalytic, she is, I believe, using "psychology" to refer to experimental psychology à la Helmholtz.

18. Harold Bloom, "The Internalization of the Quest-Romance," in *Romanticism and Consciousness: Essays in Criticism,* ed. Harold Bloom (New York: W. W. Norton, 1970), 5f. Bloom's emphasis on the quest-romance is particularly noteworthy in light of the role of Joseph Campbell, who focused almost exclusively on the myth of the hero, in the popularization of Jungian thought.

19. Kirschner, *Religious and Romantic Origins,* 163.

20. Ibid., 188.

21. See, for example, Axel Michaels, *Hinduism: Past and Present,* trans. Barbara Harshav (Princeton: Princeton University Press, 2004), 107.

22. Gerald N. Izenberg, *Impossible Individuality: Romanticism, Revolution, and the Origins of Modern Selfhood, 1787–1802* (Princeton: Princeton University Press, 1992), 8.

23. This willing submission of the individual to the state in the quest for a greater wholeness is another of the links between Romanticism and fascism.

24. Bloom, "Internalization of the Quest-Romance," 11.

25. My thanks to Jennifer Dumpert for pointing out that the most appropriate category for understanding what is known as New Age is that of folk religion.

26. Stephen Greenblatt, "Toward a Poetics of Culture," in *The New Historicism,* ed. H. Aran Veeser (New York: Routledge, 1989), 3.

27. Note, however, that Phillip Cary attributes the invention of the self as a private inner space to Augustine. Phillip Cary, *Augustine's Invention of the Inner Self: The Legacy of a Christian Platonist* (Oxford: Oxford University Press, 2000).

28. Murray Stein, *Jung's Map of the Soul: An Introduction* (Chicago: Open Court, 1998), 171.

29. Kenneth Lambert, *Analysis, Repair and Individuation,* Library of Analytical Psychology, vol. 5. (London: Academic Press, 1981), 188.

30. Lambert, 190.

31. Edward Edinger, *Ego and Archetype: Individuation and the Religious Function of the Psyche* (1972; repr., Baltimore: Penguin Books, 1974), 7.

32. Ibid., 14.

33. Ibid., 18.

34. Ibid., 7.
35. Mario Jacoby, *Individuation and Narcissism: The Psychology of Self in Jung and Kohut*, trans. Myron Gubitz and Françoise O'Kane (1990; repr., Hove, East Sussex: Brunner-Routledge, 2002), 51–55.
36. Edinger, *Ego and Archetype*, 104.
37. Lambert, *Analysis*, 193–95.
38. Ibid., 194.
39. George E. Atwood and Robert D. Stolorow, "Metapsychology, Reification and the Representational World of C. G. Jung," in *Carl Gustav Jung: Critical Assessments*, ed. Renos K. Papadopoulos, 4 vols. (London: Routledge, 1992), 1:486.
40. Ibid.
41. Ibid., 490.
42. Ann Ulanov, "Jung and Religion: the opposing Self," in *The Cambridge Companion to Jung*, ed. Polly Young-Eisendrath and Terence Dawson (Cambridge: Cambridge University Press, 1997), 296.
43. Ibid., 297.
44. Robert E. Buswell, Jr., and Robert M. Gimello, eds., *Paths to Liberation: The Mārga and its Transformations in Buddhist Thought*, Kuroda Institute Studies in East Asian Buddhism, no. 7. (Honolulu: University of Hawaii Press, 1992).
45. Daisetz T. Suzuki, "The Awakening of a New Consciousness in Zen," in *Man and Transformation*, ed. Joseph Campbell, Papers from the Eranos Yearbooks, vol. 5, Bollingen Series, no. 30 (Princeton: Princeton University Press, 1964).
46. J. Marvin Spiegelman, "The Oxherding Pictures of Zen Buddhism: A Commentary," in *Buddhism and Jungian Psychology*, ed. J. Marvin Spiegelman and Mokusen Miyuki (Phoenix, Ariz.: Falcon Press, 1987); Hayao Kawai, "The 'Ten Oxherding Pictures' and Alchemy," in his *Buddhism and the Art of Psychotherapy* (College Station: Texas A & M University Press, 1996).
47. Catherine Despeux, *Le chemin de l'éveil* (Paris: L'Asiathèque, 1981).
48. The best academic study of the path in Theravada tradition is R. M. L. Gethin, *The Buddhist Path to Awakening* (1992; repr., Oxford: Oneworld Publications, 2001).
49. David Jackson, "The *bTsan rim* ('Stages of the Doctrine') and Similar Graded Expositions of the Bodhisattva's Path," in *Tibetan Literature: Studies in Genre*, ed. José Ignacio Cabezón and Roger R. Jackson (Ithaca, N.Y.: Snow Lion, 1996).
50. These include Padmakara Translation Group, trans., *Treasury of Precious Qualities* (Boston: Shambhala Publications, 2001); Pabonka Rinpoche, *Liberation in the Palm of Your Hand*, rev. ed. (Boston: Wisdom Publications, 1993); Tsong-kha-pa, *The Great Treatise on the Stages to the Path to Enlightenment* (Ithaca, N.Y.: Snow Lion Publications, 2001); Deshung Rinpoche, *The Three Levels of Spiritual Perception* (Boston: Wisdom Publications, 1995).
51. According to Paul Williams, "Śāntideva is generally thought to have flourished some time between 685 and 763 C.E., although the reasoning behind this dating is by no means conclusive." "General Introduction: Śāntideva and his

World," in Śāntideva, *The Bodhicaryāvatāra,* trans. Kate Crosby and Andrew Skilton (Oxford: Oxford University Press, 1995), viii.

52. There are several translations and studies available in English. In addition to the Crosby and Skilton translation cited above, the translations include Vesna A. Wallace and B. Alan Wallace, trans., *A Guide to the Bodhisattva Way of Life* (Ithaca, N.Y.: Snow Lion Publications, 1997), which includes an excellent bibliographic appendix; Padmakara Translation Group, *The Way of the Bodhisattva: A Translation of the Bodhicaryāvatāra* (Boston: Shambhala, 1997); Stephen Batchelor, trans., *A Guide to the Bodhisattva's Way of Life* (Dharamsala, India: Library of Tibetan Works and Archives, 1979); Marion L. Matics, trans., *Entering the Path of Enlightenment* (New York: Macmillan, 1970). Commentaries in English include two by the Dalai Lama: *Transcendent Wisdom,* ed. and trans. B. Alan Wallace, 2nd ed. (Ithaca, N.Y.: Snow Lion, 1994); and *A Flash of Lightning in the Dark of Night: A Guide to the Bodhisattva's Way of Life,* trans. Padmakara Translation Group (Boston: Shambhala, 1994). Other studies include Geshe Kelsang Gyatso, *Meaningful to Behold: View, Meditation and Action in Mahayana Buddhism* (Ulverston, Eng.: Wisdom Publications, 1980); two works by Paul Williams, *The Reflexive Nature of Awareness: A Tibetan Madhyamaka Defence* (Richmond, Eng.: Curzon Press, 1998), and *Altruism and Reality: Studies in the Philosophy of the Bodhicaryāvatāra* (Richmond, Eng.: Curzon Press, 1998); and Francis Brassard, *The Concept of Bodhicitta in Śāntideva's* Bodhicaryāvatāra (Albany: State University of New York Press, 2000). There are also at least one translation and two studies in French: Shāntideva, *La marche vers l'éveil,* trans. Comité de traduction Padmakara (La Besse, France: Editions Padmakara, 1992); Amalia Pezzali, *Śāntideva: mystique bouddhiste des VIIe et VIIIe siècles* (Firenze: Vallecchi Editore, 1968); and Khentchen Kunzang Palden and Minyak Kunzang Seunam, *Comprendre la vacuité: deux commentaires du chapitre IX de* La marche vers l'éveil *de Shāntideva,* trans. Comité de traduction Padmakara (Saint-Léon-sur-Vézère, France: Editions Padmakara, 1993).

53. See Crosby and Skilton, *The Bodhicaryāvatāra,* 10–11, for a discussion of the *anuttarapūjā.* A popular discussion can be found in Sangharakshita, *Ritual and Devotion in Buddhism: An Introduction,* 2nd ed. (Birmingham, Eng.: Windhorse Press, 2000).

54. See Bruce Williams, *"Mea Maxima Vikalpa*: Repentance, Meditation, and the Dynamics of Liberation in Medieval Chinese Buddhism, 500–650 C.E." (Ph.D. diss., University of California, Berkeley, 2002); Claudia Weber, *Buddhistische Beichten in Indien und bei den Uiguren: Unter besonderer Berücksichtigung der uigurischen Laienbeichte und ihrer Beziehung zum Manichäismus* (Wiesbaden: Harrassowitz Verlag, 1999); and Kuo Li-ying, *Confession et contrition dans le bouddhisme chinois du Ve au Xe siècle* (Paris: École Française d'Extrême-Orient, 1994).

55. Crosby and Skilton, *The Bodhicaryāvatāra,* 30. Later Mahāyāna texts sometimes expanded the list to ten, though retaining the first six in the same order.

56. Frédéric Lenoir, *La rencontre du bouddhisme et de l'Occident* (Paris: Librarie Arthème Fayard, 1999), chap. 2, sect. 3, "Schopenhauer et le 'pessimisme bouddhique'"; Roger-Pol Droit, *Le culte du néant: les philosophes et le Bouddha* (Paris: Éditions du Seuil, 1997), chap. 6, "Francfort et le Tibet"; Volker Zotz, *Auf den Glückseligen Inseln: Buddhismus in der deutschen Kulture* (Berlin: Theseus Verlag, 2000).

57. Joseph Needham, *Science and Civilization in China*, vol. 2, *History of Scientific Thought* (Cambridge: Cambridge University Press, 1969), 417.

58. According to J. J. Clarke, Jung seems to have had some sense that the understanding of Buddhism as nihilist was itself mistaken. J. J. Clarke, *Jung and Eastern Thought: A Dialogue with the Orient* (London: Routledge, 1994), 120.

59. There are, of course, those who understand the cultural presumptions themselves to be the source of psychological dis-ease, and for whom calling those into question is itself exactly the appropriate course of action. See, for example, Philip Cushman, *Constructing the Self, Constructing America* (Boston: Addison Wesley, 1996).

Chapter 3

1. See Harvey Aronson, *Buddhist Practice on Western Ground: Reconciling Eastern Ideals and Western Psychotherapy* (Boston: Shambhala Publications, 2004); Jack Engler, "Being Somebody and Being Nobody: A Reexamination of the Understanding of Self in Psychoanalysis and Buddhism," in *Buddhism and Psychoanalysis,* ed. Jeremy Safran (Boston: Wisdom Publications, 2003); Jeffrey Rubin, "A Well-Lived Life: Psychoanalytic and Buddhist Contributions," in Safran, *Buddhism and Psychoanalysis;* and Jeremy Safran, "Psychoanalysis and Buddhism as cultural institutions," in Safran, *Buddhism and Psychoanalysis.*

2. John Reynolds, *Self-Liberation through Seeing with Naked Awareness* (Barrytown, N.Y.: Station Hill Press, 1989).

3. Suzanne Kirschner, *The Religious and Romantic Origins of Psychoanalysis: Individuation and Integration in Post-Freudian Theory* (Cambridge: Cambridge University Press, 1996).

4. Franz Metcalf, "Illusions of the Self in Buddhism and Winnicott" (presented at the conference "Between Cultures: Buddhism and Psychotherapy in the Twenty-First Century," Boston University, September 10–11, 2004).

5. Stephen Mitchell, *Hope and Dread in Psychoanalysis* (New York: Basic Books, 1993).

6. Paul Williams, *Mahayana Buddhism: The Doctrinal Foundations* (London: Routledge, 1989).

7. Stephen Batchelor, *Buddhism without Beliefs* (New York: Riverhead Books, 1997).

Chapter 4

1. Harvey B. Aronson, *Buddhist Practice on Western Ground: Reconciling Eastern Ideals and Western Psychology* (Boston: Shambhala Publications, 2004), 64–90.
2. Kalu Rinpoche, *Luminous Mind: The Way of the Buddha* (Boston: Wisdom Publications, 1997), 25.
3. Heinz Kohut, *The Analysis of the Self* (New York: International Universities Press, 1971), xv.
4. Kohut, *Analysis of the Self;* Heinz Kohut and Ernest S. Wolf, "The Disorders of the Self and Their Treatment: An Outline," *International Journal of Psycho-Analysis,* 59 (1978): 413–24; Ernest S. Wolf, *Treating the Self* (New York: Guilford Press, 1988); James F. Masterson, *The Emerging Self* (New York: Brunner Mazel, 1993); A. H. Almaas, *The Point of Existence* (Berkeley: Diamond Books, 1996).
5. Jack Engler, "Therapeutic Aims in Psychotherapy and Meditation: Developmental Stages in the Representation of Self," in *Transformations of Consciousness: Conventional and Contemplative Perspectives on Development,* ed. K. Wilber, J. Engler, and D. Brown (Boston: Shambhala, 1986), 48; Aronson, *Buddhist Practice,* 27–29.
6. Engler, "Therapeutic Aims," 31–49; Jack Kornfield, *A Path with Heart: A Guide through the Perils and Promises of Spiritual Life* (New York: Bantam, 1993), 215–26; Mark Epstein, *Thoughts without a Thinker: Psychotherapy from a Buddhist Perspective* (New York: Basic Books, 1995), 174–78; Jeffrey B. Rubin, *Psychotherapy and Buddhism: Toward an Integration* (New York: Plenum Press, 1996), 169–86; John Welwood, *Toward a Psychology of Awakening: Buddhism, Psychotherapy, and the Path of Personal and Spiritual Transformation* (Boston: Shambhala Publications, 2000), 209; Lama Surya Das, *Eight Steps to Enlightenment: Awakening the Buddha Within* (New York: Broadway Books, 1997), 283; Aronson, *Buddhist Practice,* 53–57, 191–98.
7. Almaas, *Point,* 176–77. While helpfully pointing out a main characteristic of many traditions' spiritual paths, this phenomenological characterization does fall short in what it leaves out. It leaves out the substantial approaches of mantra/visualization, tantric/yogic/Sufi physiological approaches as well as Abrahamic modes of asceticism, or the varieties of prayer/bhakti/*tariki* (not-self power) found worldwide.
8. In this essay I will not be looking at the converse issue of the numerous positive benefits to be found from meditation. Cf. Michael Murphy and Steven Donovan, *The Physical and Psychological Effects of Meditation: A Review of Contemporary Research with a Comprehensive Bibliography, 1931–1936,* 2nd ed. (Sausalito, Calif.: Institute of Noetic Sciences, 1977); Epstein, *Thoughts;* Rubin, *Psychotherapy;* Welwood, *Psychology of Awakening;* Tara Bennett-Goleman, *Emotional Alchemy: How the Mind Can Heal the Heart* (New York: Harmony Books, 2001); Aronson, *Buddhist Practice,* 27–29.

9. I will not be looking at the issue of meditation as an adjunct to therapy, though there is now a significant literature on the ways in which mindfulness and other meditations can complement therapy (for examples see the preceding note).

10. Richard Shweder, *Thinking through Cultures: Expeditions in Cultural Psychology* (Cambridge, Mass.: Harvard University Press, 1991), 108–10.

11. Ibid., 108.

12. Ibid., 108–10.

13. Richard A. Shweder, "You're Not Sick, You're Just in Love," in *The Nature of Emotions: Fundamental Questions*, ed. Paul Ekman and Richard J. Davidson (New York: Oxford University Press, 1994), 40–42.

14. Hazel Rose Markus and Shinobu Kitayama, "The Cultural Constructions of Self and Emotion: Implications for Social Behavior," in *Emotion and Culture: Empirical Studies of Mutual Influence*, ed. Shinobu Kitayama and Hazel Rose Markus (Washington, D.C.: American Psychological Association, 1994), 101–11.

15. Jack Engler, "Being Somebody and Being Nobody: A Reexamination of the Understanding of Self in Psychoanalysis and Buddhism," in *Psychoanalysis and Buddhism: An Unfolding Dialogue*, ed. Jeremy Safran (Boston: Wisdom Publications, 2003)

16. Ibid., 40.

17. Franz Aubrey Metcalf, "The Encounter of Buddhism and Psychology," in *Buddha in the West*, ed. Charles S. Prebish and Martin Baumann (Berkeley: University of California Press, 2001); Aronson, *Buddhist Practice*, 27–39.

18. Cf. Shweder, *Thinking through Cultures*, 148–52; Alan Roland, *In Search of Self in India and Japan* (Princeton: Princeton University Press, 1989).

19. Ibid., 149, 151.

20. Aronson, *Buddhist Practice*, 1–2.

21. Charles Taylor, *Sources of the Self: The Making of the Modern Identity* (Cambridge, Mass.: Harvard University Press, 1989).

22. Ibid., 159.

23. Ibid., 185–207.

24. Shweder, *Thinking through Cultures*, 122, citing Clifford Geertz, "On the Nature of Anthropological Understanding," *American Scientist*, 63 (1975): 47–53.

25. Taylor, *Sources of the Self*, 217, 228–29.

26. Ibid., 138–39.

27. Ibid., 130–31, 178.

28. Ibid., 159–84; Nicholas D. Paige, *Being Interior: Autobiography and the Contradictions of Modernity in Seventeenth-Century France* (Philadelphia: University of Pennsylvania Press, 2001).

29. Paige, *Being Interior*, 122–3.

30. Taylor, *Sources of the Self*, 211–33, 283–84.

31. On the emergence of an hedonic-based ethic in Locke, see ibid., 169; on the significance of positive feeling in America, see Markus and Kitayama, "Cultural Constructions," 109; on Bacon's contribution regarding the significance

of function over intellectualization and Locke's pragmatic vision that the religious life yields "the highest payoff of pleasure," see Taylor, *Sources of the Self*, 213, 236; on Locke's contention that reason was given to humans for them to work hard and be efficacious ("peak performance" in modern parlance), see ibid., 238; on the place of efficacy in Kohut's articulation of the self in terms of "the uninterrupted tension arc from basic ambitions, via basic talents and skills, toward basic ideals," see Heinz Kohut, *How Does Analysis Cure?* (Chicago: University of Chicago Press, 1984), 4.

32. See Shweder, *Thinking through Cultures*, 113–85; Roland, *In Search of Self*.
33. See Shweder, "You're Not Sick," 40–42; Aronson, *Buddhist Practice*, 93–104.
34. Aronson, *Buddhist Practice*, 11.
35. Ibid., 26–29.
36. Engler, "Being Somebody," 45–46.
37. Ibid., 35. Works that address are Epstein, *Thoughts;* Rubin, *Psychotherapy;* Engler, "Therapeutic Aims"; Kornfield, *Path with Heart;* Surya Das, *Awakening the Buddha Within;* Welwood, *Psychology of Awakening;* Metcalf, "Encounter"; Aronson, *Buddhist Practice*.
38. Cf. Almaas, *Point*, 177.
39. Aronson, *Buddhist Practice*, 167–72; Seigen H. Yamaoka, *Jodo Shinshu: An Introduction* (San Francisco: Buddhist Churches of America, 1989).
40. Daniel Brown and Jack Engler, "The Stages of Mindfulness Meditation: A Validation Study, Part I," in Wilber, Engler, and Brown, *Transformations of Consciousness*, 189.
41. Kornfield, *Path with Heart*, 7.
42. Engler, "Being Somebody," 47.
43. Almaas, *Point*, 184.
44. Jack Engler, "Being Somebody," 38, citing P. Kapleau, *Zen Dawn in the West* (New York: Anchor Press/Doubleday, 1979), 31.
45. Engler, "Being Somebody," 37–38.
46. Almaas, *Point*, 184–85.
47. Ibid., 224–344.
48. Ibid., 183–202.
49. Ibid., 183.
50. Ibid., 184.
51. Engler, "Being Somebody," 38.
52. Almaas, *Point*, 186–87.
53. Ibid., 186–87, 91.
54. Aronson, *Buddhist Practice*, 64–90.
55. Engler, "Being Somebody," 43. Engler presents a very interesting vignette about a woman who presented herself to a traditional meditation teacher with symptoms of anorexia and insomnia: Engler, "Therapeutic Aims," 24–25.
56. Engler, "Therapeutic Aims," 24–25, is an excellent example of an intuitive response to the symptoms of anorexia used by a traditional teacher.

57. Almaas, *Point*, 185.
58. Engler, "Being Somebody," 43.
59. A. H. Almaas, *Being and the Meaning of Life*, Diamond Heart Book Three (Berkeley: Diamond Books, 1990), 72–87.
60. Almaas, *Point*, 36.
61. Ibid., 105.
62. Almaas, *Being*, 171.
63. This is an updated paraphrase of Henry Clarke Warren's translation of the Maha Vagga, *Buddhism in Translations* (New York: Atheneum, 1963), 146.
64. Almaas, *Point*, 106.
65. Engler, in line with this, identifies the following as effects common to meditation and psychotherapy: a cohesive sense of self that is flexible and malleable, and greater acceptance of disavowed aspects of oneself; Engler, "Being Somebody," 47. Cf. Almaas, *Point*, 106–7; A. H. Almaas, *Self versus True Nature*, audiotapes (Berkeley: Almaas Publications, 1997); Aronson, *Buddhist Practice*, 80–84.
66. Almaas, *Point*, 107.
67. The way in which mindfulness meditation may be constructive of an alignment with a flexible sense of self or destructive for those with an unstable sense of self is still an area of ongoing exploration—the practice is now productively used in a structured psycho-educational program of dialectical behavioral therapy for borderline personality, yet many of us know instances of psychotic episodes induced by intense meditation retreats. See Marsha Linehan, *Cognitive-Behavioral Treatment of Borderline Personality Disorder* (New York: Guilford, 1993); Jack Engler, "The 1001 forms of self-grasping," *What Is Enlightenment?* no. 17 (Spring/Summer 2000), 98; Engler, "Therapeutic Aims," 40–43.
68. Aronson, *Buddhist Practice*, 80–84.
69. Almaas, *Point*, 106.
70. Ibid.
71. Henry Clark Warren, *Buddhism in Translations* (New York: Atheneum, 1963), 82.
72. Aronson, *Buddhist Practice*, 80–84.
73. Almaas, *Point*, 107.
74. Ibid., 106.
75. Ibid., 106–8, 26.
76. Ibid., 108.
77. Ibid., 108.
78. Ibid., 110.
79. Engler, "Being Somebody," 59.
80. Ibid., 60.
81. Ibid., 50–52, Aronson, *Buddhist Practice*, 72–79.
82. Aronson, *Buddhist Practice*, 72–84.

83. Ledi Sayadaw, "Manual of Insight *(Vipassana Dipani),*" Wheel Publications, nos. 31/32 (Kandy, Sri Lanka: Buddhist Publication Society, 1961), 79.
84. Engler, "Being Somebody," 60.
85. Ibid.; see Lama Anagarika Govinda, *The Psychological Attitude of Early Buddhist Philosophy* (London: Rider, 1969), 151; Ledi, "Manual," 79.
86. Ledi, "Manual," 79; Govinda, *Psychological Attitude,* 107–11.
87. Engler, "Being Somebody," 41.
88. Almaas, *Point,* 107.
89. Engler, "Being Somebody," 59.
90. Shimon Malin, *Nature Loves to Hide: Quantum Physics and the Nature of Reality, a Western Perspective* (Oxford: Oxford University Press, 2001), 7.
91. A. H. Almaas, *Spacecruiser Inquiry* (Boston: Shambhala, 2002).
92. Almaas, *Point,* 107; Almaas, *Spacecruiser;* Almaas, *Being,* 72–87.
93. Almaas, *Spacecruiser,* 3–196.

Chapter 5

In the notes below, I have tried to provide abundant references for editions and translations of classical sources. For the sake of efficiency and organization, they are referenced according to the following abbreviations and conventions:

A — *Aṇguttara-Nikāya.* Nyanaponika Thera and Bhikkhu Bodhi, trans., *Numerical Discourses of the Buddha: An Anthology of Suttas from the Aṇguttara Nikāya* (Walnut Creek, CA: AltaMira Press, 1999).

Abhidharma-samuccaya — Walpola Rahula, *Le Compendium de la Super-doctrine (Philosophie) (Abhidharmasamuccaya) D'Asanga* (Paris: Ecole Française d'Extrême-Orient, 1980).

AKBh — *Abhidharmakośabhāṣya.* S. D. Shastri, ed. (Varanasi: Bauddha Bharati Series, 1981); Louis de de La Vallée Poussin, trans., *L'Abhidharmakośa de Vasubandhu* (Bruxelles: Institut Belge des Hautes Etudes Chinoises, 1981); Leo Pruden, trans., *Abhidharma-kośabhāṣyam* (Berkeley: Asian Humanities Press, 1990) (English translation of Poussin's French translation). Cited by chapter, verse and page no.

ASBH — *Abhidharmasammucaya-bhāṣyam.* Tatia, Nathamala, ed. 1976. Patna: K. P. Jayaswal Research Institute.

Bh — Hsüan-tsang's Chinese trans. of Vasubandhu's *Mahāyāna-sajgraha-bhāṣya,* T, 1597.

bh — Tibetan trans. of Vasubandhu's *Mahāyāna-sajgraha-bhāṣya,* P, #5551; D, #4050.

BHSD | *Buddhist Hybrid Sanskrit Grammar and Dictionary.* Franklin Edgerton, comp. (1953; repr., Kyoto: Rinsen Book Co., 1985).

Compendium | *Compendium of Philosophy (Abhidhammattha-sangaha).* S. Z. Aung, trans. (London: Pali Text Society, 1979); Nārada, trans., Bhikkhu Bodhi, rev., *A Comprehensive Manual of Abhidhamma* (Kandy: Buddhist Publication Society, 1993).

D | *Dīgha Nikāya.* L. Walshe, trans., *Thus Have I Heard* (Boston: Wisdom Books, 1987); *Dīgha Nikāya* (1890–1911); T. W. Rhys-Davids and C. A. F. Rhys-Davids, trans., *Dialogues of the Buddha* (London: Pali Text Society, 1899–1921).

D, # | Derge edition of the Tibetan Tripitaka.

Dharmadharma-tāvibhāga-vrtti | Vasubandhu's commentary on the *Dharmadharmatāvibhāga* (P. #5529; D. #4028), attributed to Maitreya.

Kathāvatthu | (London: Pali Text Society, 1979).

M | *Majjhima Nikāya.* Nyanamoli, trans., *The Middle Length Discourses of the Buddha* (Boston: Wisdom Publications, 1997); *Majjhima Nikāya* (1948–51); I. B. Horner, trans. *Middle Length Sayings* (London: Pali Text Society, 1954–59).

MMK | *Mūlamadhyamakakārikā.* Jay Garfield, trans. *The Fundamental Wisdom of the Middle Way* (New York: Oxford University Press, 1995).

Miln. | *Milinda's Questions.* I. B. Horner, trans. (London: Pali Text Society, 1963–64).

MSg | *Mahāyānasajgraha,* T, 1594; P, 5549; D, #4048. Cited by chapter numbers and verse.

P | Peking edition of the Tibetan Tripitaka.

PED | *Pāli-English Dictionary.* T. W. Rhys-Davids and W. Stede, eds. (London: Pali Text Society, 1979).

Pravrtti Portion | Part of the *Yogācārabhūmi.* T.30 (#1579) 579c23–582a28; P. #5539 Zi.4a5–11a8; D. #4038 Shi.3b4–9b3. Cited by page number and outline in Hakamaya Noriaki, "Viniścayasaṃgrahaṇī ni okeru araya-shiki no kitei," *Tōyōbunka-kenkyūjo-kiyō,* 79 (1979).

Proof Portion | Part of the *Yogācārabhūmi,* which is also found in SBh, 11, 9–13, 20; T, 31 (#1606) 701b4–702a5; P, #5554 Si.12a2–13b5; D, #4053 Li.9b7–11a5.

S   *Saṃyutta Nikāya.* Bhikkhu Bodhi, trans., *The Connected Discourses of the Buddha* (Boston: Wisdom Publications, 2000); *Saṃyutta Nikāya* (1894–1904); C. A. F. Rhys-Davids and F. L. Woodward, trans. *The Book of the Kindred Sayings* (London: Pali Text Society, 1917–30); John D. Ireland and Bhikkhu Nyanananda, trans., *An Anthology from the Samyutta Nikāya* (Kandy: Buddhist Publication Society, 1981).

Sajdhinirmocana   Etienne Lamotte, ed. and trans., *L'Explication des Mystères* (Lou-
Sūtra   vain, 1935). Cited by chapter and section.

SN   *Suttanipāta* (London: Pali Text Society, 1948); Saddhatissa, trans. (London: Curzon Press, 1985).

T   *Taishō* edition of the Chinese Tripitaka. Takakusu Junjirō and Watanabe Kaigyoku, eds., *Taishō shinshū daizōkyō,* 100 vols. (Tokyo: Taishō Issaikyō Kankōkai, 1924–1932).

TrBh   *Trijśikā-bhāṣya of Sthiramati.* Sylvain Levi, ed., *Vijñaptimātratā-siddhi* (Paris: Librairie Ancienne Honoré Champion, 1925).

Visuddhimagga   Buddhaghosa, *The Path of Purification,* trans. Nyanamoli (Berkeley: Shambala, 1976).

U   Hsüan Tsang's Chinese translation of Asvabhāva's *Mahāyāna-saṃgraha-upanibandhana,* T, 1598.

u   Tibetan translation of Asvabhāva's *Mahāyāna-saṃgraha-upanibandhana,* P, #5552; D, #4051.

Yogācārabhūmi   Bhattacharya, ed. (Calcutta: University of Calcutta, 1957).
of Asanga   Hsüan Tsang's Chinese translation of *Yogācārabhūmi,* T, 1579.

1. William Waldron, "A Comparison of the *Ālayavijñāna* with Freud's and Jung's Theories of the Unconscious," *Annual Memoirs of Otani University Shin Buddhist Research Institute,* 6 (1998): 109–50.
2. William Waldron, *The Buddhist Unconscious: The* ālaya-vijñāna *in the Context of Indian Buddhist Thought* (London: RoutledgeCurzon, 2002).
3. This is an important qualification. I am less familiar with more current thinking on these topics, although it appears that Stephen Mitchell's work in particular suggests something similar: "The most interesting feature of contemporary psychoanalytic perspectives on self is precisely the creative tension between the portrayal of self as multiple and discontinuous and of self as integral and continuous" (Mitchell, *Hope and Dread in Psychoanalysis* [New York: Basic Books, 1993], 115).

4. For example, Descartes (*Principles* I, sec. 9) defines: "By the word *thought* I understand all that of which we are conscious of operating in us (tout ce qui se fait en nous de telle sorte que nous l'apercevons immédiatement par nous memes)"; Locke (*Essay Concerning Human Understanding* I, i.8) similarly declared an idea as "every immediate object of the mind in thinking" (Descartes and Locke cited in Richard Rorty, *Philosophy and the Mirror of Nature* [Princeton: Princeton University Press, 1980], 48). Because of such conceptions, according to Rorty, "[i]mmediacy as the mark of the mental . . . became an unquestioned presupposition in philosophy" (ibid.).

   Piatigorsky similarly characterizes Abhidharma: "the Abhidhamma does not deal with what is non-conscious, because the Abhidhamma is a 'theory of consciousness,' and the rest simply does not exist in the sense of the Abhidhamma." Alexander Piatigorsky, *The Buddhist Philosophy of Thought* [London: Curzon Press, 1984], 202, n. 17.

5. According to Gregory (Richard Gregory, ed., *The Oxford Companion to the Mind* [Oxford: Oxford University Press, 1987], 162), "For John Locke and many subsequent thinkers, nothing was more essential to the mind than consciousness, and more particularly self-consciousness. The mind in all its activities and processes was viewed as transparent to itself; nothing was hidden from its inner view. To discern what went on in one's mind, one just 'looked'—one introspected—and the limits of what one thereby found were the very boundaries of the mind. . . . For Locke, indeed, there was a serious problem of how to describe all one's memories as being continuously in one's mind, when yet they were not continuously present to consciousness." This problem, along with its presuppositions, helped Freud formulate one of his main arguments for unconscious mental processes: "We call a process unconscious if we are obliged to assume that it is being activated at the moment, though at the moment we know nothing about it."

   The Buddhist context is more complex. In contrast to earlier forms of Buddhism, in which consciousness *(vijñāna)* had a rich and multivalent range of meanings, Abhidharmic analyses of mind came to focus more and more narrowly on the cognitive processes involving immediate awareness. Thus, one of the major arguments for *ālaya-vijñāna* similarly characterized it as continuous, in contrast to those forms of conscious awareness of objects that were momentary and intermittent. *The Pravṛtti Portion* states that though the objects of *ālaya-vijñāna* are indistinct *(aparicchina)*, it "always cognizes the continuity of the world uninterruptedly," its object "always exists, yet it functions continuously in a stream of instants." *Pravṛtti Portion* I.b)A.2–1.b)B.3; T.31.580a9, a15–18; D, 4a2, a4–5. Hakamaya Noriaki, "Viniścayasaṃgrahaṇī ni okeru araya-shiki no kitei," *Tōyōbunka-kenkyūjo-kiyō,* 79 (1979): 26. Hakamaya reconstructs this last expression as '*kṣaṇika-srotaḥ-saṃtāna-vartin*'(55). See also *Saṃdhinirmocana Sūtra,* V.7.

6. Posthypnotic suggestion for Freud is exactly "the kind of occurrence we have in mind when we speak of the existence of unconscious mental processes" (Sigmund Freud, *New Introductory Lectures to Psychoanalysis* [New York: W. W. Norton., 1965], 288).

   In Yogācāra texts, both the *Proof Portion* and *Mahāyāna-saṃgraha (MSg)* I.50 cite as an argument for the presence of *ālaya-vijñāna* a sūtra where the Buddha said that "for one in the attainment of cessation *(nirodhasamāpatti)*, consciousness has not departed from the body" (Proof #7, *vijñānaṃ cāsya kāyād anapakrānatam bhavati iti; ASBh,* 13.14; T.31.701c24–5; D. 11a4; P. 13b5; *MSg,* I.50). See Hakamaya Noriaki, "Araya-shiki sonzai no hachi-ronshō ni kansuru shobunken," *Kamazawa Daigaku Bukkyō-gakubu Kenkyū-kiyō,* 16 (1978): 14.

7. "Naturally a belief in a completely unconscious mental process, like a belief in a completely unperceived physical object or process, must rest on inference; and this inference will take the form of an argument from causation and analogy" (C. D. Broad, *The Mind and Its Place in Nature* [London: Routledge and Kegan Paul, 1925], 424).

8. As Freud declares, "our mental activity moves in two opposite directions: either it starts from the instincts and passes through the system Ucs. [unconscious] to conscious thought-activity; or, beginning with an instigation from outside, it passes through the system Cs. [conscious] and Pcs. [preconscious] till it reaches the Ucs. [unconscious]" (Sigmund Freud, "The Unconscious" [1915], in *Pelican Freud Library* [London: Penguin Books, 1984], 209).

   One section of the *Proof Portion* is entitled "determining the arising [of *ālaya-vijñāna*] by reciprocal conditionality" (**anyonya-pratyayatā-pravṛtti-vyavasthāna*), while *MSg* I.27 states that "these two forms of *vijñāna* [*ālaya-vijñāna* and the traditional six manifest forms of cognitive awareness] are reciprocal conditions" *(rnam par shes pa de gnyis gi rkyen gcig yin te).*

9. *Pravṛtti Portion* of the *Yogācārabhūmi* (D, 4a3–5; T.580a12–18): "2.b)A. *ālaya-vijñāna* is linked by association *(sajprayoga)* with the five omni-present factors connected with mind *(cittasajprayukta-sarvatraga):* attention *(manaskāra),* sense-impression *(sparśa),* feeling *(vedanā),* apperception *(samjñā),* volitional impulse *(cetanā)* . . . 2.b)B. These dharmas . . . are subtle *(sūkṣma)* because they are hard to perceive *(durvijñānatva)* even for the wise ones in the world." See also *TrBh,* 19.14–15; *ASBh,* 21.9f.; Hakamaya, "Viniścayasamgrahaṇī ni okeru araya-shiki no kitei," 71nn. 6, 7; and L. Schmithausen, *Ālayavijñāna* (Tōkyō: International Institute for Buddhist Studies, 1987), 389–390.

10. C. G. Jung, *On the Nature of the Psyche,* in *The Collected Works of C. G. Jung,* vol. 8 (Princeton: Princeton University Press, 1969), para. 383.

11. Alasdair MacIntyre critiques similar assumptions in Freud's thought: "Freud retains from the Cartesian picture the idea of the mind as something distinct and apart, a place or a realm which can be inhabited by such entities as ideas" (Alasdair MacIntyre, *The Unconscious: A Conceptual Analysis* [London: Routledge & Kegan Paul, 1958], 44). To speak of mental events as *things* that happen *in* the

unconscious, he claims, is already "half-way to reduplicating the Cartesian substantial conscious mind by a substantial unconscious mind. The unconscious is the ghost of the Cartesian consciousness" (73)—a ghost, I might add, that still haunts our discourse if not our dreams.

Wittgenstein's philosophical analysis is surprisingly similar, as Stern observes: "In the *Philosophical Remarks*, Wittgenstein . . . maintains that the subject-predicate grammar of our everyday language has such a firm grip on us that we are usually quite unaware of its influence. Because the grammar of ordinary language has been shaped by the need to successfully manipulate our environment, . . . we usually understand experience in subject-predicate terms: we say such things as, 'I have a headache,' and take it for granted that the term 'I' refers to a subject, the self" (D. G. Stern, *Wittgenstein on Mind and Language* [New York: Oxford University Press, 1995], 79–80).

12. *Visuddhimagga,* XVI.90.
13. There are many passages in the Pāli texts such as the following: "'Venerable sir, who craves?' 'Not a valid question,' the Blessed One replied. 'I do not say, "One craves." If I should say, "One craves," in that case this would be a valid question: "Venerable sir, who craves?" But I do not speak thus. Since I do not speak thus, if one should ask me, "Venerable sir, with what as condition does craving [come to be]?" this would be a valid question. To this the valid answer is: "With feeling as condition, craving [comes to be]; with craving as condition, clinging; with clinging as condition, existence"'" (S, II.13).
14. M, II.32.
15. S, II.73.
16. Bertrand Russell gives a most typical analysis of perception: "There is on the one hand the thing of which we are aware . . . and on the other hand the actual awareness itself, the mental act of apprehending the thing." (Bertrand Russell, *The Problems of Philosophy* [Oxford: Oxford University Press, 1959], 65).
17. A*KBh, ad* I.42; Pruden, vol. 1, 118. Buddhaghosa similarly states in the *Visuddhimagga* (XIX, 20): "He sees no doer over and above the doing, no experiencer of the result over and above the occurrence of the result. But he sees clearly with right understanding that the wise say 'doer' when there is doing and 'experience' when there is experiencing simply as a mode of common usage."
18. Those topics of the traditional discourses that were not formulated in, or could not be transposed into, such impersonal terms, into *dharmic* terms, were considered to be merely provisional or conventional truth *(saṃvrtisatya),* whereas the doctrine as formulated in purely dharmic terms was considered to be the 'higher doctrine,' the *'abhi'*-dharma, because it is turned toward the ultimate *dharma (paramārtha-dharma),* that is, toward nirvana *(AKBh, ad* I.2b. Shastri, 12; Poussin, 4: *tadaya paramārthadharma vā nirvāṇa dharmalakṣaṇā vā pratyabhimukho dharma ityabhidharma).* The *Ahasālinī* (III, 488) of the Theravādins concurs: *abhidhammo nāmo paramatthadesanā* (as cited in

Herbert V. Guenther, *Philosophy and Psychology in the Abhidharma* [Delhi: Motilal Banarsidass, 1959], 2).

The distinction between ultimate and conventional truths or teachings has a long and important history in Buddhist thought. Jayatilleke discusses the earliest meanings of ultimate *(paramatta)* and conventional *(sammuti)* discourse and their relation to definitive teachings *(nītattha)* and interpretive, indirect teachings *(neyyattha)* (K. N. Jayatilleke, *Early Buddhist Theory of Knowledge* [Delhi: Motilal Banarsidass, 1963], 361–68). Although instances of the terms "ultimate" and "conventional" are found in the early texts [S, I.135: "Just as much as the word 'chariot' is used when the parts are put together, there is the use *(sammuti)* of the term 'being' *(satto)* when the (psycho-physical) constituents are present"], they are, Jayatilleke claims, "nowhere contrasted in the Canon" (366), and are used only to refer to "a distinction of subject matter and not a distinction of two kinds of truth" (368). See also *Kathāvatthu,* V.6; *Visuddhimagga,* XVIII; *Compendium,* 6, 11, 81n1, 200n1.

19. Sue Hamilton puts this nicely: "[S]tating that in seeking to know what you *are,* or even whether or not you *are,* you are missing the solution to the problem of cyclic continuity. . . . *That* you are is neither *the* question nor *in* question: you need to forget even the issue of self-hood and understand instead how you work in a dependently originated world of experience" (Sue Hamilton, *Early Buddhism: A New Approach. The I of the Beholder* [Surrey, U.K.: Curzon Press, 2000], 23).

20. Richard Restak, *The Modular Brain* (New York: Scribner's and Sons, 1994), 120–21.

21. Lakoff and Johnson: "The very way that we normally conceptualize our inner lives is inconsistent with what we know scientifically about the nature of mind. In our system for conceptualizing our inner lives, there is always a Subject that is the locus of reason and that metaphorically has an existence independent of the body. As we have seen, this contradicts the fundamental findings of cognitive science" (George Lakoff and Mark Johnson, *Philosophy in the Flesh: The Embodied Mind and its Challenge to Western Thought* [New York: Basic Books, 1999], 268). Similarly, the brain scientist Richard Restak argues: "Brain research on consciousness carried out over the past two decades casts important doubts on our traditional ideas about the unity and indissolubility of our mental lives" . . . particularly "the concept of ourself [sic] as a unified, freely acting agent directing our behavior" (Restak, *The Modular Brain,* 120–21).

22. These parallels help us, at least heuristically, to more fully appreciate the impersonal model of causality proposed by the Buddhists. This is true for my students, at least, who, after a mere hour's inquiry into the "dependent arising of things" in scientific terms are usually able to get a good grasp of the basic ideas of no-self, dependent arising, and provisional designation without even hearing these Buddhist concepts. This exercise consists of a insistent inquiry into

the causes and conditions that enable the arising of first a river, then a tree, a frog, a human infant, and finally the functioning personality of a human adult, accompanied by such related questions as "Who made the river?" and so on. And "What constitutes the real boundaries of the river?" and the like. See Waldron, 2002. 'An End-run 'Round Entities: Using Scientific Analogies for Teaching Buddhist Concepts,' *Teaching Buddhism in the West: From the Wheel to the Web.* Hori, V. S., Hayes, R. P., Shields, J. M. (eds.) RoutledgeCurzon, 84–91.

23. "What is consciousness for, if perfectly unconscious, indeed subject-less, information processing is in principle capable of achieving all the ends for which conscious minds were supposed to exist? . . . [This] draws our attention unmistakably to the difference between all the unconscious information processing— without which, no doubt, there could be no conscious experience—and the conscious thought itself, which is somehow directly accessible. Accessible to what or to whom? To say that it is accessible to some subsystem of the brain is not yet to distinguish it from the unconscious activities and events which are also accessible to various subsystems of the brain. If some particular and special subsystem deserves to be called the self, this is far from obvious." (Gregory, *Oxford Companion*, 162–163)

24. "Apart from conditions, there is no arising of cognitive awareness" (M I 258). *Milinda's Questions:* "Because there are vision here and material shape, size, visual consciousness arises. Co-nascent with that are sensory impingement, feeling, perception, volition, one-pointedness, the life-principle, attention; thus these things are produced from a condition and no experiencer is got at here" (*Miln.* 78) [56].

25. Lakoff and Johnson, *Philosophy in the Flesh*, 24–25.

26. Wittgenstein's attempt to forge a subjectless language entailed similar consequences: "It is because a language designed for the sole function of expressing everything that a subject might experience has no need for a term designating that subject that one cannot refer to the subject of experience from within the phenomenological language. . . . From within, one cannot individuate a subject at all. The metaphysical subject is not an object of experience, but a way of indicating the overall structure of experience. . . . The grammar of the phenomenological language ensures that all statements about experience are expressed in the same—ownerless—way." (ibid., 84).

27. See note 14 above.

28. *MMK*, XXIV.40. Also; "one who sees dependent origination sees the *dhamma* and one who sees the *dhamma*[o] sees dependent origination" (M I191). And: "Now inasmuch, brethren, as the Ariyan disciple knows the causal relation thus, knows the uprising of the causal relation thus, knows the cessation of the causal relation thus, knows the way going to the cessation of the causal relation thus, he is what we call the Ariyan disciple who has won the view, who has won vision . . . who sees this good doctrine . . . who possesses the wisdom of the trained

man, who has won to the stream of the Dharma, who has the Ariyan insight of revulsion, who stands knocking at the door of the deathless" (S II 41).

29. Although this impersonal form of discourse is seldom so strictly defined in Buddhist texts, it is useful to articulate it as an 'ideal type' with which to contrast other forms of discourse. We are of course borrowing Max Weber's concept here: "An ideal type is formed by the one-sided accentuation of one or more point of view and by the synthesis of a great many diffuse, discrete . . . individual phenomena, which are arranged accordingly to those one-sided emphasized viewpoints into a unified analytical construct. In its conceptual purity this mental construct cannot be found anywhere in reality" (Max Weber, *Theory of Social and Economic Organization* [Glencoe: Free Press, 1964], 329–36).

30. M I190: "When internally the eye is intact and external forms come into its range and there is the corresponding engagement, then there is the manifestation of the corresponding class of consciousness." Traditionally, such awareness arises in six modalities, the five senses plus mind. For the sake of simplicity I will often refer to all of these as "sense faculties, sense objects," and so on. Unless otherwise stated, this also implies mind and its correlative "mental objects" (translation taken from Nyanamoli, trans., *The Middle Length Discourses of the Buddha* [Boston: Wisdom Publications, 1995], 284).

31. This is one reason I prefer "cognitive awareness" to "consciousness." Consciousness is a nebulous enough term in English, and insofar as it connotes an active agent or faculty, as in Russell's definition above, it is misleading in a Buddhist context.

32. "Feeling, apperception, and cognitive awareness, these factors are conjoined, not disjoined, and it is impossible to separate each of these states from the others in order to describe the difference between them. For what one feels, that one apperceives; and what one apperceives, that one cognizes" (M I295; Nyanamoli, *Middle Length Discourses*, 389); terminology altered for consistency.

33. See Stephen Collins, *Selfless Persons: Imagery and Thought in Theravāda Buddhism* (Cambridge: Cambridge University Press, 1982), 43–45. Also consider the early Vedic sense of *loka* as a multidimensional "world" constructed by human action, particularly ritual action.

34. A II 48; SN, 169.

35. "Dependent on the eye-faculty and visual form, visual cognitive awareness arises; the concomitance of the three is sense-impression. Depending on sense-impression is feeling, depending on feeling is craving, depending on craving is grasping, depending on grasping is becoming, depending on becoming is birth, depending on birth, old age, death, grief, lamentation, suffering, distress and despair come about. *This is the arising of the world*" (S II73). [Emphasis added.]

36. Michael Carrithers, *Why Humans Have Cultures* (New York: Oxford University Press, 1992). This is a pattern which the neurophysiologist Terrence Deacon notes "has been invoked by most theories of human cognitive evolution" (T. W.

Deacon, *The Symbolic Species: The Co-evolution of Language and the Brain* [New York: W. W. Norton, 1997], 352).

37. "The Elder traced a circle *(cakka)* on the ground and spoke thus to King Milinda: 'Is there an end to this circle, sire?' 'There is not, revered sir.' 'Even so, sire, are those cycles *(cakka)* that are spoken of by the Lord: "Visual consciousness arises because of eye and material shapes, the meeting of the three is sensory impingement; conditioned by sensory impingement is feeling; conditioned by feeling is craving; conditioned by craving is kamma [karma]; vision [*chakkhu*, lit.: eye] is born again from kamma"—is there thus an end of this series?' 'There is not, revered sir.' . . . 'Even so, the earliest point of [samsaric] time cannot be shown either.'" (*Miln.*, 22).

38. This refers to a previous passage in the same text. *(AKBh, ad* IV.1a; Shastri, 567; Poussin, 1: *sattvabhājanalokasya bahudhā vaicitryamuktaj tat kena kṛtam . . . sattvānāj karmajaṃ lokavaicitryam.)*

39. *AKBh, ad* V.1a; Shastri 759; Poussin 106: *karmajaṃ lokavaicitrayam iti uktam. tāni ca karmāṇi anuśayavaśād upacayaṃ gacchanti, antareṇa ca anuśayān bhavābhinirvartane na samarthāni bhavanti. ato veditavyāḥ mūlaṃ bhavasya anuśayāḥ.*

40. "The mental stream," Vasubandhu's euphemism for evolving individuals, "increases gradually by the afflictions and by actions, and goes again to the next world. In this way, the circle of existence is without beginning." *(AKBh* III.19a–d. Poussin, 57–59; Shastri, 433–34: *yathā ākṣepaj kramād vṛddhaḥ santānaḥ kleśakarmabhiḥ paralokaj punar yāti . . . iti anādibhavacakrakam.)*

41. William Waldron, "Beyond Nature/Nurture: Buddhism and Biology on Interdependence," *Contemporary Buddhism*, 1, no. 2 (2000): 199–226.

42. See Waldron, *Buddhist Unconscious*, for a book-length treatment.

43. The *Pravṛtti Portion* of the *Yogācārabhūmi*: "1.b)B.2. *[ālaya-vijñāna]* always has an object, it is not sometimes this and sometimes that *(*anyathātva).* However, from the first moment of appropriation [of the body at conception] for as long as life lasts *(yāvaj jīvam)* [its] perception (Skt. *vijñapti;* Tib. *rigs pa)* arises always having one flavor *(ekarasatvena)* [that is, homogeneously]. 1.b) B.3. It should be understood that *ālaya-vijñāna* is momentary regarding [its] object, and though it arises continuously in a stream of instants, it is not unitary *(ekatva)"*(D. 4a3–5; T.580a12–18).

44. *Pravṛtti Portion*: "A1.b)A.2. The 'outward perception of the external world, whose aspects are indistinct' *(bahirdhā-aparicchinnākāra-bhājana-vijñapti)* means the continuous, uninterrupted perception of the continuity of the world based upon that very *ālaya-vijñāna* which has the inner substratum as a cognitive support" (D. 3b7–4a3; T.580a2–12).

45. This closely parallels passages describing *vijñāna* in Pāli texts, e.g., S III 53; D III 228.

46. *Saṃdhinirmocana Sūtra*, V.2. All the Sanskrit terms in this passage are reconstructed from the Chinese and Tibetan.

Schmithausen has reconstructed the Sanskrit of this last phrase as: *nimitta-nāma-vikalpa-vyavahāra-prapañca-vāsanā-upādāna, the import of which is well summarized in his definition of the first term, nimitta, as: "in this context, objective phenomena as they are experienced or imagined, admitting of being associated with names, and being (co-) conditioned by subjective conceptual activity (vikalpa), which has become habitual so that it permeates all (ordinary) perceptions and cognitions" (Schmithausen, Ālayavijñāna, 357, n.511).

47. Ālaya-vijñāna is one of the bases upon which the six manifest forms of cognitive awareness arise. The Saṃdhinirmocana Sūtra (V.4–5) states, "The six groups of cognitive awareness (ṣad-vijñāna-kāya) . . . occur supported by and depending upon (sajniśritya pratisthāya) the appropriating consciousness (ādāna-vijñāna) [a synonym of ālaya-vijñāna]."

48. Ad MSg I.58; U 397a24–b4; u 266b4–267a1; Bh 336c5f.; bh 168b7f.

49. And it appears to be precisely this, our ability to maintain a common object of attention, which is both the prerequisite for and reinforced result of language use, that separates human forms of cognitive awareness from those of our closest primate cousins. The primatologist and child developmentalist Michael Tomasello concludes that "the uniquely human forms of thinking do not just depend on, but in fact derive from, perhaps even are constituted by, the interactive discourse that takes place through the medium of intersubjective and perspectival linguistic symbols, constructions, and discourse patterns."(Tomasello, The Cultural Origins of Human Cognition [Cambridge: Harvard University Press, 1999], 215).

50. Ad MSg I.60; U 397c12f.; u 267a8–268a1.

51. Elsewhere, Asanga explicitly states that it is the common and uncommon actions of sentient beings that bring about the common (bhājana-) and individual worlds (sattva-loka) respectively.
    Abhidharma-samuccaya (T.31.679b24B7; P. 102b6B8f.: las thun mong ba zhes kyang byung/ las thun mong ma yin pa zhes kyang byung/ . . . thun mong ba gang zhe na/ gang snod kyi jig rten rnam par byed pa'o// thun mong ma yin pa gang zhe na/ gang sems can gyi jig rten rnam par byed pa'o). See Schmithausen, Ālayav-ijñāna, 491–92 n1302f.

52. Bh 337a28ff.; bh 169b5. de lta bu "i rnam pa can gyi kun gzhi rnam par shes pa med na gang sems can thams cad kyi thun mong gi longs spyod kyi rgyur gyur pa snod kyi jig rten yod par mi gyur ro.

53. As my perceptive sister pointed out on first hearing the term, perhaps even inter-subjectivity itself already implies isolated subjects only subsequently coming into contact.

54. As the eminent Japanese Buddhologist Nagao observes: "If the doctrine of non-self is treated from merely its theoretical, logical aspect, without religious concerns, the result will be a mere denial of the self in which religious subjectivity tends to get lost" (Nagao Gadjin, Mādhyamika and Yogācāra [Albany: SUNY Press, 1991], 8). Similarly, Georges Dreyfus points out that such personalist discourse

"provides the Tibetan tradition with the framework that makes a narrative of spiritual progress possible and introduces an element of closure without which the commitment required by Buddhist practices cannot be sustained" (Georges Dreyfus, "Tibetan Scholastic Education and the Role of Soteriology,"*Journal of the International Association of Buddhist Studies,* 20, no. 1 [1997]: 62).

55. *AKBh* I.3; Shastri, 14; Poussin, 5; Pruden, 1988, 57: "Apart from the discernment of the *dharmas,* there is no means to extinguish the defilements, and it is by reason of the defilements that the world wanders in the ocean of existence. So it is with a view to this discernment that the Abhidharma has been, they say, spoken [by the Master]. . . . without the teaching of the Abhidharma, a disciple would be incapable of discerning the *dharmas.*"

   Vasubandhu also states in another of his texts, the *Dharmadharmatāvibhāga-vṛtti,* that there needs to be a (at least some) basis of designation for individuals who have realized Nirvana just as one designates the aggregates of individuals who are said to be coursing in samsara (D, #4028.37b.4: *gor ba'i gang zag la gor ba'o zhes phung po rnams dogs pa de bzhin du yongs su mya ngan las das pa'i gang zag la yang gdags pa'i gzhi yod dgos so*).

56. But, as Nagao has clearly stated, unlike the essentialist concept of *ātman,* in Buddhism "the existential subject must be purely individual, historical, and temporal, and not universal and permanent. Existence is opposite to essence. The existential subject must be, by name, anti-universal and anti-metaphysical" (Nagao, *Mādhyamika and Yogācāra,* 8–9).

57. K. Wilber, Jack Engler, Daniel Brown, *Transformations of Consciousness* (Boston: Shambala, 1986), 24.

58. I wish to thank David Lawrence for referring me to this provocative and his own evocative article.

59. Edwin Gerow, "What Is Karma (Kim Karmeti): An Exercise in Philosophical Semantics," *Indological Taurinensia,* 10 (1982): 97.

60. Gerow, "What Is Karma," 98.

61. Even in standard sentences, the "effect is the result *(phala)* that is understood to occur in the direct object *(karman)*" (David Lawrence, "The Mythico-Ritual Syntax of Omnipotence," *Philosophy East & West,* 48, no. 4 [1998]: 599).

62. Gerow describes the process whereby, in the case of intransitive sentences, the object of a verb becomes identified with its result. According to the medieval grammarians,

> In every act designated by a verbal root (e.g. <<to go>> or <<to cook>>) are two complementary semantic aspects: a function/process or vyāpāra, indicating the change per se, and the fruit, or phala, indicating the tendency or end of that change. . . . The two aspects of the verbal action look to different external substrates for their practical realization: whereas the vyāpāra is based typically in the agent (kartṛ), or in the examples, in the *cook,* or the *walker,* the phala usually finds its substrate or basis in the object

of the verb, the karma, or in the examples, in the rice or place reached. In this way . . . the karma is linked closely to the <<objective>> phala, whereas the more internal or processual aspect of the verbal idea is associated with the kartṛ. . . . [But intransitive] verbs in effect have no <<karma>>, no <<external>> [direct] object although they most certainly do have a *phala;* it is precisely this relationship of karma to phala that defines the class of intransitives (Gerow, "What Is Karma," 94–95).

63. "The vyāpāra, the <<processual meaning>> of the verb, is boldly identified with the verb in its resultative guise: karman" (ibid., 114).

64. This development is paralleled in the Buddhist lexicon in a series of "process-result" or "process-product" nouns, such as *citta, saṃskārā,* and *upādāna,* that have long been noted but never adequately explained by Buddhist scholars. The PED, for example, defines *citta* as "the centre and focus of man's emotional nature as well as that intellectual element which inheres in and accompanies its manifestations: thought. In this wise *citta* denotes both the agent and that which is enacted" (PED 266–267). Edgerton describes *sankhārā (saṃskārā)* as "predispositions, the effect of past deeds and experience as conditioning a new state," as both "conditionings [and] conditioned states" (BHSD 542); Collins similarly describes *sankhārā* as "both the activity which constructs temporal reality *[loka]* and the temporal reality thus constructed" (*Selfless Persons,* 202). Rune Johansson has similar observations (*Dynamic Psychology of Early Buddhism* [Oxford: Curzon Press, 1979], 50–51). And, finally, *upādāna* also evinces both an active, affective sense of "grasping, holding on, attachment," as well as a resultant sense of "fuel, supply, substratum by means of which an active process is kept alive or going." Together they convey the senses of "finding one's support for, nourished by, taking up" (PED 149).

These are not peculiar to Sanskrit. The philosopher A. W. Sparkes describes what he calls "'process-product ambiguity', i.e., it is used to refer both to the *process* (or, more accurately, *activity*) . . . and to the *product* of that activity" (A. W. Sparkes, *Talking Philosophy: A Wordbook* [London: Routledge, 1991], 76). Participial words such as painting or building often exhibit this ambiguity (or, perhaps more precisely, bivalence).

65. "Wittgenstein's response to these difficulties [of overcoming the subject-predicate grammar of our everyday language] is to suggest that we imagine talking about one's experiences without using the word 'I'.... [I]nstead of saying 'I have a toothache,' one says, 'There is toothache.' More generally, in talking about one's experience, one dispenses with the first-person pronoun and simply states that the experience in question has occurred. The point of the imagined reconstrual is that the new sentences now have a dummy subject and so conform to the subject-predicate conventions of our language, but do not have a logical subject. We are to think of the 'there is' in 'there is toothache' as like

the 'it is' in 'it is snowing': in both cases something is going on, but there is no subject" (Stern, *Wittgenstein on Mind,* 79–80).

66. Gerow, "What Is Karma," III.

67. Ibid., 102.

68. Ibid., 112.

69. Ibid.

70. See note 20 above.

71. Gerow, "What Is Karma," 113

72. Ibid.

73. Ibid.

74. Lawrence, "Mythico-Ritual Syntax," 592–622.

75. Ibid., 603, 604.

76. "At a fundamental level, the Buddhist division of the world into dharmas of various types may be criticized as a selection, from experience, of categories as arbitrary as any others. And, most basically, it may be that Buddhist descriptions of the world are based on unstated assumptions about, e.g. the ultimate 'impersonality' of reality that simply would not be shared by those who select 'personal' metaphors, like agency, as a way of understanding things" (Roger Jackson, *Is Enlightenment Possible?* [Ithaca, N.Y.: Snow Lion, 1993], 141).

77. "Even [the act of cognition] 'I cognize this to be blue' really amounts to 'I am aware' *[prakāśe]*"(Lawrence, "Mythico-Ritual Syntax," 604, citing the *Īśvara-pratyabhijñavimarśinī,* 1.5.17, 1:279, of Abhinavagupta).

78. Gerow, "What Is Karma," 116.

79. S II 20; John D. Ireland and Bhikkhu Nyanananda, trans., *An Anthology from the Samyutta* [Kandy: Buddhist Publication Society, 1981], 20.

80. This is the impetus behind introducing 'first-person' accounts into laboratory experiments, such as discussed by Francisco Varela and Jonathan Shear (Varela and Shear, eds., *The View from Within: First-Person Approaches to the Study of Consciousness* [Exeter, U.K.: Imprint Academic, 1999]).

81. "There is no lack of highly persuasive books whose objective is to demonstrate why organisms are not what they seem to be—integrated entities with lives and natures of their own—but complex molecular machines controlled by the genes carried within them, bearers of the historical record of the species to which they belong" (Brian Goodwin, *How the Leopard Changed Its Spots: The Evolution of Complexity* [London: Phoenix Press, 1994], x).

Chapter 6

1. Shimazono Susumu, *Gendai shūkyō no kanōsei* (Tokyo: Iwanami Shoten, 1997), 65.

2. Ibid., 192.

3. Ibid., 25ff.

4. Ibid., 37ff, 255ff.

5. Ishii Kenji, *Deeta bukku—gendai Nihonjin no shūkyō* (Tokyo: Shinyosha, 1997), 3.

6. D. T. Suzuki, *Nihonteki reisei* (Tokyo: Iwanami Shoten, 1944), 70.

7. Ama Toshimaro, *Why Do Japanese Lack Religion* (Tokyo: Chikuma Shobo, 1996).

8. Suzuki Daisetz, *Nihonteki Reisei* (Tokyo: Iwanami Bunkōban, 1977), 94ff.

9. William James, *Varieties of Religious Experience* (New York: Collier Books, 1961).

10. Yanagida Seizan, *Zen shisō* (Tokyo: Chūōkōron, 1975), 11, 49; Hisao Inagaki, ed., *A Glossary of Zen Terms* (Kyoto: Nagata Bunshodo, 1991), 90 (s.v. *gyōnyū*).

11. Shimazono, *Gendai shūkyō no kanōsei*, 41, 157ff.

12. Ibid., 162

13. Hirose Hirotada, *Kokoro no senzairyoku—placebo kouka* (Tokyo: Asahi Shimbunsha, 2001).

14. The following account of Hara Inashiro is indebted to Okuwa Hitoshi, "Bakumatsu zaison chishikijin to Shinshū—Hara Inashiro ni okeru 'ga' no keisei," *Nihon shisōshigaku*, 29 (1997).

15. Okuwa, "Bakumatsu zaison chishikijin," 46.

16. Ibid., 39.

Chapter 7

1. Myōe Kōben, *Recommending Faith in the Sand and the Mantra of Light,* trans. Mark Unno, in his *Shingon Refractions* (Boston: Wisdom Publications, 2004), 224.

2. *Kōjien,* ed. Shinmura Izuru, 3rd ed. (Tokyo: Iwanami Shoten, 1969), s.v. "suna."

3. Hōshū Matsubayashi, trans., *The Sukhāvatīvyūha Sūtra* (Union City, Calif.: Samgha Press, 1985).

4. R. Bower, "The Importance of Sand in the World Technique Experiment," *British Journal of Psychology,* 29 (1959): 162–64.

5. Akita Itsuki, "Suna dake no zōkei: Shinkeishō shokushi fushinshō no keesu yori," *Hakoniwa ryōhōgaku kenkyū,* 4, no. 2 (1991): 49–59.

6. Yokoyama Takashi, "Suna nomi ni yotte hyōgen sareta naiteki kosumorojii— Bamen genmokushō no shinriryōhō katei wo tōshite," *Hakoniwa ryōhōgaku kenkyū,* 2, no. 1 (1989): 15–27.

7. Yamanaka Yasuhiro, "Suna dake no hyōgen ga tenki to natta hakoniwa ryōhō no shōrei," *Rinshō seishin igaku,* 20, no. 7 (1991): 1149–57.

8. P. Heidenrich, "Furui tsuchi dewa nai—Boku ga ima asondeiru, kore wa atarashii tsuchi da," trans. Nakano Yūko, *Hakoniwa ryōhōgaku kenkyū,* 14, no. 2 (2001): 75–106.

9. Takuma Yukiko, "Yūki ryōhō ni okeru suna—'Utsuwa' to shite no hakoniwa to chiryōsha," *Hakoniwa ryōhōgaku kenkyū,* 10, no. 1 (1997): 4–14.

10. Abe Kōbō, *Suna no onna* (Woman in the Dunes) (Tokyo: Shinchōsha, 1978).

11. Matsumoto Seichō, *Suna no utsuwa,* 2 vols. (Tokyo: Shinchōsha, 1973).

12. Edith Nesbit, *Five Children and It* (Cutchogue, N.Y.: Buccaneer Books, 1996).

13. Myōe Kōben, *Recommending Faith,* in *Shingon Refractions,* 232.

Chapter 8

1. Albert Camus, *The Plague,* trans. Gilbert Stuart (N.Y.: Vintage Books, 1972), 84–91.
2. Ibid., 115, 116.
3. Ibid., 133.
4. *Therigatha Atthakatha,* X.1, trans. Andrew Olendzki, http://www.accesstoinsight.org/noncanon/comy/index.html (August 14, 2005).
5. Jay Haley, *Uncommon Therapy: The Psychiatric Techniques of Milton H. Erickson* (NY: Norton, 1986), 115.
6. Ibid., 71–72.
7. Taitetsu Unno, *Tannisho: A Shin Buddhist Classic* (Honolulu: Buddhist Study Center Press, 1984), 11 (sec. 6); translation adapted.
8. Unno, *Tannisho,* 35 (epilogue).
9. *Diagnostic and Statistical Manual of Mental Disorders DSM-IV-TR* (Text Revision), 4th ed. (Washington, D.C.: American Psychiatric Association, 2000).

Chapter 9

1. Thanks are due to Mark Unno for direction and suggestions on this paper.
2. This view of Zen practice seems more applicable to Suzuki's Rinzai orientation than that of Dōgen and Sōtō Zen.
3. Taitetsu Unno, *Tannisho: A Shin Buddhist Classic* (Honolulu: Buddhist Study Center Press, 1996), 11.
4. Yoshifumi Ueda, *Mahayana Buddhism: An Approach to Its Essence* (Los Angeles: Pure Land Publications, 1989), 5–11.
5. Briefly described by Chiba Jōryū as *hiji-hōmon* (secret teaching) in "Orthodoxy and Heterodoxy in Early Shinshū: *Kakushi Nembutsu and Kakure Nembutsu,*" in *The Pure Land Tradition: History and Development,* by Richard Payne et al., Berkeley Buddhist Studies Series, no. 3 (Fremont, California: Asian Humanities Press, 1996), 463–96. See also Suzuki's own view of his mother's faith in *Suzuki Daisetsu no Hito to Shisō* (Tokyo: Shunjūsha, 1961), 166–81.
6. See Yoshimoto Ishin, *Naikanhō* (Tokyo: Shinjisha, 1989). I wish to thank Greg Krech, director of ToDo Institute in Vermont, for suggesting this work on Naikan therapy.
7. See David Reynolds, *Naikan Psychotherapy* (Chicago: University of Chicago Press, 1983).
8. Greg Krech, *Naikan: Gratitude, Grace, and the Japanese Art of Self-realization* (Berkeley: Stone Bridge Press, 2002), 13.
9. Dennis Hirota et al., trans. and ed., *The Collected Works of Shinran* (Kyoto: Jōdo Shinshū Hongwanji-ha, 1997), 1:421.
10. Ibid., 64.

11. The best comprehensive work on the subject in English is Minor L. Rogers and Ann T. Rogers, *Rennyo: The Second Founder of Shin Buddhism,* Nanzan Studies in Asian Religions, no. 3 (Berkeley: Asian Humanities Press, 1991).

12. *The Words of St. Rennyo,* trans. Koshō Yamamoto (Tokyo: The Karinbunkō, 1968), 105.

13. Rogers and Rogers, *Rennyo,* 75.

14. Ibid., 37.

15. Ibid., 28.

16. Hirota et al., *Collected Works,* 1:453.

17. Ibid., 371.

18. Rogers and Rogers, *Rennyo,* 381.

19. D. T. Suzuki, *Mysticism: Christian and Buddhist* (New York: Harper and Row, 1956), 185.

20. Ibid., 185.

21. Ibid.

22. Ibid., 211.

23. Kaneko on Suzuki's view of Shin Buddhism, in *Suzuki Daisetsu: Hito to Shisō* (Tokyo: Iwanami, 1971), 31.

24. Kaneko's citation of the *Tannishō* does not include bibliographic information. The English translation is taken from: Taitetsu Unno, trans., *Tannisho: A Shin Buddhist Classic* (Honolulu, Hawaii: Buddhist Study Center Press, 1996), 10.

Chapter 10

1. Thanks to Richard Payne, whose response to my paper at the conference addressed this distinction. Thanks to Tomoyasu Naitō from Japan, who during the conference provided me with an outline of how Western views of energy shifted in relation to Mesmer and Freud. Thanks to Lisa Grumbach, for her gracious and expert late-night translation. Thanks to Jeremy Safran and Jack Engler for their comments during the conference on the theoretical constellation of different therapeutic perspectives.

2. *Thig le gnyag gcig.* This is a term widely used in the Great Completeness (rDzogs-chen) traditions of Tibet to refer to the ground or base (Tib. *gzhi;* Skt. *sthāna or ālaya*) of all the subjects and objects known to the ordinary senses. Failing to recognize that only this unbounded wholeness is genuine, we identify infinitely with what is finite, false.

3. Jung, while articulating a theory of psychic energy, found it difficult to bridge this with the material and physical realm. In an attempt to bridge the subjective psyche and objective matter, he posited the existence of an "objective psyche," something akin to Kant's transcendental object "X." In essence, Jung's theories in this area enter into the realm of speculative metaphysics under the banner of necessary postulates.

4. See Harvey B. Aronson, *Buddhist Practice on Western Ground: Reconciling Buddhist Ideals and Western Psychology* (Boulder: Shambhala, 2005).

5. A detailed discussion of this in the context of contemporary Western understandings of self is the central subject of Anne C. Klein, Kathryn Milun, and Phyllis Pay, *The Knowing Body: Subtleties of the Self* (forthcoming).

6. Thus, in Tibetan one term for extreme anxiety is "life-wind" *(srog rlung).*

7. Kenneth G. Zysk, "Science of Respiration and the Doctrine of Bodily Winds," *Journal of the American Oriental Society,* 113, no. 2 (1993): 205.

8. Jung as well as transpersonal psychologists such as Ken Wilber have written about the intersections of Asian thought and their own psychological perspectives, seeking to integrate the former into the latter. There is not room here to elaborate on their attempts. Suffice it to note the following: (1) Whatever the theoretical similarities, the various practices involved, meditative and nonmeditative, differ widely. In order to confirm theoretical parallels, there must be ways to bridge these paradigms practically. (2) Western thinkers' attempts to integrate Asian thought often occur on the basis of Western metaphysical and epistemological assumptions, assumptions that may not map perfectly onto the Asian paradigms they examine. For example, Western ontology is generally dualistic and teleological in a linear sense, seeking to establish a basis for being and a discursive goal for the realization of that being. Just to give one example from the Asian side, Tibetan Buddhist ontology is based on emptiness and the transcendence of discursive or dualistic assumptions and seeks to realize buddhahood, not in a linear fashion, but as an all-embracing awakening that works endlessly in this world to dissolve dualistic assumptions.

9. Shin Buddhism's views of the vital principle of receptivity to the other-power of Amida were eloquently relayed at the conference by Rev. Seigen Yamaoka, contributor to this volume. These views are very helpful in articulating the psychologically expanded capacity that an allegiance to a transcendent divine encourages. Gregory Bateson suggested something very similar in his analysis of why, in Alcoholics Anonymous, establishing a relation to a "higher power" is so epistemologically transformative. Gregory Bateson, "The Cybernetics of 'Self': A Theory of Alcoholism," in *Steps to an Ecology of Mind* (New York: Ballantine Books), 309–37.

10. Jack Engler, "Being Somebody and Being Nobody: A Reexamination of the Understanding of Self in Psychoanalysis and Buddhism," in *Buddhism and Psychoanalysis: An Unfolding Dialogue,* ed. Jeremy Safran (Boston: Wisdom Publications, 2003).

11. Although *ātman* is generally considered the object of critique in Buddhist doctrine, Buddhists, especially Mahāyāna Buddhists, freely use terms that, in the spirit of *upāya,* appropriately address a particular context. Thus, terms such as "Brahma-faring" and "eternal" describe the path of nonduality as much as *anātman* and impermanence.

12. William B. Parsons, *The Enigma of the Oceanic Feeling: Revisioning the Psychoanalytic Theory of Mysticism* (New York: Oxford University Press 1999).

13. Engler, "Being Somebody and Being Nobody," 35–79.

14. See discussion of confidence and surety in Klein & Wangyal, 2006.

15. Lopon Tenzin Namdak, *Ma rgyud ye shes thig le'i mchan 'grel thar lam rab gsal: An expository treatise on Ma rgyud Ye shes thig le* (Delhi: Bön Monastic Centre, Dolanji, n.d.), 8–9. Although this text in general is from the viewpoint of the seventh vehicle, its discussion here accords with the Great Completeness. This discussion is drawn from conversations I had with Lopon Tenzin Namdak and is discussed in detail in Anne C. Klein and Geshe Tenzin Wangyal Rinpoche, *Unbounded Wholeness: Dzogchen, Bon, and the Logic of the Nonconceptual* (New York: Oxford University Press, 2006) (forthcoming).

16. According to Lopon Tenzin Namdak, criticism of Dzogchen often assumes that its reflexive open awareness is discussed like the Cittamātra view, but it is not. For a concise discussion of the types of sense perception in the context of Dharmakirti's own views, see Roger Jackson, *Is Enlightenment Possible?: Dharmakirti and Rgyal Tshab Rje on Knowledge, Rebirth, No-Self and Liberation* (Ithaca, New York: Snow Lion Publications, 1993), 122–26. As he notes, "apperception" or perception of perception itself *(rang rig)* is the most basic context of these categories; it is in a sense the consequent malleability of this rubric that gives the *gTan tshigs gal mdo rig pa'i tshad ma (Authenticity of Open Awareness)* philosophical room to maneuver within it.

17. Lopon Tenzin Namdak, *Ma rgyud ye shes thig le'i mchan 'grel,* 9.8ff.

18. Mitchell, Stephen A., "Commentary: Somebodies and Nobodies," in Safran, *Buddhism and Psychoanalysis,* 83–85.

19. Lopon Tenzin Namdak, *Ma rgyud ye shes thig le'i mchan 'grel,* 56.9.

20. Cited in the *Gal mDo,* 97.3; translation in Anne Klein and Geshe Wangyal, *Unbounded Wholeness.*

21. A crucial element in the sudden/gradual debate that has so many permutations in Buddhist thought is how buddha-nature is located in relation to the ordinary self. For a discussion of sudden discovery versus gradual development, and some of the issues the debate raises for structurings of the path, see Anne C. Klein, *Meeting the Great Bliss Queen: Buddhists, Feminists, and the Art of the Self* (Boston: Beacon Press, 1995).

22. One critical difference lies in the fact that Buddhism calls "it" emptiness, a term that contains within itself a nondual logic of self-negation such that emptiness cannot be regarded as a fixed idea. Although Almaas's "Being" also implies that which cannot be conceptually reified, in the actual articulation of the concept within the mind, it may be subject to subtle reification. Nevertheless, as a concept that bridges emptiness/buddha-nature and Western psychology, it is highly sophisticated and effective.

23. A. H. Almaas, *Facets of Unity: The Enneagram of Holy Ideas* (Berkeley, Diamond Books, 1998), 17.

24. Engler, "Being Somebody and Being Nobody," 77.
25. As Engler pointedly puts it: Why do we repeatedly construct identity out of an illusory self? ("Being Somebody and Being Nobody," 77).
26. The most classical formulation can be found in Longchenpa's *Tshig don mDzod.* See Gregory Hillis, "The Rhetoric of Naturalness: A Critical Study of the *gNas Lugs mdzod*" (Ph.D. diss., University of Virginia, 2002). For detailed discussion of the esoteric system of winds and essences, see also David Germano, "Poetic Thought, The Intelligent Universe, and the Mystery of Self: The Tantric Synthesis of rDzogs Chen in Fourteenth Century Tibet" (Ph.D. diss., University of Wisconsin–Madison, 1992).
27. A. H. Almaas, *The Pearl beyond Price* (Berkeley: Diamond Books, 1988), 230.
28. Ibid., 230.
29. By now, it should be apparent that "metaphysical" means something other than the objective entity pursued by speculative metaphysics as found in the Western tradition of a Leibniz or a Hegel. Rather, it points to an all-encompassing awareness that is beyond the finite, physical (material) world that is nevertheless real and confirmable through contemplative or mystical experience.
30. *The Primordially Existent Sky (Nam mkha' ye srid),* cited in *Authenticity of Open Awareness (gTan tshigs gal mdo rig pa'i tshad ma),* translated and discussed in Klein and Wangyal, *Unbounded Wholeness.*
31. Klein and Wangyal, *Authenticity of Open Awareness,* 14.10–18.
32. This became a term of art in the work of Michael Gearin-Tosh who, when diagnosed with a fatal disease, took medical matters into his own hands. He not only survived but recovered and wrote a book in which he explored the logic of scientific verification, which would have denied him life, and contrasted it with his own method. He himself was, of course, the living proof. See Michael Gearin-Tosh, *Living Proof: A Medical Mutiny* (New York: Simon & Schuster, 2002).
33. *Sems nyid me long gi mdzod phug (Mirror of Mindnature Treasure),* 55.1, http://datastore.lib.virginia.edu (May 2005).
34. According to the noted Nyingma Dzogchen scholar Tulku Thondup, the term *thig le nyag gcig* in Nyingma Dzogchen variously signifies *dharmakāya* or great bliss. Further, its roundness, innocent of edges, symbolizes freedom from extremes. Khenbo Palden Sharab, among the most respected Nyingma Dzogchen scholars today, notes that the term *thig le nyag gcig* is found in Longchen-ba, especially in the *chos dbyings mdzod,* [Klong-chen-pa Dri-med-'od-zer (1308-1363), *The Precious Treasury of the Basic Space of Phenomena (chos dbyings rin po che'i mdzod)* (trans. Richard Barron a.k.a. Lama Chokyi Nyima) (Junction City, California: Padma Publishing, 2001)], as synonymous with *dbyings, rang 'grol,* and *spros pa dang 'grel ba.* Further study, especially of *chos dbyings mdzod,* is necessary to develop this comparison.
    Herbert Guenther (*Wholeness Lost and Wholeness Regained: Forgotten Tales of Individuation from Ancient Tibet* [Albany: SUNY Press, 1994], 2–3, 18n10) cites

several very early Buddhist sources in his survey of meanings of this term. He notes that according to the *Byang-chub tu sems skyod pa*, attributed to 'Jam-dpal bshes-gnyen and preserved in the *rGyud 'bum* of Vairocana (Vol. 7 pp. 287–340), the *le* of *thig le* means totality, arising as anything, that *nyag* means "profound and subtle," and *gcig* refers to the continuity between subject and object. Shri Sinha concurs, as does a passage form Padmasambhava's *sPros-bral don-gsa* (see Klein and Wangyal, *Unbounded Wholeness*).

35. The text, *The Scripture of the Blissful Samantabhadra*, is cited in *Authenticity of Open Awareness;* see Klein and Wangyal, *Unbounded Wholeness* (forthcoming).

36. This has been the focus of a series of Buddhism in the Body workshops taught by myself and Phyllis Pay.

37. *Gal mDo* 52.5, in Klein and Wangyal, *Unbounded Wholeness.*

38. Almaas discusses the difference in some detail in his chapter on "Merging" in *Pearl Beyond Price*, 223–44.

39. The last verse of "New Moon, Hillal," in *The Essential Rumi*, trans. Coleman Banks (New York: HarperCollins, 1995), 151.

40. *Essential Rumi*, 177.

41. This and related issues will be discussed in detail in Klein, Pay, and Milun, *The Knowing Body*, a manuscript in progress.

Chapter 11

1. Andrew Olendzki, trans., *Therigatha Atthakatha*, X.1, http://www.accesstoinsight.org/noncanon/comy/index.html.

2. I have chosen to use the etymological root of *dukkha*, "not at ease," to refer to a lack of ease, or "dis-ease." I explore the full meaning of this term in the rest of this paper.

3. While these statements are intended to be genuinely helpful or supportive, these phrases are often used to avoid the mental and emotional realities of a situation. My citation of them here is not to condemn or endorse them.

4. Shinran, *The True Teaching, Practice, and Realization,* trans. Dennis Hirota et al., in *The Collected Works of Shinran,* vol. 1, *The Writings* (Kyoto: Jōdo Shinshū Hongwanji–Ha, 1997), 120.

5. *A Record in Lament of Divergences (Tannishō),* in *Collected Works of Shinran*, 665 (sec. 9).

6. To read the story, see *Collected Works of Shinran*, 89.

7. I will address the doctrinal ramifications of these questions in further detail in a future paper.

8. "Family of origin" refers to our families prior to entering into a marriage or long-term partnership, i.e. the families in which we were raised. We often bring messages from our families of origin without realizing how they affect us in our marriages and new families.

9. The various aspects of the Eightfold Path are usually translated as "right": *right* views, *right* thoughts, *right* speech, and so on. I have deliberately chosen not to use the word "right," as it sets up a dualistic mind-set that one does it right or wrong, correctly or incorrectly. Based on the Sanskrit original, *samyak*, meaning to "go with" nirvana or transformation of blind passions, I prefer the translation "appropriate."

Chapter 12

1. *Shinshū Shōgyō Zensho* (hereafter *SSZ*) (Kyoto: Kokyo Shoin, 1963), 2:4; *Ryukoku Translation Series* (*RTS*) 2:36.
2. Haruo Yamaoka, *Awakening of Gratitude in Dying* (San Francisco: BCA Research and Educational Committee, 1978), 25–28.
3. Shinran, *Notes on 'Essentials of Faith Alone'* (Yuishinshō-mon'i) (Kyoto: Honganji International Center, 1979).
4. *SSZ*, 2:630; *Shin Buddhism Translation Series (SBTS)*, 2:42–43.
5. Shinran, *Shōzōmatsu wasan*, *SSZ*, 2:530; *RTS*, 7:117.
6. Jack Engler, "Being Somebody and Being Nobody," in *Psychoanalysis and Buddhism: An Unfolding Dialogue*, ed. Jeremy D. Safran (Boston: Wisdom Publications, 2003), 76.
7. Rennyo, *Goichidai Kikigaki*, *SSZ*, 3:554
8. Jeremy D. Safran, "Psychoanalysis and Buddhism as Cultural Institutions," in Safran, *Psychoanalysis and Buddhism*, 12.
9. Engler, "Being Somebody and Being Nobody," 47.
10. Rennyo, *Gobunsho*, *SSZ*, 3:494.
11. Engler, "Being Somebody and Being Nobody," 95.
12. *SSZ*, 2:2–3; *RTS*, 5:30.
13. *SSZ*, 2:588; *RTS*, 7:97–99.
14. *SSZ*, 2:80; *RTS*, 5:132.
15. *SSZ*, 2:5; *RTS*, 5:41.
16. *SSZ*, 2:5; *RTS*, 5:40.
17. *SSZ*, 2:71; *RTS*, 5:118.
18. *SSZ*, 2:202; *RTS*, 5:211.
19. *SSZ*, 2:44; *RTS*, 1:30.
20. *SSZ*, 2:4; *RTS*, 5:36. *Shinjin*, true entrusting, is said to be endowed by Amida to the practitioner. That is, even the ability to entrust the self to other-power comes from other-power.
21. Seigen H. Yamaoka, *The Transmission of Shin Buddhism to the West* (San Francisco: Federation of Dharma School Teacher's League, 2005).
22. *SSZ*, 2:631; *SBTS*, *Yuishinshō-mon'i*, 44.
23. Shinran, *Shōzōmatsu Wasan*, *SSZ*, 2:558; *RTS*, 7:97.

Chapter 13

1. Kamei Katsuichiro, *Ai to inori ni tsuite* (On love and prayer) (Tokyo: Daiwa Shobō, 1967), 146.

2. "Nihonjin no heikin yomyō" (Life expectancy of Japanese people), Kōsei rōdō shō tōkeijōhōbu, 2002), http://www.mhlw.go.jp/toukei/saikin/hw/life/life02/index.html.

3. As of May 5, 2003, according to government statistics, 23.3 percent of Japanese households are single households, 59.7 percent are nuclear families, 10.4 percent are families with three generations, and 6.6 percent have some other composition (*Heisei 15 Kokumin seikatsu kisochōsa gaiyō* [Overview of Research on the Fundamentals of Citizens Living, 2003], Kōsei rōdō shō, 2003, http://www.mhlw.go.jp/toukei/saikin/hw/k-tyosa/k-tyosa03/1-1.html.

4. *Kōsei rōdō shō tōkeihyō deetabeesu* (Database of statistical charts of the Ministry of Health, Labor and Welfare), http://wwwdbtk.mhlw.go.jp/toukei/index.html.

5. Zenkoku hosupisu kanwa kea byōtō renraku kyōgikai (National Council of Hospice and Palliative Care Facilities), ed., *Hosupisu te nāni?* (What is hospice?) (Tokyo: NHK Kōsei Bunka Jigyōdan, 2003), 5.

6. Jōdo Shinshū Hongwanji-ha, Dendō Shakai-bu, "Vihara katsudō no rinen to hōkōsei" (The ideals and the direction of the Vihara movement), http://www2.hongwanji.or.jp/social/vihala/html/rinen.html.

7. The "Increasing-by-One Āgama Sutra" (Pali: Aṅguttara Nikāya), vol. 40: *Taishō shinshū daizōkyō*, ed. Takakusu Junjirō and Watanabe Kaigyoku (Tokyo: Taisho Issaikyō Kankōkai, 1924–32), 2:767b.

8. *Eshin sōzu zenshū* (Kyoto: Shibunkaku, 1973), 1:170–72; *Ōjōyōshū*, vol. 2, *Nihon Jōdokyō no yoake*, trans. Ishida Mizumaro (Tokyo: Heibonsha, 1981), 133–36; *Shinshū shōgyō zensho*, vol. 1 (Kyoto: Ōyagi Kōbundō, 1941), 854–55; *Jōdo Shinshū seiten: Shichiso hen chūshaku ban* (Kyoto: Hongwanji Shuppansha, 1988), 1044–45.

"The Fraternity of the Twenty-five Samādhi" means that twenty-five fellow human beings support each other until death, and aspire to transcend the twenty-five samsaric states of darkness through the *nembutsu*. The fraternity was originally founded in 986 by twenty-five monks. After Genshin, the imperial officers and thirty other monks joined this *nembutsu* society. The members met on the fifteenth of each month, and after chanting sutras they recited the *nembutsu* from the evening until the next morning. Then they continued to chant sutras and recite the *nembutsu* until noon. If a member became ill, he was cared for at the Birth Hall *(ōjōin)*. To make concentration on Amida Buddha easier, other members gathered around his bedside, offering flowers and incense and reciting the *nembutsu*. The number twenty-five indicates twenty-five states of samsaric existence, which cover all the realms of sentient beings. The society aimed at transcending these states and reaching the Pure Land.

9. *Eshin sōzu zenshū*, 1:172–81; *Ōjōyōshū*, vol. 2, trans. Ishida Mizumaro, 139–49; *Shinshū shōgyō zensho*, 1:855–61; *Jōdo Shinshū seiten: Shichiso hen chūshaku ban*, 1045–46:

> Again, aspirants, when you are about to die with sickness or otherwise, follow, with mind and body, the above-stated method of the *samādhi* of recollecting the Buddha. Turn your face to the west, and, with concentration of mind, focus your thought on Amida Buddha. Making your mental act agreeable with the oral one, recite (the Name) uninterruptedly, and resolutely think of attaining birth in the Pure Land and of the sages' coming to receive you. If the sick person sees a realm, let him tell the nursing man about it. When he has told it, record his story. If the sick person cannot talk, let the nursing man ask him various questions, saying, "What realm did you see?" If he tells of the visions of his karmic evils, let the man on the bedside recite the Name and himself repent in order to help the sick man repent; thereby, you can definitely purge him of the karmic evils. If, having extinguished the karmic evils, he sees the sages on the lotus-base appear before him in response to his recitation of the Name, record it in writing as I have prescribed above. When the aspirant's relatives and kinsmen come to nurse him, let not those who have drunk wine or eaten meat or any of the five kinds of acrid food enter (the room). If there is such a man, never allow him to go to the sick man's bedside. For the sick man may lose his right recollection, be confounded by the spirits, and, after having died in a state of madness, fall into the three evil realms. May the aspirants restrain themselves, uphold the Buddha's teachings, and perform the causal practice for seeing the Buddha. The above are the rules for practicing in the hall and for nursing a sick man. ("Shan-tao's [Shandao] *Exposition of the Method of Contemplation on Amida Buddha*, Part 1," trans. Hisao Inagaki, *Pacific World*, 3rd ser., 1 [1999]: 86)

10. Nabeshima Naoki, "Hōnen ni okeru shi to kanshi no mondai, 2" (Death and care for the dying in Hōnen's writing, part 2), *Ryūkoku daigaku ronshū*, no. 436 (1990).

11. *Ōjō Jōdo yōjin*, in *Shōwa shinshū: Hōnen Shōnin zenshū* (Kyoto: Heirakuji Shoten, 1987), 564.

12. "Gorinjū no toki monteito ni shimesareru okotoba," in *Hōnen Shōnin zenshū*, 724–25.

13. *Nembutsu ōjō yōgishō*, in *Hōnen Shōnin zenshū*, 687–88.

14. "Saihōshinanshō," *Shinran Shōnin zenshū*, 5 (Kyoto: Hōzōkan, 1984), 121.

15. *Lamp for the Latter Ages*, 14, in CWS, 1:545.

16. *Lamp for the Latter Ages*, 12, in CWS, 1:539. See also *Mattōshō*, 12, in *Jōdo Shinshū seiten: Chūshakuban* (Kyoto: Jōdo Shinshū Hongwanji-ha, 1988), 795.

17. *Lamp for the Latter Ages*, 1, in CWS, 1:523. See also *Mattōshō*, 1, in *Jōdo Shinshū seiten: Chūshakuban*, 735.

18. Asai Jōkai, "Shinran no shōji kan" (Shinran's view of life and death), in *Bukkyō no shōji kan*, ed. Nihon Bukkyō Gakkai (Kyoto: Heirakuji Shoten, 1981), 343.

19. *Lamp for the Latter Ages*, 6, in CWS, 1:531. See also *Mattōshō*, 6, in *Jōdo Shinshū Seiten: Chūshakuban*, 771.

20. *A Record in Lament of Divergences*, chap. 9, in CWS, 1:666. See also *Tannishō*, chap. 9, in *Jōdo Shinshū Seiten: Chūshakuban*, 837.

21. *Mattōshō*, 6, in *Jōdo Shinshū Seiten: Chūshakuban*, 771; see also Nabeshima Naoki, "Shinran to sono montei ni okeru shi no chōkoku," *Shinshūgaku*, 97 and 98 (1988): 357.

22. *Lamp for the Latter Ages*, 14, in CWS, 1:545.

23. World Health Organization, *Gan no itami kara no kaihō*, 2nd ed. (Tokyo: Kanehara Shuppan, 1996); World Health Organization, *Gan no itami kara no kaihō to pariatibu kea* (Tokyo: Kanehara Shuppan, 1993).

24. Sawada Aiko, "Shi to kodoku: Makki kanja no shinriteki kumon wo mitsumete," in *Sei to shi no kyōiku: Death Education no susume*, ed. Higuchi Kazuhiko and Hirayama Masami (Osaka: Sōgensha, 1984), 114.

25. Yamazaki Fumio, *Byōin de shinu to iu koto* (Tokyo: Bunshun Bunko, 1996), 214.

26. Nakamura Hajime, *Gautama Buddha*, 2, Nakamura Hajime Senshū, vol. 12 (Tokyo: Shunjūsha, 1992), 188.

27. Suzuki Akiko, *Gan kokuchi no ato de* (Kyoto: Tankyūsha, 1989), 80.

28. Ibid., 201.

29. Ibid., 31.

30. Ibid., 232.

31. Hirano Keiko, *Kodomo tachi yo arigatō* (Kyoto: Hōzōkan, 1990), 7.

32. Ibid., 18–19.

33. Ibid., 36, 37–38.

34. Nihon Ishikai Dai Hachiki Seimei Rinri Kondankai: The Bioethics Committee of the Japan Medical Association, *Iryō no jissen to seimei rinri ni tsuite no hōkoku*, 25, 20, http://www.med.or.jp/nichikara/seirin15.pdf. The author is one of the bioethics committee members.

35. Ibid., 20.

36. Ryōkan (1758–1831) was a Zen monk and a Shin Buddhist. He died at the age of seventy-three on the sixth day of the first month, 1831. Ryōkan is one of the best known of Japan's poets. At the age of seventeen he left his home and from then until his death lived as a Zen monk. Most of the time he supported himself by begging rice from door to door. He was always content with his lot. At times he would take part in the village children's game, or gather herbs with the women. Near the end of his life he became attached to a young Zen nun named Teishinni who tended and fed him in his illness. Another poet may have composed his death poem; Ryōkan spoke it to Teishinni in his last moments. The following poems are recorded in *Hachisu no tsuyu* (Dew Drops on a Lotus Blossom), written by Teishinni. Teishinni read this poem to Ryōkan: "Ikishini no sakai hanarete sumuminimo saranu wakare no aruzo kanashiki" (You and I free

from the unenlightened state of birth and death / However, I am so sad at this unavoidable parting from you). Ryōkan replied in a haiku poem to Teishinni: "Ura o mise omote o misete chiru momiji" (First one side, then the other—thus falls, an autumn maple leaf).

37. Malcolm David Eckel, "Is There a Buddhist Philosophy of Nature?" in *Buddhism and Psychotherapy*, ed. Mary Evelyn Tucker and Duncan Ryuken Williams (Cambridge, Mass.: Harvard University CSHR Publications, 1997), 343.

38. Memorial services for the deceased are held every seventh day during the first forty-nine days after death. Then annual memorial services are often held on the day that the loved one passed away. Moreover, memorial services usually will be held at various intervals during the fifty years after death (first, third, seventh, thirteenth, twenty-fifth, and fiftieth years, in addition to various daily and monthly services during the first year) for each family that lost a loved one. Such services are acts of healing confirming the long-term transformation of the feeling of the family members. The Buddhist altar is a place where they can reflect upon the feelings in the depth of their minds. Through the memorial services, the surviving family will realize feelings of their own as well as memories of the deceased. And through the memory of the deceased, they can move on to explore a new future.

39. Naoki Nabeshima, *Shinran's Approaches towards Bereavement and Grief: Transcendence and Care for the Pain of Separating from Loved Ones in Shinran's Thought*, CCSBS On-line Publication Series 3 (Berkeley: Institute of Buddhist Studies, 2001), http://www.shin-ibs.edu/ccsbs4.htm.

Ōtani Kōshin, the abbot of Jōdo Shinshū Hongwanji-ha, says,

Then, is it only their memory which connects us with the deceased? Not at all. We can live our lives together with the deceased. People die and will attain buddhahood. According to the teaching of Jōdo Shinshū, people who listen to the teaching of Amida Buddha and recite the *nembutsu*, at the moment that their lives in this world are over, are born in the Pure Land to become a buddha. The buddha here means "power" or "working." Perhaps, it is easier to understand if I say that it is just like the changing of the seasons. . . . The Buddha is the same. The existence of the Buddha cannot be known by his image or shape. But, by studying the teaching of Buddhism, participating in services held at the temples, or chanting the sutras, in the process of developing such conditions, we will gradually be able to feel the existence of the Buddha. The ashes and the memories of the deceased are simply their legacies of the past. But communicating through your heart with those who have become buddhas is possible in the present, in the future, and forever. The buddhas and we can always stay together. (Ōtani Kōshin, *Ashita niwa kōgan arite* [Tokyo: Kadokawa Shoten, 2003], 150–52).

Appendix I

1. Jeremy D. Safran, ed. *Psychoanalysis and Buddhism: An Unfolding Dialogue* (Boston: Wisdom Publications, 2003).

2. Safran, Jeremy D. "Introduction: Psychoanalysis and Buddhism as Cultural Institutions," in Jeremy D. Safran, ed. *Psychoanalysis and Buddhism: An Unfolding Dialogue*, 1–34 (Boston: Wisdom Publications, 2003).

3. Jack Engler, "Being Somebody and Being Nobody: A Reexamination of the Understanding of Self in Psychoanalysis and Buddhism," in Jeremy D. Safran, ed. *Psychoanalysis and Buddhism: An Unfolding Dialogue*, 35–79 (Boston: Wisdom Publications, 2003).

4. This is literally true. Participants at the conference, "Between Cultures: Buddhism and Psychology in the 21st Century," were asked to read these contributions in preparation for attending. That reading proved so provocative to me, I made it the subject of my contribution. I want to express my thanks to the participants for their comments on my work. Also, and importantly, to Joseph Bobrow for his thoughtful responses to an earlier draft of this appendix and to material developed in "An Object-Relations Psychology of Zen Practice," in Damien Keown, ed., *Buddhist Studies from India to America: Essays in Honor of Charles S. Prebish*, 191–206 (London and New York: Routledge/Curzon, 2006), some of which material also found its way here. Bows to all.

5. Charles S. Prebish and Martin Baumann, eds. *Westward Dharma: Buddhism beyond Asia* (Berkeley and Los Angeles, University of California Press, 2002).

6. Safran, "Introduction," 3.

7. Peter Homans, *The Ability to Mourn: Disillusionment and the Social Origins of Psychoanalysis* (Chicago: University of Chicago Press, 1989).

8. Suzanne Kirschner, *The Religious and Romantic Origins of Psychoanalysis: Individuation and Integration in Post-Freudian Theory* (Cambridge: Cambridge University Press, 1996).

9. D. W. Winnicott On the Use of an Object, Parts II–VII 228–246, Part IV, "The Use of the Word 'Use'." In *Psycho-Analytic Explorations*, eds. Clare Winnicott, Ray Shepherd and Madeleine Davis (Cambridge: Harvard University Press, 1989 [1968]) 233.

10. Jack Engler, "Therapeutic Aims in Psychotherapy and Meditation: Developmental Stages in the Representation of Self," in Ken Wilber, Jack Engler, and Daniel P. Brown, eds., *Transformations of Consciousness: Conventional and Contemplative Perspectives on Development* (New Science Library. Boston and London: Shambhala Books Publications, 1986), 24 and 49; and Engler, "Being Somebody and Being Nobody," 35.

11. D. W. Winnicott, "The Location of Cultural Experience," in *Playing and Reality* (London and New York: Routledge, 1971 [1967]) 99.

12. Metcalf, "The Encounter of Buddhism and Psychology," 360.

13. Engler, "Being Somebody and Being Nobody," 73.

14. Ibid., 67–71.
15. Ibid., 73.
16. Ibid., 71.
17. To claim that Hindu and Buddhist meditative experiences are identical would seem to mean one of two things. The first option is that *anātman* and *ātman* (and Brahman) are fundamentally different and yet the experiences of them are identical. This would allow Engler to save his argument and examples, but it seems to me ontologically and psychologically incoherent. I don't believe Engler is making this odd claim, so that leaves us with the second option: *anātman*, the sine qua non (or perhaps better: sine qua sum) of Buddhism, is fundamentally *ātman* and thus Brahman. Engler claims "that which observes in silence and wonder . . . is not, cannot be, the result of constructive activity itself" (Jack Engler, "Can We Say What the Self "Really" Is?", in Jeremy D. Safran, ed. *Psychoanalysis and Buddhism: An Unfolding Dialogue* [Boston: Wisdom Publications, 2003], 95). If this silent observer truly is what remains after the impermanent has been stripped away, then there can be no flux, no selves, no arising and passing away within it. What can this now permanent, lucid, infinite, unitive observer be but Brahman? Engler may *call* it *anatta*, but Freud surely, and perhaps the Buddha as well, would see this as a form of backdoor theism and eternalism.

   I was pleased to see Engler accept Stephen Mitchell's criticism and at least begin to back away from this ontological claim at the end of his "Reply" to Mitchell (Ibid., 94–95). There, Engler refers to his colleague Dan Brown's work showing the no-self arrived at in Raj Yoga is continuous, not discontinuous as in *vipassanā*. Still, Engler's words on the silent observer, quoted above, are taken from this "Reply," Engler's final word, so far. This signals to me that if Engler is not conflating these two experiences of Self/no-self, he may well still be collapsing the Buddhist experience into the Hindu one. If so, there is that eternalism, again.
18. Engler, "Being Somebody and Being Nobody," 67.
19. Daniel Capper, *Guru Devotion and the American Buddhist Experience* (Lewiston, NY: Edwin Mellon Press, 2002).
20. From Louis Macneice's poem, "Snow," which I admit was surely not written about Buddhism, but just as surely was written more evocatively than whatever sentence I would have produced here.
21. Metcalf, "The Encounter of Buddhism and Psychology," 363.
22. Engler, "Being Somebody and Being Nobody," 52.
23. Ibid., 53.
24. Ibid., 78.
25. Ibid., 58–59.
26. Ibid., 58.

27. D. W. Winnicott, "The Fate of the Transitional Object," in *Psycho-Analytic Explorations*, ed. Clare Winnicott, Ray Shepherd and Madeleine Davis (Cambridge: Harvard University Press, 1989 [1959]), 58.
28. Engler, "Being Somebody and Being Nobody," 53–73.
29. Ibid., 77.
30. Winnicott, "The Fate of the Transitional Object," 54.
31. D. W. Winnicott, "Primary Maternal Preoccupation," in *Collected Papers: Through Paediatrics to Psycho-Analysis*, 300–305 (New York: Basic Books, 1958 [1956]).
32. Of course by "mother" here I refer to any primary caregiver. In fact, as I write these words, my daughter is 16 weeks old and, holding her in my arms and gaze, I feel the truth of Winnicott's words. We are not-two.
33. D. W. Winnicott, "Playing: Creative Activity and the Search for the Self," in *Playing and Reality*, 64.
34. D. W. Winnicott, "Transitional Objects and Transitional Phenomena," in *Playing and Reality*, 14–15.
35. D. W. Winnicott, "The Place where We Live," in *Playing and Reality*, 108.
36. Ibid.
37. D. W. Winnicott, "Transitional Objects," 5.
38. Ibid., 3.
39. D. W. Winnicott, "Primitive Emotional Development," in *Collected Papers: Through Paediatrics to Psycho-Analysis* (New York: Basic Books, 1958 [1945]), 150n.
40. Winnicott, "Location," 100.
41. D. W. Winnicott, "Ideas and Definitions," in *Psycho-Analytic Explorations* [early 1950s], 43.
42. D. W. Winnicott, "Ego Distortion in Terms of True and False Self," in *The Maturational Processes and the Facilitating Environment* (London: Hogarth Press and the Institute for Psycho-Analysis, 1965 [1960]), 148.
43. Ibid.
44. Joseph Bobrow, "Psychoanalysis, Mysticism, and the Incommunicado Core." *fort da* 8, 2: 62–71, 2002.
45. I'm suggesting here that the experience of non-duality is real and that the transpersonal non-dual experience is more real or accurate than the pre-personal non-dual experience. I'm using a Buddhist word ("non-duality") here, rather than a monotheistic word (say, "union") because my evidence, coming from Zen practice, supports it. Other researchers' evidence may support the use of "union." These words each impart a distinctive theological flavor. I can't, right now, conceive of evidence that would support a definitive choice between them; that would go beyond the limit of psychological research. After all, who can falsify the sacred?
46. James H. Austin, *Zen and the Brain: Toward an Understanding of Meditation and Consciousness* (Cambridge: M.I.T. Press, 1999).

47. Jeffrey B. Rubin, "A Well-lived Life: Psychoanalytic and Buddhist Contributions," in *Psychoanalysis and Buddhism: An Unfolding Dialogue*, 387–410.
48. Joseph Bobrow, "Moments of Truth, Truths of Moment," in *Psychoanalysis and Buddhism: An Unfolding Dialogue*, 199–221.
49. Franz Metcalf, "Why Do Americans Practice Zen Buddhism?" Ph.D. dissertation, University of Chicago, 1997.
50. Madeleine Davis and David Wallbridge, *Boundary and Space: an Introduction to the Work of D. W. Winnicott* (New York: Brunner/Mazel, 1981), 172.
51. D. W. Winnicott, "Ego Integration in Child Development," in *The Maturational Processes and the Facilitating Environment* [1962], 56–63.
52. Note that "illusion" derives from the Latin *"ludere,"* "to play."
53. How can *bodhi*, direct experiencing, be an illusion in the potential space? If it is unconditioned it should be the direct experiencing of the external world, a kind of experiencing Winnicott would never have credited as an achievement. So it is ironic that Buddhism agrees with Winnicott that normal human experience is illusory, but disagrees about perfected human experience, saying it is *not* illusory just where Winnicott would say it *is*. This is more than a language problem. I think there are ontological issues at stake. Winnicott thought the deepest experience was created from shared illusion and so had to occur in the potential space. To generalize wildly, Buddhism thinks the deepest experience is direct perception of the external world in a way that breaks down the distinction of internal and external. So the deepest Buddhist experience ought to be anything but illusory; it ought to be an experience of the real thing, the flux of existence. These progressions go opposite ways.

This apparent contradiction is, I think, resolved by *anātman*. If the delusion of the permanent self is broken through, the strict division between internal and external experience no longer applies, at least on the ultimate level. When inner "fantasy" and outer "reality" cease being ultimately separable, then surely we have a breakthrough into the third realm of experiencing, the potential space. Daniel Capper, another toiler in the field of Buddhism and psychology, cautions me here, warning that Winnicott's third realm may ontologically depend on the existence of the first two: if they evaporate, so does it. He's wisely trying to pull me back from the brink of metaphysical assertion. But I seem to want to assert that the potential space in some sense pre-exists its creation/discovery in each person in whom it's experienced as arising.

In this sense, in ongoing awakened experience, the high level Zen practitioner lives in the potential space, but does so in *fact*, not in illusion. She does so without any dependence on the illusion of internal and external. Winnicott never imagined such a possibility, but I don't know if he'd disbelieve it. What he might caution is that such a way of experiencing stands in danger of leaving behind closeness, affect, meaning, in short the things that make life worth the time it takes. Some forms of Buddhist practice fall prey to this impoverishment, as Engler, Jeffrey Rubin, Joseph Bobrow, Robert Suler, Mark Finn, and others have pointed out. Zen does not so fall prey (or it does, but it shouldn't). In fact, it is precisely in its rich involvement in the stuff of life that I believe Zen makes its greatest (non-)spiritual contributions.

54. Engler, "Being Somebody and Being Nobody," 75.

55. Joseph Bobrow, "The Fertile Mind," in *The Couch and the Tree: Dialogues between Psychoanalysis and Buddhism*, ed. Anthony Molino (San Francisco: North Point Press, 1999), 319.

56. Engler, "Being Somebody and Being Nobody," 73.

57. Richard A. Shweder, *Thinking Through Cultures: Expeditions in Cultural Psychology* (Cambridge: Harvard University Press, 1991).

Appendix II

1. According to texts such as the *Great Collection Sutra*, Moon Matrix Section (*Daijikkyō*, Gatsuzō-bun, in *Taishō shinshū daizōkyō*, eds. Takakusu Junjirō and Watanabe Kaigyoku [Tokyo: Taishō Issaikyō Kankōkai, 1924–32], 13:376b), the concept of *mappō* explains the process of gradual decline of Buddhism after the demise of the Buddha. In Chinese Buddhism the first Buddhist master who propagated this concepts is considered to be Huisi (Jpn. Nangaku Eji, 515–77) According to his *Passages on Establishing Vows (Ryūseiganmon):* "The period of the Right Dharma Age is between the years of Senior Wood/Dog and Junior Water/Snake, which lasts for five hundred years. The period of the Semblance Dharma Age is between the years of Senior Wood/Ox, and Junior Water/Cock, which lasts for a thousand years. The period of the Last Dharma Age is between the years of Senior Wood/Dog, and Junior Water/Ox, which lasts for ten thousand years" (*Taishō*, 46:786c). Other theories count the Right Dharma Age and the Semblance Dharma Age as lasting five hundred years each or as a thousand years each, so the number of years preceding the Last Dharma Age is indeterminate. There are also different theories on the year of the Buddha's death. So the beginning of the Last Dharma Age can differ by more than a thousand years, depending on the theory.

The state of Buddhism in each period is also discussed differently. To summarize, in the True Dharma Age, teaching, practice, and realization are complete; in the Semblance Dharma Age, there are teaching and practice but no realization; in the Last Dharma Age, there is teaching, but practice and realization do not exist. Shinran, in his *Hymns of the Dharma-ages (Shōzōmatsu Wasan),* says:

Now, amid the five defilements in the last dharma-age,
Sentient beings are incapable of practice and realization;
Hence the teachings that Sakyamuni left behind
Have all passed into the *naga's* palace.

See *Collected Works of Shinran* (Kyoto: Jōdo Shinshū Hongwanji-ha, 1997), 339 (hereafter *CWS*). And in the "Chapter on Transformed Buddhas and Lands" in the *Kyōgyōshinshō*, Shinran says, "Truly we know that the teachings of the Path of Sages were intended for the period when the Buddha was in the world and for the right dharma-age; they are altogether inappropriate for the times and beings of the semblance and last dharma-ages and the age when the dharma has become extinct. Already their time has passed; they are no longer in accord with beings" (*CWS*, 240). And: "I see that in the various teachings of the Path of Sages, practice and enlightenment died out long ago, and that the true essence of the Pure Land way is the path to realization now vital and flourishing" (*CWS*, 289). According to Shinran, the self-power teaching of the Path of Sages declines after Śākyamuni's death, but the Pure Land teaching of other-power does not decline no matter how much time passes.

2. The development of the Pure Land teaching in China and Japan tends to emphasize the evilness of human existence, especially the evilness within one-self. The following are examples:

Regarding the phrase "the manifestation of true merit," there are two kinds of merit. First is the merit which accrues from the activity of a defiled mind and is not in accordance with the Dharma-nature. Such merit arises from the various good acts of ordinary men and heavenly beings. It also refers to the reward of human and heavenly states of existence. Both the cause and effect of such good acts are inverted and false; hence they are called "false merit." (Tanluan, *Commentary on the Discourse on the Pure Land*, trans. Hisao Inagaki [Kyoto: Nagata Bunshōdō, 1998], 135; slightly modified.)

The reason why the Buddha originally provided this glorious merit of purity was that [when he was a bodhisattva] he saw that the three worlds were characterized by illusion, incessant samsaric change and the endless round of suffering, like measuring-worms moving in a circle or silkworms spinning themselves into cocoons. He saw that pitiable sentient beings were bound to the three worlds and were entangled in inverted thinking and moral impurity. (Tanluan, *Commentary*, 137.)

Since the beginningless time, I have been transversing the three worlds because of the circle of delusion.
The karma I create in every thought moment binds my feet to the six realms and mires me in the three realms of suffering. (Tanluan, *Verses in Praise of Amida Buddha (San Amida Butsu ge)*, in *Jōdo Shinshū Seiten gentenban: Shichiso hen* [Kyoto: Jōdo Shinshū Hongwanji-ha, 1992], 200.)

Further no one among all sentient beings is able to weigh [his own spiritual abilities]. If we rely on the Mahāyāna [doctrines of attaining enlightenment], then no one has yet contemplated suchness, the true reality, or ultimate empti-ness. From the Hinayana point of view, one must enter into the Path of Insight and the Path of Practice, then one must [toil one's way up] through [the stage of] the *anāgāmin* to [that of] the arhat, severing the five [bonds of the] lower [world of desire] and leaving behind the five [bonds of the] higher [worlds of form and formlessness]. Until now, however, neither monk nor layperson has ever been able to reach these goals. True, there are those who enjoy the benefit of being born as human and heavenly beings. But this benefit is achieved only by having practiced the five precepts and the ten good acts. Now, however, even those who continue to observe these precepts and virtues are very rare. But when we consider people's evil doings and sinful deeds are they not raging everywhere like the storm's winds and lashing rains? (Daochuo, *Passages on the Land of Hap-piness [Anraku-shū]*, in *Hōnen's Senchakushū* [Honolulu: University of Hawai'i Press, 1998], 57.)

Deep mind is the deeply entrusting mind. There are two aspects. One is to believe deeply and decidedly that you are a foolish being of karmic evil caught in birth-and-death, ever sinking and ever wandering in transmigration from innumerable kalpas in the past, with never a condition that would lead to emancipation. (Shandao, *Commentary on the Contemplation Sutra*, Chapter on Non-Meditative Practice [*Kangyō-sho*, Sanzengi], cited in the *Kyōgyōshinshō*, in *CWS*, 85.)

Yet the teaching [for attaining birth in the Pure Land] expounded in the exo-teric and esoteric Buddhist literature is not single. As for the methodologies and principles regarding the creation of karmic causes [for attaining birth in the Pure Land], there are many different practices. For wise and diligent people, it is not difficult. But how could a stubborn and ignorant man such as myself pos-sibly follow the teaching? (Genshin, *Essentials for Attaining Birth (Ōjōyōshū)*, in *Jōdo Shinshū Seiten gentenban*, 891.)

[The master says] "I, Hōnen-bō, who accumulate the ten evil deeds, can attain birth in the Pure Land by reciting the *nembutsu*." He also says, "This ignorant Hōnen-bō is going to attain birth in the Pure Land by reciting the *nembutsu*." (Genkū [Hōnen], *Wagotōroku*, "Shōnin densetsu no kotoba," in *Shinshū shogyū zensho*, vol. 4 [Kyoto: Ōyagi Kōbundō, 1941], 677.)

How sad, how sad. What can I do, what can I do? I, myself, am not a person who can uphold the three learnings to cultivate discipline, meditation and wis-dom. (Ibid., 680.)

3. In the Eighteenth Vow, the phrase "even ten *nien*" *(naishi jū-nen)* is considered the cause for birth in the Pure Land. There are various interpretations regard-ing the meaning of "ten *nien*," one of which is that *nien* is the mindful practice of compassion, etc., only suitable for the sages. Shandao, however, interprets this ten *nien* as ten recitations of Amida's name *(nembutsu)*. And since the word

"even" is added to the word "ten," he understands that the number of recitations is not limited to ten, but rather refers to even just a single utterance of the
nembutsu as well as the practice of recitation throughout one's life. Hōnen also
follows Shandao's interpretation.

4. In the *Hymns of the Pure Land Masters (Kōsō Wasan)*, Shinran uses this metaphor:

> Through the benefit of the unhindered light,
> We realize *shinjin* of vast, majestic virtues,
> And the ice of our blind passions necessarily melts,
> Immediately becoming the water of enlightenment.
> Obstructions of karmic evil turn into virtues;
> It is like the relation of ice and water:
> The more the ice, the more the water;
> The more the obstructions, the more the virtues.
>
> (*CWS*, 371)

5. In *Passages on the Land of Happiness (Anraku-shū)* Daochuo says, "There is only
a single gate of the Pure Land path recommended for the mind of ordinary
beings to seek to enter" (*Jōdo Shinshū seiten gentenban*, 209).

6. Richard Crouter, ed., *Schleiermacher: On Religion: Speeches to its Cultured Despis-
ers*, Cambridge Texts in the History of Philosophy (Cambridge: Cambridge
University Press, 1996).

7. For example, Shinran, in citing Shandao's *Commentary on the Contemplation
Sutra*, alters the traditional reading to clarify that it is impossible to attain birth
in the Pure Land through the self-power practices.

We should not express outwardly signs of wisdom, goodness, or diligence
while inwardly being possessed of falsity. [Shinran's reading: We should not
express outwardly signs of wisdom, goodness, or diligence, for inwardly we are
possessed of falsity.] We are filled with all manner of greed, anger, perversity,
deceit, wickedness, and cunning, and it is difficult to put an end to our evil
nature. In this we are like poisonous snakes or scorpions. Though we perform
practices in the three modes of action, they must be called poisoned good acts
or false practices. They cannot be called true, real, and sincere action. Firmly
setting our minds and undertaking practice in this way—even if we strive to
the utmost with body and mind through the twelve periods of the day and night,
urgently seeking and urgently acting as though sweeping fire from our heads—
must all be called poisoned good acts. To seek birth in the Buddha's Pure Land
by directing the merit of such poisoned practice is completely wrong. (*Kyōgyōshinshō*, in *CWS*, vol. 1, 84, and vol. 2, 260).

The first reading means to admonish practitioners not to seek birth in the
Pure Land simply by pretending that they possess wisdom, goodness, or diligence *while* inwardly being possessed of falsity. Shinran alters the reading to
express the idea that it is impossible to attain birth in the Pure Land through

self-power practices, and he strongly criticizes practitioners who express out-wardly signs of wisdom, goodness, or diligence.

In the *Kyōgyōshinshō*, "Chapter on *Shinjin*," he also says, "In all small fool-ish beings, at all times, thoughts of greed and desire incessantly defile any good-ness of heart; thoughts of anger and hatred constantly consume the dharma-treasure. Even if one urgently acts and urgently practices as though sweeping fire from one's head, all these acts must be called 'poisoned and sundry good [acts]' and 'false and deceitful practice.' They cannot be called 'true and real action.' To seek to be born in the land of immeasurable light through such false and poisoned good is completely wrong" (*CWS*, 98). In this passage, Shin-ran also implies the impossibility of birth through self-power practices.

8. In the *Kyōgyōshinshō*, "Chapter on Realization," Shinran begins with the sub-title "The Vow of Necessary Attainment of Nirvana: The Birth That Is Incon-ceivable" (*CWS*, 152), and he explains that the significance of this chapter is "to reveal, with reverence, the true realization: It is the wondrous state attained through Amida's perfect benefiting of others; it is the ultimate fruition of supreme nirvana" (*CWS*, 153). Later he remarks, "Second is Amida's directing of virtue for our return to this world. This is the benefit we receive, the state of benefiting and guiding others" (158). These passages imply both ultimate enlightenment and the ability to freely save others that follows from it.

9. For example, in the *Passages on the Land of Happiness (Anraku-shū)* [*Jōdo Shinshū seiten gentenban*, 244], Daochuo compares birth in Tuṣita Heaven to birth in Amida's Pure Land of the West, explaining that in Amida's Pure Land those who attain birth reach the bodhisattva stage of non-retrogression. He adds that the water, birds, and trees described as being in the Pure Land also convey the teach-ing themselves to help the practitioners seek the path.

Also, in *Commentary on the Contemplation Sutra*, "Chapter on the Essential Meaning of the Sutra," Shandao does not acknowledge that practitioners can attain buddhahood solely through the *nembutsu*. He understands that those who attain birth in the Pure Land become holy beings but do not attain buddhahood simply by being born in the land.

10. For example, in the *Passages on the Pure Land Way (Jōdomon ruijushō)*, Shinran says, "Truly we know that the supreme, perfect fruit of enlightenment is not difficult to attain; it is pure *shinjin*, true and real, that is indeed difficult to real-ize" (*CWS*, 299). In this passage, he implies that, compared to the immediate attainment of buddhahood at the moment of birth in the Pure Land in the future, it is more urgent for practitioners to accomplish the cause for birth here and now.

11. *CWS*, 662.

12. Shinran expresses his joyfulness in various passages in the *Kyōgyōshinshō*. For example, in the "General Introduction," he says,

Ah, hard to encounter, even in many lifetimes, is the decisive cause of birth, Amida's universal Vow! Hard to realize, even in myriads of kalpas, is pure *shinjin* that is true and real! If you should come to realize this practice and *shinjin*, rejoice at the conditions from the distant past that have brought it about. . . . How joyous I am, Gutoku Shinran, disciple of Śākyamuni! Rare is it to come upon the sacred scriptures from the westward land of India and the commentaries of the masters of China and Japan, but now I have been able to encounter them. Rare is it to hear them, but already I have been able to hear. (*CWS*, 4)

And in the "Chapter on Practice,"

Thus, when one attains the true and real practice and *shinjin*, one greatly rejoices in one's heart. This attainment is therefore called the stage of joy. It is likened to the first fruit: sages of the first fruit, though they may give themselves to sleep and to sloth, will still never be subject to samsaric existence for a twenty-ninth time. Even more decisively will the ocean of beings of the ten quarters be grasped and never abandoned when they have taken refuge in this practice and *shinjin*. Therefore the Buddha is called "Amida Buddha." This is other-power. (*CWS*, 54)

And again in the "Chapter on the Transformed Bodies and Lands," "Having entered forever the ocean of the Vow, I now realize deeply the Buddha's benevolence. To respond with gratitude for the supreme virtues, I collect the crucial passages expressing the true essence of the Pure Land way, constantly saying, out of mindfulness [the Name that is] the inconceivable ocean of virtues. Ever more greatly rejoicing, I humbly receive it" (*CWS*, 240). It is clear that these passages express the joyfulness of his encountering the true teaching.

13. *Kyōgyōshinshō*, "Chapter on Practice," in *CWS*, 56.
14. In the *Kyōgyōshinshō*, "Chapter on the True Buddha and Land," Shinran says, "Since there are thousands of differences in the causes of birth in the provisional Buddha-lands, there are thousands of differences in the lands" (*CWS*, 203).
15. *Lamp for the Latter Age*, in *CWS*, 539.
16. *Uncollected Letters*, in *CWS*, 579.
17. *CWS*, 429.
18. The following poem by the myōkōnin Asahara Saichi (Myōkōnin means "wondrous, excellent person of *nembutsu*") expresses that the poet accepts birth in the Pure Land in such occasions:

My father, at the age of eighty-four,
Attained birth in the Pure Land.
My mother, at the age of eighty-three,
Attained birth in the Pure Land.
And I am going there in the course of time.
Parents and a child, the three of us all together,

become beings to save sentient beings.
How grateful I am for the benevolence [of the Buddha].
Namu Amida Butsu.

19. In another poem, Myōkōnin Asahara Saichi says of himself,

What a shameful person I am!
Deeply in the darkness like mud, with no abilities.
Drifting in the darkness between heaven and earth,
Living without knowing that I am falling,
Drifting through my life, what a shameful person I am!

He also repents in a poem that

I am a pitiless, shameful, ogre.
That is the truth of Saichi.
How shameful, shameful, shameful!

But at the same time, he also wrote a poem expressing his deep feeling of
oneness with the Buddha:

How shameful! In the fire of Saichi's heart,
The great compassionate parent must stay up all night.
Embracing a burning being
With the compassion of a parent.

Appendix III

1. Yoshifumi Ueda, ed., *Letters of Shinran—a Translation of Mattoshō* (Kyoto: Honganji International Center, 1978), 31.
2. *Saihōshinanshō, Shinran Shōnin zenshū* 5 (Kyoto: Hōzōkan, 1984), 121.
3. *Saihōshinanshō*, 131.
4. Taitetsu Unno, trans., *Tannishō* (Honolulu: Buddhist Studies Center Press,
   1984), sec. 10. Note: T. Unno translates this as "No selfworking is true working."
5. Ueda, *Letters of Shinran*, 30.
6. Taitetsu Unno, trans., *Tannishō—a Shin Buddhist Classic* (Honolulu: Buddhist
   Study Center Press, 1996).

Abe Kōbō	安部公房
Agonshū	阿含宗
akunin	悪人
Ama Toshimaro	阿満利磨
Amitojing/Amidakyō	阿弥陀経
annyō	安養
Asahara Shōkō	麻原彰晃
asamashii	浅ましい
Aum Shinrikyō	オウム真理教
bonbu	凡夫
bonnō	煩悩
bonnō soku bodai	煩悩即菩提
byōdōshin	平等芯
Chan/Sŏn/Zen	禅
Chihara Satoshi	千原明
chōmon	聴聞
daihi	大悲
danwaku shōri	断惑証理
Dao	道
Dawuliangshoujing/Daimuryōjukyō	大無量寿経
dokusan	独参
engi	縁起
Fukushima	福島
funbecchi	分別知
futaiten	不退転
Genshin	源信
gōman	傲慢

goshō no ichidaiji	後生の一大事
Guanwuliangshoujing/Kanmuryōjukyō	観無量寿経
hakoniwa ryōhō	箱庭療法
Hamamatsu	浜松
hazukashii	恥ずかしい
Hara Inashiro	原稲城
Hara Yoshio	原義雄
Heian Bukkyō	平安仏教
hijiri	聖
Hirano Keiko	平野恵子
hisō hizoku	非僧非俗
hōben	方便
Hōnen	法然
hongan	本願
hongan riki	本願力
Hsinshin ming	信心銘
ichijōdō	一乗道
ishi	石
jakumetsu byōdō	寂滅平等
jakumetsu hosshō	寂滅法性
jiriki	自力
Jōdo-Shin	浄土
Jōdo-Shinshū	浄土真宗
Jōdo-shū	浄土宗
Kai Wariko	甲斐和里子
Kakushin-bō	覚信房
Kamakura Bukkyō	鎌倉仏教
Kamei Katsuichirō	亀井勝一郎
Kaneko Daiei	金子大榮
Kannen bōmon	観念法門
Kashiwagi Tetsuo	柏木哲夫
kōan	公安

kongōshin	金剛心
kokoro naoshi	心直し
konjō naoshi	根性直し
konpon mufunbecchi	根本無分別智
kue issh	倶会一処
kusōgan	九相観
kyōgaku	教学
Kyōgyōshinshō	教行信証
Kyūma Kazutake	久馬一剛
Linji	臨済
Matsumoto Seichō	松本清張
mi-shirabe	身調べ
mitsugimono	貢物
monpō	聞法
muchi	無智
muryō kōmyōdo	無量光明土
musō	無相
Myōe	明恵
myōgō	名号
myōkōnin	妙好人
Nagaoka Nishi Hospital	長岡西病院
Naikan	内観
Nakazawa Shin'ichi	中沢新一
Namu Amida Butsu	南無阿弥陀仏
Namu Fukashigikō Nyorai	南無不可思議光如来
Namu Mugekō Nyorai	南無無碍光如来
Nanquan	南泉
Nanto Bukkyō	南都仏教
nembutsu	念仏
Nichiren-shū	日蓮宗
Nijūgozanmai-e	二十五三昧会
ōjō	往生

ōjōden	往生伝
Ojōyōshū	往生要集
Okuwa Hitoshi	大桑斉
ondōbō ondōgyō	御同朋御同行
oroka	愚か
qi	気
Rennyo	蓮如
Rinzai-shū	臨済宗
Saichi	才市
Seirei Mikatagahara Hospital	精霊三方原病院
Shandao	善導
shigyō	四行
shinenjo	四念所
Shingon-shū	真言宗
shinjin	信心
shinjitsu-chie mui-hosshin	真実智慧無為法身
shinnyo	真如
Shinran, Gutoku	愚禿親鸞
shitsurau	設らう
shōji soku nehan	生死即涅槃
shōjōju	正定聚
shoshin	初心
Shōzōmatsu wasan	正像末和讃
shūkyō	宗教
Shuryōgon	首楞厳
songenshi	尊厳死
sōshiki Bukkyō	葬式仏教
Sōtō-shū	曹洞宗
suna	砂
suna dango	砂団子
Suna no onna	砂の女
Suna no utsuwa	砂の器

Suna no yōsei	砂の妖精
Suzuki Akiko	鈴木章子
Suzuki Shōsan	鈴木正三
taishi ichiban	大死一番
tamashii	魂
Tamiya Masashi	田宮仁
Tannishō	嘆異鈔
tariki	他力
Tendai-shū	天台宗
tenmei kaigo	転迷開悟
tongyō	頓教
Tsuboi Hospital	坪井病院
tsuchi	土
tsumaranai	つまらない
usōshōgon	有相荘厳
Vihara Care	ビハーラ・ケア
wagamama	我がまま
Wŏnhyo	元曉
Yodogawa Christian Hospital	淀川キリスト教病院
Yoshimoto Ishin	吉本威信
Yuien-bō	唯円房
zenbun tariki	全分他力
zengyō	漸教
Zhaozhou	趙州

Contributors

Harvey Aronson has a private clinical practice in Houston, Texas, using an integrative model of psychotherapy that spans both brief solution-oriented therapy and longer-term psychodynamic work. He is, with Anne Klein, founder and residential teacher of Dawn Mountain, a center for Buddhist study and practice in Houston (www.dawnmountain.org) where they meet with students twice a month for practice and several times a year for more intensive practice with Tibetan masters and lamas. He has also taught at the University of Virginia and Stanford University. He is author of *Buddhist Practice on Western Ground: Reconciling Eastern Ideals and Western Psychology* (Shambala, 2004), and *Love and Sympathy in Theravada Buddhism* (Motilal Banarsidass, 1999). He has engaged in Buddhist practice in the Theravadin and Tibetan Gelukba and Nyingma traditions. He received his Masters in Social Work from Boston University School of Social Work and his Ph.D. in Buddhist Studies from the University of Wisconsin, Madison.

Jack Engler is Instructor in Psychology, Harvard Medical School. He teaches and supervises psychotherapy trainees at Harvard Medical School, and has a private psychotherapy practice in Cambridge, Massachusettes. He is on the faculty of Deep Streams Institute and is a former board member of Barre Center for Buddhist Studies. He is the co-author, among other books, of *Transformations of Consciousness* (Shambala, 1986) with Ken Wilber and Daniel Brown. Among his recent articles is "Being Somebody and Being Nobody: A Reexamination of the Understanding of Self and No-Self in Psychoanalysis and Buddhism," in *Buddhism and Psychoanalysis,* ed. Jeremy Safran (Wisdom Publications, 2003).

Julie Hanada-Lee is a Jōdo Shinshū Hongwanji-Ha priest. She is an Association of Clinical Pastoral Education Supervisor who completed her candidacy at the Providence Portland Medical Center in Portland, Oregon. She was still in candidacy at the time of writing the essay included in this volume. She has served as minister at Los Angeles Hompa Hongwanji Buddhist Temple and as resident minister at Oregon Buddhist Temple. Her clinical training was at the Portland Veterans Administration Medical Center. She completed the research level at Chūō Bukkyō Gakuin in Kyoto, Japan, has a Masters in Buddhist Studies from the Institute of Buddhist Studies, and a bachelors in Public Relations from San Jose State University.

Anne Carolyn Klein is Professor of Religious Studies at Rice University and has also been chair of the Department of Religious Studies. She is, with Harvey Aronson, founding director and residential teacher of Dawn Mountain, a center for Buddhist study and practice in Houston (www.dawnmountain.org). Her publications include *Knowledge and Liberation, Path to the Middle* (Snow Lion Publications, 1987), *Meeting the Great Bliss Queen: Buddhists, Feminists, and the Art of the Self* (Beacon Press, 1996), and *Unbounded Wholeness: Dzogchen, Bön, and the Logic of the Nonconceptual* (Oxford University Press, 2006), a six-chapter introduction and translation (with Geshe Tenzin Wangyal Rinpoche) which for the first time translates a scholarly Dzogchen text from the early Bön tradition. She received an M.A. in Buddhist Studies from the University of Wisconsin and her Ph.D. in Religious Studies from the University of Virginia.

Franz Aubrey Metcalf is review editor for the *Journal of Global Buddhism;* past chair of the Person, Culture, and Religion Group of the American Academy of Religion; author of chapters, reviews, and articles on Buddhism and psychology; and instructor in comparative religion at California State University, Los Angeles. His first book, *What Would Buddha Do?* (Ulysses Press, 1999), is now out in ten languages. His most recent book, *Just Add Buddha* (Ulysses Press, 2004), he lobbied to title *Shallow Practice.* He is also founding member of The Forge Guild of Spiritual Leaders and general editor of its newsletter, and he has written four popular press books applying a deeply Winnicottian Buddhism to our everyday lives. He received his Ph.D. from the University of Chicago, asking why Americans practice Zen Buddhism.

Nabeshima Naoki is Professor of Shin Buddhist Studies, Faculty of Law, Ryukoku University, and Vice Director, Open Research Center for Humanities, Science and Religion, Ryukoku University. His research focuses on the Pure Land Buddhist thought of China and Japan, in particular Shin Buddhism, founded by Shinran (1173–1262). He has been developing Shin Buddhist approaches to end-of-life care. He is also interested in bioethics of interdependence, Buddhist perspectives on the emancipation of evil beings, and Shinran's view of King Ajātaśatru. He is author of The *Emancipation of King Ajātaśatru: In the Depths of the Tragedy at Rajagṛha Castle* (in Japanese) (Hōjōdō Shuppan, 2004), "Bioethics of Interdependence: Shin Buddhist Reflections on Human Cloning" in Jensine Andressen, ed. *Issues for the Millennium, Cloning and Genetic Technologies* (forthcoming), and many other articles on Shin Buddhism, bioethics, and end-of-life care.

Naitō Chikō is Professor, Shin Buddhist Studies, Faculty of Letters, Ryukoku University, and Director, Educational Research Organization, Ryukoku University. He seeks to understand the interface of Buddhism and psychotherapy as both a scholar and a minister working with the spiritual and psychological ills of contemporary Japanese Buddhists. His research interests include Shinran's view on Birth in the Pure Land, Shin Buddhist doctrine and spiritual repose, and Rennyo's thought on *kami,* or local gods. He completed advanced doctoral work in Shin Buddhist studies at Ryukoku University.

Okada Yasunobu is Dean of the Counseling Center and Professor in the Graduate School of Education, Kyoto University. Although he is broadly engaged in the training of psychotherapists and counselors at Kyoto University, his special area of expertise is Sandplay therapy. He is editor and contributor to *Contemporary Significance of Sandplay* (Shibundō, 2002), and *The Essence and Ramifications of Sandplay Therapy* (Shibundō, 2002) (both in Japanese), and is author and editor of numerous publications on clinical psychotherapy and Sandplay therapy. He received his Doctorate in Education from Kyoto University.

Richard K. Payne is Dean and Professor of Buddhist Studies of the Institute of Buddhist Studies, Graduate Theological Union, and a Core Doctoral Faculty Member of the Graduate Theological Union. He is the author of *Tantric Ritual of Japan* (Aditya Prakashan, 1991), editor of *Re-Visioning "Kamakura" Buddhism* (University of Hawai'i Press, 1998), co-editor with Kenneth Tanaka of *Approaching the Land of Bliss: Religious Praxis in the Cult of Amitabha* (University of Hawai'i Press, 2004), editor of *Tantric Buddhism in East Asia* (Boston: Wisdom Publications, 2005), and editor and author of numerous other books and articles. He specializes in clarifying the context of ritual practice in East Asian Buddhism with a particular focus on Shingon Buddhism. He traveled to Japan to study the Tantric tradition for his doctoral research, and in order to gain access to the temples of Mount Koya to study Shingon, an initiatory, esoteric tradition, Payne was required to enter the training process as a monk. It was, he says, "the ultimate participant-observer situation." He received his Ph.D. from the Graduate Theological Union.

Jeremy D. Safran is Professor of Psychology in the Graduate Faculty of New School University, where he has directed the Clinical Psychology Program. He is also Senior Research Scientist at Beth Israel Medical Center in New York City. Much of his theoretical and empirical work in the last fifteen years has focused on the topic of therapeutic impasses, and together with collaborators he has conducted a number of studies examining the processes through which therapists and their patients are able to successfully resolve therapeutic impasses. He has trained in both Zen and Tibetan Buddhist traditions. He is editor of *Psychoanalysis and Buddhism: An Unfolding Dialogue* (Wisdom Publications, 2003), co-author with J. C. Muran of *Negotiating the Therapeutic Alliance: A relational treatment guide* (Guilford, 2000), and other books and articles on psychotherapy and clinical psychology. He received his Ph.D. in clinical psychology at the University of British Columbia.

Tarutani Shigehiro is Associate Professor of Theory of Human Nature and Philosophy in the Department of Humanities and Social Sciences, Maizuru National College of Technology. His research has focused on the analysis of Jung's psychological theories from the perspective of religious studies. His recent publications include "Chapter 2, Section II: 'Healing in the Context of Self-enclosure,'" in *The Fount of Religion and the Contemporary Age: Vol. 3* (Shōyō Shobō, 2002), and "Dimensions of the Sacred and Holism in the Context of Healing," *Research Report, Ministry of Education Research Fund: Section B1* (2001–2003) (both articles in Japanese). He received his Master's Degree and completed advanced doctoral work in Religious Studies at Kyoto University.

Mark Unno is Associate Professor of East Asian Religions in the Department of Religious Studies at the University of Oregon. His primary research is in medieval Japanese Buddhism, and he has a strong secondary interest in the field of Buddhism and psychotherapy. He is the author of *Shingon Refractions: Myōe and the Mantra of Light* (Wisdom Publications, 2004). His other publications include articles on Pure Land Buddhism, Zen Buddhism, comparative religious thought, and Buddhism and psychology. He has previously taught at the Institute of Buddhist Studies, Brown University, Carleton College, and Kyoto University, and he received his Ph.D. in Religious Studies from Stanford University.

Taitetsu Unno retired from Smith College in Massachusetts in 1998 as the Jill Ker Conway Professor Emeritus of Religion and East Asian Studies. He is author of *River of Fire, River of Water* (Doubleday, 1996), co-editor with James Heisig of *The Religious Philosophy of Nishitani Keiji: Encounter with Emptiness* (Asian Humanities Press, 1990), and numerous other books and articles on East Asian Buddhism, Japanese religion, and Japanese philosophy. He continues his research on Hua-yen Buddhism and is involved with Shin Buddhist activities in Northampton, Massachusetts and the American Buddhist Study Center in New York City. He has a strong secondary interest in the interface between Buddhist practices and psychotherapy. He graduated from the University of California, Berkeley and received his master's and doctoral degrees in Buddhist Studies from Tokyo University.

William S. Waldron teaches South Asian religions and Buddhist philosophy at Middlebury College, Vermont. His research focuses on the Yogacara school of Indian Buddhism, and comparative psychologies and philosophies of mind. His publications include *The Buddhist Unconscious: The Ālaya-vijñāna in the Context of Indian Buddhist Thought* (RoutledgeCurzon, 2003), "Buddhist Steps to an Ecology of Mind: Thinking about 'Thoughts without a Thinker,'" *Eastern Buddhist*, 2002, Vol. XXXIV, No. 1 (available online), and "Common Ground, Common Cause: Buddhism and Science on the Afflictions of Identity," in *Buddhism and Science: Breaking New Ground,* ed. B. Alan Wallace (Columbia University Press, 2003). He has been engaged personally, practically, and intellectually with the Buddhist/psychology interface since 1972. He received his Ph.D. in Buddhist Studies from the University of Wisconsin after studying extensively in India and Japan.

Seigen H. Yamaoka has been a minister of the Buddhist Churches of America (BCA) for forty years. He has served at the Buddhist Church of Oakland, Stockton Buddhist Buddhist Temple, as Bishop of BCA, and as President of the Institute of Buddhist Studies. Presently, he is minister at Buddhist Church of Oakland. His publications include *The Transmission of Shin Buddhism to the West* (Federation of Dharma School Teacher's League, 2005), and *Awakening of Gratitude in Dying* (BCA Research and Educational Committee, 1978). He received his Doctorate in Literature in Shin Buddhist Studies at Ryūkoku University and his Doctorate in Ministry from the Pacific School of Religion.

Index

Psychoanalysis and Buddhism
An Unfolding Dialogue
Edited by Jeremy D. Safran
456 pp, ISBN 0-86171-342-7, $19.95

"This is a beautifully conceived work—it is innovative, provocative, fascinating, and useful. Jeremy Safran deserves much praise."—Mark Epstein, author of *Thoughts without a Thinker*

Includes contributions from Jack Engler, Neil Altman, Robert Langan, Barry Magid, Polly Young-Eisendrath, Joseph Bobrow, and more.

Mindful Therapy
A Guide for Therapists and Helping Professionals
Thomas Bien, Ph.D.
272 pp, ISBN 0-86171-292-7, $17.95

"Bien explains Buddhist psychology in language that should make sense to beginners, seasoned practitioners, and clients alike. A rich and timely contribution to our understanding of how to integrate the ancient practice of mindfulness into modern-day psychotherapy."—Christopher K. Germer, Ph.D., co-editor of *Mindfulness and Psychotherapy*

Minding What Matters
Psychotherapy and the Buddha Within
Robert Langan | Foreword by Robert Coles
224 pp, ISBN 0-86171-353-2, $16.95

"These wonderfully literate, compelling pages summon the reader to wonder about life's purposes and meanings. A shining, even entrancing vision of what it is possible to do and to be."— Robert Coles, author of *The Spiritual Lives of Children*

WISDOM PUBLICATIONS, a nonprofit publisher, is dedicated to making available authentic works relating to Buddhism for the benefit of all. We publish books by ancient and modern masters in all traditions of Buddhism, translations of important texts, and original scholarship. Additionally, we offer books that explore East-West themes unfolding as traditional Buddhism encounters our modern culture in all its aspects. Our titles are published with the appreciation of Buddhism as a living philosophy, and with the special commitment to preserve and transmit important works from Buddhism's many traditions.

To learn more about Wisdom, or to browse books online, visit our website at www.wisdompubs.org.

You may request a copy of our catalog online or by writing to this address:

Wisdom Publications
199 Elm Street
Somerville, Massachusetts 02144 USA
Telephone: 617-776-7416
Fax: 617-776-7841
Email: info@wisdompubs.org
www.wisdompubs.org

The Wisdom Trust

As a nonprofit publisher, Wisdom is dedicated to the publication of Dharma books for the benefit of all sentient beings and dependent upon the kindness and generosity of sponsors in order to do so. If you would like to make a donation to Wisdom, you may do so through our website or our Somerville office. If you would like to help sponsor the publication of a book, please write or email us at the address above.

Thank you.

Wisdom is a nonprofit, charitable 501(c)(3) organization affiliated with the Foundation for the Preservation of the Mahayana Tradition (FPMT).